PRINCE2®

Study Guide

David Hinde

WILEY

John Wiley & Sons, Ltd.

Executive Comissioning Editor:
   Birgit Gruber
Assistant Editor: Ellie Scott
Development Editor: Kathi Duggan
Technical Editors: Gina Abudi and Duncan Wade
Production Editor: Dassi Zeidel
Copy Editor: Liz Welch
Editorial Manager: Pete Gaughan
Production Manager: Tim Tate
Vice President and Executive Group Publisher:
   Richard Swadley
Vice President and Publisher: Neil Edde
UK Tech Publishing
   VP Consumer and Technology Publishing Director:
   Michelle Leete

Associate Director—Book Content Management:
   Martin Tribe
Associate Publisher: Chris Webb
Marketing
Associate Marketing Director: Louise Breinholt
Senior Marketing Executive: Kate Parrett
Media Project Manager 1: Laura Moss-Hollister
Media Associate Producer: Marilyn Hummel
Media Quality Assurance: Josh Frank
Book Designers: Judy Fung and Bill Gibson
Proofreader: Paul Sagan, Word One New York
Indexer: Ted Laux
Project Coordinator, Cover: Kristie Rees
Cover Designer: Ryan Sneed

Dear Reader,

Thank you for choosing *PRINCE2 Study Guide*. This book is part of a family of premium-quality Sybex books, all of which are written by outstanding authors who combine practical experience with a gift for teaching.

Sybex was founded in 1976. More than 30 years later, we're still committed to producing consistently exceptional books. With each of our titles, we're working hard to set a new standard for the industry. From the paper we print on, to the authors we work with, our goal is to bring you the best books available.

I hope you see all that reflected in these pages. I'd be very interested to hear your comments and get your feedback on how we're doing. Feel free to let me know what you think about this or any other Sybex book by sending me an email at nedde@wiley.com. If you think you've found a technical error in this book, please visit http://sybex.custhelp.com. Customer feedback is critical to our efforts at Sybex.

Best regards,

Neil Edde
Vice President and Publisher
Sybex, an Imprint of Wiley

To Louise,

Thanks for all your help and support whilst I was writing this book.
I couldn't have done it without you.

Love, Dave

Acknowledgments

Whilst writing this book I have had the help and support of many people. Firstly I would like to thank my partner, Louise, for putting up with me this past year. Without her advice, support, and love, I could not have written this book.

Then, I need to thank the fantastic team at Wiley. First, there is Birgit Gruber for encouraging me to start this project in the first place. Next, Kathi Duggan, the development editor, for all your fantastic comments and advice while I was preparing the manuscript. Thank you to the project manager gurus, Gina Abudi and Duncan Wade, for all your invaluable advice on how to describe PRINCE2. Thanks to Dassi Zeidel, Pete Gaughan, and Ellie Scott, for all your help with the editorial and production process.

I would also like to thank Learning Tree, who five years ago sponsored me when I applied for the PRINCE2 teacher qualification and continue to support me in keeping that qualification up-to-date and providing me with PRINCE2 courses to teach. Particular thanks to Duncan Wade (again) for writing such a great course for me to teach and also Graham Williams for helping me through the early stages of becoming an accredited PRINCE2 teacher.

Finally, I must thank the people in the APMG. Although I have never met you, without your hard work and dedication in compiling the latest version of *Managing Successful Projects with PRINCE2* (Stationery Office, 2009) and continually striving to achieve such high standards with accreditation exams, this book would not have been possible.

About the Author

 David Hinde has more than 20 years of experience in directing and managing projects and change programmes in the digital industry. He spent the early years of his career working for Mars Global before switching to the world of software development, broadcast, and IT. He worked in the engineering departments of MFN and RedBox, delivering projects to clients such as Deloitte and Touche, BP, and GroupTrade. He has had many years of experience in implementing best-practice approaches such as PRINCE2, PMI, Scrum, XP, Six Sigma, and MSP.

In 2002, David founded the consultancy practice Orgtopia and has since led many projects working with clients such as Citi, Eli Lilly, and the BBC. His work focuses on pragmatic implementations of best-practice approaches in change, programme, and project management. He believes in a holistic approach that includes improving both processes and people skills. Another part of his work with Orgtopia is training and coaching. He has trained over a thousand people in PRINCE2, coaching skills, project management, and strategic directing and governance. He is a qualified management coach with the Association for Coaching and a PRINCE2 qualified trainer, and was certified as a Project Management Professional with the Project Management Institute in 2001. He also works regularly for Learning Tree International, running their project management courses.

When David isn't working, he likes to spend his time reading, watching films, and searching out good places to eat in London. He is also a keen skier and tries to spend some time each winter in the Alps.

Contents at a Glance

Contents

Introduction

PRINCE2 is a globally recognized approach to successfully managing projects. It is widely adopted across many countries, industries, and sectors. Many projects have found that adopting the approach considerably increases the likelihood of project success.

Becoming PRINCE2 accredited is an important career development objective for anyone connected with project work. Increasingly, job ads for project-related work are asking for people with the PRINCE2 accreditation.

This study guide will help you pass the PRINCE2 accreditation exams. It has been written by someone who has trained hundreds of individuals from many different backgrounds to prepare for the Foundation and Practitioner PRINCE2 exams. It provides explanations of all parts of the PRINCE2 approach, lots of examples that show you how the method is applied in practice, and a whole range of mock examination questions for you to test your knowledge.

Introduction to PRINCE2

PRINCE2 is a best-practice project management approach. It can be used on any type of project in any type of environment. PRINCE2 is used to deliver projects in industries as diverse as IT, banking, pharmaceuticals, telecommunications, and construction. It has been implemented widely both in the private and the public sector. In the private sector, companies such as Deloitte and Touche, Citi, KPMG, and Eli Lilly have used the method. In the public sector, the UK, Canadian, Dutch, Danish, and German governments are using PRINCE2.

Since its creation in 1996, PRINCE2 has become one of the most widely adopted project management methods in the world and is currently used in over 50 countries. More than 250,000 accredited PRINCE2 professionals have passed the PRINCE2 examinations. The exams are available in 16 different languages, among them English, French, Dutch, German, Chinese, Polish, Danish, Italian, and Spanish. More than 120 training organizations provide PRINCE2 training in over 17 different languages.

PRINCE stands for *PRojects IN a Controlled Environment*. PRINCE2 was derived from PRINCE, a method created in 1989 as a project management approach for the UK government's Central Computer and Telecommunications Agency (CCTA). PRINCE2 took the commonsense ideas of PRINCE and widened the method so that it could be used across all industries. It has been updated a number of times so as to take account of the latest ideas in project management. The last major revision was in 2009. This new version has vastly improved the method, making it far easier to apply, more concise, and a lot more flexible. This study guide is based on the PRINCE2 2009 edition.

Why Should You Use PRINCE2?

Managing projects is a notoriously difficult thing to do. The news is full of high-profile projects failing to deliver successfully. Why is this?

The main reason is that project work is much more difficult than business as usual. Business-as-usual work tends to be repetitive. What happens this month is pretty similar to what happened last month. Projects, however, often involve working with new people, sometimes in other organizations. They often involve working in new ways with new management processes. They involve creating new products and services and maybe new technologies. All this unfamiliarity leads to uncertainty. It is difficult to predict how long things will take, how things will work out, or whether people will accept new ways of doing things.

What PRINCE2 provides is a structured way of working through this uncertainty. It says, OK, your project involves a great deal of unpredictability, but there are many things that are the same as any other project. Whether you are building a hotel, a new IT system, or a nuclear-powered submarine, you will have to go through these similar processes. For example, any team needs to decide what the objectives of their project are at the outset and have management mechanisms to check throughout the project that things are on track, and at the end of the project, to check that the objectives have been met. Many other commonalties exist across projects, such as approaches for managing risk, quality, changes, and so on. PRINCE2 has captured these common steps and set them out in a process model. It also describes a range of management roles with responsibilities to carry out these steps and provides a range of management documents to hold and report on project information.

Following the PRINCE2 framework does not guarantee project success. However, it does substantially increase the likelihood of any project achieving its objectives.

PRINCE2 provides a lot of ideas, some of which might not be practical to follow. However, comparing how your project is being managed against how PRINCE2 says it should be managed provides an excellent diagnostic tool to see what might be missing in your project management approach. Some (not all) of these gaps might be beneficial to fill.

In the uncertain world of managing projects, PRINCE2 provides a solid, tested, structured approach for the project management team to decide on the way forward.

The PRINCE2 Accreditations

There are three PRINCE2 accreditations: the Foundation level, the Practitioner level and the Professional level. Candidates must first pass the Foundation level before attempting the Practitioner level. Similarly candidates need the Practitioner level before trying to pass the Professional level. In order to gain the Foundation and Practitioner level candidates need to pass an exam. The Professional level is different; candidates are observed whilst working through a project case study over a two and a half day period and then, if they met the required level, are awarded the Professional qualification. This Study Guide will focus on the first two levels: the Foundation and the Practitioner. However in order to pass the Professional level a candidate requires a thorough knowledge of PRINCE2 which the reader will gain from working through this book.

I will talk about the Foundation and Practitioner exams later in this Introduction, in the section "The Accreditation Exams".

Reasons to Become PRINCE2 Certified

These days, most work environments are subject to rapid change. Most of this change will be implemented through project work. As I said at the beginning of this Introduction, PRINCE2 has become a very widely recognized and adopted approach for managing projects. This makes it a very valuable career progression accreditation to hold. The following benefits are associated with PRINCE2 accreditation:

- Demonstrates proof of project management competency
- Increases career marketability
- Raises customer confidence

Demonstrates Proof of Project Management Competency

You must have a thorough understanding of the best-practice approach to managing projects in order to pass the Foundation and Practitioner levels of PRINCE2. Those holding the PRINCE2 accreditations are showing that they are capable of managing a project in a way that substantially increases the likelihood of project success.

Increases Career Marketability

PRINCE2 is globally recognized as a professional best-practice approach for project management. When an organization is recruiting project managers, a PRINCE2 accreditation is often a prerequisite. Even if this is not the case, a PRINCE2-accredited candidate will probably be looked on more favorably.

Many senior managers need to be able to demonstrate that they can successfully implement change programs within their departments and organizations. PRINCE2 is a best-practice way of implementing change, so holding the accreditation also makes senior directing level employees more marketable.

Raises Customer Confidence

Many businesses deliver project work to their clients. The project itself can include anything from building a hotel, to creating new software, to building an aircraft carrier, for example. These businesses need to be able to demonstrate to their clients not just a technical ability in their specialist area, but also an ability to competently deliver projects. Potential clients will often expect to see proof that the business follows best-practice approaches when managing projects. An excellent way of doing this is to train project managers in PRINCE2 and align in-house project delivery approaches to the PRINCE2 model.

How to Become Accredited

The first step is to thoroughly review PRINCE2 by reading this study guide. You then have one of two choices.

- Contact a PRINCE2 Accredited Training Organization (ATO). (For a full list of ATOs, refer to the APMG-International website http://www.apmg-international .com.) ATOs have been licensed by APMG-International to deliver PRINCE2 training and to provide PRINCE2 exam testing centers. APMG-International is the group that administers PRINCE2 exams. There are ATOs in most major countries. ATOs may provide any of the following products:
    - A 2- or 3-day training course, providing last-minute revision and an invigilated Foundation exam
    - A 2- or 3-day course, providing last-minute revision and an invigilated Practitioner exam for those already holding the Foundation level
    - A 5-day course that includes an invigilated Foundation and Practitioner exam (usually on different days) and last-minute revision training for both
    - An invigilated Foundation or Practitioner exam without any revision training
2. Contact APMG-International and attend an Open Center Exam. (You can get full contact details at http://www.apmg-international.com.) These examinations are held in centers across the world.

Who Is APMG-International?

The APMG-International is a global examination institute. They have regional offices in Australia, China, Denmark, Germany, the Netherlands, Malaysia, the United States, and the United Kingdom. They manage a portfolio of best-practice qualifications, including PRINCE2®, ITIL®, MSP®, M_o_R®, and P3O®. In addition, they provide a host of specialist management qualifications such as Change Management, Agile Project Management, and Service Catalogue. They accredit training organizations, trainers, and training materials, and certify examination candidates through a variety of methods. They also set, mark, and certify the relevant examinations.

About this Study Guide

This study guide will help you prepare and (if you work hard enough!) pass the PRINCE2 Foundation and Practitioner accreditation exams. This section tells you about the objectives and content of the book and gives general advice about how best to approach your exam preparation.

Objectives of the Study Guide

The overall objective of this study guide is to provide the resources necessary for an individual to prepare for and successfully pass the PRINCE2 Foundation- and Practitioner-level accreditations.

The Foundation level examines whether a candidate has the necessary knowledge to work within (but not lead) a project team. To demonstrate this level, a candidate must have a firm understanding of the theory of the PRINCE2 model. This study guide explains this theory by setting out the model in an informal, accessible way, explaining the terminology in simple, everyday language.

The Practitioner level examines whether the candidate can not only explain the theory of PRINCE2, but also demonstrate how the model is applied in practice. A PRINCE2 Practitioner candidate should be able to justify his application of the model. This level of understanding is required for someone leading a project team. This study guide sets out many examples of how the theory is used in practice, both throughout the main body of the text using simple examples and by providing case studies from actual projects where PRINCE2 was used.

The final objective of this guide is to give readers plenty of practice with the types of questions they will encounter in the PRINCE2 accreditation exams. There are over 200 mock Foundation questions and over 150 mock Practitioner questions in the book for you to test your knowledge.

Contents of the Study Guide

The study guide covers all the areas of the syllabus for the Foundation- and Practitioner-level accreditations. The information is set out in an accessible style, using plenty of examples to help you understand both the theory of the topic and how it is applied. Each chapter contains the following useful elements:

- Exam Objectives—A description of what you must achieve in order to thoroughly understand that chapter's topic.

- Case Studies—Real-life applications of that chapter's topic, to help you understand how PRINCE2 works in practice. This is an essential skill for the Practitioner level.

- Exam Spotlights—Tips and techniques to help you tackle the PRINCE2 exams.

- Summary—An overview of all the relevant PRINCE2 topics covered within that chapter.

- Exam Essentials—All the key revision points relating to that chapter's topic.

- Review Questions—A set of mock Foundation- and Practitioner-level questions. (The answers and explanations are provided in Appendix A, "Answers to Review Questions.")

There are 15 examinable syllabus areas: the seven PRINCE2 themes, the seven PRINCE2 processes, and an area covering an overview of projects and PRINCE2. These are covered in this study guide in the following way:

- The overview of PRINCE2 is covered in Chapter 1, "Overview of PRINCE2" and Chapter 12, "Tailoring PRINCE2 to the Project Environment."

- The seven PRINCE2 processes are covered in Chapter 2, "Starting a Project Successfully with PRINCE2"; Chapter 10, "Managing the Middle of a Project Successfully with PRINCE2"; and Chapter 11, "Managing the End of a Project Successfully with PRINCE2."

- The seven PRINCE2 themes are covered in Chapter 3, "Organization Theme"; Chapter 4, "Business Case Theme"; Chapter 5, "Plans Theme"; Chapter 6, "Quality Theme"; Chapter 7, "Risk Theme"; Chapter 8, "Change Theme"; and Chapter 9, "Progress Theme."

There are also some useful appendices that will help you prepare for the exams:

- Appendix A, "Answers to Review Questions"—This appendix not only gives you the answers to the mock Foundation and Practitioner questions at the end of each chapter, but also provides you with a useful explanation of each question and answer.

- Appendix B, "Management Products in PRINCE2"—This appendix gives you a useful summary of all of the management products that are used in PRINCE2, such as the records, plans, registers, and logs.

- Appendix C, "Passing the Accreditation Exams"—Of course, you need a good knowledge of PRINCE2 to pass the exams, but good exam technique helps as well. This appendix gives you lots of useful tips and techniques on how to tackle the rather unusual style of questions in a PRINCE2 exam.

- Appendix D, "Sample Foundation Examinations"—You should do plenty of practice questions before doing the exams. This appendix gives you two further Foundation exams on top of all the Foundation questions that you can do at the end of each chapter.

The companion website is home to many tools such as a glossary, practice exams, and flashcards. See Appendix E, "About the Additional Study Tools," for more details on the contents and how to access them.

How to Use this Study Guide

The good news when it comes to revising PRINCE2 is that none of the material is particularly complex. The bad news is that there is a lot of it! Also, many parts of PRINCE2 are interrelated. So when you're first reviewing a topic in this study guide, you may run across references to things you haven't learned about yet.

Therefore, I suggest that you first read Chapter 1, "Overview of PRINCE2," to understand the whole PRINCE2 model in a high-level way, followed by Chapter 2, "Starting a Project Successfully with PRINCE2," and Chapter 3, "Organization Theme," to understand the beginning of a PRINCE2 project. You can then tackle the other chapters and topics in any order you wish.

(Throughout this book, I have predominantly used the male pronoun. This is only to make the text easier to read; not to imply any difference between male and female project management professionals.)

Other Resources You Will Need

This study guide provides a full explanation of PRINCE2 in enough detail for you to pass the accreditation exams. However, you will also need a copy of the official PRINCE2 manual, *Managing Successful Projects with PRINCE2* (Stationery Office, 2009).

The reason for this is that during the Practitioner examination, you are allowed to refer to *Managing Successful Projects with PRINCE2*. You are not allowed to take in any other reference material, including this study guide. This means that part of your exam preparation should include familiarizing yourself with how the topics are set out in the manual. In the Exam Spotlights throughout this book as well as in Appendix C, "Passing the Accreditation Exams," I explain how to use the manual to help you pass the exams.

The Accreditation Exams

There are two accreditation exams: the Foundation level and the Practitioner level.

Foundation Exam

The Foundation-level exam is the lower-level accreditation. It must be taken and passed in order to take the Practitioner exam. Here are some key facts about the Foundation exam:

- It is a one-hour exam.
- The exam consists of 75 multiple-choice questions. You are given four possible answers to each question, only one of which is correct.
- You need to get 50 percent to pass the exam.
- The exam tests to see if you have the ability to act as a member of a project team running a project with PRINCE2. It requires you to understand the theory of PRINCE2.
- You are not allowed to refer to any material during the exam.

Practitioner Exam

The Practitioner exam is the higher-level accreditation. Here are some key facts about the Practitioner exam:

- The exam is two and a half hours.
- It has nine main questions. Each of the main questions is subdivided into 12 mini-questions. Each of the nine questions is focused on a particular syllabus topic. Possible examinable syllabus topics are Starting up a Project/Initiating a Project processes, Controlling a Stage/Managing Product Delivery processes, Managing a Stage Boundary/Directing a Project/Closing a Project processes, Business Case theme,

Organization theme, Quality theme, Plans theme, Risk theme, Change theme, or Progress theme. Each syllabus topic will only be asked once in any one exam.

- The exam includes a project scenario that each question will refer to.

- The exam tests to see if you are capable of leading a project according to PRINCE2. To pass the exam, you not only need to understand the theory of PRINCE2 but also you need to know how to apply it and justify its application.

- You need to get 55 percent to pass this exam.

- You are allowed to refer to *Managing Successful Projects with PRINCE2*. You are not allowed to use any other reference material.

Example Practitioner Scenario

This section contains an example Practitioner exam scenario. All the Practitioner questions at the end of each chapter use this scenario, so you will need to refer back to it while doing the review questions in each chapter. Read through it once now. Don't worry if it doesn't make much sense yet. Come back to it again when you do your first set of Practitioner-style mock questions.

Scenario—Website Project

 The companies and people described in this scenario are fictional.

Quality Furniture Limited produces handcrafted wooden furniture from locally sourced timber. They sell their products through their four shops and via a mail-order catalog. Their sales figures are good, but the Chief Executive feels that they are missing a major business opportunity by not selling products via the Internet. Their current website has a number of problems, very few people visit the site, and it is difficult to use. There is also no facility to buy products over the Web.

The Chief Executive employed a digital marketing consultancy called FirstTech to review their website and make recommendations. They created a feasibility study that suggested the following:

- Redesign the website system so that customers can easily browse information about furniture and the Quality Furniture marketing team can quickly upload new product information.

- Link the site to the Quality Furniture sales system and add a shopping facility onto the website so that customers can order via the Web.

- Increase the rankings of the website in the major search engines.

They also recommended that the project be managed using PRINCE2 and consist of the following stages:

- Stage 1: Initiation.

- Stage 2: Develop the requirements document for the website. Send out a request for tender document to suitable web design companies for the design and development of the new website. Receive and evaluate proposals. Select a Supplier.

- Stage 3: Design the website, including page designs and informational content.

- Stage 4: Build the website.

- Stage 5: Launch the site onto the Internet and increase the site's ranking in major web search engines.

The project has just finished Starting up a Project and the Chief Executive has recruited a PRINCE2-accredited project manager. Initial estimates are that the project will cost $150,000 and take 6 months to complete. There is a project cost tolerance of +$20,000, a time tolerance of +2 weeks/–3 weeks, and a change budget of $10,000. The project is forecast to increase the sales of furniture by 20 percent over the next three years.

How to Contact the Author

I welcome feedback from you about this book or about books you'd like to see from me in the future. You can reach me by writing to davidhinde@orgtopia.com. For more information about my work, visit my website at www.orgtopia.com.

Sybex strives to keep you supplied with the latest tools and information you need for your work. Please check their website at www.sybex.com/go/prince2studyguide, where we'll post additional content and updates that supplement this book should the need arise.

PRINCE2 Syllabus Areas Covered in this Study Guide

The following tables list the Syllabus Areas and Learning Outcomes defined in The APM Group (APMG)'s 2011 PRINCE2 Syllabus. The Learning Outcomes are shown in bold and describe what a Foundation-level or Practitioner-level candidate will be expected to know, understand, or do. Under each Learning Outcome is a more specific list of what is required of the candidate in order to demonstrate that the Learning Outcome has been achieved.

The tables also specify whether a requirement is applicable to the Foundation or Practitioner exam, as well as which chapter in this Study Guide covers that topic.

Syllabus area: overview, principles, and tailoring PRINCE2 to the project environment

Learning Outcome	Foundation	Practitioner	Chapter
Know facts, terms, and concepts relating to the overview, principles, and tailoring PRINCE2 to the project environment.			
Specifically to recall the:			
Six aspects of project performance to be managed	X		1
Definition of a project	X		1
Four integrated elements of principles, themes, processes, and the project environment upon which PRINCE2 is based	X		1
Customer/supplier context of a PRINCE2 project	X		3
Understand terms and concepts relating to the overview, principles, and tailoring PRINCE2 to the project environment, and explain how these are applied on/are involved with a project.			
Specifically to identify the:			
Benefits of using PRINCE2	X		1
Seven principles	X		1
Characteristics of a project	X		1
Difference between embedding and tailoring PRINCE2		X	12
Context of a customer/supplier environment and how it affects the application of the themes, processes, and management products within a project		X	3, 12

Syllabus area: Business Case (BC) theme

Learning Outcome	Foundation	Practitioner	Chapter
Know facts, terms, and concepts relating to the Business Case theme.			
Specifically to recall the:			
Definition of a project output, an outcome, a benefit, and a dis-benefit	X		4

Learning Outcome	Foundation	Practitioner	Chapter
Understand how the Business Case theme relates to the principles; the approach to the treatment of this theme; how it is applied throughout the project life cycle and the responsibilities involved.			
Specifically to identify:			
The purpose of the Business Case theme	X		4
The purpose of a:			
1. Business Case	X		4
2. Benefits Review Plan			
The recommended composition of a:		X	4
1. Business Case, and in which process(es) it is developed, verified, maintained, and confirmed, and which roles are responsible for this			
2. Benefits Review Plan, and in which process(es) it is developed, used, and reviewed, and which roles are responsible for this			
The relationship between a programme's business case and a project's Business Case		X	4
Be able to apply and tailor the relevant aspects of the Business Case theme to a project scenario, when creating products or making decisions related to this theme, in any or all of the processes.			
Specifically to:			
Identify appropriate information, using the recommended composition, for inclusion in the Business Case and Benefits Review Plan		X	4
Identify outputs, outcomes, benefits, and dis-benefits		X	4
Be able to identify, analyze, and distinguish between appropriate and inappropriate application of the Business Case theme throughout the life cycle of a project scenario.			
Specifically to analyze:			
Whether the Business Case and Benefits Review Plan, using the recommended composition, are fit for purpose, with reasons, and whether the appropriate roles have been involved in their development and maintenance throughout the life of a project		X	4

Syllabus area: Organization (OR) theme

Learning Outcome	Foundation	Practitioner	Chapter
Know facts, terms, and concepts relating to the Organization theme.			
Specifically to recall the:			
Roles within the Organization theme	X		3
Understand how the Organization theme relates to the principles; the approach to the treatment of this theme; how it is applied throughout the project life cycle and the responsibilities involved.			
Specifically to identify:			
The purpose of the Organization theme	X		3
The three project interests and how these are represented within the three levels of the project management team structure	X		3
The responsibilities and characteristics of the role of the:			
1. Project Board			
2. Project Manager	X		3
3. Project Assurance			
4. Change Authority			
5. Team Manager			
6. Project Support			
What a stakeholder is	X		3
The purpose of the Communication Management Strategy	X		3
How the four levels of the project management structure apply to the process model		X	3
The relationship between the Communication Management Strategy and other products and themes		X	3
The recommended composition of a Communication Management Strategy, in which process(es) it is developed, used, and reviewed, and which roles are responsible for this		X	3
Be able to apply and tailor the relevant aspects of the Organization theme to a project scenario, when creating products or making decisions related to this theme, in any or all of the processes.			

Learning Outcome	Foundation	Practitioner	Chapter
Specifically to:			
Identify an appropriate project management team structure and role descriptions, including acceptable role consolidations or sharing		X	3
Identify appropriate information, using the recommended composition, for inclusion in a Communication Management Strategy		X	3
Be able to identify, analyze, and distinguish between appropriate and inappropriate application of the Organization theme throughout the life cycle of a project scenario.			
Specifically to analyze:			
Whether the following products, using the recommended composition, are fit for purpose, with reasons, and whether the correct roles have been involved in their development and maintenance throughout the life of a project:		X	3
1. Project management team structure			
2. Communication Management Strategy			

Syllabus area: Quality (QU) theme

Learning Outcome	Foundation	Practitioner	Chapter
Know facts, terms, and concepts relating to the Quality theme.			
Specifically to recall the:			
Recommended quality review team roles	X		6
Understand how the Quality theme relates to the principles; the approach to the treatment of this theme; how it is applied throughout the project life cycle and the responsibilities involved.			
Specifically to identify:			
The purpose of the Quality theme	X		6
The difference between quality assurance and Project Assurance	X		6

(continued)

Learning Outcome	Foundation	Practitioner	Chapter
The objectives of the quality review technique	X		6
The difference between quality planning, quality control, and quality assurance	X		6
The difference between customer's quality expectations and acceptance criteria	X		6
The purpose of a:	X		6
1. Project Product Description			
2. Product Description			
3. Quality Register			
4. Quality Management Strategy			
The PRINCE2 approach to quality: quality audit trail		X	6
The recommended composition of a:			
1. Project Product Description			
2. Product Description			
3. Quality Register		X	6
4. Quality Management Strategy			
and in which process(es) they are developed, used, and reviewed, and which roles are responsible for this			
Be able to apply and tailor the relevant aspects of the Quality theme to a project scenario, when creating products or making decisions related to this theme, in any or all of the processes.			
Specifically to:			
Identify appropriate information, using the recommended composition, for inclusion in the Project Product Description, Product Description, Quality Register, and Quality Management Strategy		X	6
Identify appropriate actions and responsibilities when applying the quality review technique to a given product		X	6
Identify appropriate actions and responsibilities when applying quality planning and quality control to a given project		X	6
Be able to identify, analyze, and distinguish between appropriate and inappropriate application of the Quality theme throughout the life cycle of a project scenario.			

Learning Outcome	Foundation	Practitioner	Chapter
Specifically to analyze:			
Whether the Project Product Description, Product Description, Quality Register, and Quality Management Strategy, using the recommended composition, are fit for purpose, with reasons, and whether the appropriate roles have been involved in their development and maintenance throughout the life of a project		X	6
Use of the quality review technique for a given product		X	6
Whether quality planning activities have been, or are scheduled to be, undertaken appropriately during the execution of a project, with reasons, and whether the appropriate roles have been involved, including:		X	6
1. Understanding and documenting the customer's quality expectations and the project's acceptance criteria in the Project Product Description			
2. Formulating a Quality Management Strategy and setting up a Quality Register			
Whether quality control activities have been, or are scheduled to be, undertaken appropriately during the execution of a project, with reasons, and whether the appropriate roles have been involved. Including:		X	6
1. Carrying out the quality methods			
2. Maintaining quality and approval records			
3. Gaining acceptance			

Syllabus area: Plans (PL) theme

Learning Outcome	Foundation	Practitioner	Chapter
Know the facts, terms, and concepts relating to the Plans theme.			
Specifically to recall the:			
Levels of plan recommended by PRINCE2	X		5
Four tasks of product-based planning	X		5
Understand how the Plans theme relates to the principles; the approach to the treatment of this theme; how it is applied throughout the project life cycle and the responsibilities involved.			

(continued)

Learning Outcome	Foundation	Practitioner	Chapter
Specifically to identify:			
The purpose of the Plans theme	X		5
The levels of plans, their purpose, and the interrelationship between the:			
1. Project Plan			
2. Stage Plans	X		5
3. Team Plans			
4. Exception Plan			
The tasks within the product-based planning technique	X		5
The recommended composition of a Plan, in which process(es) it is developed, used, and reviewed, and which roles are responsible for this		X	5
Be able to apply and tailor the relevant aspects of the Plans theme to a project scenario, when creating products or making decisions related to this theme, in any or all of the processes.			
Specifically to:			
Identify appropriate information, using the recommended composition, for inclusion in a Plan (excluding the schedule)		X	5
Identify the appropriate actions and responsibilities when applying the product-based planning technique, including the creation of Product Descriptions, a product breakdown structure, and a product flow diagram		X	5
Be able to identify, analyze, and distinguish between appropriate and inappropriate application of the Plans theme throughout the life cycle of a project scenario.			
Specifically to analyze:			
Whether a Plan (excluding the schedule), using the recommended composition, is fit for its purpose, with reasons, and whether the appropriate roles have been involved in its development and maintenance throughout the life of a project		X	5
Whether the product-based planning technique has been applied appropriately. This should include analyzing the appropriate application of Product Descriptions, a product breakdown structure, and a product flow diagram, with reasons		X	5

Syllabus area: Risk (RK) theme

Learning Outcome	Foundation	Practitioner	Chapter
Know facts, terms, and concepts relating to the Risk theme.			
Specifically to recall:			
The definition of a risk and the difference between a threat and an opportunity	X		7
The recommended risk response types and whether they are used to respond to a threat or an opportunity	X		7
The difference between a risk owner and a risk actionee	X		7
Understand how the Risk theme relates to the principles; the approach to the treatment of this theme; how it is applied throughout the project life cycle and the responsibilities involved.			
Specifically to identify:			
The purpose of the Risk theme	X		7
The steps within the recommended risk management procedure. This should include:	X		7
1. Identify the context and therefore the influences on a project's Risk Management Strategy			
2. Identify the threats and opportunities that may affect a project's objectives			
3. Estimate risks to assess their probability, impact, and proximity			
4. Evaluate the net effect of all risks on a project when aggregated together			
5. Plan risk management responses			
6. Implement planned risk management responses, identifying an appropriate risk owner and/or risk actionee			
7. Communicate information related to risks, both within the project and externally to stakeholders			
The purpose of a risk budget	X		7
The risk probability, risk impact, and risk proximity	X		7
The difference between cause, event, and effect when expressing a risk	X		7
The purpose of a:			
1. Risk Management Strategy	X		7
2. Risk Register			
The concept of risk appetite and risk tolerance	X		7

(continued)

Learning Outcome	Foundation	Practitioner	Chapter
The recommended composition of a 1. Risk Management Strategy 2. Risk Register and in which process(es) they are developed, used, and reviewed, and which roles are responsible for this		X	7
The concept of inherent, secondary, and residual risks		X	7
Be able to apply and tailor the relevant aspects of the Risk theme to a project scenario, when creating products or making decisions related to this theme, in any or all of the processes.			
Specifically to:			
Identify appropriate information, using the recommended composition, for inclusion in the Risk Management Strategy and Risk Register		X	7
Identify the appropriate actions and responsibilities when applying the steps within the recommended risk management procedure, as listed above		X	7
Identify primary and secondary risks and estimate inherent and residual risks		X	7
Be able to identify, analyze, and distinguish between appropriate and inappropriate application of the Risk theme throughout the life cycle of a project scenario.			
Specifically to analyze:			
Whether the Risk Management Strategy and Risk Register, using the recommended composition, are fit for purpose, with reasons, and whether the appropriate roles have been involved in their development and maintenance throughout the life of a project		X	7
Whether activities undertaken during the execution of the recommended risk management procedure are appropriate, with reasons, and whether the appropriate roles have been involved		X	7

Syllabus area: Change (CH) theme

Learning Outcome	Foundation	Practitioner	Chapter
Know facts, terms, and concepts relating to the Change theme.			
Specifically to recall:			
Three types of issues	X		8
Five typical activities of a configuration management procedure	X		8
Understand how the Change theme relates to the principles; the approach to the treatment of this theme; how it is applied throughout the project life cycle and the responsibilities involved.			
Specifically to identify:			
The purpose of the Change theme	X		8
The purpose of a change budget	X		8
The purpose of a:			
1. Configuration Management Strategy			
2. Configuration Item Record	X		8
3. Issue Report			
4. Issue Register			
5. Product Status Account			
The steps in the recommended issue and change control procedure	X		8
In which process(es) issues are captured and managed, and which roles are responsible		X	8
In which process(es) a change budget and a Change Authority are agreed and which roles are responsible		X	8
The recommended composition of a:			
1. Configuration Management Strategy			
2. Configuration Item Record			
3. Issue Report		X	8
4. Issue Register			
5. Product Status Account			
and in which process(es) they are developed, used, and reviewed, and which roles are responsible for this			
Be able to apply and tailor the relevant aspects of the Change theme to a project scenario, when creating products or making decisions related to this theme, in any or all of the processes.			

(continued)

Learning Outcome	Foundation	Practitioner	Chapter
Specifically to:			
Identify appropriate information, using the recommended composition, for inclusion in the Configuration Management Strategy, Configuration Item Record, Issue Report, Issue Register and Product Status Account		X	8
Identify the appropriate type for a given issue		X	8
Identify the appropriate actions and responsibilities when applying the recommended issue and change control procedure		X	8
Identify appropriate resource(s) for the role of Change Authority		X	8
Identify the appropriate actions and responsibilities when applying the typical activities of a configuration management procedure		X	8
Be able to identify, analyze, and distinguish between appropriate and inappropriate application of the Change theme throughout the life cycle of a project scenario.			
Specifically to analyze:			
Whether the Configuration Management Strategy, Configuration Item Record, Issue Report, Issue Register, and Product Status Account, using the recommended composition, are fit for purpose, with reasons, and whether the appropriate roles have been involved in their development and maintenance throughout the life of a project		X	8
Whether activities undertaken during the execution of the recommended issue and change control procedure are appropriate, with reasons, and whether the appropriate roles have been involved, including activities associated with:			
1. Capturing and analyzing to determine the type of issue and whether it can be managed informally or formally		X	8
2. Examining an issue to determine its impact			
3. Proposing a course of action			
4. Deciding on appropriate course of action			
5. Implementing agreed action			

Learning Outcome	Foundation	Practitioner	Chapter
Whether the typical activities of a configuration management procedure have been undertaken appropriately, with reasons, and whether the appropriate roles have been involved, including activities associated with:			
1. Planning what level of configuration management is required		X	8
2. Identifying configuration items			
3. Controlling configuration items			
4. Status accounting			
5. Verifying and auditing configuration items			

Syllabus area: Progress (PG) theme

Learning Outcome	Foundation	Practitioner	Chapter
Know facts, terms, and concepts relating to the Progress theme.			
Specifically to recall the:			
Lines of authority and reporting between the four levels of management	X		9
Understand how the Progress theme relates to the principles; the approach to the treatment of this theme; how it is applied throughout the project life cycle and the responsibilities involved.			
Specifically to identify:			
The difference between event-driven and time-driven controls	X		9
The purpose of the Progress theme	X		9
The concept of management stages and the difference between management and technical stages	X		9
The factors to consider in identifying management stages	X		9
Tolerance(s): when and how tolerances are set and exceptions reported, in which management products tolerances are documented, and how management by exception applies to the different levels of management	X		9

(continued)

Learning Outcome	Foundation	Practitioner	Chapter
The purpose of a:	X		9
1. Daily Log			
2. Lessons Log			
3. Work Package			
4. Lessons Report			
5. Exception Report			
The purpose of a:	X		10
1. End Stage Report			
2. Checkpoint Report			
3. Highlight Report			
The purpose of an:	X		11
1. End Project Report			
The recommended composition of a:		X	9
1. Lessons Log			
2. Work Package			
3. Lessons Report			
4. Exception Report			
and in which process(es) they are developed, used, and reviewed, and which roles are responsible for this			
The recommended composition of a:		X	10
1. End Stage Report			
2. Checkpoint Report			
3. Highlight Report			
and in which process(es) they are developed, used, and reviewed, and which roles are responsible for this			
The recommended composition of an:		X	11
1. End Project Report			
and in which process(es) it is developed, used, and reviewed, and which roles are responsible for this			
Be able to apply and tailor the relevant aspects of the Progress theme to a project scenario, when creating products or making decisions related to this theme, in any or all of the processes.			
Specifically to:			
Identify appropriate information, using the recommended composition, for inclusion in the Work Package, Lessons Log, Exception Report, and Lessons Report		X	9

Learning Outcome	Foundation	Practitioner	Chapter
Identify appropriate information, using the recommended composition, for inclusion in the Checkpoint Report, Highlight Report, and End Stage Report		X	10
Identify appropriate information, using the recommended composition, for inclusion in the End Project Report		X	11
Identify the appropriate actions and responsibilities when applying the concept of management by exception		X	9
Be able to identify, analyze, and distinguish between appropriate and inappropriate application of the Progress theme throughout the life cycle of a project scenario.			
Specifically to analyze:			
Whether the Work Package, Lessons Log, Exception Report, and Lessons Report, using the recommended composition, are fit for purpose, with reasons, and whether the appropriate roles have been involved in their development and maintenance throughout the life of a project		X	9
Whether the Checkpoint Report, Highlight Report, and End Stage Report, using the recommended composition, are fit for purpose, with reasons, and whether the appropriate roles have been involved in their development and maintenance throughout the life of a project		X	10
Whether the End Project Report, using the recommended composition, is fit for purpose, with reasons, and whether the appropriate roles have been involved in their development and maintenance throughout the life of a project		X	11
Whether activities undertaken to manage by exception during the execution of the project were applied appropriately, with reasons, and whether the appropriate roles have been involved		X	5, 9

Syllabus area: Starting up a Project (SU) process

Learning Outcome	Foundation	Practitioner	Chapter
Understand the SU process and how it can be applied and tailored on a project.			
Specifically to identify:			
The purpose of the SU process	X		2
The objectives of the SU process	X		2

(continued)

Learning Outcome	Foundation	Practitioner	Chapter
The context of the SU process	X		2
The purpose of a Project Brief	X		2
The following activities within the SU process and the responsibilities within them:			
1. Appointing the Executive and the Project Manager			
2. Capturing previous lessons			
3. Designing and appointing the project management team		X	2
4. Preparing the outline Business Case			
5. Selecting the project approach and assembling the Project Brief			
6. Planning the initiation stage			
How the seven themes may be applied within the SU process		X	2
The recommended composition of a Project Brief and in which process(es) it is developed, used, and reviewed, and which roles are responsible		X	2
Be able to apply the SU process, tailoring the recommended activities and actions where appropriate, to a project scenario.			
Specifically to:			
Identify appropriate information, using the recommended composition, for inclusion in the Project Brief		X	2
Identify the recommended SU process actions when carrying out the activities listed above		X	2
Be able to identify, analyze, and distinguish between appropriate and inappropriate application of the SU process to a project scenario.			
Specifically to analyze:			
Whether the Project Brief, using the recommended composition, is fit for its purpose, with reasons, and whether the appropriate roles have been involved in its development and maintenance throughout the SU process		X	2
Whether the recommended SU process actions have been undertaken appropriately, with reasons, and whether the appropriate roles have been involved when carrying out the activities listed above		X	2

Syllabus area: directing a Project (DP) process

Learning Outcome	Foundation	Practitioner	Chapter
Understand the DP process and how it can be applied and tailored to a project.			
Specifically to identify:			
The purpose of the DP process	X		1, 2, 10, 11
The objectives of the DP process	X		1, 2, 10, 11
The context of the DP process	X		1, 2, 10, 11
The following activities within the DP process and the responsibilities within them:			
1. Authorizing initiation			
2. Authorizing the project		X	1, 2, 10, 11
3. Authorizing a Stage or Exception Plan			
4. Giving ad hoc direction			
5. Authorizing project closure			
How the seven themes may be applied within the DP process		X	1, 2, 10, 11
Be able to identify, analyze, and distinguish between appropriate and inappropriate application of the DP process to a project scenario.			
Specifically to analyze:			
Whether the recommended DP process actions have been undertaken appropriately, with reasons, and whether the appropriate roles have been involved when carrying out the activities listed above		X	10

Syllabus area: Initiating a Project (IP) process

Learning Outcome	Foundation	Practitioner	Chapter
Understand the IP process and how it can be applied and tailored to a project.			
Specifically to identify:			
The purpose of the IP process	X		2
The objectives of the IP process	X		2
The context of the IP process	X		2

(continued)

Learning Outcome	Foundation	Practitioner	Chapter
The purpose of Project Initiation Documentation (PID)	X		2
The following activities within the IP process and the responsibilities within them:			
1. Preparing the Risk Management Strategy			
2. Preparing the Configuration Management Strategy			
3. Preparing the Quality Management Strategy		X	2
4. Preparing the Communication Management Strategy			
5. Setting up the project controls			
6. Create the Project Plan			
7. Refining the Business Case			
8. Assembling the Project Initiation Documentation			
How the seven themes may be applied within the IP process		X	2
The recommended composition of the Project Initiation Documentation, and in which process(es) it is developed, used, and reviewed, and which roles are responsible		X	2
Be able to apply the IP process, tailoring the recommended activities and actions where appropriate, to a project scenario.			
Specifically to:			
Identify the recommended IP process actions when carrying out the activities listed above		X	2
Be able to identify, analyze, and distinguish between appropriate and inappropriate application of the IP process to a project scenario.			
Specifically to analyze:			
Whether the Project Initiation Documentation, using the recommended composition, is fit for its purpose, with reasons, and whether the appropriate roles have been involved in its development and maintenance throughout the IP process		X	2
Whether the recommended IP process actions have been undertaken appropriately, with reasons, and whether the appropriate roles have been involved when carrying out the activities listed above		X	2

Syllabus area: Controlling a Stage (CS) process

Learning Outcome	Foundation	Practitioner	Chapter
Understand the CS process and how it can be applied and tailored to a project.			
Specifically to identify:			
The purpose of the CS process	X		10
The objectives of the CS process	X		10
The context of the CS process	X		10
The following activities within the CS process and the responsibilities within them:			
1. Authorizing a Work Package			
2. Reviewing Work Package status			
3. Receiving completed Work Packages		X	10
4. Reviewing the stage status			
5. Reporting Highlights			
6. Capturing and examining issue and risks			
7. Escalating issues and risks			
8. Taking corrective action			
How the seven themes may be applied within the CS process		X	10
Be able to apply the CS process, tailoring the recommended activities and actions where appropriate, to a project scenario.			
Specifically to:			
Identify the recommended CS process actions when carrying out the activities listed above		X	10
Be able to identify, analyze, and distinguish between appropriate and inappropriate application of the CS process to a project scenario.			
Specifically to analyze:			
Whether the recommended CS process actions have been undertaken appropriately, with reasons, and whether the appropriate roles have been involved when carrying out the activities listed above		X	10

Syllabus area: Managing Product Delivery (MP) process

Learning Outcome	Foundation	Practitioner	Chapter
Understand the MP process and how it can be applied and tailored to a project.			
Specifically to identify:			
The purpose of the MP process	X		10
The objectives of the MP process	X		10
The context of the MP process	X		10
The following activities within the MP process and the responsibilities within them:			
1. Accepting a Work Package		X	10
2. Executing a Work Package			
3. Delivering a Work Package			
How the seven themes may be applied within the MP process		X	10
Be able to apply the MP process, tailoring the recommended activities and actions where appropriate, to a project scenario.			
Specifically to:			
Identify the recommended MP process actions when carrying out the activities listed above		X	10
Be able to identify, analyze, and distinguish between appropriate and inappropriate application of the MP process to a project scenario.			
Specifically to analyze:			
Whether the recommended MP process actions have been undertaken appropriately, with reasons, and whether the appropriate roles have been involved when carrying out the activities listed above		X	10

Syllabus area: Managing a Stage Boundary (SB) process

Learning Outcome	Foundation	Practitioner	Chapter
Understand the SB process and how it can be applied and tailored on a project.			
Specifically to identify:			
The purpose of the SB process	X		10
The objectives of the SB process	X		10

Learning Outcome	Foundation	Practitioner	Chapter
The context of the SB process	X		10
The following activities within the SB process and the responsibilities within them:			
1. Planning the next stage			
2. Updating the Project Plan		X	10
3. Updating the Business Case			
4. Reporting stage end			
5. Producing an Exception Plan			
How the seven themes may be applied within the SB process		X	10
Be able to apply the SB process, tailoring the recommended activities and actions where appropriate, to a project scenario.			
Specifically to:			
Identify the recommended SB process actions when carrying out the activities listed above		X	10
Be able to identify, analyze, and distinguish between appropriate and inappropriate application of the SB process to a project scenario.			
Specifically to analyze:			
Whether the recommended SB process actions have been undertaken appropriately, with reasons, and whether the appropriate roles have been involved when carrying out the activities listed above		X	10

Syllabus area: Closing a Project (CP) process

Learning Outcome	Foundation	Practitioner	Chapter
Understand the CP process and how it can be applied and tailored to a project.			
Specifically to identify:			
The purpose of the CP process	X		11
The objectives of the CP process	X		11

(continued)

Learning Outcome	Foundation	Practitioner	Chapter
The context of the CP process	X		11
The following activities within the CP process and the responsibilities within them:			
1. Preparing planned closure			
2. Preparing premature closure		X	11
3. Hand over products			
4. Evaluate the project			
5. Recommend project closure			
How the seven themes may be applied within the CP process		X	11
Be able to apply the CP process, tailoring the recommended activities and actions where appropriate, to a project scenario.			
Specifically to:			
Identify the recommended CP process actions when carrying out the activities listed above		X	11
Be able to identify, analyze, and distinguish between appropriate and inappropriate application of the CP process to a project scenario.			
Specifically to analyze:			
Whether the recommended CP process actions have been undertaken appropriately, with reasons, and whether the appropriate roles have been involved when carrying out the activities listed above		X	11

Exam specifications and content are subject to change at any time without prior notice and at The APM Group (APMG)'s sole discretion. Please visit APMG's website (www.prince-officialsite.com/) for the most current information on exam content.

Assessment Test

1. Which of these processes occurs before the project has been commissioned?

   A. Initiating a Project

   B. Managing a Stage Boundary

   C. Starting up a Project

   D. Controlling a Stage

2. During which PRINCE2 process is the project's management team designed?

   A. Starting up a Project

   B. Initiating a Project

   C. Controlling a Stage

   D. Managing Product Delivery

3. Which information does **NOT** appear in the PRINCE2 Business Case?

   A. Business options

   B. Delivery options

   C. Project costs

   D. Duration over which benefits will be measured

4. In which process is the Stage Plan for the initiation stage created?

   A. Starting up a Project

   B. Initiating a Project

   C. Managing a Stage Boundary

   D. Directing a Project

5. The fact that project work often spans multiple organizations and functional divisions relates to which characteristic of a project?

   A. Change

   B. Risk

   C. Cross-functional

   D. Uncertainty

6. Which of the following are **NOT** examples of situations that PRINCE2 can be tailored for?

   A. Multi-organization projects

   B. Small projects

   C. Commercial customer/supplier environment

   D. Business as usual

7. Which of the following is **NOT** a quality review technique activity?

    A. Review preparation

    B. Review meeting

    C. Review follow-up

    D. Review approval

8. Which PRINCE2 process is used to review and, if necessary, update the project management team?

    A. Managing a Stage Boundary

    B. Directing a Project

    C. Controlling a Stage

    D. Managing Product Delivery

9. In which process would a change budget for a stage be authorized?

    A. Initiating a Project

    B. Managing a Stage Boundary

    C. Controlling a Stage

    D. Directing a Project

10. Which PRINCE2 risk response type cannot be applied to an opportunity?

    A. Accept

    B. Enhance

    C. Reject

    D. Share

11. Which of the following is a task in the product-based planning technique?

    A. Prepare estimates

    B. Identify activities and dependencies

    C. Create the product breakdown structure

    D. Document the plan

12. Which role might the Project Manager consult during the activities of Initiating a Project to ensure that the various sections of the Project Initiation Documentation meet the needs of the Project Board?

    A. Project Assurance

    B. Project Support

    C. Change Authority

    D. Team Manager

13. The person who is responsible for managing, monitoring, and controlling all aspects of a particular risk is the _____.

   A. Risk Owner

   B. Risk Manager

   C. Risk Actionee

   D. Project Manager

14. Which is **NOT** one of the six aspects of project performance that needs to be managed?

   A. Quality

   B. Contracts

   C. Scope

   D. Timescales

15. A PRINCE2 risk is _____.

   A. A certain event that will affect the project in a positive or negative way

   B. A certain event that will affect the project in a negative way

   C. An uncertain event that will affect the project in a positive or negative way

   D. An uncertain event that will affect the project in a negative way

16. Which management product is used by the Project Manager to pass responsibility for the delivery of the products to the Team Manager or team member?

   A. Product Descriptions

   B. Team Plans

   C. Work Package

   D. Configuration Item Record

17. Which management product sets out the procedures, responsibilities, and tools and techniques necessary to ensure that the project delivers what users expect?

   A. Project Product Description

   B. Quality Management Strategy

   C. Product Descriptions

   D. Quality Register

18. Which management product does the Project Manager regularly create during the Controlling a Stage process to report progress to the Project Board?

   A. Checkpoint Report

   B. Highlight Report

   C. End Stage Report

   D. Exception Report

19. Which of the following management products might be used to capture an issue?

   1. Daily Log

   2. Issue Register

   3. Issue Report

   4. Risk Register

   A. 1, 2, 3

   B. 1, 2, 4

   C. 1, 3, 4

   D. 2, 3, 4

20. The purpose of which theme is to provide a forecast for the project's objectives and control any unacceptable deviations?

   A. Business Case

   B. Plans

   C. Quality

   D. Progress

21. Which process is the Quality Register created in?

   A. Starting up a Project

   B. Initiating a Project

   C. Controlling a Stage

   D. Managing Product Delivery

22. How would the Project Manager escalate a situation where stage tolerances are forecast to be exceeded?

   A. Exception Report

   B. Highlight Report

   C. Exception Plans

   D. End Stage Report

23. Which role is responsible for assembling the Project Initiation Documentation?

   A. Executive

   B. Project Manager

   C. Project Support

   D. Senior User

24. Which level of management would make a decision regarding a breach of project tolerances?

   A. Corporate or programme management

   B. Project Board

   C. Project Manager

   D. Team Manager

25. Which is the only PRINCE2 role within the project management team that has post-project responsibilities?

    A. Senior User

    B. Executive

    C. Senior Supplier

    D. Project Manager

26. During which process are specialist products created?

    A. Initiating a Project

    B. Controlling a Stage

    C. Managing Product Delivery

    D. Managing a Stage Boundary

27. The three types of issue are request for change, off-specification, and _____.

    A. Potential opportunity

    B. Dis-benefit

    C. Problem or concern

    D. External product

28. Which of these is a purpose of the Quality theme?

    A. Ensure that issues affecting quality are appropriately managed

    B. Identify, assess, and control uncertainty that might affect the quality of the project's products

    C. Establish mechanisms to provide a forecast for the project's objectives

    D. Ensure that the project's products meet business expectations

29. Which is **NOT** one of the benefits provided by PRINCE2?

    A. Presents a generic approach that can be applied to any type of project

    B. Improves leadership capabilities

    C. Provides a thorough and economical set of reports

    D. Provides explicit recognition of project responsibilities

30. Which of the following management products may be updated during the Managing a Stage Boundary process?

    1. Project Brief

    2. Configuration Management Strategy

    3. Business Case

    4. Project Approach

    A. 1, 2, 3

    B. 1, 3, 4

    C. 1, 2, 4

    D. 2, 3, 4

31. Which principle does the Organization theme primarily implement?

   A. Continued business justification

   B. Learn from experience

   C. Tailor to suit the project environment

   D. Defined roles and responsibilities

32. Which plan provides the Business Case with planned costs and timescales?

   A. Project Plan

   B. Stage Plans

   C. Team Plan

   D. Exception Plan

33. The Project Manager reviews the _____ to identify any organization that needs to be informed when the project is closing.

   A. Communication Management Strategy

   B. Work Package for Closing a Project

   C. Configuration Management Strategy

   D. Notification from the Project Board

34. Weighing a project's benefits against ongoing operational and maintenance costs is one aspect of _____.

   A. Benefits Review Planning

   B. Investment Appraisal

   C. Cost Planning

   D. Sensitivity Analysis

35. Which of the following are the three primary interests that are represented on a PRINCE2 Project Board?

   1. Business

   2. Customer

   3. User

   4. Supplier

   A. 1, 2, 3

   B. 1, 3, 4

   C. 1, 2, 4

   D. 2, 3, 4

36. Which of the following statements describes the general approach to tailoring PRINCE2?

1. Using PRINCE2 with a lightness of touch

2. Omitting elements of PRINCE2 to suit the situation

3. Avoiding introducing unnecessary bureaucracy

4. Adapting the method to external and project factors

A. 1, 2, 3

B. 1, 2, 4

C. 1, 3, 4

D. 2, 3, 4

37. Which of the following are **NOT** examples of PRINCE2 reports?

A. Risk Register

B. Product Status Account

C. Highlight Report

D. Checkpoint Report

38. Which one of the following is **NOT** a step in the PRINCE2 risk management procedure?

A. Communicate

B. Plan

C. Identify

D. Mitigate

39. Which is the first plan that is created during the PRINCE2 process model?

A. Project Plan

B. Stage Plan for the initiation stage

C. Stage Plan for the first delivery stage

D. Programme Plan

40. Which of the following is the fundamental philosophy behind the PRINCE2 approach to plans?

A. Just-in-time planning

B. Product-based planning

C. Brainstorming

D. Use of work breakdown structures

41. Which role is responsible for producing the outputs from the Closing a Project process?

A. Corporate or programme management

B. Project Board

C. Project Manager

D. Team Manager

42. Which process describes the work of the Project Manager in handling the day-to-day management of each delivery stage?

    A. Starting up a Project

    B. Initiating a Project

    C. Controlling a Stage

    D. Managing Product Delivery

43. During which PRINCE2 process is the outline Business Case created?

    A. Starting up a Project

    B. Initiating a Project

    C. Controlling a Stage

    D. Managing a Stage Boundary

44. Which process is used to create the Configuration Management Strategy?

    A. Starting up a Project

    B. Initiating a Project

    C. Controlling a Stage

    D. Managing a Stage Boundary

Answers to Assessment Test

1. **C.** The Starting up a Project process occurs before the project has been commissioned. The process's purpose is to collate information upon which the Project Board can make a decision whether to commission the project during the authorizing initiation activity. See Chapter 2, "Starting a Project Successfully with PRINCE2."

2. **A.** The project management team is designed in the Starting up a Project process during the Design and appoint the project management team activity. Refer to Chapter 2, "Starting a Project Successfully with PRINCE2."

3. **B.** Delivery Options will appear in the Project Approach, not the Business Case. See "The Contents of the Business Case" in Chapter 4, "Business Case Theme."

4. **A.** The Stage Plan for the initiation stage is created in the Starting up a Project process in order for the Project Board to review the work necessary for the initiation stage before authorizing it. See Chapter 5, "Plans Theme."

5. **C.** The cross-functional characteristic of a project means that often projects involve several groups of people who don't usually work together. The groups could come from different functional divisions or even different organizations. See Chapter 1, "Overview of PRINCE2."

6. **D.** PRINCE2 is not used to manage business-as-usual situations. See Chapter 12, "Tailoring PRINCE2 to the Project Environment."

7. **D.** The quality review technique has three steps: review preparation, review meeting, and review follow-up. See Chapter 6, "Quality Theme."

8. **A.** At the end of each stage, the Project Manager reviews the project management team to see if it needs to be updated for the next stage. Refer to Chapter 3, "Organization Theme."

9. **D.** A change budget, along with the stage budget and any risk budget for that stage, would be authorized by the Project Board during Directing a Project in the Authorize a stage activity. See Chapter 8, "Change Theme."

10. **A.** To answer this question, you need to know the various terms that PRINCE2 uses for risk responses to threats and for opportunities. Intuitively you might pick option C, reject. But in fact, the correct answer is option A, accept, because PRINCE2 reserves this word for a type of threat response. See the "Plan" section of the Risk Management Procedure in Chapter 7, "Risk Theme."

11. **C.** The product-based planning technique includes four tasks: writing the Project Product Description, creating the product breakdown structure, writing the Product Descriptions, and creating the product flow diagram. See Chapter 5, "Plans Theme."

12. **A.** Project Assurance will check and audit the work of the Project Manager during the project, to ensure that it will be acceptable for the people on the Project Board. See Chapter 2, "Starting a Project Successfully with PRINCE2."

13. A. The Risk Owner's role is to manage and monitor an assigned risk. See the "Implement" section under "Risk Management Procedure" in Chapter 7, "Risk Theme."

14. B. According to PRINCE2, the six aspects of project performance that need to be managed are costs, timescales, quality, scope, risk, and benefits. See Chapter 1, "Overview of PRINCE2."

15. C. In PRINCE2, a risk is something that may or may not happen—in other words, it is uncertain. Normally you might think of a risk as a negative event, but in PRINCE2 it could also have a favorable impact on the project. See "How Does PRINCE2 Use the Word *Risk*?" in Chapter 7, "Risk Theme."

16. C. The Work Package is used by the Project Manager to pass on information to the teams in order for them to understand what to deliver and how to do it. It is used to pass authority to the teams for the delivery of one or more products. See the "Project Manager Controls" section in Chapter 9, "Progress Theme."

17. B. The Quality Management Strategy sets out how the project will be managed to ensure it delivers products that meet the users' expectations. See Chapter 6, "Quality Theme."

18. B. The Project Manager creates the Highlight Report to regularly report progress to the Project Board during the Controlling a Stage process. See Chapter 10, "Managing the Middle of a Project Successfully with PRINCE2."

19. A. If the issue is informal, it might be captured in the Daily Log. If it is to be treated formally, an entry in the Issue Register would be created as well as a corresponding Issue Report. The Risk Register is used to capture risks, not issues. See Chapter 8, "Change Theme."

20. D. The purpose of the Progress theme is to establish mechanisms to monitor and compare actual achievements against those planned; provide a forecast for the project objectives and the project's continued viability; and control any unacceptable deviations. See Chapter 9, "Progress Theme."

21. B. The Quality Register is created in the Prepare the Quality Management Strategy activity in the Initiating a Project process. See Chapter 6, "Quality Theme."

22. A. The Project Manager uses the Exception Report to escalate to the Project Board situations where stage tolerances are forecast to be exceeded. See the "Tolerances and Exceptions" section in Chapter 9, "Progress Theme."

23. B. The Project Manager is responsible for assembling the Project Initiation Documentation. This is the final activity in the Initiating a Project process. See Chapter 2, "Starting a Project Successfully with PRINCE2."

24. A. Corporate or programme management makes decisions regarding a breach of project level tolerances. See the "Tolerances and Exceptions" section in Chapter 9, "Progress Theme."

25. A. The Senior User must demonstrate that the forecast benefits have been realized. In most projects, many of the benefits will not occur until after the project. See the "Business Case Responsibilities" section in Chapter 4, "Business Case Theme."

26. C. The teams create specialist products during the Execute a Work Package activity in the Managing Product Delivery process. See Chapter 10, "Managing the Middle of a Project Successfully with PRINCE2."

27. C. There are three types of issues in PRINCE2: request for change, off-specification, and problem or concern. See Chapter 8, "Change Theme."

28. D. Ensuring that the project's products meet business expectations is a purpose of the Quality theme. See Chapter 6, "Quality Theme."

29. B. PRINCE2 does not focus on people-management or leadership skills. See Chapter 1, "Overview of PRINCE2."

30. D. All elements of the Project Initiation Documentation may be updated during the Managing a Stage Boundary process. The Configuration Management Strategy, the Business Case, and the Project Approach are all elements of the Project Initiation Documentation. The Project Brief is not updated after the Starting up a Project process. See Chapter 10, "Managing the Middle of a Project Successfully with PRINCE2."

31. D. The Organization theme ensures that everyone involved in the project's team—at the directing, managing, and delivering levels—is clear about what is expected of them. Refer to Chapter 3, "Organization Theme."

32. A. The Project Plan provides the Business Case with planned costs and timescales. See Chapter 5, "Plans Theme."

33. A. Option A is correct—the Communication Management Strategy details the requirements for reporting to the project's stakeholders, including the stakeholders who must be notified of the project closing. See Chapter 11, "Managing the End of a Project Successfully with PRINCE2."

34. B. One of the key sections of the Business Case is Investment Appraisal. This balances the forecast benefits against project costs and ongoing operational and maintenance costs. See "The Contents of the Business Case" in Chapter 4, "Business Case Theme."

35. B. The three primary interests of stakeholders that are represented on the Project Board are *business*, represented by the Executive; *user*, represented by Senior Users; and *supplier*, represented by the Senior Suppliers. Refer to the section "The Three Project Interests" in Chapter 3, "Organization Theme."

36. C. Tailoring PRINCE2 consists of applying the method to the level required, not omitting elements of the method (which would weaken the approach). See Chapter 12, "Tailoring PRINCE2 to the Project Environment."

37. A. A Risk Register is a record, not a report. See Chapter 1, "Overview of PRINCE2."

38. D. Although you may talk about mitigating a risk in everyday speech, this is not a PRINCE2 term. The steps in the PRINCE2 risk management procedure are identify, assess, plan, implement, and communicate. See the "Risk Management Procedure" section in Chapter 7, "Risk Theme."

39. B. The Stage Plan for the initiation stage is created in Starting up a Project, so it is the first one that is created. The Project Plan is created later in the Initiating a Project process, the delivery Stage Plans are created later in the Managing a Stage Boundary process, and the Programme Plan is not created within the PRINCE2 model. See Chapter 5, "Plans Theme."

40. B. A fundamental philosophy behind the PRINCE2 approach to plans is that the products required are identified before the activities and resources to deliver those products are identified. This is known as product-based planning. Just-in-time planning, brainstorming, and work breakdown structures are not PRINCE2 techniques or approaches. See Chapter 5, "Plans Theme."

41. C. The Project Manager is responsible for producing the management products within the Closing a Project process. See Chapter 11, "Managing the End of a Project Successfully with PRINCE2."

42. C. The Controlling a Stage process contains a set of activities that are used by the Project Manager to manage each delivery stage. See Chapter 10, "Managing the Middle of a Project Successfully with PRINCE2."

43. A. During the Starting up a Project process, the Executive will draft the outline Business Case. Refer to the section "Using the Business Case Theme" in Chapter 4, "Business Case Theme."

44. B. The Configuration Management Strategy is created along with the other strategies in Initiating a Project. See Chapter 8, "Change Theme."

Chapter

1

Overview of PRINCE2

PRINCE2 EXAM OBJECTIVES COVERED IN THIS CHAPTER:

- ✓ Understand the six aspects of project performance that need to be managed.

- ✓ Define what a project is and the characteristics of project work that distinguish it from business as usual.

- ✓ Understand that the four integrated elements of PRINCE2 are the principles, the processes, the themes, and tailoring PRINCE2 to the project environment.

- ✓ Understand the benefits of using PRINCE2.

- ✓ Explain the seven principles of PRINCE2.

This is a really important chapter—it sets out the overall framework of PRINCE2. You will learn about the main components of the PRINCE2 model and see how they all fit together. Each section of PRINCE2 often has many relationships with other parts of the methodology, so the first step in learning the approach is to understand how the structure links together. Then when I discuss a particular PRINCE2 topic, you will see how it fits into the model.

In this chapter, I will also introduce some of the main PRINCE2 terms. You have quite a lot of terminology to learn! You might need to do some translation between the project management vocabulary you are familiar with and the PRINCE2 terms.

PRINCE2 is a management method that is used in project situations. In this chapter, you will see how PRINCE2 defines a project and how it differs from "business as usual." I will describe the main groups of project management activities as well as what needs to be achieved for a successful project.

The PRINCE2 model adheres to seven principles. I will describe the details of these principles and show you why they contribute to successful project management.

Finally, I will use an example project scenario to walk you through each step of a PRINCE2 project.

Project Work

In this section, you will see how PRINCE2 defines a project. This is important: only project situations are managed with PRINCE2, so the first task is to understand whether a piece of work is a project or business as usual. You will then learn how PRINCE2 defines project management. Finally, you will see what objectives can be set for a project.

What Is a Project?

PRINCE2 is *only* used to manage projects. So the first step for a Project Manager is to ensure that the situation they are faced with is indeed a project. Sometimes, this is not so easy. If an IT manager is asked to update a website, is that a project? If the update is quite small, the work might be considered a normal operational task. If it's a larger piece of work, then it might be treated as a project. At what point does the small update become too big to be business as usual?

The answer to this question relates to risk. An approach such as PRINCE2 provides a management framework that considerably increases the likelihood of project success. However, for small jobs, the framework might introduce a large and unnecessary management overhead. So deciding whether to treat a situation as a project is all about balancing the management overhead that would be introduced against such things as the decrease in the level of risk, the importance of the work, and the increase in the likelihood of success.

PRINCE2 defines a *project* as "a temporary organization that is created for the purpose of delivering one or more business products according to an agreed Business Case." The definition mentions a temporary organization. In PRINCE2, a group of people called the *project management team* come together for the duration of the project. Business products are ones that will ultimately deliver some return for the organization running the project. Also note that the definition mentions a Business Case. PRINCE2 places a great deal of importance on the justification of the project. Anyone involved with the project should be able to justify why they are doing it.

Certain characteristics of project work distinguish it from business as usual.

Change   The organization will be different after the project. For example, if the project implements a new invoice-processing system, the finance department will be working in quite a different way after the project than it did before it.

Temporary   Projects don't go on forever (although a few I've worked on have felt as if they have!). They should have a start and an end point. The end point occurs when the desired change has been implemented.

Cross-functional   *Cross-functional* projects often involve a collection of people drawn from many different sets of skills, different departments, and sometimes even different organizations.

Unique   To some extent, all project work is unique. On the one extreme, the project could be completely unique, such as the 1960s Apollo missions to send a man to the moon. Alternatively, the project could be just slightly different from what has been done before. For example, the installation of a new version of office software might be similar to the installation of the last version; however, this time the software is a little different and maybe new people are involved.

Uncertainty   The previous four characteristics introduce a great deal of uncertainty into project work. It is not quite clear how things will turn out. All sorts of unforeseen threats might occur. This uncertainty introduces a lot more risk compared with business as usual.

> ### 🌐 Real World Scenario
>
> **Cross-Functional Aspect of Project Work**
>
> My consultancy was involved in a project that was a good example of one with cross-functional characteristics. The project's objective was to install a new Internet system in a UK government education department. The site was to hold examination syllabus information for the various national curriculums. Within the government department, two main divisions were involved: the IT division and an information division. There were also a number of senior managers. The website was being built by a third-party software house. The teaching unions were represented, because they needed to specify their informational requirements. There was a government quality assurance group who audited the project to ensure it met UK government standards. We all came from different backgrounds, saw the project with different perspectives, and had our own way of working. All these parties had to come together and work as a unified team on a temporary basis. They did, and the project was a success, although at times it was difficult. The key was to pay particular attention to how we all communicated with each other throughout the project. I will talk about how PRINCE2 meets this challenge in Chapter 3, "Organization Theme."

What Is Business as Usual?

PRINCE2 is not used to manage situations that could be regarded as *business as usual*. Business as usual is any work that is part of an organization's normal operations—for example, supporting a company's IT systems, cleaning the rooms of a hotel, or running a call center. It has no predefined end. It usually involves people from the same area of the business and doesn't introduce any major change into the organization. It isn't unique—what was done last week is pretty much what will be done next week. Therefore, far less uncertainty exists regarding the work.

Project work often leads to business-as-usual work. For example, if there is a project to build a hotel, once that hotel opens, there will be a lot of business-as-usual work. This normal operational work might consist of a range of activities, including supporting the hotel's IT systems, manning the reception desk, dealing with clients' queries, running the restaurant, and so on.

What Is Project Management?

There are four main areas of *project management*: plan, delegate, monitor, and control. The four areas ensure that the specialist work of the project is co-coordinated in an effective way so as to deliver what is required within certain constraints, such as budgets and delivery dates. For example, if the project is to build a hotel, it ensures that all the hundreds of tasks, people, and resources work together to produce a hotel of the right quality. Here are some brief descriptions of each of the four areas of project management.

Plan   The first area is to plan what needs to be created and how this will be done. This ensures that all the work is effectively coordinated. In the hotel example, it stops situations such as the painters arriving on site before the builders have finished building the hotel walls.

Delegate   Effective delegation by the Project Manager ensures that the right people do the right work at the right time. Delegating must communicate all the information that the person doing the work needs to know, such as what to create, how much time they have, what budget that have, how often to report progress, and so on. (In PRINCE2, the Project Manager uses Work Packages to delegate work—more on this in Chapter 10, "Managing the Middle of a Project Successfully with PRINCE2.")

Monitor   It would be a naïve Project Manager who believes that once the work has been delegated, it will all be completed to plan. The Project Manager needs to constantly monitor the ongoing progress of the project, spotting problems that might delay things as well as opportunities to move the project forward.

Control   Through the previous three areas, project management exerts *control* over the project. It controls all the work of all the people involved. It ensures the right activities occur at the right time to create the right products. Control is also about taking corrective action when the project looks like it will go off course.

Figure 1.1 shows the four areas of project management in a wheel to signify that they will need to be done again and again throughout a project.

FIGURE 1.1   Project management

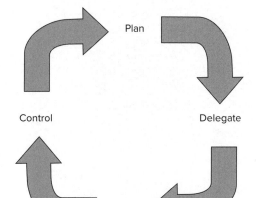

Based on Cabinet Office PRINCE2® material. Reproduced under licence from the Cabinet Office.

Measuring the Performance of a Project

A project's performance can be measured in six areas:

- How much money it spends; this relates to a project's costs.

- How ahead or behind schedule it is; this relates to a project's timescales.

- How well the project's products meet the required specification; this relates to a project's quality.

- How many of the required products have been delivered and whether any products have been delivered that were not asked for; this relates to a project's scope.

- How much uncertainty the project has that might lead to the project being negatively impacted; this relates to the level of project risk.

- How much value a project has delivered to the organization either during or after the project; this relates to a project's benefits.

It may be not possible to judge how well a project has performed against its benefits' targets until sometime after the initiative has finished. For example, if the project was to build a website to sell a company's products, online sales can't be measured until after the website has been launched.

Figure 1.2 shows these six different areas. PRINCE2 calls these areas the six aspects of project performance that need to be managed.

FIGURE 1.2 Six project objectives

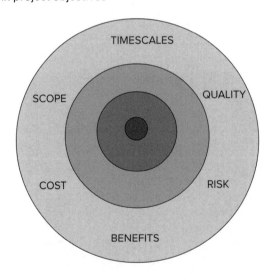

🌐 Real World Scenario

The Benefits of the London 2012 Olympics

As I said earlier, the benefit objective is the hardest one to meet. There are a number of reasons for this. First, the products of the project can become an end in themselves. So much effort, time, and money is involved in creating them that people forget they are there as a means to an end, not the end itself. Second, the achievement of the benefit objective can usually be measured only after the project has finished. Of course, by this time, the project team has been disbanded and members have moved on to the next big thing. No one is left to report on the achievement (or lack of it) of the project's returns.

In the months preceding the 2012 London Olympics there was a good example of a project nearly not delivering one of its major benefit objectives. One of the main stated benefits of the project was to create venues that could be used for British athletics events for many years to come. The Olympic Delivery Authority (the public body in charge of the project) had been looking for companies to take ownership of the main stadium after the Olympics. In 2011, two bids were put forward, both from London football (or soccer, for readers in the United States) teams. One bid was to turn the central grounds within the stadium into a football pitch but to keep the running tracks. Then the venue could be used for football and athletics events. The other bid, from a rival London club, proposed to demolish the stadium and build a new, football-only stadium in its place. Of course, if this happened, the legacy benefit for British athletics would not be met. Thankfully, in the end the football only-bid was not successful. One of the results of this was that London was awarded the hosting of the 2017 World Athletics Championships during which the main stadium would be used.

Introducing PRINCE2

In the previous section, we looked at projects. I explained that project work involves a lot of uncertainty and risk. When a project is started, it can be difficult to see ahead. It can be hard to know what to do next. Where PRINCE2 helps is that it says no matter what project you are involved with, you have certain steps that must be carried out to ensure success. Many of these steps are just common sense. For example, at the outset of all projects, those involved should agree on its objectives. Then at the end of the project, everyone should meet again to decide whether the objectives have been met. Another set of commonsense steps is that all projects should involve those who will ultimately use the project products, so that they can define what they require and later can verify that the products that have been created are fit for their purpose. There are many other commonalities in how all projects are managed, such as general approaches to managing areas like risks, changes, quality, and communication.

The PRINCE2 model combines all these commonsense ideas about managing projects. It gives a range of processes with steps to ensure the right management activities are done, defines role to ensure the right people take responsibility for doing the steps, and suggests a range of management documents to hold and report on useful management information. It disciplines everyone on the project to follow these commonsense ideas by appointing an assurance role, which checks whether the steps are being followed.

The Structure of PRINCE2

PRINCE2 is made up of four main parts, or what PRINCE2 refers to as *integrated elements*. These are the *principles*, the *themes*, the *processes*, and the *project environment*. These integrated elements are shown in Figure 1.3.

FIGURE 1.3   The structure of PRINCE2

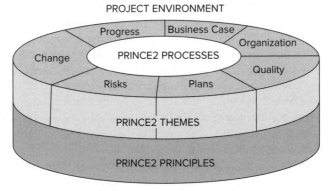

Based on Cabinet Office PRINCE2® material. Reproduced under licence from the Cabinet Office.

The Principles

The first integrated element of PRINCE2 is the principles. You can think of these as the core concepts that the rest of PRINCE2 adheres to. There are seven PRINCE2 principles, which are described in detail later in this chapter. An example is "learn from experience," which means (rather obviously!) that before anything is done to manage a project, it is always worth considering any prior experience that might be useful.

The Processes

The second integrated element of PRINCE2 is the seven processes. All of these processes provide a set of activities showing how to manage various parts of a project. The processes cover the management work from the time just before the project starts (when the question is whether the project should be done) to the end of the project. The processes show which roles should be responsible for each activity and what management documents (such as plans or reports) would be useful to create, review, or update at this time.

Each process covers a specific time during the project. For example, the Starting Up a Project process gives six activities that should be considered for a successful start to a project. The Closing a Project process, as the name suggests, covers the management activities that need to take place at the end of the project.

I describe the seven PRINCE2 processes in more detail in the "An End-to-End Walkthrough of PRINCE2" section later in this chapter. In the meantime, here's a brief overview of each process:

Starting Up a Project   *Starting Up a Project* covers the activities you use to investigate whether to start the project. I describe this process in detail in Chapter 2, "Starting a Project Successfully with PRINCE2."

Directing a Project   *Directing a Project* covers the activities of the *Project Board*, who are the main decision-making body on a PRINCE2 project. It includes making decisions such as whether the project should start, whether to move on to the next stage of the project, and whether the project can close.

Initiating a Project   *Initiating a Project* covers the planning activities done at the beginning of the project. I describe this process in detail in Chapter 2, "Starting a Project Successfully with PRINCE2."

Controlling a Stage   *Controlling a Stage* covers the Project Manager's day-to-day work, such as delegating work, reporting, and dealing with issues and risks. I describe this process in detail in Chapter 10, "Managing the Middle of a Project Successfully with PRINCE2."

Managing Product Delivery   *Managing Product Delivery* covers the day-to-day work of the people creating products in the project. The activities detail accepting work, creating it, reporting progress, and delivering work. I describe this process in detail in Chapter 10, "Managing the Middle of a Project Successfully with PRINCE2."

Managing a Stage Boundary   *Managing a Stage Boundary* covers the work of the Project Manager at the end of a major part or stage of the project. It involves activities such as reporting on the achievements in the last stage and detailed planning for the next stage. I describe this process in detail in Chapter 10, "Managing the Middle of a Project Successfully with PRINCE2."

Closing a Project   *Closing a Project* covers the work that the Project Manager does to prepare for the end of the project. It involves work such as preparing the End Project Report, handing the products to the operational teams, and archiving project documents. I describe this process in detail in Chapter 11, "Managing the End of a Project Successfully with PRINCE2."

The Themes

The third integrated element of PRINCE2 is the themes. The themes describe how PRINCE2 recommends carrying out various aspects of project management. For example, the Risk theme describes how PRINCE2 recommends managing risk throughout a project, and the

Organization theme describes how PRINCE2 recommends defining the project management team's roles and responsibilities.

Each of these themes may be useful throughout all the processes. For example, the risk management approach described in the Risk theme is used in all the processes. And any one process may use numerous themes. For example, in the Starting Up a Project process, the project management team is appointed (the organization structure and the accompanying roles are described in the Organization theme), risks for the project will need to identified (risk identification and estimation approaches are described in the Risk theme), and the outline Business Case is created (the composition of the Business Case is described in the Business Case theme).

There are seven themes in PRINCE2, and this study guide has a chapter explaining each one. Here's a brief overview of each theme:

Business Case   The *Business Case theme* describes how to ensure the project has a solid justifiable reason to exist, not just at the outset of the project, but throughout its life. It shows how to create a Business Case and how to plan the tracking of the project's benefits using a Benefits Review Plan. It sets out various activities related to justifying the project and shows which roles should be responsible for them. I describe this theme in detail in Chapter 4, "Business Case Theme."

Organization   The *Organization theme* defines the project management team structure. It describes the various roles within the structure and sets out their responsibilities. I describe this theme in detail in Chapter 3, "Organization Theme."

Quality   The *Quality theme* describes how to ensure that the project's products are fit for the purpose for which they will be used. I describe this theme in detail in Chapter 6, "Quality Theme."

Plans   The *Plans theme* describes how to plan what products to create and what activities are needed to build those products. I describe this theme in detail in Chapter 5, "Plans Theme."

Risk   The *Risk theme* describes how to manage potential threats and opportunities to the project. I describe this theme in detail in Chapter 7, "Risk Theme."

Change   The *Change theme* describes how to control and manage changes to the project's products. I describe this theme in detail in Chapter 8, "Change Theme."

Progress   The *Progress theme* describes how to track the progress of a project, what mechanisms to use to keep the project on track, and what to do when things go astray. I describe this theme in detail in Chapter 9, "Progress Theme."

The Project Environment

The fourth integrated element of PRINCE2 is the project environment and how to tailor PRINCE2 to that situation.

There are many types of projects and many environments in which they might run. Examples include very large, complex initiatives, involving various organizations and running over many years. In contrast, there are much smaller activities involving a few people over a number of days. Every possible industry you could think of runs projects, each creating very different products or services. Some projects run in the private sector, others in the public sector, and still others run in charities. Some projects use a variety of specialist approaches alongside PRINCE2, such as the one set out in the Project Management Institute's (PMI) *A Guide to the Project Management Body of Knowledge* (2009) or the agile approaches in computer software development.

PRINCE2 can be applied to all of these types of situations for two reasons. First, as I discussed earlier in the chapter, no matter what type of project you are running, there will be a common set of activities that need to be done, which are set out in PRINCE2. Second, the framework is flexible so that it can be tailored in many ways to suit the various situations described previously.

I will look at tailoring PRINCE2 to the project environment in more detail in Chapter 12, "Tailoring PRINCE2 to Particular Environments."

Exam Spotlight

How to tailor PRINCE2 to the multitude of potential project environments is a very important subject. However, the range of tailoring situations examined for the PRINCE2 accreditation is fairly limited. You may be asked how to tailor PRINCE2 to manage a small project, or how to tailor PRINCE2 for a project being run as part of a programme. (A programme is a collection of projects being run in a coordinated way.) You may also be asked to consider situations where there are multiple organizations involved in a project. With the latter case, PRINCE2 uses the term *customer/supplier environment*. This means that when a project involves multiple parties, some can be categorized as customers of the project's products and some can be categorized as suppliers of the products. I will discuss the tailoring topic in more detail in Chapter 12, "Tailoring PRINCE2 to Particular Environments."

Other Parts of PRINCE2

In addition to the four main integrated elements of PRINCE2 covered previously (processes, themes, principles, and the project environment), there are two other main parts to PRINCE2: the roles and the management products.

Exam Spotlight

There are four integrated elements to PRINCE2: the principles, the themes, the processes, and the project environment. The roles and the management products are also important parts of the method, but PRINCE2 does not define them as integrated elements.

Roles

I will discuss the PRINCE2 management roles in more detail in Chapter 3, "Organization Theme," but it is important to understand the basic details at this point.

PRINCE2 gives a recommended project management team structure. It looks like a company organization chart, as shown in Figure 1.4.

FIGURE 1.4 Project management team structure

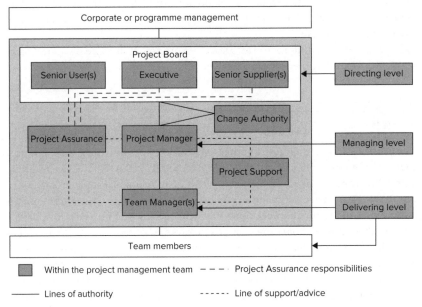

Based on Cabinet Office PRINCE2® material. Reproduced under licence from the Cabinet Office.

The four levels of hierarchy in the PRINCE2 project management structure are as follows:

Corporate or Programme Management This level sits outside and above the project management team.

Directing Level The Project Board is responsible for this. It is the top level of the project management team.

Managing Level The Project Manager is responsible for this, the middle level of the project management team.

Delivering Level The Team Manager and their teams are responsible for this. It is the bottom level of the project management team.

At the top of the project organization structure is *corporate or programme management*. (A *programme* is a collection of related projects being run in a coordinated way.) This consists of a rather ambiguous group of people—all we know about them is that they are "high up"—that is, they have enough authority to start a project. How "high up" they are in their organizations depends on the size of the project and how much authority is needed to start it. If it is a very large project, corporate or programme management might be the board of directors of the company; if it is a smaller project, they may be the head of a department. It is important to note that they trigger the start of the PRINCE2 process model, but corporate or programme management are not part of the project management team. All the levels below corporate or programme management, however, *are* part of the project management team.

Below corporate or programme management in the project management structure is the directing level. The Project Board is responsible for this level. The Project Board is given authority for the overall direction and management of the project by corporate or programme management. They are the main decision-making body on the project. They make key project decisions such as whether or not the project should start, whether it should it go on to its next major part, and finally, whether it is ready to close. They need to be high enough up in their own organization's hierarchy so as to have the authority to make these decisions.

There are a number of people who make up the Project Board. Between them, they must represent three key perspectives on the project: the business perspective, the user perspective, and the supplier perspective.

The business perspective focuses on the returns the project will give their organization. For example, if the project is to build a hotel for a leisure company, the business perspective is concerned with factors such as the potential sales of rooms. They would also be interested in how much investment is needed to get those returns—in other words, what value they might get for their money. This business view is represented by the *Executive* role. The Executive sits on the Project Board. There is always *only* one Executive, who is considered the leader of the project.

The user perspective focuses on how the project's products will be used post-project. This perspective is represented on the Project Board by the *Senior User* role. In the hotel example, the Senior User role could be carried out by representatives of those who will stay in the hotel or who understand these travelers' needs, such as a tourist board or a market research person specializing in tourism. There might be a number of people on the Project Board who share the Senior User role.

Finally, the supplier perspective focuses on creating the project's products. This is represented on the Project Board by the *Senior Supplier* role. In the hotel example, the Senior Supplier role could be taken by operational managers from architectural or construction firms. Like the Senior User role, there might be a number of people who share the Senior Supplier role.

Below the Project Board in the project management structure is the managing level. It is the responsibility of the *Project Manager* to manage the project on a day-to-day basis within the constraints set by the Project Board. There is only *one* Project Manager in a PRINCE2 project. This individual is responsible for project planning, delegating work, reporting on the project's progress, managing risks and issues, and creating and updating the project management documents.

At the bottom of the project management structure is the delivering level. This is the responsibility of the *teams* who actually create the products of the project. In the hotel project, there could be teams of architects, builders, electricians, plumbers, and so on. In some cases, such as a small project, the Project Manager might manage the teams directly. In other, larger projects, the Project Manager might delegate work to several *Team Managers* who will in turn delegate work to the teams.

As illustrated earlier in Figure 1.4, there are several other roles, such as Project Assurance, Change Authority, and Project Support. I will explain these roles in Chapter 3, "Organization Theme."

Management Products

Management products are things that help the project management team manage the project, such as plans, registers, logs, and reports. They are a means to an end, not the end itself. Although you might think of these items as management documents, PRINCE2 calls them *management products* because the management information could be communicated verbally. In fact, you could run a PRINCE2 project without any documents at all.

Examples of PRINCE2 management products are the Project Plan that is used to track and monitor the work of the project, Product Descriptions that help to specify the products to be delivered, and the Risk Register that contains information on all the identified risks to the project. There are 26 management products in all—you can find further information on each one of them throughout this study guide as well as in Appendix B, "Management Products in PRINCE2."

PRINCE2 defines three types of management products: baselines, records, and reports.

Baseline management products might go through a number of versions during the life of a project. If someone needs to make an update to a baseline management product, the amendments are made to a new version of the document. Then at the end of the project, the project team can review all the versions of the document (the latest and all the old ones) and see how the information has evolved. An example of a baseline management product is a Plan.

Records are the registers and the logs that the Project Manager uses to record information on things such as risks, issues, and lessons. An example of a record is the Issue Register. As with all records, there is only one Issue Register document; new versions are not made of the document when it needs to be updated. The updates are just added to the bottom of the register as a new line.

Reports are ... well, reports! They are the progress reports that are sent during the project to update various people of the latest situation on the project. An example of a report is the Highlight Report that the Project Manager sends to the Project Board on a regular basis.

Specialist Products

In addition to the management products, there is another type of product called *specialist products*. These are the deliverables from the project. For example, in a project to build a hotel, there are lots of deliverables such as the architectural plans, the rooms, the furniture, the swimming pool, and a hotel brochure.

What PRINCE2 Does Not Cover

A whole range of skills and approaches are needed to manage projects successfully. PRINCE2 by no means covers all of them. It does not focus on any specialist techniques that might be needed in specific industries, such as an IT project as opposed to a construction project. The framework does not provide any specific techniques, such as stakeholder analysis or critical path analysis. It also does not cover motivational approaches, team building, or leadership development.

Benefits of Using PRINCE2

The benefits of using PRINCE2 to manage a project include the following:

- The ideas in PRINCE2 have been developed over many years and tested successfully on many types of projects. It is highly likely that any project will benefit from these ideas. Because the methodology is generic, PRINCE2 can be applied to many different types of projects.

- PRINCE2 provides a common vocabulary of project terms. This makes it easier to communicate on projects, especially when several different organizations and people are involved.

- PRINCE2 defines specific project management responsibilities and shows how a project management team should be structured. This ensures that those involved in the management team are clear on their responsibilities. It also ensures that all the people who are needed to manage a project are included in the management team.

- PRINCE2 focuses attention on what needs to be created. This ensures that there is clarity and agreement on the outputs from the project.

- PRINCE2 provides a range of reports and plans as well as other management documents to meet the needs of different levels of management.

- The PRINCE2 management-by-exception approach ensures the efficient and economic use of management time. (I describe management by exception in more detail in the next section.)

- Before, during, and after a project, PRINCE2 focuses attention on the justification for undertaking that project. This ensures that projects are run as a means to an end rather than as an end in themselves. It also ensures that organizations take on projects that provide value.

- Adopting PRINCE2 allows people within an organization to learn how to improve their management skills. It provides consistency in project work, which means that project management assets can be reused, and reduces the impact of changes in management personnel. Many PRINCE2 accredited consultants and Project Managers are available around the world.

- PRINCE2 provides a theoretical management framework through which actual projects can be viewed. This helps you identify problems and missing elements of the project's approach to management.

PRINCE2 Principles

I introduced the seven PRINCE2 principles earlier in this chapter. These are guiding concepts that the rest of the model adheres to. All of the other elements and parts of PRINCE2 ensure that one or a number of these principles are implemented.

As you work through this study guide and learn about the different parts of the PRINCE2 model, ask yourself which principle each part is supporting. This will help you answer the exam questions about the linkages between the various parts of PRINCE2. For example, Chapter 4, "Business Case Theme," covers the Business Case theme, which helps to implement the principle of continued business justification.

Continued Business Justification

The principle of *continued business justification* ensures that there is a documented justification for starting a project. It ensures that this justification is reviewed and possibly updated throughout the life of the project. You should use the latest version of the justification to decide whether to move on to each major stage of the project.

PRINCE2 provides a range of activities with associated responsibilities to ensure continued business justification. These are described throughout the process model and also in the Business Case theme. PRINCE2 provides two important business-related management products: the Business Case, which documents the justification for undertaking the project, and the Benefit Review Plan, which plans the reviews of the project's benefits.

Learn from Experience

When you're managing a project, it is a good idea to take into account the good practice and the mistakes made in past projects. It is also a good idea to collate the lessons learned during the management of the current project and pass them on to teams managing subsequent projects. During many of the management activities throughout the process model, PRINCE2 constantly highlights the need to take account of past experience and collate new knowledge. It provides two important management products to help implement the "*learn from experience*" principle: the Lessons Log, which is used to record both previous and current experience, and the Lessons Report, which is used to pass on experience from the current project to those who will manage subsequent projects. The Progress theme (covered in Chapter 9, "Progress Theme") describes how to control the flow of experience.

Defined Roles and Responsibilities

It is important that each role in the project management team be performed by someone who understands what is expected of them and who is willing to take on that role. This is the PRINCE2 principle of *defined roles and responsibilities*. The project management team must include people from a broad range of stakeholder perspectives, especially those viewing the project from business, user, and supplier perspectives. The project management team should include appropriate roles for the various management levels of the organizations involved.

PRINCE2 provides a project management team structure. For each role within the structure, it sets out a range of responsibilities. For each of the activities in the process model, there is a defined role (or roles) responsible for that activity. The project management team structure and the associated roles are first set out in the Project Brief and then in the Project Initiation Documentation. The Communication Management Strategy (covered in Chapter 3,"Organization Theme") describes how the communication between these people will be managed.

Manage by Stages

The *manage by stages* principle ensures that PRINCE2 projects are divided into a number of time periods called *stages*. These stages could last days, weeks, or even months (or, in some of the military projects I've been involved with, years!). A collection of specialist products is created within each stage. The Project Board gives the Project Manager the authority to manage one stage at a time. After a stage is complete, the Project Manager must report back to the Project Board members, who then review the stage's performance and decide whether to authorize the next stage. The project management team decides *how* to divide the project into stages when preparing the Project Plan at the outset of the project.

For example, if the project is to build a hotel, it could be divided into four stages:

- During stage 1, the project is planned.
- During stage 2, the hotel is designed.
- During stage 3, the hotel is built.
- During stage 4, the interior of the hotel is decorated and fitted out with electricity, plumbing, furniture, and so on.

This approach has two benefits. First, it helps with planning. There is always a planning horizon, beyond which it is difficult to forecast. For example, at the beginning of the designing work in stage 2, it is impossible to plan in detail the building work of stage 3, because at this point, the specification of the hotel has not been decided. With the PRINCE2 manage-by-stages approach, the detailed Stage Plan for each stage is not created until the end of the previous stage. The Project Plan, which covers the whole project and is created at the outset, is done from a high-level perspective.

The other major benefit is that the senior managers taking on roles in the Project Board do not need to get involved with the day-to-day management of the stages. However, they can retain control of the project by authorizing progress a stage at a time. This is an efficient way of using senior management time. Senior managers can also vary the amount of control they have by shortening or lengthening the stages.

Every PRINCE2 project always has at least two stages: a planning stage (or what PRINCE2 calls the initiation stage) and at least one other stage where specialist products are delivered.

Manage by Exception

In PRINCE2, each management level manages the level below using the *manage by exception* principle. As I discussed in the "Roles" section earlier in this chapter, the PRINCE2 project management structure has four levels of management. At the top is a group called corporate, or programme, management, who instigate the project. Below them is the main decision-making body on the project, the Project Board. Then comes the Project Manager, who manages the project on a day-to-day basis. Finally, at the bottom, are the Team Managers and their teams, who create the project's products. So corporate or programme management manage the Project Board by exception, then the Project Board manages the Project Manager by exception, and then, finally, the Project Manager manages the Team Manager by exception.

Manage by exception means that the upper level of management gives the level of management below them a piece (or all) of the project to manage on their behalf. The upper level of management also sets certain boundaries around the lower level of management's authority. The lower level of management then only needs to report back to the level of management above them in one of two circumstances: either they have finished delivering their piece of the project or they realize that a situation has arisen that breaches the boundaries of their delegated authority.

The upper level of management defines the authority that they give to the level of management below them by setting constraints around six areas: time, cost, scope, quality, risk, and benefits. A certain amount of leeway, or what PRINCE2 calls *tolerances*, may be allowed around these constraints. If at any time it appears that these constraints may be breached, the lower level of management must escalate the situation to the level of management above them. This situation is called an *exception*. Here are some examples of the six areas where constraints can be set:

Time   The upper level of management gives the level of management below them a certain amount of time to carry out their work within certain tolerances. For example, the work must be finished in 6 months, with a permissible early delivery of two weeks and late delivery of one week. If the lower level of management believes they cannot deliver the work within this three-week range, they must escalate the situation to the level of management above them.

Cost   The upper level of management gives the level of management below them a certain budget to spend, possibly with some permissible leeway. For example, the budget could be $10,000 with an allowable under spend of $1,000 and no allowable overspend. If the lower level of management forecasts that they cannot deliver their work for $9,000 to $10,000 they must escalate the situation to the level of management above them.

Scope   The upper level of management gives the level of management below them a set of products that need to be delivered with any possible variation allowed. For example, create a website with pages that contain information on all the company's primary services and, if time permits, the secondary services. If the lower level of management realizes they will not be able to deliver even the primary service pages, they must escalate the situation to the level of management above them.

Quality The upper level of management gives the level of management below them a set of specifications for all the products that should be created. These are specified in an appropriate manner to an appropriate level of detail for that management level. Any tolerance around the specifications will also be shown. For example, create an Olympic stadium with between 90,000 and 100,000 seats. (Obviously you'd have a few more details to work with than this!) If the lower level of management cannot deliver products within these specification ranges, they must escalate the situation to the level of management above them.

Risk The upper level of management gives the level of management below them a threshold level of aggregated risk. An example is that expected costs of the predicted threats must not exceed $20,000. (For more information on risk tolerances, see Chapter 7, "Risk Theme.") If the lower level of management realize this threshold level of risk will be breached, they must escalate the situation to the level of management above them.

Benefits The objectives for the project's benefits may also be given some allowable deviation by corporate or programme management. An example is that sales resulting from the project must be in the range of $500,000 to $600,000. If this forecast looks as though it won't be possible, the situation should be escalated back to corporate or programme management.

Management by exception provides for efficient use of the senior managers' time. They don't have to get involved in the day-to-day work of the level below. However, they can control the work of the level below by setting tolerances around these six areas.

Focus on Products

The principle of *focus on products* ensures that through every step of the project, what the project is creating is clearly defined and agreed to. In PRINCE2, these product specifications are set out in Product Descriptions. The Product Descriptions are then used as the basis of planning the activities needed to create the products, manage proposed changes to the products, and verify approval and acceptance of the products once they have been built.

This seems like a rather obvious thing to do. However, many projects miss this simple approach, and as a result, disputes occur over the acceptance of the products, uncontrolled changes are introduced, or the wrong outputs are created.

Tailor to Suit the Project Environment

I provided an overview of how the project management team can *tailor [PRINCE2] to suit the project environment* in "The Project Environment" section earlier in this chapter and, as mentioned, I'll discuss this topic in more detail in Chapter 12, "Tailoring PRINCE2 to Particular Environments." In addition to defining this important approach as an integrated element of the model, PRINCE2 restates it as one of the seven principles.

An End-to-End Walk-through of PRINCE2

Thus far in this chapter, you've learned about some of the major parts of PRINCE2, including its underlying principles, processes, themes, roles, and management products. Now it's time to see how these parts fit together in a project.

In this section, I use a sample project—constructing a new hotel for a leisure company—to show you how the processes are used both before and during the project. I will also discuss where each role becomes involved in the model and how some of the main management products are used.

At this point, I am going to discuss the various areas at a high level. To use an analogy, I want you to see how the major pieces of the jigsaw puzzle fit together before I discuss each piece on its own. It will then be easier, when I discuss a particular part of PRINCE2 in the later chapters, to show you how that part fits into the whole model.

For this section, I will use the process overview diagram shown in Figure 1.5.

Take a look at the composition of Figure 1.5. First, there are four horizontal rows that correspond to the four levels of the project management structure.

The various rectangles and squares on the diagram represent the seven processes. The processes are positioned to show which level of management is involved with that process. For example, all the activities in the Directing a Project process occur at the Project Board level, and all the activities of the Managing Product Delivery level occur at the Team level. Some processes are carried out by a number of the management levels. For example, Starting Up a Project involves corporate or programme management, the Project Board, and the Project Manager.

The four columns in Figure 1.5 show the work that is done during four different times in the project, as follows:

- Work that happens before the project (pre-project)
- Work that happens at the beginning of the project (initiation stage)
- Work that happens in the middle of the project (subsequent delivery stages)
- Work that happens at the end of the project (final delivery stage)

Pre-Project Activities

Figure 1.6 highlights the work that takes place before a PRINCE2 project. The numbered circles on the diagram correspond to the five steps described in this section.

FIGURE 1.5 PRINCE2 process model

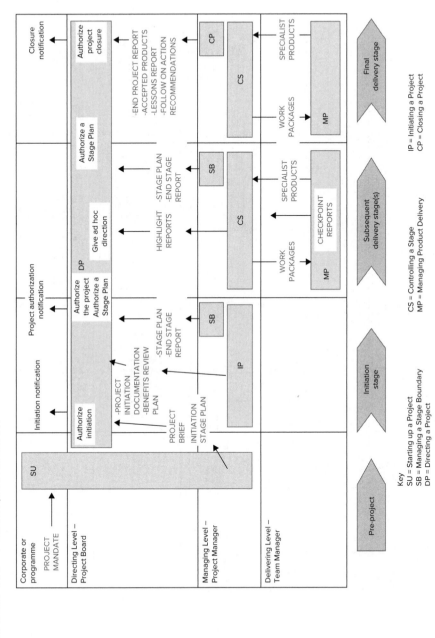

Based on Cabinet Office PRINCE2® material. Reproduced under licence from the Cabinet Office.

21

FIGURE 1.6 Activities before the project

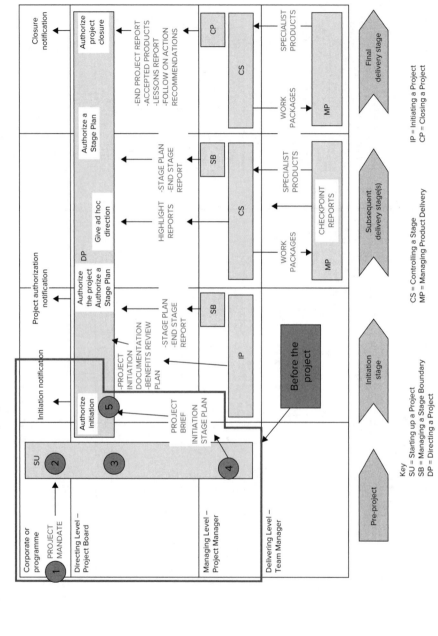

Based on Cabinet Office PRINCE2® material. Reproduced under licence from the Cabinet Office.

Step 1: Corporate or Programme Management Creates a Project Mandate

In PRINCE2, before a project can start, a number of activities and authorizations must occur. First, someone (or a group of people) with an appropriate level of authority to authorize this project must create a project mandate. The project mandate will begin to answer basic questions about the project, such as the following:

- What is the project all about? What is it creating?
- Who will be involved in the project? Who will be using the project's products after the project?
- Where will the project happen? Where will the products be built?
- When will the project start and finish? When will there be any return from this project?
- How will the project be done? How will the products be built?
- Why do this project? What is the justification for it?

The project mandate will answer these basic what, why, when, who, where, and how questions. At one extreme, the information might be high-level, in which case, as you will see, the first set of activities in PRINCE2 is partly about refining and expanding these details. At the other extreme, the information in the project mandate might be in great detail, in which case the first set of activities in PRINCE2 will be more about checking that it is correct. The latter is more likely in a programme situation, where the project is part of a group of projects. In this case, the specific definitions of each project will probably be agreed to at the beginning of the programme.

For our hotel project example, let's say someone in the leisure company has an idea for a new hotel. They may have many hotels across the world, but they decide they would like to create one in Shanghai because they see China as a growing market. Someone who has the authority to start a project of this size will create a project mandate. In this example, the head of business development in the Asia Pacific region is assigned this task.

Step 2: Corporate or Programme Management Appoints the Executive

Once the project mandate is created, the PRINCE2 process model starts. The very first process is Starting Up a Project. I will describe the Starting Up a Project process in much more detail in Chapter 2, "Starting a Project Successfully with PRINCE2."

The first thing to do in Starting Up a Project is for corporate or programme management to appoint a senior-level person to the Executive role. This person should see the initiative from a business perspective and will act as the key decision maker for the project. (The Executive role will be described in more detail in Chapter 3, "Organization Theme.")

Let's say in the example project, the head of business development in the Asia Pacific region is appointed as Executive. He is now straddling two of the PRINCE2 management levels: he created the project mandate while sitting in the corporate or programme management level and now takes on the Executive role that sits in the Project Board level.

Step 3: The Executive Appoints the Project Manager

The next step in Starting Up a Project is for the Executive to appoint the Project Manager. The Executive can then focus on directing, decision-making, and business-related activities, and the Project Manager can focus on the day-to-day management of the pre-project work.

Step 4: The Executive and the Project Manager Create the Project Brief and Recruit the Project Management Team

The remaining activities in Starting Up a Project are focused on answering the following question: Is the project idea set out in the project mandate worthwhile and viable? With regard to the hotel project example, is it worth committing major resources to start a project to build a new hotel in Shanghai? As such, a PRINCE2 project doesn't actually start during the Starting Up a Project process. Instead, Starting Up a Project is a set of activities that are performed *before* the project to decide whether or not to do that project.

To begin, the project mandate needs to be reviewed, and if necessary, the information needs to be expanded so as to provide enough details to form the basis of the decision of whether to commission the project. The output of this work goes into a new management product called the Project Brief. The Project Brief will answer exactly the same set of what, why, when, who, where, and how questions about the project that the project mandate did.

The "why" question is answered by creating an outline Business Case, which forms part of the Project Brief. This will start to show, at a high level at least, the justification for undertaking the project. It is the Executive's responsibility to create this section of the Project Brief.

The rest of the project management team members are now appointed. So people are assigned to the other two Project Board roles of Senior User and Senior Supplier. (These roles will be described in more detail in Chapter 3, "Organization Theme.") Some of the Project Board members might appoint separate Project Assurance roles who will monitor the project to find out if it is being run in the correct way for their perspective on the project. A Project Support person or people might also be appointed.

This initial project management team might get updated and added to as the initiative proceeds. However, at this point, the team needs to reflect the range of stakeholder perspectives of business, user, and supplier at the right level of authority. That way, a thorough analysis of the project idea can be done and a meaningful authorization can occur if the project idea looks to be worthwhile and viable.

For the hotel project example, let's say the leisure company's marketing director for Asia is appointed a Senior User and will use the hotel to increase his sales figures. A travel market research consultant is also appointed as a Senior User to represent the needs of the tourists and business travelers who might stay in the hotel. To represent the interests of the supplier side of the project, the head of procurement for Asia Pacific is appointed as Senior Supplier. (Later on, people from the suppliers contracted to do work on the hotel might also take on the Senior Supplier role.)

Once the Project Brief has been finished, the Project Board will review it and make a decision on whether to authorize things to go any further. If they decide to allow the initiative to proceed, the project will officially start with what PRINCE2 calls the initiation stage. In this stage, the project will be planned out, at least at a high level. (Remember that the "manage by stages" principle means that more detailed planning is done before each stage.) Before committing resources to the initiation stage, the Project Board will want to see a plan for the work that will be involved. So the final activity in the Starting Up a Project process is for the Project Manager to create a Stage Plan for the initiation stage, detailing the time, effort, and costs needed to plan the project.

Step 5: The Project Board Authorizes Initiation

Now that Starting Up a Project is complete, the PRINCE2 model moves on to the Directing a Project process. Directing a Project covers the work of the Project Board. This work mainly involves making decisions.

The Project Board's first decision is called "Authorize initiation." The Project Board reviews the Project Brief to see whether the project is a worthwhile and viable initiative. If they think it is, they then review the Stage Plan for the initiation stage to see what would be involved in planning this project. If they decide that the resources requested for the initiation (planning) stage are reasonable, they authorize the Project Manager to proceed. In effect, they are giving the Project Manager the authority to manage just the initiation stage, after which the Project Manager must ask the Project Board, once again, for authority to continue any further.

Activities at the Beginning of the Project

Figure 1.7 shows the process diagram once again, with the initiation stage highlighted and its steps numbered.

FIGURE 1.7 Activities at the beginning of the project

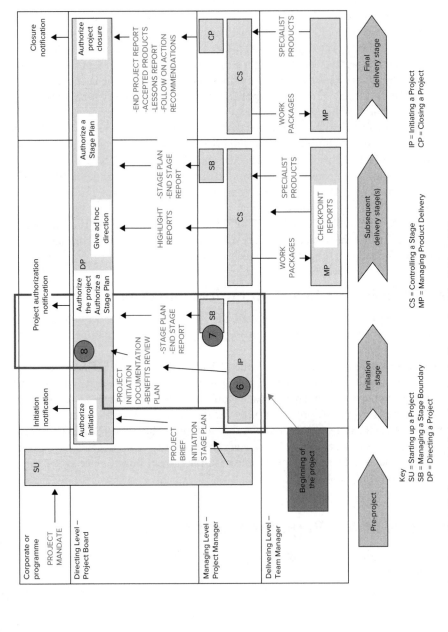

Based on Cabinet Office PRINCE2® material. Reproduced under licence from the Cabinet Office.

Step 6: The Project Manager Creates the Project Initiation Documentation

The Initiating a Project process describes a set of activities to create the Project Initiation Documentation (PID). The Project Manager does most of the work to create the PID. The information in the PID answers the same what, why, when, where, who, and how questions that the project mandate and then the Project Brief answered. This time, the document has greater detail because now that the project has been authorized, the project team will have more time and resources to consider these questions.

The PID is actually a collection of documents. It contains the following information:

- The Project Plan, which describes the major products and the activities and resources required to create them, as well as how the project will be divided into stages. This plan can be high-level, because the "manage by stages" principle of PRINCE2 allows for more detailed planning to be left until just before a particular stage.

- A set of strategy documents that set out how the project will be managed with regard to such areas as risk, change, quality, and communication.

- A detailed Business Case.

- Information on the project management team.

- Information on how the project will be delivered (project approach).

- A project definition, giving information on such areas as the background to the project, the project's objectives, and the project's scope.

- Information on how the project will be controlled, such as how to monitor the progress of the project and what reports are required.

- Information on how PRINCE2 will be tailored for the project.

With regard to the hotel project, the Project Plan section might set out the individual delivery stages like this:

Delivery Stage 1   Create architectural plans for the hotel. Obtain planning permission for construction. Create tender documents for outsourced contractors and send to potential suppliers. Select suppliers.

Delivery Stage 2   Construct hotel exteriors.

Delivery Stage 3   Decorate interior of the hotel; fit out with electrics, plumbing, furniture, and so on.

In addition to creating the PID, the Project Manager will create the Benefits Review Plan during the Initiating a Project process. The Benefits Review Plan specifies how and when the project will be reviewed with regard to whether it's achieving the stated benefits. Many of these reviews might be planned for some time after the project. In the hotel project example, a review might be scheduled for a year after the hotel opens, to see if the hotel is meeting its targets for room sales, restaurant sales, and so on—but the planning for that review would start at this point in the project.

Step 7: The Project Manager Creates a Plan for the First Delivery Stage

Once the Project Manager has almost finished the PID, he can start planning the next stage of the project. In the hotel example, he will plan in detail the work for the first delivery stage, which is when architectural plans for the hotel are created and the tender process takes place. This work is done in the Managing a Stage Boundary process.

At this point, the Project Manager might have two focuses: finishing off the PID using the Initiating a Project process, and creating the plan for the first delivery stage using the Managing a Stage Boundary process. The Managing a Stage Boundary process is described in detail in Chapter 10, "Managing the Middle of a Project Successfully with PRINCE2."

Step 8: The Project Board Authorizes the Project and the First Delivery Stage

The Project Manager sends the PID and the Stage Plan for the first delivery stage to the Project Board. The Project Board reviews both of these management products in their Directing a Project process.

The Project Board has two Directing a Project activities to carry out at this point. First, they review the information in the PID and decide whether to authorize the project. Second, they review the information in the Stage Plan and decide whether to authorize the first delivery stage of the project.

The way that PRINCE2 has set out the Directing a Project activities at this point can be confusing for two reasons. First, it says that the Project Board authorizes the project here. However, the project has already started at this point. (It has just finished the initiation stage.) What PRINCE2 means is that the Project Board needs to decide whether to authorize the delivery part of the project where specialist products are created.

The second reason it can be confusing is that although the Project Board authorizes the delivery part of the project, the Project Manager cannot move ahead and manage the whole project. The Project Manager only has authority to manage the next delivery stage, after which he must ask the Project Board, once again, for authority to continue further. So in the hotel example, the Project Manager will only have authority to manage the work to create the architectural plans, obtain planning permission, and carry out the tender process.

Activities in the Middle of the Project

In Figure 1.8, I have highlighted the section of the process model we are now focusing on: delivering specialist products. In the hotel example, this will involve creating deliverables such as tender documents, architectural plans, parts of the hotel building, computer software to run the booking system, and so on. The delivery of these specialist products will be managed on a stage-by-stage basis.

FIGURE 1.8 Activities in the middle of the project

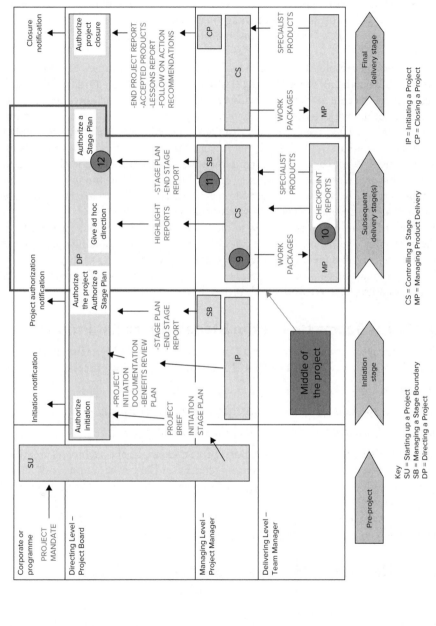

Based on Cabinet Office PRINCE2® material. Reproduced under licence from the Cabinet Office.

29

Step 9: The Project Manager Manages a Delivery Stage

The Project Manager will manage each delivery stage using the activities in the Controlling a Stage process. This process sets out management activities such as how the Project Manager delegates work to various teams, reports on progress, and deals with problems and issues.

With the hotel example, the Project Manager will use Controlling a Stage to manage the first delivery stage (and all the other stages, too, once they've been authorized). The Project Manager might delegate work to an architectural firm to create the hotel designs. He might also delegate work to the leisure company's procurement department to create and issue the tenders as well as delegate work to the people who are dealing with the planning authorities in Shanghai. In PRINCE2, the Project Manager assigns work to teams using a Work Package. A Work Package gives team members all the information they need to know in order to do some work, such as what to create, how much time and money they have, how often to report back to the Project Manager, and so on. Teams are not authorized to do any work until they have received a Work Package.

The Project Manager reports progress to the Project Board throughout the stage by creating Highlight Reports. The Project Board decides how regularly they would like to receive these reports, but let's say, in our example, they are sent every week.

The Controlling a Stage process is described in a lot more detail in Chapter 10, "Managing the Middle of a Project Successfully with PRINCE2."

Step 10: The Teams Create the Stage's Specialist Products

The Team Managers and their teams carry out their work in the Managing Product Delivery process. The teams carry out three PRINCE2 activities during this process:

- Accept the work from the Project Manager via the Work Packages
- Create the specialist products as instructed in the Work Packages
- Deliver the specialist products back to the Project Manager

During the first delivery stage in the hotel project example, the architects creating the hotel's plans, the procurement team creating tenders for the construction work, and the team dealing with the Chinese planning authorities will all use the Managing Product Delivery process.

The teams must also regularly report on the progress of their work to the Project Manager. They do this by creating Checkpoint Reports.

Step 11: The Project Manager Plans the Next Stage

This step is similar to step 7. Once the Project Manager sees that the work of the current delivery stage is nearly finished, he will start planning the next delivery stage. In the hotel example, the Project Manager will plan in detail the work to construct the hotel's exteriors. Just as in step 7, this work is done in the Managing a Stage Boundary process.

Also just as in step 7, at this point, the Project Manager might have two focuses: finishing off managing the work in the current delivery stage using the Controlling a Stage process, and creating the stage plan for the next delivery stage using the Managing a Stage Boundary process.

The Project Manager also creates an End Stage Report for the delivery stage just ending and, if necessary, updates some of the major management products within the PID, such as the Project Plan and the Business Case.

Step 12: The Project Board Authorizes Another Delivery Stage

Once all the specialist products of the stage have been delivered, the Project Manager will send the End Stage Report, the next Stage Plan, and the updated PID to the Project Board. In the hotel example, this will take place when the architectural designs for the hotel are finished, contractors have been sourced for the construction work, and planning permission for the hotel has been obtained.

The Project Board will review the next Stage Plan in their Directing a Project process and decide whether to authorize the next delivery stage. So in our hotel example, they will decide whether the project can move on to building the hotel's exteriors.

Steps 9, 10, 11, and 12 Again and Again and...

Steps 9, 10, 11, and 12 are repeated again and again, managing the delivery of each stage of the project, until the project team reaches the last stage. The final stage is handled a little differently, as you will see in the next section.

So in our hotel example, which has an initiation stage and then three delivery stages, steps 9, 10, 11, and 12 will be carried out twice: first to manage delivery stage 1, and then again to manage delivery stage 2.

Activities at the End of the Project

The final delivery stage is managed slightly differently. In our hotel example, this would correspond to the management of delivery stage 3, when the hotel is decorated and the electrics, plumbing, furniture, IT systems, and so on are installed. Figure 1.9 highlights the section of the process model I will discuss in this section.

Step 13: The Project Manager Manages the Final Delivery Stage

This step is exactly the same as step 9 from the previous delivery stages. The Project Manager uses the Controlling a Stage process to create Work Packages that delegate the final stage's delivery work to the appropriate teams. In the hotel project example, the Project Manager might give out work to the electrical fitters, the plumbers, the furniture moving companies, and so on. The Project Manager also reports to the Project Board using Highlight Reports and deals with problems and issues.

FIGURE 1.9 Activities at the end of the project

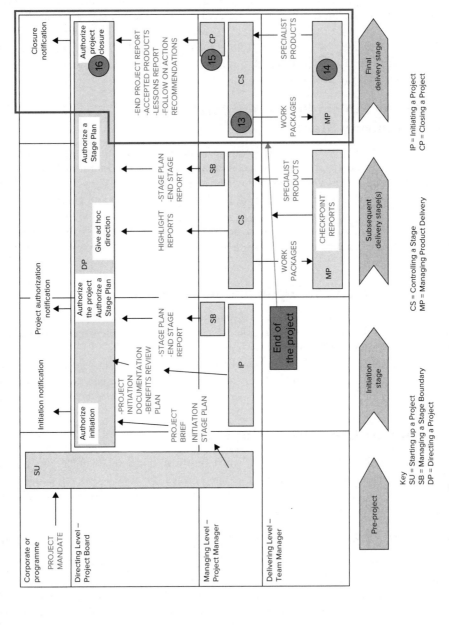

Based on Cabinet Office PRINCE2® material. Reproduced under licence from the Cabinet Office.

Step 14: The Teams Create the Specialist Products of the Final Stage

This step is exactly the same as step 10 from the previous delivery stages. The teams involved with creating this delivery stage's specialist products use the Managing Product Delivery process to accept work via Work Packages, create the specialist products, and give them back to the Project Manager. They also report on progress to the Project Manager using Checkpoint Reports.

In the hotel example, the teams involved with creating the last delivery stage's specialist products will now be involved. These could be decorators painting the hotel, electricians wiring the lighting, IT specialists installing software, and so on.

Step 15: The Project Manager Prepares for the End of the Project

The first difference between the final delivery stage and the previous delivery stages is that at the end of this last stage, instead of using the Managing Stage Boundary process to prepare for the next stage, the Project Manager uses the Closing a Project process to prepare for the end of the project.

During the Closing a Project process, the Project Manager will do the following:

- Ensure that the project's products are signed off and accepted by the ultimate clients. In the hotel example, the ultimate clients might be the head of the Asia Pacific region that ultimately will need to accept the new hotel.

- Create an End Project Report. This report will review the project's performance against the original objectives that were set out in the first version of the PID.

- Update the Benefits Review Plan to check that all of the post-project benefit reviews are included.

- Give a list of Follow-on Action Recommendations to the people who will operate the project's products.

- Create a Lessons Report that can be passed on to subsequent projects.

- Archive the project documentation.

Step 16: The Project Board Authorizes the Project to Close

The second difference between the final delivery stage and the previous delivery stages is that at the end of it, the Project Board will authorize the closure of the project rather than another stage. Board members will review all the management products prepared by the Project Manager in the Closing a Project process, and if they are satisfied that everything is complete, they will authorize the end of the project. The Project Board will carry out this authorization in the Directing a Project process.

Summary

This chapter presented a broad summary of all the features of PRINCE2 and showed you how they fit together. I described the main sections of PRINCE2: principles, themes, processes, roles, and management products.

Projects have five key characteristics that distinguish them from business as usual: they change the organization; they are temporary, with a start and an end; they involve different functions and divisions within an organization; they involve unique work that has not been done before; and they involve a lot of uncertainty.

Given all the challenges that projects introduce, project management attempts to lower the risks and increase the likelihood of a successful outcome. As you saw, there are four main areas of project management activity: planning work, delegating work, monitoring the progress, and controlling the project. These four main areas of project management work attempt to deliver the project to its objectives. In PRINCE2, there are six ways of describing a project objective: in terms of cost, time, scope, quality, risks, and benefits.

After discussing what constitutes a project, I introduced a tool that you can use to manage them: PRINCE2. The PRINCE2 method consists of four integrated elements: principles, processes, themes, and the project environment.

As you learned in this chapter, there are seven principles of PRINCE2: continued business justification, learn from experience, defined roles and responsibilities, manage by stages, manage by exception, focus on products, and tailor to suit the project environment. These are core concepts that the rest of the PRINCE2 model adheres to.

Next, you learned about the PRINCE2 processes, which describe the activities to be performed by the various project roles both before and during a project. The chapter then covered the seven themes—Business Case, Organization, Quality, Plans, Risk, Change, and Progress—which explain how certain aspects of project management should be approached throughout a PRINCE2 project.

Then, you learned how to tailor PRINCE2 to a project environment. PRINCE2 can be applied in different ways depending on such factors as the scale of the project, the industry the project is operating within, and the other specialist techniques and approaches that are being used.

In addition to the four integrated elements of PRINCE2, you learned that there are a number of other important parts. There are certain roles that need to be carried out on each project, such as a Project Manager who manages the project on a day-to-day basis. There are also 26 PRINCE2 management products, including plans, registers, logs, strategies (showing how the project will be managed), and a variety of reports. The chapter covered the whole range of benefits that PRINCE2 can bring to a project. These range from providing a common vocabulary for project management to providing a tested best-practice approach to managing projects.

Finally, you saw how the major parts of PRINCE2 are used throughout the life of a project. I suggest that you review this section a number of times—it will give you a good idea how all the parts of PRINCE2 fit together.

Exam Essentials

Define the six aspects of project performance that need to be managed.   Know that the six objectives of a project can be written in terms of cost, timescales, risk, benefits, quality, and scope.

Define what a project is, how it is different from business as usual, and the characteristics of a project.   Be able to define a project as a temporary organization created for the purpose of delivering one or more business products according to an agreed Business Case. Be able to name the five characteristics of a project: change, temporary, cross-functional, unique, and uncertainty. These characteristics distinguish project work from business as usual.

Define the four integrated elements of PRINCE2.   Know that the four integrated elements of PRINCE2 are the principles, the processes, the themes, and tailoring to the project environment.

Understand the benefits of using PRINCE2.   The PRINCE2 framework provides a range of benefits to help increase the likelihood of project success; be able to describe these benefits.

Explain the seven principles of PRINCE2.   Be able to list the seven principles of PRINCE2: continued business justification, learn from experience, defined roles and responsibilities, manage by stages, manage by exception, focus on products, and tailor to suit the project environment. Explain how adhering to these principles helps increase the likelihood of project success.

Review Questions

The rest of this chapter contains mock exam questions for the Foundation exam.

Foundation Exam Questions

1. Which theme helps to ensure that the project's products are fit for purpose?
   A. Risk theme
   B. Quality theme
   C. Organization theme
   D. Progress theme

2. Which is **NOT** one of the integrated elements of PRINCE2?
   A. Management products
   B. Processes
   C. Principles
   D. Tailoring to the project environment

3. Which aspect of project performance that needs to be managed helps to set the objectives for the expected return on the project?
   A. Costs
   B. Risks
   C. Benefits
   D. Scope

4. Which option represents a characteristic of projects?
   A. Involves work with no defined end point
   B. Involves work across multiple functional divisions
   C. Predictable, recurring work
   D. Involves work that brings little change to an organization

5. Which principle ensures that the range of stakeholder perspectives are represented within the project management team?
   A. Defined roles and responsibilities
   B. Continued business justification
   C. Learn from experience
   D. Tailor to suit the project environment

6. Delegating authority from one management level to the next supports which principle?

   A. Continued business justification

   B. Learn from experience

   C. Manage by stages

   D. Manage by exception

7. Which principle addresses the problem that planning beyond a certain planning horizon is difficult?

   A. Continued business justification

   B. Manage by stages

   C. Manage by exception

   D. Tailor to suit the project environment

8. What is **NOT** a type of management product?

   A. Blueprint

   B. Baseline

   C. Report

   D. Record

9. Which one of the integrated elements of PRINCE2 provides a stepwise progression through the project life cycle?

   A. Principles

   B. Themes

   C. Processes

   D. Tailoring to the project environment

10. What is one of the benefits provided by PRINCE2?

   A. Sets out how to manage projects in particular industries

   B. Provides motivational techniques

   C. Provides a way of diagnosing problems in projects

   D. Shows how to manage business as usual

Chapter 2

Starting a Project Successfully with PRINCE2

PRINCE2 EXAM OBJECTIVES COVERED IN THIS CHAPTER:

✓ **Understand the purpose, objectives, and context of the Starting up a Project process and the Initiating a Project process.**

✓ **Understand the following six activities of the Starting up a Project process and know which role has responsibilities within each activity:**

  ▪ Appoint the Executive and the Project Manager.

  ▪ Capture previous lessons.

  ▪ Design and appoint the project management team.

  ▪ Prepare the outline Business Case.

  ▪ Select the project approach and assemble the Project Brief.

  ▪ Plan the initiation stage.

✓ **Understand the following eight activities of the Initiating a Project process and know which role has responsibilities within each activity:**

  ▪ Prepare the Risk Management Strategy.

  ▪ Prepare the Configuration Management Strategy.

  ▪ Prepare the Quality Management Strategy.

  ▪ Prepare the Communication Management Strategy.

  ▪ Set up the project controls.

  ▪ Create the Project Plan.

  ▪ Refine the Business Case.

  ▪ Assemble the Project Initiation Documentation.

✓ **Understand the purpose and the composition of the Project Brief.**

  ▪ Know in which processes the Project Brief is developed, used, and reviewed.

  ▪ Know which roles are responsible for creating and reviewing the Project Brief.

✓ **Understand the purpose and the composition of the Project Initiation Documentation.**

  ▪ Know in which processes the Project Initiation Documentation is developed, used, and reviewed.

  ▪ Know which roles are responsible for creating and reviewing the Project Initiation Documentation.

✓ **Understand how the seven themes may be applied within the Starting up a Project process and the Initiating a Project process.**

In this chapter, you'll see how PRINCE2 recommends that you begin a project. The two main steps are using the Starting up a Project process to investigate whether the project idea is a worthwhile and viable one, and then using the Initiating a Project process to plan the project at a high level.

You use two key management products at the beginning of a PRINCE2 project: the Project Brief and the Project Initiation Documentation. In this chapter, you'll learn how to create them and then use them to define and gain consensus on what your project is all about.

Beginning a PRINCE2 Project

Figure 2.1 is taken from the "An End-to-End Walk-through of PRINCE2" section in Chapter 1, "Overview of PRINCE2." If you haven't read that section yet, I recommend that you do so before reading this chapter, as it gives a high-level overview of the PRINCE2 process model. You will then be able to understand the context of the two processes discussed in this chapter: *Starting up a Project* and *Initiating a Project*. In Figure 2.1, I've highlighted where those two processes sit within the whole model. You can see that Starting up a Project happens before the project starts. It contains a set of activities that help the Project Board determine whether to do the project. If the board decides to proceed with the project, then the activities in the Initiating a Project process are done. This is the official start of the project, during which you plan the project at a high level.

Starting up a Project Process

As you can see in Figure 2.1, Starting up a Project is the first process in the PRINCE2 model. It contains the following six activities, which are carried out before a project starts:

- *Appoint the Executive and the Project Manager.*
- *Prepare the outline Business Case.*
- *Capture previous lessons.*
- *Design and appoint the project management team.*
- *Select the project approach and assemble the Project Brief.*
- *Plan the initiation stage.*

FIGURE 2.1 Pre-project and beginning of the project

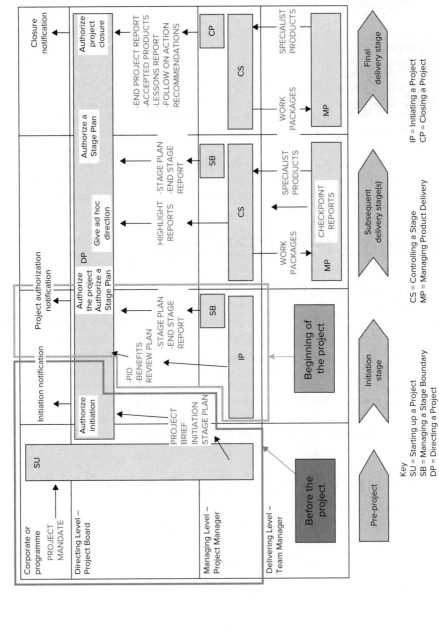

Based on Cabinet Office PRINCE2® material. Reproduced under licence from the Cabinet Office.

42

You'll learn about these activities in more detail in the following section. Their main purpose is to help you consider the project idea and decide whether it is a viable and worthwhile proposal.

The activities in the Starting up a Project process shouldn't take too long relative to the potential length of the project. That way, time and money won't be wasted on initiatives that aren't taken any further. Starting up a Project is as much about stopping poorly conceived initiatives as it is about identifying good ones.

Exam Spotlight

The Foundation and Practitioner exams are based on the information in the official PRINCE2 manual: *Managing Successful Projects with PRINCE2* (Stationery Office, 2009). The manual provides a great deal of detail regarding each of the 40 activities that are found within the seven separate processes. So how much of this do you need to know before tackling the exams?

For the Foundation exam, you should memorize what happens in each individual process, but not necessarily what happens within each of the processes' activities. This is the level of detail that I discussed in the "An End-to-End Walk-Through of PRINCE2" section in Chapter 1, "Overview of PRINCE2." This gives you the high-level detail for each process, and shows you how they all fit together. Then for each individual process, I suggest you read the relevant chapters in this study guide:

- Chapter 1, "Overview of PRINCE2," which covers Directing a Project in the "An End-to-End Walk Through of PRINCE2" section

- Chapter 2, "Starting a Project Successfully with PRINCE2," which covers Starting up a Project and Initiating a Project

- Chapter 10, "Managing the Middle of a Project Successfully with PRINCE2," which covers Controlling a Stage, Managing Product Delivery, and Managing a Stage Boundary

- Chapter 11, "Managing the End of a Project Successfully with PRINCE2," which covers Closing a Project

Each of these chapters gives you a detailed description of what happens in each activity, which you need to read and understand but not necessarily memorize. Also within these chapters, I give you a key facts table for each process. I recommend that you *do* memorize these key facts.

The Practitioner exam is a different matter. It will ask you detailed questions about the activities. However, in this exam, you'll be able to refer to *Managing Successful Projects with PRINCE2*. So in this case, you don't need to memorize all the activity detail—instead, you need to know how to use that manual to find the answers during the exam.

In *Managing Successful Projects with PRINCE2*, you'll find a chapter on each of the processes. Within each of those chapters is a section on each activity. These sections describe what happens in the activity and include a table of responsibilities. A flow diagram accompanies each description.

For example, the following illustration shows the flow diagram for the first activity of the Starting up a Project process: Appoint the Executive and the Project Manager. You can see that it shows that the Project Mandate is needed for this activity—it is an input to the activity. You can also see what is created by the work done in the activity—the outputs of this activity. The outputs are the Executive and Project Manager role descriptions, an appointed Executive and Project Manager, and finally, the Daily Log.

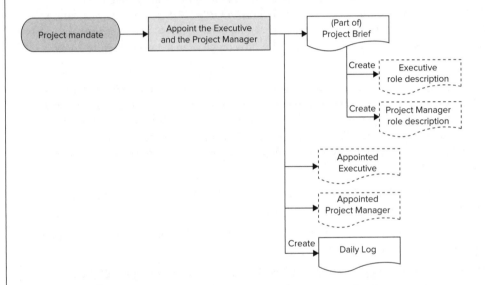

Based on Cabinet Office PRINCE2® material. Reproduced under licence from the Cabinet Office.

These flow diagrams are very useful. You can quickly flick through them and see which management products are involved in which activity. If you need further information, you can then refer to the activity section's text or the table of responsibilities.

When you come to the review Practitioner questions at the end of this chapter, you might want to practice using the *Managing Successful Projects with PRINCE2* process chapters as a reference.

Starting up a Project Process Activities

Figure 2.2 shows an overview of the activities in the Starting up a Project process. As you can see, dependencies exist between some of the activities, indicated by arrows. For example, the "Appoint the Executive and the Project Manager" activity needs to be done before the "Capture previous lessons" activity. Apart from these dependency constraints, you can accomplish the activities in any order: sequentially, simultaneously, or iteratively.

FIGURE 2.2   Overview of Starting up a Project

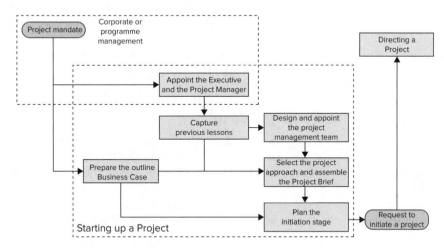

Based on Cabinet Office PRINCE2® material. Reproduced under licence from the Cabinet Office.

As you can see in Figure 2.2, the Starting up a Project process is triggered when corporate or programme management creates the project mandate. The six activities of the Starting up a Project process are then carried out. When this process is completed, the Project Manager sends the Project Board a request to initiate the project. This triggers the *Directing a Project* process, during which the Project Board decides whether to proceed further with the initiative.

The following sections describe each Starting up a Project activity in detail. You should read through each of these sections, but you don't have to memorize all the details. After these sections, you'll find a Starting up a Project facts table that you *do* need to memorize for the exams.

Appoint the Executive and the Project Manager

This is the first step of the PRINCE2 process model. It occurs after the project mandate has been created by someone in the corporate or programme level of management.

The first step in this activity is for corporate or programme management to recruit the Executive. This is a critical role in the project management team. This person will have the necessary authority, budget, and resources to move the initiative from just an idea to a fully funded project with the necessary resources to deliver the products. The Executive will also represent the commissioning organization's business perspective to ensure that the idea represents value for money and will provide an adequate return on investment. Corporate or programme management will create a role description for the Executive based on the PRINCE2 Executive role description and then recruit a suitable candidate.

The Executive will probably be a senior-level manager, so it is unlikely that they will want to involve themselves in the day-to-day management of the project. Therefore the Executive will create a job description based on the PRINCE2 Project Manager role description and then recruit a suitable candidate.

The Project Manager creates a *Daily Log*. They will use it to track personal action points and informal issues that are not tracked in the other PRINCE2 registers and logs. During the Starting up a Project process, the Daily Log also has another use. At this point in the initiative, the Risk Register and the Issue Register have not been created. (They are created later in the Initiating a Project process.) Until the registers are created, the Daily Log acts as a repository to record information for all project risks and issues.

Prepare the Outline Business Case

There are two major focuses in this activity. First, the Executive is responsible for creating an outline Business Case and, if necessary, getting it approved by corporate or programme management. Second, the Project Manager is responsible for creating the Project Product Description.

The Executive sets out the justification for the project in the outline Business Case. The exact composition of the Business Case is covered in Chapter 4, "Business Case Theme." For now, you should know that it will contain the forecast returns that the project will give the organization balanced against the time, cost, and risk that need to be taken on to get those returns. For example, if the project involves building a hotel, the Business Case will contain a forecast of the likely room sales compared to the cost of the hotel construction, how long the hotel will take to build, and the risks of building it. It will also consider how the project will be funded.

Remember that the time taken to carry out the activities during Starting up a Project should be less compared to the rest of the processes. This is so time isn't wasted on initiatives that shouldn't go further. So as the name suggests, the Business Case will only be in outline form at this point. But it must have sufficient detail for the Project Board to decide the viability of the project. The Business Case will be refined if the project is given authorization to move to the initiation stage.

The other main focus in this activity is the Project Manager creating the *Project Product Description*. This document should specify the product(s) that are capable of delivering the returns set out in the outline Business Case. For example, for the hotel project, if the forecasts in the Business Case include very high room rates, then the Project Product Description would probably describe a luxury hotel. During its creation, the Project Manager liaises with the Senior Users to find out their product requirements.

The exact composition of the Project Product Description is covered in Chapter 6, "Quality Theme." It has a number of sections, but the two sections that I'll look at now are the customer quality expectations and the acceptance criteria.

The customer presents their *customer quality expectations* to indicate what they require. In the hotel example, the client might say that their expectations are for a luxury hotel. However, the word "luxury" is ambiguous. My idea of what luxury means could be very different from yours. So in order to avoid disputes at the end of the project about what should have been created, the Project Manager and the Senior Users review the customer quality expectations and define a set of measurable specification criteria for the project's products. In PRINCE2, these are called *acceptance criteria*. These criteria are used at the end of the project to verify that the correct products have been delivered.

In the hotel example, acceptance criteria could be things such as the number of rooms the hotel will have or the size of the lobby. When the project is finished, the end customers can use these acceptance criteria to determine whether the "right" hotel has been built.

The final task for the Project Manager is to put together a high-level schedule to deliver the project. This schedule will include important delivery milestones and risks. At this point in the initiative, this information will go into the outline Business Case. Later on, if the initiation stage is authorized, a more detailed version of this schedule will go into the Project Plan.

Capture Previous Lessons

The Project Manager captures useful experiences that could help the project. These lessons could come from numerous sources, such as the following:

- Looking at Lesson Reports from previous projects

- Running workshops or talking to people with relevant experience

- Seeking lessons from the corporate or programme management level in the organization

- Talking to external organizations

During this activity, the Project Manager creates the *Lessons Log*, which acts as a repository for any lessons learned. The Project Manager can refer to this log throughout the PRINCE2 process model, to guide and direct how he manages the project and how to create the variety of management products. He can also use it to record lessons learned during the current project that might be useful to other projects or the organization.

As the project moves through its life and more becomes known about what lies ahead, it might be useful to repeat the exercise of capturing previous lessons.

Design and Appoint the Project Management Team

During this activity, the Executive and the Project Manager work together to design an appropriate project management team structure and develop descriptions for all the roles in the structure (with the exception of the role descriptions for the Executive and the Project Manager, which were written in the Appoint the Executive and the Project Manager activity). The Executive then appoints people who have the level of authority necessary to move the project forward as well as the time to dedicate to the project.

You were introduced to the PRINCE2 project management team structure in Chapter 1, "Overview of PRINCE2." This is the basis on which the project's team structure is designed. This structure ensures that the three main perspectives on the project—the business, the ultimate users of the project's products, and the suppliers of the project's products—are represented on the main decision-making unit, the Project Board.

All PRINCE2 Project Boards include Senior Users and Senior Suppliers. The Senior Users are senior-level people who represent those who will use the final outputs of the project. The Senior Suppliers are senior-level people who control the resources that will create the outputs of the project. The Project Manager should create job descriptions for both these roles based on the recommended PRINCE2 job descriptions. The Executive then approves these job descriptions.

The Project Manager and the Executive must next decide what other roles will be necessary to ensure that the project is effectively managed. At this point, job descriptions might be developed for Project Assurance (the people who monitor the project to ensure it is being run correctly), Project Support (those who provide a range of support to help the Project Manager manage the project), and Team Managers (people who manage the teams).

The next step is to recruit skilled people into the roles. Not all of these roles are filled at this time. For example, the project might involve using an external supplier who at this point has not been contracted. Later in the project, people from this external contractor might take on the Senior Supplier and Team Manager roles.

More than one person might fill any of the roles being created in this activity. That means the project might have two or three Senior Users. (Remember that the Executive and the Project Manager roles created earlier in the process are different—each project has only one Executive and one Project Manager.)

Having multiple Senior Users and Senior Suppliers ensures a broader range of perspectives are represented on the Project Board. However, it might take longer for the Project Board to come to a decision.

When looking for suitable candidates for the project roles, the Project Manager should perform a thorough analysis of all the people who might be impacted by the project. Some of these people might be suitable for the project management team. If they don't wish to take on roles in the project, they will at least probably want to be informed of its progress. This is called *stakeholder analysis*. This analysis will be done again, in more depth, if the project reaches its initiation stage during the "Prepare the Communication Management Strategy activity."

The people appointed to the project management team should clearly understand and accept what is expected of them. They might need some training in order to carry out their roles.

Chapter 3, "Organization Theme," covers the project management team structure in even more detail.

Select the Project Approach and Assemble the Project Brief

This activity has two focuses: create a project approach showing how the project will be delivered, and assemble the *Project Brief*, which the Project Board will use as the basis of their decision regarding whether to proceed to the first stage of the project.

The Project Manager creates the *project approach*. It answers how the project's products will be delivered and how they will be brought into the operational environment, if there is one. For example, will the products be created in-house, outsourced, or bought as an off-the-shelf solution? For the hotel project, a reasonable approach might be to outsource the hotel's construction to a building firm. The project approach might also look at technical approaches used in particular industries. For example, in the construction of a hotel, the rooms might be built as individual units and then shipped to the site rather than being built at the hotel location. Finally, the project approach specifies any supplier, organizational, or industry delivery standards.

PRINCE2 sometimes refers to the project approach as the *delivery solution*. This terminology can be rather confusing, because the word "solution" typically refers to the end result, not how the end result is delivered. So remember, in PRINCE2, delivery solution is synonymous with project approach.

At the end of this activity, the Project Manager assembles the Project Brief. Figure 2.3 shows the composition of this management product. Many of the sections of the Project Brief will have been created during the previous activities—such as the Project Product Description, the outline Business Case, the project management team structure, the role descriptions, and the project approach. The only section that needs to be created at this point is the project definition, which describes the project's background, objectives, scope, and the amount of flexibility for the delivery dates and budgets.

FIGURE 2.3   The composition of the Project Brief

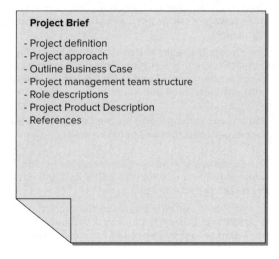

Project Brief

- Project definition
- Project approach
- Outline Business Case
- Project management team structure
- Role descriptions
- Project Product Description
- References

Plan the Initiation Stage

After the Starting up a Project process is complete, the Project Board reviews the information in the Project Brief and decides whether the project should start. The first stage of the project is the *initiation stage*, where the detailed planning is addressed. In addition to the Project Brief, the Project Board will want to see a plan for this first stage, to understand the time and resources needed to plan the project. In effect, they will want to see a plan for the planning! In this activity, the Project Manager creates the *Stage Plan for the initiation stage*.

Key Facts for Starting up a Project

For the Foundation exam, you do not have to memorize all the details from the Starting up a Project activity sections. You should, however, learn the important facts for this process specified in Table 2.1

TABLE 2.1   Starting up a Project—key process facts

Activity	Key facts
Appoint the Executive and the Project Manager	Corporate or programme management appoints the Executive. The Executive appoints the Project Manager. The Project Manager creates the Daily Log. This log is used by the Project Manager as a personal project diary, recording personal actions and informal issues.
Prepare the outline Business Case	The Executive creates the outline Business Case. This justifies the undertaking of the project, although at this point, it may be quite high-level. The Project Manager liaises with the Senior User(s) to create the Project Product Description. This outlines the specifications for the major products. It is used at the end of the project to verify that the right products have been created.
Capture previous lessons	The Project Manager creates the Lessons Log and populates it with past experience that will help the management of the project.
Design and appoint the project management team	The Executive and the Project Manager design the project management team structure and create job descriptions for all the roles. They appoint as many people to the project management team as is possible at this early point in the initiative. This will include recruiting who they can to the Project Board.
Select the project approach and assemble the Project Brief	The Project Manager creates the project approach. This describes the overall approach to delivering the products, such as in-house development or outsourcing the work. The Project Manager assembles the Project Brief. This defines the scope and objectives of the project. It contains some of the outputs from previous activities, such as the project management team structure, role descriptions, outline Business Case, Project Product Description, and the project approach.
Plan the initiation stage	The Project Manager creates the Stage Plan for the initiation stage. This plan shows the Project Board what resources, money, and time would be needed to carry out the next step, the initiation stage. The initiation stage is when the project is planned to a high level. The Project Board reviews the Stage Plan for the initiation stage to decide whether to authorize the initiation stage.

Authorizing Initiation

Once all the activities of the Starting up a Project process are finished, the Project Manager will send a request to initiate a project to the Project Board. The Project Board considers this request in the Directing a Project process in the "Authorize initiation" activity. (Refer to Figure 2.1.) They may or may not do this in a formal meeting. The basis of their decision will be all the information in the Project Brief. They can also use Project Assurance to review this material and test its validity.

Sometimes in this early stage, there may be no Senior Supplier representative—for example, if an outsourced supplier has not been contracted at this point. Even without the Senior Supplier, PRINCE2 allows the Project Board to authorize the initiation stage (although I think it would be a good idea to represent the outsourced supplier by a proxy—maybe using the procurement department).

If the Project Board decides to proceed, they will obtain the resources required by the Stage Plan for the initiation stage. Then the Executive will give the Project Manager documented instructions to proceed with the delivery of just the initiation stage. At this point, they should inform all stakeholders that the project is being initiated.

Initiating a Project

In Figure 2.1, you can see that once the Project Board has authorized initiation, the next process is Initiating a Project. This is where the project begins. The Project Manager uses this process to run the first stage of the project, the initiation stage. It contains the following eight activities:

- *Prepare the Risk Management Strategy*
- *Prepare the Quality Management Strategy*
- *Prepare the Configuration Management Strategy*
- *Prepare the Communication Management Strategy*
- *Set up the project controls*
- *Create the Project Plan*
- *Refine the Business Case*
- *Assemble the Project Initiation Documentation*

The main focus of these activities is to plan the project. PRINCE2's definition of the purpose of this process is "to establish solid foundations for the project, enabling the organization to understand the work that needs to be done to deliver the project's products before committing to a significant spend."

The main output from the Initiating a Project process is the Project Initiation Documentation. You will learn about the exact composition of this management product in the "Assemble the Project Initiation Documentation" activity section later in this chapter. Many of the sections from the Project Brief will be transferred to the Project Initiation Documentation, although at this point, there will be more time to refine them. Additional information needs to be added, such as the Project Plan, the project's strategies, and how PRINCE2 will be tailored for this particular situation.

After the Initiating a Project process is completed, the Project Initiation Documentation is passed to the Project Board. The board then uses this documentation to decide whether to authorize the project to proceed. All the activities in Initiating a Project create information that goes into the Project Initiation Documentation. Rather than wait until the document has been finished, the Project Board might decide to review the information as it is created themselves, or they may ask their Project Assurance representatives to do so for them.

 Real World Scenario

Using PRINCE2 to Sell Projects

Many companies sell projects, such as building firms that sell their ability to deliver construction projects, software companies that deliver bespoke software, and office moving companies that deliver projects to move office furniture.

I was involved with a company of this type several years ago. They created the IT infrastructure used by large organizations for their websites. They would procure a range of types of computers and software for their clients and then install this hardware and software in secure data centers, making sure there were all sorts of fail-safes incorporated to keep the websites up in an emergency—for example, gas generators that would start if there was a blackout. They would then maintain and operate the infrastructure on behalf of their clients.

One of the challenges for the project teams was that the sales teams would often promise potential clients unrealistic delivery dates and miscommunicate the scope of the products that would be delivered. This, of course, caused a lot of problems when the project was handed over from the sales team to the delivery team.

To resolve this problem, I set up a handover process between the sales team and the project teams based on PRINCE2. Every time a salesperson felt a potential client was about to sign up for the company's services, they had to put a proposal together for that client. A representative from the project team helped them. This proposal was based on the PRINCE2 Project Brief. In effect, the pre-sales work was the Starting up a Project process. Then if the client decided to proceed with the work, it was with the understanding that there would be some time devoted to expanding on this proposal to create the Project Initiation Documentation. At this point, if any significant new pieces of information arose, the quote might be allowed to change.

This approach allowed for a much more consistent message to be given to the clients through the pre-sales and project work. This approach led to more satisfied customers.

Initiating a Project Activities

Figure 2.4 shows an overview of the activities in the Initiating a Project process. As you can see, there is a certain sequence in which these activities are carried out. First, the strategies are created, and then the Project Plan and project controls are set up. Finally, the Business Case is refined and the Project Initiation Documentation assembled.

FIGURE 2.4   Overview of Initiating a Project

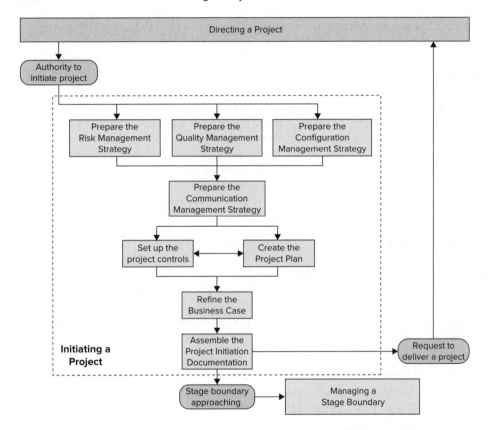

Based on Cabinet Office PRINCE2® material. Reproduced under licence from the Cabinet Office.

You'll learn about each of the eight activities over the following sections. You should read these sections and make sure you understand them, but again, you don't necessarily need to memorize the details. After these sections, you will find an "Initiating a Project— key process facts" table that you *do* need to memorize for the exams.

Preparing the Strategies

The first four activities in Initiating a Project create four strategies, as follows:

- Prepare the Risk Management Strategy creates the Risk Management Strategy.
- Prepare the Quality Management Strategy creates the Quality Management Strategy.

- Prepare the Configuration Management Strategy creates the Configuration Management Strategy.
- Prepare the Communication Management Strategy creates the Communication Management Strategy.

These four management products will show how the project team will manage risks and quality, how they will assess and authorize proposed changes to the project, how they will track the project's products, and how they will communicate effectively with all the project's stakeholders. You will learn about the contents of each strategy later in the book. (The Risk Management Strategy is covered in Chapter 7, "Risk Theme"; the Quality Management Strategy is covered in Chapter 6, "Quality Theme"; the Configuration Management Strategy is covered in Chapter 8, "Change Theme"; and the Communication Management Strategy is covered in Chapter 3, "Organization Theme.") However, this section will give you a brief overview of what a strategy is.

A strategy provides all the information needed to describe an approach to management. For example, if the Project Manager wanted to describe how quality on the project should be managed, what information would they need to provide? PRINCE2 recommends that each strategy contain six sections: procedure, timings, roles and responsibilities, tools and techniques, reporting, and records. The following list presents examples of the type of information that might go into these six sections for a Quality Management Strategy. Of course, you'd need a lot more information in each category to fully describe an approach to quality management, but these examples will give you an idea of how to set up a strategy:

Quality Management Procedure   This is basically the set of activities that the project needs to do (maybe a number of times) to ensure it builds the right products. The project team identifies who will use the products, talks to them to find out their requirements, documents those requirements, ensures that those creating the products use the documented requirements when they are deciding what to build, and finally, gets the users back at the end of the project to agree that the products that have been built are what was initially specified. All of these activities together form a basic quality procedure.

Timing of Quality Management Activities   Are there any particular dates, times, or schedules that are important to ensuring the project is building the correct products? For example, maybe at the end of each stage of the project, Project Assurance will carry out an audit of all the quality checks that have occurred.

Quality Management Roles and Responsibilities   Who will be involved during the project to ensure the right products are built? What responsibilities will these people have? For example, maybe one role will represent those who will use the products. That individual's responsibilities will be to fully specify what all the users require from the products, check the products as they are being built to ensure they are being created correctly, and finally, sign off on the product.

Quality Management Tools and Techniques   Will any special techniques be used in quality management? For example, if the project involves building software, a particular technical test may be available that measures whether the product is sufficiently robust to be used in operations.

Quality Management Reporting   What quality reports need to be created, who do they need to be sent to, and what sort of format will they have? For example, maybe the Project Manager's regular progress report should include a section describing how the products are progressing through their quality checks.

Quality Management Records   What information does the project need to record on the quality activities carried out throughout the project? For example, many quality checks may be done during the project. It would be useful to record who was involved in those checks, what date the checks occurred, what each check revealed, and whether the quality check passed or failed.

The preceding examples deal with quality management. However, you could use the same six categories to describe how to manage risk, configuration, and communication.

Prepare the Risk Management Strategy

The Project Manager creates the *Risk Management Strategy*, which defines how to manage risk. In particular, it describes how to decrease the likelihood and/or the impact of potential threats to the project. Threats are potential problems that would detrimentally affect the project's objectives. But risks could also be opportunities—potential events that could positively affect the project's objectives. So the Risk Management Strategy also looks at how to increase the likelihood and/or impact of potential opportunities to the project. (You'll learn more about risk in Chapter 7, "Risk Theme.")

The Risk Management Strategy sets out the six pieces of information common to all strategies, which were discussed in the previous section: procedure, timings, roles and responsibilities, tools and techniques, reporting, and records. Chapter 7, "Risk Theme" describes what type of information goes into each of these sections.

This strategy also specifies the threshold of risk that the corporate or programme level and the Project Board are willing to accept—in other words, their risk tolerance levels. Risk can be measured in a variety of ways, such as adding together the expected financial impact of all the potential threats to the project. If this overall level goes over the risk tolerance levels, the Project Manager needs to ensure that this situation is escalated to the correct management level.

In addition, the Risk Management Strategy considers how risks will be assessed in terms of their probability, their impact on the project, what category of risk they are, and how their likelihood will vary over time. It will specify whether there will be any money set aside to fund responses to risks. Early warning indicators will be taken into account, which if monitored, might indicate an increase or decrease of the project's exposure to risk.

Finally, the Project Manager creates the *Risk Register*. You will learn how to compose this management product in Chapter 7, "Risk Theme." For now, think of it as containing all the details of the identified threats and opportunities that might affect the project objectives. There might be a number of risks that were identified in the Starting up a Project process and that the Project Manager recorded in the Daily Log; in that case, these risks will now be transferred to the Risk Register.

Prepare the Quality Management Strategy

In the next step, the Project Manager creates the *Quality Management Strategy*, which describes how the project management team will ensure that the end result of the project will be a product (or products) that are suitable for their intended purpose. This strategy should include information in the six categories previously described in "Preparing the Strategies": procedure, timings, roles and responsibilities, tools and techniques, reporting, and records.

To develop the Quality Management Strategy, the Project Manager should review the Project Product Description that was created in the Starting up a Project process. This describes, at a high level, the specification for the main product or products that the project will need to create. The Project Manager will also need to take into account any organizational quality approaches of both the customers and suppliers involved with the project.

In addition to the strategy, the Project Manager creates an empty *Quality Register*. As the project progresses, this register will be used to record information on the quality checks that are carried out on the products that are created. You will learn more about how the Quality Register is used in Chapter 6, "Quality Theme."

Prepare the Configuration Management Strategy

Creating the *Configuration Management Strategy* is also the job of the Project Manager. This strategy describes how the project team will manage all the project's products.

In any project, there might be hundreds of individual parts to what is being created. For example, if the project is to create a car, all sorts of individual parts will have to be bought or built separately (the engine, the body, the seats, and so on) and then put together, or *configured*, to form the completed car. You can think of "configuration" as referring to all the various parts that make up the final product. An important part of project management is to keep track of and control all of these parts—what PRINCE2 calls *configuration management*. Configuration management includes the following aspects:

Identifying   The project team must ensure that all the items that are necessary to create the final product are identified during the project. At this stage, probably only the major products can be identified, but as the project progresses, smaller and smaller components of the major products will be identified.

Tracking   Once any item that needs to be created has been identified, the project team must be clear about what state it is in at any point in time.

Protecting   Once the parts of the final product have been finished, the project team must ensure that no unauthorized changes are made to them. The team also needs to have a process for considering the impact of proposed changes to the products and deciding whether to authorize them.

The Configuration Management Strategy specifies how all three aspects of configuration management will be done on the project. This strategy should include the six categories of strategy information—procedures, timings, roles and responsibilities, tools and techniques, reporting, and records.

Two procedures are described in the Configuration Management Strategy. First is the procedure for keeping track of and controlling all of the project's products. This includes such tasks as identifying all the products, controlling access to the products, and reporting information on the state of the products. Second is the procedure used to manage changes to the project's products. This includes steps to capture proposed changes, evaluate them, and then authorize them at an appropriate level of authority. In most projects, the Project Board is responsible for authorizing changes to the products. However, the board may decide that this will require too much of their time and will instead delegate some or all of this authority to a separate group of people. PRINCE2 calls this group a Change Authority.

The Configuration Management Strategy also describes two types of records: Issue Register and Configuration Item Record. The *Issue Register* is used to record and track all proposed changes, as well as unauthorized changes that have been made to the product by mistake. The *Configuration Item Record* is used to track information about a product, such as the product's status and who is working on it. Each product should have its own Configuration Item Record.

The Project Manager creates the project's Issue Register at this point. Some issues may have already been recorded in the Daily Log; if so, these will be transferred to the Issue Register. In addition, the Project Manager creates a set of Configuration Item Records for the project's management products, such as the Project Initiation Documentation.

You will learn more about configuration management and the associated concepts of change management in Chapter 8, "Change Theme."

Prepare the Communication Management Strategy

Finally, the Project Manager creates the *Communication Management Strategy*, which describes how the project will manage communication between the people on the project management team as well as between the project and stakeholders outside the project team. The Project Manager should create this strategy last, since the preceding three strategies might have identified various reports that should be included in the Communication Management Strategy.

You will learn how to create the Communication Management Strategy in more detail in Chapter 3, "Organization Theme." For now, remember that it also contains the six common types of strategy information: procedures, timings, roles and responsibilities, tools and techniques, reporting, and records.

Remember that the Project Manager might have conducted a stakeholder analysis during the Starting up a Project process (while designing and appointing the project management team). If this is the case, the Project Manager should review the results of that work and, if necessary, conduct further analysis. If no stakeholder analysis was done in Starting up a Project, the Project Manager will have to do it here.

Set Up the Project Controls

Anything that ensures that the project is heading toward its objectives is a *project control*. For example, the Project Board controls the Project Manager by giving them only one stage of the project to manage at a time, setting specific objectives for that stage in terms of the products that must be built and the time and money that are available for that stage. So one of the controls established in this activity is how the Project Plan will be divided into stages and when the end-stage assessment meetings between the Project Board and the Project Manager will occur.

Many of the ways of controlling the project will have already been defined in the four strategies. For example, the reporting system, defined in the Communication Management Strategy, allows the project to be monitored. Monitoring is an important aspect of control—it allows the monitoring body to get an early warning of problems, which they can then rectify in a timely manner.

The strategies might also set out new responsibilities for the various project management team roles. In this activity, the Project Manager adds these responsibilities to the role descriptions and makes sure the individuals concerned accept these amendments.

Create the Project Plan

Next, the Project Manager creates the *Project Plan*. It shows how the major products in the project will be delivered. It covers the time directly after the initiation stage to the end of the project and will probably be fairly high-level. Remember that the more detailed planning is done on a stage-by-stage basis. (Refer to the "Manage by Stages" section in Chapter 1, "Overview of PRINCE2.") If the project is short, the Project Manager might be able to plan the entire project in detail at this point.

The Project Plan should be based on the work that was done in Starting up a Project. The Project Brief will have specified important delivery dates and the project approach. The Project Plan needs to be consistent with both of these.

The Project Manager needs to decide how to format the Project Plan. There are many ways of presenting the information in a plan, including the popular Gantt chart format (a graphical way of showing a schedule), spreadsheets, or purely text-based. You don't need to know about these formats for the PRINCE2 exam—you just need to know that this is when the Project Manager decides on the plan format.

The Project Manager should also decide what estimating techniques will be used. For example, some projects use the Delphi method to estimate durations. (The Delphi method is a process used to come to a consensus estimate with a group of people.) Once again, estimating techniques are not covered in the PRINCE2 syllabus—you just need to know that this is the point at which the Project Manager decides which techniques to use.

PRINCE2 plans contain not only schedule information such as tasks, dates, and resources, but also detailed specifications of the products that will be built during that plan. In PRINCE2, these specifications are the Product Descriptions. Remember that the Project Plan is probably fairly high-level, so at this point, the Project Manager will only be able to identify the major deliverables. The Project Manager will create Product Descriptions for these major deliverables. These descriptions need to be consistent with the higher-level Project Product Description created in Starting up a Project and agreed to by the Senior Users. For each major product identified in the plan, the Project Manager should create a corresponding Configuration Item Record, which will be used to track status information on that product.

Refine the Business Case

Creating a detailed Business Case—using the information in the outline Business Case created in Starting up a Project and the more detailed estimates of costs and timescales available from the newly created Project Plan—is also the task of the Project Manager. They will confer with the Executive to do this.

The Project Manager also creates the *Benefit Review Plan*. This management product will be covered in more detail in Chapter 4, "Business Case Theme." For now, you just need to know that the Project Manager uses this plan to specify how achievements of the project's benefits will be measured. Many of the activities in this plan are likely to occur after the project has finished, because many benefits from projects aren't realized until after all the products have been built.

Assemble the Project Initiation Documentation

During this activity, the Project Manager gathers all the information needed for the *Project Initiation Documentation*. Figure 2.5 shows the composition of the Project Initiation Documentation. Many of the sections come directly from the Project Brief, although the information within them might be more detailed at this point. The new sections are the strategies, a Project Plan, a detailed Business Case, and a summary of how PRINCE2 will be tailored for this project. The Project Initiation Documentation might be a collection of individual documents.

FIGURE 2.5   The composition of the Project Initiation Documentation

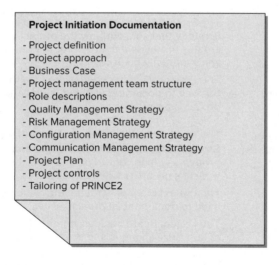

As the project progresses, the Project Manager will create a new version of the Project Initiation Documentation at the end of each stage. The Project Board will authorize these new versions. However, the first version of the Project Initiation Documentation is particularly important. It describes the stakeholder's expectations of the project at the point it was authorized. PRINCE2 recommends that the Project Board review this first version at the end of the project, in order to evaluate how the project performed.

At the end of this activity, the Project Manager will use the Managing a Stage Boundary process to prepare for the next stage. (Refer back to Figure 2.1 to see how the process model fits together at this point.) The Managing a Stage Boundary process is covered in more detail in Chapter 10, "Managing the Middle of a Project Successfully with PRINCE2." At this point, all that you need to know about this process is that it is used to create a detailed plan for the next stage. The Project Manager will show this Stage Plan to the Project Board and ask them for permission to manage that section of the project.

Finally, the Project Manager sends a request to deliver the project to the Project Board.

Key Facts for Initiating a Project

For the Foundation exam, you do not need to memorize all details contained in the Initiating a Project activity sections. Read through those sections and make sure the information makes sense. You should, however, learn the important facts for this process set out in Table 2.2.

TABLE 2.2 Initiating a Project—key process facts

Activity	Key facts
Prepare the Risk Management Strategy	The Project Manager creates the Risk Management Strategy that sets out how risk will be managed during the project.
	The Project Manager creates the Risk Register that will be used to document the project risks.
Prepare the Quality Management Strategy	The Project Manager creates the Quality Management Strategy that sets out how the project will ensure it creates products that are fit for the purpose for which they will eventually be used.
	The Project Manager creates the Quality Register that will be used to document all the quality checks made on the project's products.
Prepare the Configuration Management Strategy	The Project Manager creates the Configuration Management Strategy that sets out how changes to the project's products will be controlled and how the status of the project's products will be tracked.
	The Project Manager creates the Issue Register that will be used to document all project issues.
	The Project Board decides whether to delegate any authority to authorize changes and so create a Change Authority.
Prepare the Communication Management Strategy	The Project Manager creates the Communication Management Strategy that sets out how communication between those involved with the project and other stakeholders will be managed.

Activity	Key facts
Set up the project controls	The Project Manager documents how they and the Project Board will control work on the project and make sure the right things are done.
Create the Project Plan	The Project Manager creates the Project Plan.
Refine the Business Case	The Project Manager creates the first version of the detailed Business Case and the Benefit Review Plan
Assemble the Project Initiation Documentation	The Project Manager assembles all the information from the preceding activities to create the Project Initiation Documentation.

Authorizing the Project and Authorizing the Stage

Once the Initiating a Project process has finished, the Project Manager sends a request to the Project Board asking them to authorize the delivery part of the project. The process model then moves on to the Directing a Project process and, in particular, to two activities that the Project Board are responsible for: "Authorize the project" and "Authorize a Stage Plan." (Refer to Figure 2.1 to see how the process model works at this point.)

In "authorize the project," the Project Board decides whether to authorize the delivery part of the project. If the answer is yes, they then decide whether to give the Project Manager authorization to commit resources to the next delivery stage, in the "Authorize a Stage Plan" activity. If the answer is yes to this as well, the Project Manager will then be allowed to manage the next delivery stage, after which he must report back to the Project Board.

Authorize the Project

During this activity, the main management product that the Project Board or their Project Assurance representatives will review is the Project Initiation Documentation. They look through all the information and make sure they are happy with it. They will want to see evidence that any previous experience in the Lessons Log was taken into account when the Project Manager assembled the Project Initiation Documentation.

The Project Board also reviews the Benefits Review Plan to ensure that there is adequate planning for the review of the achievements of the project's benefits.

The board will then need to decide whether or not to authorize the project. If they decide not to, they will instruct the Project Manager to close the project prematurely. In this case, the Project Manager will start the Closing a Project process. You will learn more about this process in Chapter 11, "Managing the End of a Project Successfully with PRINCE2." For now, all you need to know is that during this process, the Project Manager performs various activities to close the project, such as creating the End Project Report. After the Closing a Project process, the Project Manager goes back to the Project Board for a final time to request authorization to close the project.

The alternative is, of course, that the Project Board decides that, based on the information in the Project Initiation Documentation, this project is a viable and worthwhile initiative. In that case, they will obtain or commit the resources needed for the project. However, remember that they will only release these resources to the Project Manager on a stage-by-stage basis.

Finally, the Project Board will notify corporate or programme management and any other interested parties that the project has been authorized.

Authorize a Stage

After deciding to authorize the project, the Project Board will then move on to reviewing the Stage Plan for the first delivery stage and decide whether to authorize this work.

During this activity, the Project Board (or their Project Assurance representatives) will review the plan for the next stage and any new Product Descriptions for products that will be created in that stage. They will also want to check that any risks associated with this stage are covered by suitable countermeasures.

Then they will either approve the Stage Plan and set time, cost, and scope tolerances that the Project Manager must abide by, or they will ask the Project Manager to revise the plan and give guidance on what would make it acceptable.

Finally, the Project Board will notify corporate or programme management and any other interested parties that a new stage is starting.

Themes Used to Start a Project Successfully

All of the seven themes are used throughout the activities at the beginning of the project. It is important for you to understand how these themes link to the activities of the Starting up a Project and Initiating a Project processes, because this will be a potential topic for exam questions.

Business Case Theme

The Business Case theme describes how to ensure that the project is desirable, viable, and achievable throughout the project's life. It shows how to write the project's Business Case, assigns a variety of business-related responsibilities to the roles within the project management team, and shows where in the process model the major business-related activities should occur. This section describes how the Business Case theme is implemented at the beginning of the project.

Prior to starting a PRINCE2 project, corporate or programme management creates a project mandate. In a programme situation, this might be a detailed document that includes a detailed Business Case. However, for most projects, this is a very high-level document that includes the reasons the project is being considered and the background of the project, both of which will be transferred into the Business Case.

During the Starting up a Project process, corporate or programme management appoints an Executive for the project. The Executive should represent the commissioning organization's business viewpoint. Their responsibility is to check that the project represents value for money and will give adequate returns given the investment needed. The Executive will create an outline Business Case, which will justify the undertaking of the project.

During the Initiating a Project process, the Project Manager refines the outline Business Case to create the first detailed Business Case. The Project Manager will also create the Benefits Review Plan, which describes how the achievements of the project's benefits will be measured.

During the Directing a Project process, the Project Board has a number of decisions to make. First, they authorize initiation, then the project, and finally, the first delivery stage. In all of these decisions, they must verify that there is a solid justification for carrying on with the project based on the information in the Business Case.

You will learn about the Business Case theme in more detail in Chapter 4, "Business Case Theme."

Organization Theme

The Organization theme sets out a project management team structure with associated roles and responsibilities. During the Starting up a Project process, the project management team is designed and then appointed. Corporate or programme management appoints the Executive, the Executive appoints the Project Manager, and then together, they design the rest of the project management team and appoint as many people to the roles as is possible at this early point in the initiative.

During the Initiating a Project process, the Project Manager will carry out a full stakeholder analysis, identifying anyone who will be impacted by the project, the type of information that the project management team requires from them, and also the type of information that they require from the project management team. The output of this analysis work is put into the Communication Management Strategy.

You will learn about the Organization theme in more detail in Chapter 3, "Organization Theme."

Quality Theme

The Quality theme shows how a project should be managed to ensure it creates the right products. It covers how to specify what products to build, how to check the quality of the products, and who will be involved in product-focused activities. This section describes how the Quality theme is implemented at the beginning of the project.

The Project Manager creates the Project Product Description during the Starting up a Project process. This will set out the high-level specifications for the major project outputs. The Project Manager will work with the Senior Users in order to create this management product. The Project Product Description contains the customer's quality expectations and the measurable acceptance criteria that the final products should conform to when finished.

During the Initiating a Project process, the Project Manager creates the Quality Management Strategy. This shows how the project will be managed to ensure that the correct products are created. The Project Manager also creates a blank Quality Register, which is used to record information on all the product quality checks that will take place throughout the project. The Project Manager also creates the Project Plan during this process. This plan includes Product Descriptions for the major products to be delivered.

You will learn about the Quality theme in more detail in Chapter 6, "Quality Theme."

Plans Theme

The Plans theme shows how to plan the work of the project using three different levels of plans: the Project Plan, the Stage Plan, and the Team Plan. It describes the roles involved with planning as well as the steps needed to create a plan. This section describes how the Plans theme is implemented at the beginning of the project.

Plans are created during the following processes at the outset of a project:

- During the Starting up a Project process, the Stage Plan for the initiation stage is created; it plans the work needed to create the Project Initiation Documentation.

- During the Initiating a Project process, the Project Plan is created, which plans at a high level the work for the entire delivery part of the project.

- During the Managing a Stage Boundary process that occurs at the end of the initiation stage, the first delivery Stage Plan is created.

You will learn about the Plans theme in more detail in Chapter 5, "Plans Theme."

Risk Theme

The Risk theme identifies, assesses, and controls the potential threats to and opportunities of the project, and thus improves the likelihood of project success. This section shows how the Risk theme is implemented at the beginning of the project.

During the Starting up a Project process, the Project Manager logs identified threats or opportunities in the Daily Log. The Executive then summarizes the risk situation in the outline Business Case.

During the Initiating a Project process, the Project Manager creates the Risk Management Strategy, which describes how risk will be managed during the project. The Project Manager also creates a Risk Register and transfers into it any threats or opportunities logged in the Daily Log. The Risk Register is then used to record details of identified risks throughout the project. The Project Manager summarizes the risk situation in the detailed Business Case.

You will learn about the Risk theme in more detail in Chapter 7, "Risk Theme."

Change Theme

The Change theme covers two aspects of project management: how to track and control all of the project's products, and how to control changes to the project's products. This section describes how the Change theme is implemented at the beginning of the project.

During the Initiating a Project process, the Project Manager will create the Configuration Management Strategy, which describes how changes to the project will be managed and how the project's products will be controlled. The Project Manager also creates the Issue Register, which is used to record all requested changes to the project's products.

During the Initiating a Project process, Configuration Item Records for the project's management products and the specialist products identified in the Project Plan will be created. These records will be used to track the status of these products throughout their life.

Also during Initiating a Project, the Project Board decides whether to establish a separate Change Authority. The individual(s) with Change Authority will be able to authorize some changes to the project's products.

You will learn about the Change theme in more detail in Chapter 8, "Change Theme."

Progress Theme

The Progress theme shows how the work of the project is controlled and kept on track. It covers the topic of tolerances, which are used to delegate authority with certain constraints. (See the "Manage by Exception" section in Chapter 1, "Overview of PRINCE2.") The Progress theme also describes how to use stages that help the Project Board to control and monitor a project. (See the "Manage by Stages" section in Chapter 1, "Overview of PRINCE2.") This section describes how the Progress theme is implemented at the beginning of the project.

In the Initiating a Project process, the Project Manager creates the project controls section in the Project Initiation Documentation. This sets out how the project will be controlled and monitored. It shows how the Project Plan will be divided into stages and specifies the various decision-making responsibilities in the project. Corporate or programme management sets cost, time, and scope tolerances for the objectives in the Project Plan. The Project Board sets cost, time, and scope tolerances for the objectives in the Stage Plan for the first delivery stage.

You will learn about the Progress theme in more detail in Chapter 9, "Progress Theme."

Using the PRINCE2 Principles to Successfully Start a Project

The seven PRINCE2 principles are used at the beginning of the project as follows:

- *Continued business justification* is implemented by the creation of the outline Business Case and then the detailed Business Case, the appointment of the Executive to represent the business interest, and the verification that a Business Case exists during all the Directing a Project authorization points.

- *Learn from experience* is implemented during Starting up a Project by the creation of the Lessons Log, which is populated with previous useful experience, and by considering lessons when carrying out any of the activities in the Starting up a Project and Initiating a Project processes.

- *Defined roles and responsibilities* is implemented by the establishment of a project management team in the Starting up a Project process, appointing people to the various roles and ensuring that they understand their project responsibilities.

- *Manage by stages* is implemented by creating a Project Plan divided into various management stages, and by the Project Board authorizing the Project Manager's work one stage at a time—first for the initiation stage and then for the first delivery stage.

- *Manage by exception* is implemented by the Project Board defining certain tolerances within which the Project Manager must manage the initiation stage and the first delivery stage. It is also implemented by corporate or programme management setting tolerances for the Project Board for the project.

- *Focus on products* is implemented first by specifying the overall output of the project in the Project Product Description, then by specifying the major products in their Product Descriptions, and finally by creating the Quality Management Strategy that defines how the project will be managed to ensure that the right products are created.

- *Tailor to suit the project environment* is implemented by including a section in the Project Initiation Documentation that shows how PRINCE2 will be tailored for this particular project.

Summary

In this chapter, you learned how to start a project successfully with PRINCE2. You saw that the Starting up a Project, Initiating a Project, and Directing a Project processes include activities that ensure a disciplined beginning to a project.

Starting up a Project was the first process you learned about. The Executive and the Project Manager work together in this process to ensure that the project's scope and objectives are clearly defined. They also design a project management team and appoint people to the roles. The Executive creates an outline Business Case containing a justification for the project. The main outputs from the Starting up a Project process are a Project Brief, which defines the project idea, and a Stage Plan for the initiation stage that specifies the resources necessary for the initiation stage.

You then saw that during the Directing a Project process, the Project Board reviews the Project Brief and Stage Plan for the initiation stage. They will use these documents to come to a decision about whether to authorize the initiative to continue.

The Project Manager then carries out the Initiating a Project process. You saw that this covers the work of planning the project, at least at a high level. The Project Manager creates four strategies: the Risk Management Strategy, the Quality Management Strategy, the Configuration Management Strategy, and the Communication Management Strategy. These show how the project will be managed. In addition, the Project Manager creates a Project Plan and refines the Business Case. All of these outputs are assembled into the Project Initiation Documentation.

After the Initiating a Project process, the Project Manager uses the Managing a Stage Boundary process to create a Stage Plan for the next delivery stage. The Project Manager then takes this plan along with the Project Initiation Documentation to the Project Board. The board reviews both of these management products and decides whether to authorize the Project Manager to move on with the project.

The final part of the chapter covered how the PRINCE2 themes and principles are implemented in these early parts of a project. You saw that all seven themes and principles are used throughout the processes covered in this chapter.

Exam Essentials

Understand the purpose, objectives, and context of the Starting up a Project process.   The purpose of the Starting up a Project process is to answer the question, "Do we have a worthwhile and viable project?" It has a number of objectives: ensuring that there is business justification for the project, understanding the scope of the project, investigating the various ways of delivering the project, appointing the project management team, planning the work for the initiation stage, and ensuring that time is not wasted initiating a project that is not viable or worthwhile.

Starting up a Project is a pre-project process that starts once the project mandate has been created. After Starting up a Project, the Project Board decides whether to continue the project.

Understand the purpose, objectives, and context of the Initiating a Project process.   The purpose of the Initiating a Project process is to establish a solid foundation for the project that enables all stakeholders to understand the work that needs to be done to create the project's products. It has a number of objectives to ensure that there is a common understanding of: the business case for the project; the scope of the project; the plan for the project; the approach to risk, quality, configuration, and communication management; and how PRINCE2 will be tailored to meet the needs of this particular project.

This process occurs during the initiation stage, which is the first stage of the project.

Define which roles have responsibilities within the Starting up a Project process and know what main activities occur within the process.   The main activities within the Starting up a Project process are that corporate or programme management appoints the Executive, who, in turn, appoints the Project Manager. The Executive creates an outline Business Case, and the Project Manager creates the Project Product Description. The Executive and the Project Manager together design and appoint the project management team. The Project Manager puts the Project Brief together, which refines and expands on the information in the project mandate and defines what the project is all about. The Project Manager also creates a Stage Plan for the initiation stage to plan out the work to create the Project Initiation Documentation.

Define which roles have responsibilities within the Initiating a Project process and know what main activities occur within the process.   The main activity within the Initiating a Project process is that the Project Manager will create the Project Initiation Documentation. Within the Project Initiation Documentation, the Project Manager will create a number of strategies for managing the project, a Project Plan that will plan at a high level the delivery parts of the project, and a detailed Business Case. The Project Manager will also create a Risk, Issue, and Quality Register plus the Benefit Review Plan. The Project Board must decide whether to set up a Change Authority.

Describe the purpose and composition of the Project Brief.   The Project Brief provides a full and firm foundation for the initiation of the project. It contains a number of sections: project definition, outline Business Case, Project Product Description, project approach, project management team structure, and role descriptions. It is developed in the Starting up a Project process by the Executive and the Project Manager and is reviewed in the Directing a Project process by the Project Board when they are deciding whether to initiate the project.

Understand the purpose and the composition of the Project Initiation Documentation. The Project Initiation Documentation forms the contract between the Project Manager and the Project Board regarding the definition of the project. It can be used at the end of the project to see how successfully the project performed. It contains a number of sections: project definition, project approach, Business Case, project management team structure, role descriptions, Quality Management Strategy, Risk Management Strategy, Configuration Management Strategy, Communication Management Strategy, Project Plan, project controls, and tailoring of PRINCE2. The Project Manager develops the Project Initiation Documentation in the Initiating a Project process. The Project Board reviews it in the Directing a Project process when they are deciding whether to authorize the delivery part of the project.

Understand how the seven themes may be applied within the Starting up a Project process and the Initiating a Project process.   Know that the seven themes are applied throughout the Starting up a Project and Initiating a Project processes to manage their specific areas of project management.

Review Questions

The rest of this chapter contains mock exam questions, first for the Foundation exam and then for the Practitioner exam.

Foundation Exam Questions

1. Which product can be used to assess how the project performed at the end of the project?
   - **A.** Project Brief
   - **B.** Project Initiation Documentation
   - **C.** Risk Register
   - **D.** Quality Management Strategy

2. Which of the following is a purpose of the Initiating a Project process?
   - **A.** Answers the question, "Do we have a viable and worthwhile project?"
   - **B.** Prevents poorly conceived projects from being initiated
   - **C.** Makes key decisions and exercises overall control in the project
   - **D.** Establishes a solid foundation for the project, enabling the organization to understand the work that needs to be done

3. Which of the following actions from Starting up a Project implements the quality theme?
   - **A.** Design and appoint the project management team
   - **B.** Create the Project Approach
   - **C.** Create the Project Product Description
   - **D.** Draft the outline Business Case

4. Which of the following are objectives of the Initiating a Project process?
   1. Ensure that there is common understanding of how the quality required will be achieved.
   2. Identify who needs information, in what format, and at what time.
   3. Ensure that all the necessary authorities exist for initiating the project.
   4. Identify how risks will be identified, assessed, and controlled.
   - **A.** 1, 2, 3
   - **B.** 1, 3, 4
   - **C.** 1, 2, 4
   - **D.** 2, 3, 4

5. Which product defines how PRINCE2 will be tailored to suit the project?

    A. Project Initiation Documentation

    B. Project Brief

    C. Project Product Description

    D. Business Case

6. Which activity in Starting up a Project might be repeated later in the project?

    A. Appoint the Executive and the Project Manager

    B. Capture previous lessons

    C. Prepare the outline Business Case

    D. Select the project approach and assemble the Project Brief

7. Which role should the Project Manager consult with when preparing the Project Product Description during the Starting up a Project process?

    A. Project Support

    B. Senior Supplier

    C. Team Manager

    D. Senior User

8. When the Project Plan is divided into management stages in the Initiating a Project process, which theme is primarily being applied?

    A. Business Case

    B. Organization

    C. Quality

    D. Progress

9. Which process provides base information needed to make a rational decision on the commissioning of the project?

    A. Directing a Project

    B. Starting up a Project

    C. Initiating a Project

    D. Managing a Stage Boundary

10. What is an objective of the Starting up a Project process?

    A. Evaluate the various ways the project can be delivered.

    B. Decide whether to appoint a Change Authority.

    C. Ensure that there is common understanding of how the quality required will be achieved.

    D. Prepare a plan to show how the achievement of the project's benefits will be measured.

Practitioner Exam Questions

The Practitioner questions in Sections 1, 2, and 3 are based on the Practitioner exam scenario that you will find in the Introduction to this book.

Section 1: Classic Multiple Choice Questions on PRINCE2 Theory

Answer the following two questions about the relationship between the Initiating a Project process and the PRINCE2 themes.

1. Which statement correctly describes how the Organization theme is addressed in the Initiating a Project process?

   A. An analysis of who will be impacted by the web project is carried out when the Project Manager prepares the Communication Management Strategy.

   B. The project management team's lack of experience running IT projects is recorded in the Risk Register as a threat.

   C. A decision is made on whether a separate group of people has authority to authorize changes to the project's scope.

   D. The escalation procedures between the different project management team levels will be established during setting up the project controls.

2. Which statement correctly describes how the Change theme is addressed in the Initiating a Project process?

   A. The Product Descriptions of the various parts of the website are created when the Project Manager creates the Project Plan. Once the parts of the website have been defined, they cannot change.

   B. The Issue Register is created while the Project Manager is preparing the Configuration Management Strategy. This will be used to record parts of the website that are forecast not to meet their specifications.

   C. The Project Manager creates the Configuration Item Records for all the project's products during the Initiating a Project process, so as to track their status.

   D. The Project Manager will record in the Risk Register the fact that the Marketing Director's lack of experience in IT projects might lead him to frequently change his mind on the requirements for the website.

Section 2: Classic Multiple-Choice Questions Based on Applying PRINCE2 to the Scenario

Using the project scenario that you will find in the Introduction to this book, answer the following four questions about the Starting up a Project process.

Decide whether the actions taken represent an appropriate application of PRINCE2 for this project and select the response that supports your decision.

1. After creating a project mandate, Quality Furniture's board of directors appointed a PRINCE2-qualified Project Manager. The Project Manager then appointed an Executive for the Project Board. Is this an appropriate application of PRINCE2 for this project?

    A. No, the Quality Furniture's board of directors should appoint the Executive, and then the Executive should appoint the Project Manager.

    B. No, the Project Manager will not be appointed until the first stage of the project, the initiation stage.

    C. Yes, the Project Manager's expertise in PRINCE2 means that he is an appropriate person to appoint the Executive role.

    D. Yes, the Project Manager designs and appoints the project management team.

2. During the "Prepare the outline Business Case" activity, the Project Manager should document what will make the website acceptable to the marketing director, who has taken on the Senior User project role. Is this an appropriate application of PRINCE2 for this project?

    A. No, only the draft Business Case should be created during this activity.

    B. No, it is the responsibility of the Senior User to produce the Project Product Description, which contains their requirements for the website.

    C. Yes, the Project Manager should create the Project Product Description during the "Prepare the outline Business Case" activity.

    D. Yes, because the Project Manager will be responsible for giving the ultimate approval of the project's products.

3. When preparing the outline Business Case during Starting up a Project, the Executive will consider whether it is possible to secure a loan on the factory premises in order to fund the project. Is this an appropriate application of PRINCE2 for this project?

    A. No, because the Starting up a Project is a lighter process, so funding arrangements are left to the initiation stage, when the detailed Business Case is produced.

    B. No, because the corporate or programme level will always secure the funds for the project when they create the project mandate.

    C. Yes, because how the project will be funded should be set out in the outline Business Case.

    D. Yes, because if the project is authorized, then the Project Board must have secured the funds in order to release the project's entire budget to the Project Manager for all the delivery stages.

4. During the Starting up a Project process, the Project Manager creates a Project Plan showing how to deliver the main parts of the website and associated specialist products. Is this an appropriate application of PRINCE2 for this project?

    A. No, the Project Plan should show the delivery of the management products as well as the major specialist products.

    B. No, the Project Plan should be created in the initiation stage.

    C. Yes, during the Starting up a Project process, the Project Manager needs to consider the key milestone dates.

    D. Yes, the Project Plan forms part of the Project Brief.

Section 3: Practitioner Assertion/Reason Questions

Exam Spotlight

Generally, out of all five types of questions in a Practitioner exam, candidates find the assertion/reason type the most confusing. I would recommend a two-step approach to answering these sorts of questions. First, read the assertion statement and the reason statement given in each question as two entirely separate statements. All you need to do in step 1 is work out whether, on its own, each statement is true or false. Then write on the question paper a "T" or an "F" next to each statement to indicate whether it is true or false.

Having done step 1, you might now be able to choose an option. If the assertion is true and the reason is false, the answer is option C. If it is the assertion that is false and the reason that is true, then the answer is option D. Or if both statements are false, the answer is option E.

However, if you find that both the assertion and the reason statements are true, then you need to do another step to find the answer. You now need to see if the reason is a good explanation of the assertion statement. For example, if I were to make an assertion such as "you should set your alarm clock tomorrow morning," a reasonable reason for this might be "you mustn't be late for your job interview."

A good trick to see if the reason statement explains the assertion statement is to reread the assertion statement and ask yourself the question, "Why is that?" If your answer to "Why is that?" is similar to the reason statement given in the question, then the reason explains the assertion.

The final part of the second step is to pick option A if the reason explains the assertion and option B if the reason does not explain the assertion.

Rows 1 to 6 in the following table consist of an assertion statement and a reason statement. For each line, identify the appropriate option, from options A to E, that applies. Each option can be used once, more than once, or not at all.

A. The assertion is true and the reason is true, *and* the reason explains the assertion.

B. The assertion is true and the reason is true, *but* the reason does not explain the assertion.

C. The assertion is true and the reason is false.

D. The assertion is false and the reason is true.

E. Both the assertion and the reason are false.

Assertion		Reason
1. If the Chief Executive Officer feels this is a very important project, they should take on the Executive and the Project Manager role.	BECAUSE	The Executive is the single point of accountability for the project.
2. During the Starting up a Project process, the Project Manager should record in the Daily Log that Quality Furniture's procurement department has no experience in dealing with IT suppliers and this could lead to them selecting a poor supplier.	BECAUSE	The Daily Log acts as a repository for all project risks before the creation of the Risk Register.
3. The Project Manager will need to create detailed specifications for the tender documents during the Starting up a Project process.	BECAUSE	The Project Product Description that forms part of the Project Brief contains detailed descriptions of all the project's products.
4. The fact that Quality Furniture will outsource the building of the website to an external supplier should be recorded in the Project Brief.	BECAUSE	The Project Brief contains the Project Approach, which sets out the delivery solution for the project.
5. The Project Manager should only consider the information needs of the Quality Furniture personnel when creating the Communication Management Strategy, as they are stakeholders in the project.	BECAUSE	Those impacted by the project are stakeholders.
6. The Project Manager should prepare the Stage Plans for the tendering of suppliers and the design and building of the website during the initiation stage.	BECAUSE	A plan for the project is created during the initiation stage.

Chapter

3

Organization Theme

PRINCE2 EXAM OBJECTIVES COVERED IN THIS CHAPTER:

✓ **Understand the different PRINCE2 project roles and the responsibilities that they carry out.**

✓ **Know that the Organization theme supports the PRINCE2 principle of defined roles and responsibilities and establishes accountability and responsibility for those involved with the project.**

✓ **Understand how the three project interests are represented in the project management team structure.**

✓ **Understand the responsibilities and characteristics of the Project Board, Executive, Senior User, Senior Supplier, Project Manager, Project Assurance, Change Authority, Team Manager, and Project Support.**

✓ **Explain the meaning of the term "stakeholder."**

✓ **Understand the purpose and composition of the Communication Management Strategy.**

  ▪ Know which other management products have a relationship with the Communication Management Strategy.

  ▪ Know in which processes the Communication Management Strategy is created, used, and reviewed.

  ▪ Know which roles are responsible for creating, using, and reviewing the Communication Management Strategy.

✓ **Understand how the four different management levels are represented within the project management team structure and know which processes they are involved in.**

✓ **Understand how the project management structure is applied to a customer and supplier environment.**

✓ **Know how to apply the Organization theme to a scenario.**

  ▪ Know how to design and appoint relevant people to a project management team.

  ▪ Know how to create a Communication Management Strategy.

In this chapter, you'll learn who gets involved in a PRINCE2 project and what roles and responsibilities they might be given. PRINCE2 calls the information described in this chapter the Organization theme. PRINCE2 recommends a project management team structure that ensures that all the relevant levels of management are involved. It also ensures that a broad range of stakeholder interests are represented.

This chapter takes you through each of the PRINCE2 roles and shows what their responsibilities are throughout the project (and sometimes pre- and post-project). You'll learn about the management products that are important for organizing people, such as the Communication Management Strategy. As usual, this chapter describes a number of case studies to illustrate how all this works in practice and gives you plenty of example exam questions.

Common Project Organizational Challenges

What are the challenges when it comes to organizing people on projects? First, losing contact with senior stakeholders (those who have an interest in the project) is one of the prime reasons projects fail. For example, very often, a senior manager who funds the project only gets involved at the beginning. After this, he expects the Project Manager to be totally responsible for the project. However, the Project Manager is nearly always at a fairly low or middle level of the organization. He won't have enough authority to overcome all the challenges of the project. At various times, he needs the help of senior managers.

Another reason projects need continual involvement of senior managers is that they operate in a dynamic environment, and there will be times when the original direction needs to be refocused. PRINCE2 deals with both these challenges by describing roles for senior managers in the project team and ensuring their involvement at key points.

Another challenge is finding a way to involve the ultimate users of the project's products. Sometimes, these people are only involved at the outset of a project, when they are asked what they want, and then at the end, when they are shown the product. Of course, in the interim, their requirements might have changed. Another challenge here is that people often don't understand exactly what they want until they start to see some initial work that shows them what is possible. To mitigate both these challenges, PRINCE2 sets out specific roles for the users of the products and gets them involved in the important decisions throughout the project.

Many projects suffer from unrealistic schedules. PRINCE2 reduces this problem by giving roles to those with authority over the resources that deliver the project's products. They must agree to the project's plans.

Even in small projects, the day-to-day coordination of all the different types of work and people involved can be complicated. PRINCE2 helps this situation by appointing one key person, the Project Manager, to be responsible for this task. However, on difficult, time-consuming projects, PRINCE2 provides another role, Project Support, to help the Project Manager with his work.

The Three Project Interests

In any project, there may be many people who have an interest in the outcome. These people are called *stakeholders*. They might support or oppose the project for all sorts of reasons. PRINCE2 groups these stakeholders into three main categories. First are those who are looking at the project from a business point of view, thinking about whether the project gives good value for money or, in other words, a good return given the money invested in it. Next are those who will be using the project's products and services on an ongoing basis after the project has finished. Finally, there are those who will be supplying resources and people to create the project's products. PRINCE2 ensures that these three perspectives on the project are represented in the project's decisional body, the Project Board. Figure 3.1 shows these three interests.

FIGURE 3.1   The three project interests

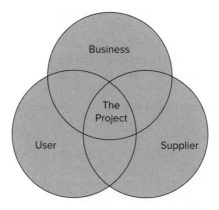

Based on Cabinet Office PRINCE2® material. Reproduced under licence from the Cabinet Office.

The Business Interest

The Executive represents the business interest on the project. The Executive sits on the Project Board and, unlike the Senior Supplier and the Senior User, there can only be one person carrying out this role. The Executive is focused on whether the project is providing good value for the money invested in it and whether an adequate return on the project's investment will be achieved. PRINCE2 sees this as the primary interest, outranking the needs of the users and the suppliers. As such, the Executive is the ultimate level of authority within the Project Board. However, the Executive should take into account the views of the user and supplier interests (represented on the Project Board by the Senior User and Senior Supplier) when making decisions.

For example, in a project to build a new hotel, the Executive should be thinking about such things as whether the cost of the hotel represents good value compared to other hotels that have been built of an equivalent standard and whether the forecast sales will pay back the initial investment in a reasonable amount of time. Rather than focusing on the quality of the hotel for its own sake, the Executive will be thinking about whether the hotel will be capable of achieving the estimated returns.

The User Interest

This perspective is involved with using the products and services created by the project. The user interest is represented by the Senior User role on the Project Board. This stakeholder category can include a number of subcategories, such as the following:

- Those who will use the products and services directly
- Those who might use the products and services as a tool to create value for themselves or their organizations
- Those who might maintain and support the products in their operational use

As such, there might be several people who carry out the Senior User role.

Let me give you an example. Let's suppose a project's aim is to create a website for a company. The website will sell the company's products. Who has a user interest in this initiative? First, there are the company's clients. They will go onto the website and buy products. The company might have hundreds or even thousands of clients. They can't all take on Senior User roles. Instead, the project might represent them using a market research company who, by doing research, understands these people's requirements.

Another type of user interest will be those who will use the website as a tool to sell products. The company's marketing director could represent this perspective. Finally, the company's IT department, who will support the website in operational use, is another potential Senior User.

All of these various perspectives have one thing in common: Suppliers are interested in specifying the project's products and services. They also want to get involved in validating the products and services when they are finished.

The Supplier Interest

The supplier interest is the final perspective on the project. Suppliers create the project's products and services by providing resources and the necessary skills. The Senior Supplier role represents this interest on the Project Board. A number of people might take on the Senior Supplier role. This is because there could be several groups of people creating different types of products and services. All of these groups should be represented on the Project Board. The Senior Suppliers are senior people from these groups who have authority over the supplier resources. The suppliers may be internal to the organization running the project or an external third party.

For example, in a project to build a new hotel for a leisure company, there might be a building firm doing the construction work. The building firm's operations manager could assume a Senior Supplier role. Also, if the leisure company's PR department is doing work to promote the hotel, the head of PR could also take on a Senior Supplier role.

The supplier perspective is focused on ensuring that the products meet the quality standards set by the project and that the project's targets—in terms of time, cost, and scope—are feasible.

Achieving Consensus Between the Project Interests

The three project interests will probably not initially agree. For example, the user's requests for product features might not represent value for money as far as the business is concerned. The business's idea of a reasonable project cost might be well below what the suppliers are quoting. It is the role of the Project Board to come to an agreement on these differing and sometimes inconsistent points of view when they are making decisions about the project. But remember, it is the Executive who has ultimate authority. When conflict exists between the three interests, it is the business perspective that has the final word.

The Four Levels of Management

In any PRINCE2 project, there are four distinct levels of management, as shown in Figure 3.2. As you go up the levels, the authority of the managers increases.

FIGURE 3.2   The four levels of management

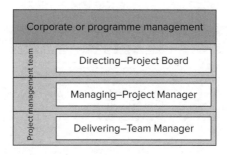

Based on Cabinet Office PRINCE2® material. Reproduced under licence from the Cabinet Office.

Corporate or Programme Management

Corporate or programme management is the top level of management in a PRINCE2 project. They instigate the project by creating the project mandate. This management product is the first document to describe the project. Its details may be very high-level, and it is up to the Project Board and the Project Manager to refine them. However, in some instances, particularly when the project is part of a programme (a collection of projects with a coherent aim), the project mandate may be quite detailed. This is because a programme should be clear on the definition of upcoming projects in order to coordinate them.

After corporate or programme management has created the project mandate, they will then appoint the Executive. From that point on, the Executive is responsible for taking the project forward. Corporate or programme management will set certain boundaries that the Executive (and, once the Executive has appointed the Senior Users and Senior Suppliers, the whole Project Board as well) needs to keep the project within. PRINCE2 calls these boundaries project tolerances. These tolerances are mainly leeway around the project's forecast budget and delivery time. If the Executive or the whole Project Board thinks the project tolerances will be breached, they no longer have authority to continue with the project and must escalate the situation back up to corporate or programme management. (You'll learn more about tolerances in Chapter 9, "Progress Theme.")

Once corporate or programme management has appointed the Executive, they only become involved with the project if the project tolerances are forecast to be breached. The Project Board will send regular notifications to corporate or programme management about significant project events, such as the decision to move on to the next major part of the project (stage). Corporate or programme management may also choose to receive regular progress reports from the Project Manager.

Figure 3.3 shows the PRINCE2 project management team structure. One important thing to note about this diagram is that the project management team includes the Project Board, the Project Manager, and the Team Manager levels, but not the corporate or programme management level. Corporate or programme management is separate from the project management team.

FIGURE 3.3   PRINCE2 project management structure

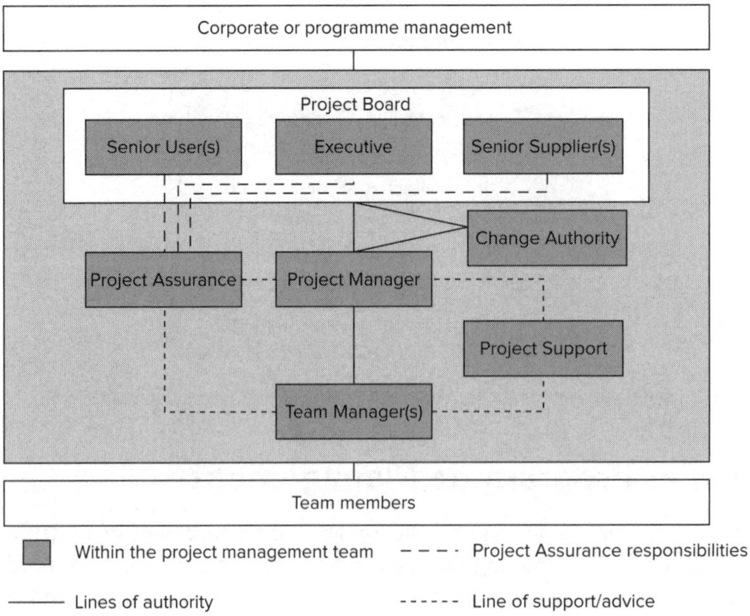

Based on Cabinet Office PRINCE2® material. Reproduced under licence from the Cabinet Office.

Directing

The directing level is the responsibility of the Project Board. The board makes the important project decisions, such as authorizing the beginning of the project, the beginning of each stage, and finally, the end of the project. The Project Board delegates the day-to-day management of the project to the Project Manager. They do this by authorizing the Project Manager to manage a stage of the project on their behalf within predefined limits or tolerances. These tolerances are usually defined in terms of costs or timescales. For example, the Project Board might say to the Project Manager: "You have 3 months and $100,000 to deliver the next part of the project. If you forecast that you will breach these targets by more than 10 percent, please refer to us for a decision." (For a full discussion on tolerances, see Chapter 9, "Progress Theme.")

In Figure 3.3, you can see where the Project Board sits in the project management team structure. You can also see that the Project Board is made up of three roles: the Executive, the Senior User, and the Senior Supplier.

Managing

The Project Manager is responsible for managing the project on a day-to-day basis within the tolerances that have been given to him by the Project Board. He focuses on ensuring that the project creates the required products by planning, delegating, and monitoring all the separate activities that need to be done. He also regularly updates the project management team and outside stakeholders on the progress of the project.

There should be only one Project Manager assigned to each project. If there were more than one Project Manager, there would be a risk that work on the project would lack coordination.

Delivering

In PRINCE2, the Team Managers are responsible for the delivering level. They manage the teams who are creating the project's products. In some circumstances, such as a small project, there may be no need for separate people to take on the Team Manager role. In this case, the Project Manager will manage the teams directly. When there are Team Managers, the Project Manager delegates work to them, and they, in turn, delegate work to their teams.

The Project Management Team

The PRINCE2 project management team consists of a variety of roles that ensure a broad perspective is represented when making key project decisions and that the right collection of skill is available to direct, manage, and deliver the project. In this section, you'll see the responsibilities of all the PRINCE2 roles.

The Project Board

The Project Board consists of three main roles: the Executive, the Senior Users, and the Senior Suppliers. I'll show you how these roles come together to ensure that the project is directed effectively and that important project decisions are made in a timely, informed way.

Executive

As stated earlier, in the section "The Business Interest," the Executive role represents the business interest in the project. The Executive is focused on whether the project is delivering value for money and creates an adequate return on the project's investment.

The Executive is ultimately responsible for the project. Only one person should assume this role so there will be clear accountability and responsibility for the project. The Executive is also the chief decision maker. He makes decisions supported by the other members of the Project Board, the Senior Users, and the Senior Suppliers—but ultimately, he has the final say.

The Executive is also responsible for securing the funding for the project.

The Senior Users

The Senior Users are responsible for representing those who will ultimately use the project's products. As discussed earlier, in the section "The User Interest," there could be a number of different types of "users." PRINCE2 defines three types of Senior Users. Here is a brief description of each user type, along with examples relating to a project to build a new hotel for a leisure company:

- Those users who will directly use the project's products (such as the people who might stay in the hotel)

- Those users who might maintain or support the products when they go into their operational life (such as the people who might maintain the hotel's systems, like the heating system or the computer booking software)

- Those users for whom the project will achieve an objective or a benefit (such as the marketing director of the leisure company, who will use the hotel to increase his sales figures)

The Senior Users should be in a position to have authority over the people who will be using the products. They must ensure that these people are available to define the characteristics and requirements of the products and then to review the products once they've been built to see whether they meet these requirements.

In addition, the Senior Users have an important role in connection with the Business Case. They are responsible for forecasting the project's benefits and then demonstrating that those benefits have occurred. Many benefits might not occur until after the project has finished. For example, the hotel doesn't start selling rooms until after it has been built. As such, fulfilling the Senior User role is likely to involve a commitment beyond the life of the project.

Why should the Senior Users be involved with forecasting and then tracking benefits? Let me give you an example. In the hotel project, the marketing director is a Senior User. He will use the hotel as a tool to create benefits for the leisure company, such as room sales. Putting the project to one side for a moment, as a marketing director, this individual is involved in projecting and tracking sales for the leisure company. He is thus in an ideal position to do this for the project as well.

 Real World Scenario

Identifying Senior Users in a Pharmaceutical Project

My consultancy company recently worked on a project to build a pharmaceutical company's website. On the site, there would be medical information on a range of drugs. The information was for doctors and nurses to read when they were using the drugs to treat their patients.

In this project, there were numerous types of "uses" of the website. First, there were the doctors and nurses. Of course, there are thousands of health-care practitioners, so how did we represent them on our Project Board? We used a market research company, which carried out a range of focus groups with doctors to understand their requirements. A senior consultant from this company was assigned a Senior User role.

The pharmaceutical company's marketing department would use the website to propagate information on the drugs, which might ultimately lead to more drugs being prescribed. The website was to roll out across Europe, and within each country, there was a separate marketing department with a separate brand manager in charge of their territory. A collection of brand managers in key countries took on another set of Senior User roles. Because the website didn't launch in all the countries at the same time, the brand manager for the next territory to launch would be involved in the Project Board just for his part of the project.

In the pharmaceutical company was a department called Medical Information. Their responsibility was to build a database of information on all the company's drugs and distribute it to doctors and nurses. They would use the website as a tool to carry out this objective, so they were interested in the editing and storage features of the web system. A senior person from this department also took on a Senior User role.

Finally, there was the pharmaceutical company's IT department. They wouldn't be building the website, because this task was outsourced to a third-party supplier, but they would be involved in maintaining the site. Their focus was on how easy the website was to maintain and operate once it had been built.

In the end, our Project Board had six people who represented all these perspectives on using the website.

The Senior Suppliers

The Senior Suppliers represent those who will be delivering the project's products. As you learned in the section "The Supplier Interest," these are people who have authority over the resources used to create the project's products. They are able to commit and authorize the supplier resources. They could be people from the organization that has commissioned the project or external third-party organizations.

One of the common challenges for Project Managers is that they often have to delegate work to teams over whom they have no authority. Senior Suppliers are useful for overcoming this problem. For example, what does the Project Manager of a construction project do if the builders are working ineffectively? In a PRINCE2 project, he could escalate this situation to the head of the building company who has taken on a Senior Supplier role. This person is the boss of the builders, so he should be in a position to manage his workers.

There could be problems sharing confidential information if the Senior Suppliers are from organizations external to the commissioning organization. Would the third-party supplier want to share with the Project Board how much profit he is making? I doubt it! In this case, there might be two types of project meetings: meetings that are held to discuss confidential information (which take place in the separate customer and supplier organizations) and meetings that are attended by all those involved in the project. It can be quite challenging to have all external suppliers represented on the Project Board, but the important decisions in the project must take account of their views. They can point out unreasonable deadlines or cost budgets.

Project Assurance

Project Assurance is a role that checks and monitors that the project is being run correctly and is capable of delivering the project's objectives in terms of time, cost, quality, scope, risks, and benefits. Each of the Project Board roles is responsible for a Project Assurance role that aligns to their area of interest. So the Executive, Senior Users, and Senior Suppliers are responsible for business, user, and supplier assurance, respectively.

What does this checking and monitoring entail? A Project Assurance role could involve a range of activities, such as meeting with the Project Manager and Team Managers and discussing their activities, auditing project documents, or observing project meetings and quality reviews.

Who assumes the Project Assurance roles? If they have enough time, the Project Board members might choose to do so themselves. Otherwise, they might delegate the day-to-day assurance activities to other people. The Project Board will still be accountable for the Project Assurance actions aligned to their area of interest, even if they delegate them to separate individuals.

The *business assurance* role checks that the project is providing value for money and that the project's products are capable of delivering the benefits forecast in the Business Case. They are interested in things such as the amount of money being spent, how realistic the project's Business Case is, and whether risks are being effectively managed.

The *user assurance* role checks that the project is building products that will be fit for their ultimate purpose. They are interested in whether all the user perspectives were represented when the products were specified, whether the requirements for the products have been captured in the project documentation, whether suppliers are using the correct specifications to carry out their product-creation work, and whether there is an effective user acceptance process for signing off the products when they are finished.

The *supplier assurance* role checks the project from a delivery perspective. They look at whether the supplier resources are capable of delivering the project on time and to the budget agreed. They consider the technical feasibility of the products. If the supplier is external to the organization that commissioned the project, there could actually be two perspectives on supplier assurance: the commissioning organization will want to check how the external organization is carrying out their work, and the external organization will want to check their own work.

It is important that the Project Assurance role be independent of the Project Manager and the teams and Team Managers. However, as part of their role, Project Assurance will be expected to provide advice and guidance to these people.

Structuring the Project Board

It is a good idea to keep the Project Board fairly small, say six or seven people. Anything above this makes it more difficult to get agreement on decisions. If you have a large number of users and suppliers, it might be better to create separate *user groups* and *supplier groups* who send representatives to Project Board meetings.

If the same people are paying for and using the project's products, one person might take on the role of Senior User and Executive.

Allocating the Right People to the Project Board

PRINCE2 talks about an effective Project Board displaying four key characteristics: authority, credibility, an ability to delegate, and availability. Let's look at each of these in turn.

Without the right level of authority, the Project Board will be unable to drive the project forward. If they have to constantly refer to people above them in their organizations in order to make decisions, this can cause unnecessary delay to the project. Without the right level of authority, they will not be able to provide resources and money to the project and sort out potential conflicts. However, if the people on the Project Board are too high up within their organizations, the project might not be important enough for them to get involved.

Credibility is closely linked to authority. Without credibility, the people on the Project Board may not be able to influence others to provide the resources and budgets that might be necessary to achieve the project's objectives.

The ability to delegate is another important characteristic of an effective Project Board member. Project Board members rarely have the right expertise to make management- and delivery-level decisions. Unfortunately, if the Project Board *does* involve themselves too heavily in the day-to-day management and delivery of the project, team members tend to follow their bad advice out of respect for their level in the organization. It is usually far better if Project Board members concern themselves with strategic project decisions and leave the management and delivery to those who have the relevant skills.

Finally, Project Board members must be available for the project. They do not need to get involved on a day-to-day basis, but only when the key decisions need to take place. If they are busy on other work, then the project will likely stall while it waits for a key authorization.

In addition to these four PRINCE2 characteristics, remember that Project Board members must be looking at the project from the correct perspective. The Executive must keep track of whether the project is delivering value for the money invested in it, the Senior User must keep track of whether the project is delivering products that are fit for their purpose, and the Senior Supplier must ensure that the supplier resources are capable of delivering products of the required quality.

Change Authority

From time to time within a project, someone asks for a change to one of the project's products. In the hotel project discussed earlier in the chapter, say the marketing director of the leisure company asks for an upgrade to the room design. Or the construction manager wants to change the type of materials used to build the foundations of the hotel because he realizes the original materials won't meet safety standards. PRINCE2 calls these *requests for change*.

The Project Board is the ultimate authorization body for requests for change. However, on a project where there may be many requests for change, they can delegate part of this authority to a group called the *Change Authority*. This group is allowed to authorize changes within certain limits. It is up to the Project Board to specify these limits. Examples of such limits might be that the Change Authority can authorize changes up to a preagreed cost or changes that don't impact the project plans by more than a certain number of days.

The Project Manager might also be given some authority to authorize changes. For example, a project might have a number of levels of change authority: the Project Board authorizes large changes, the Change Authority authorizes medium-sized ones, and the Project Manager authorizes the smaller ones. Also, when faced with a large requested change to the project's products or scope, the Project Board might escalate the decision as to whether to implement the change to the corporate or programme management.

The Change Authority and requests for change are discussed in more detail in Chapter 8, "Change Theme."

The Project Manager

The Project Manager manages the project on a day-to-day basis on behalf of the Project Board. He is given authority by the Project Board to run a part of the project, referred to as a stage in PRINCE2, at any one time. (For a full discussion of PRINCE2 stages, see Chapter 9, "Progress Theme.") After each stage, the Project Manager must ask the

Project Board for authority to move on to the next stage. As previously mentioned, to avoid problems with coordination of tasks, there should be only one Project Manager per project.

The Project Manager will carry out the following roles:

- Delegate work to the teams using *Work Packages*. Work Packages are a management product that tells the team what work they need to do.

- Deal with issue and change control management.

- Deal with reporting. The Project Manager will receive progress reports from the teams. These progress reports from the team are called *Checkpoint Reports*. The Project Manager sends progress reports to the Project Board. These progress reports from the Project Manager are called *Highlight Reports*.

- Track the status of the products that are being created, the project costs, the schedule, and the scope of the project.

- Ensure that the project is being managed in line with the strategy documents. Remember that PRINCE2 has four strategy documents that set out how various aspects of project management should be approached: the Risk Management Strategy (described in Chapter 7, "Risk Theme"), the Quality Management Strategy (described in Chapter 6, "Quality Theme"), the Configuration Management Strategy (described in Chapter 8, "Change Theme"), and the Communication Management Strategy (described later in this chapter).

The Project Manager will manage any team that does not have a Team Manager. If no one is available to carry out the Project Support role, the Project Manager will have to do this as well.

Project Support

The Project Support role is the responsibility of the Project Manager. The Project Manager can delegate the work of Project Support to a separate person or people. If no one is available to delegate Project Support activities to, the Project Manager will need to carry them out himself.

The Project Support role supports the Project Manager and the Team Manager(s) in their day-to-day management work. Their responsibilities can consist of the following:

- Providing administration services

- Providing advice or guidance on the use of project management or configuration management tools

- Providing specialist management functions such as planning or risk management

- Maintaining the configuration management procedure

In some organizations, Project Support will be supplied by a project office that provides support for all of the organization's projects.

Team Manager

The Team Manager role is optional. It may be that the team is small enough for the Project Manager to manage it directly. However, for large projects, it would not be feasible for the Project Manager to delegate work to each individual, so the PRINCE2 project management team structure allows for another level of management: the Team Manager.

In fact, there are a variety of other reasons that Team Managers might be required. The team might be in another town or even another country. It might make sense to have a Team Manager at the same location as the rest of the team. Another reason is that the Project Manager might not have the knowledge to fully understand the technical nature of the team's work. In such cases, it is useful to have an expert in that specialist area as a Team Manager.

The Team Manager role is responsible for the following activities:

- Accepting work on behalf of the team via a Work Package from the Project Manager. A Work Package is a management product that tells the team what is expected of them.

- Planning, delegating, monitoring, and controlling the team's work.

- Reporting to the Project Manager on a regular basis (as defined in the Work Package) by creating Checkpoint Reports. A Checkpoint Report is a report on the progress of the team's work.

Other Stakeholders

A stakeholder is any individual, group or organization that can affect, be affected by, or perceive itself to be affected by, a project. He can be an advocate of the project or against the project. All the people who are allocated roles on the project management team are stakeholders, but there may be many other people outside the team who are stakeholders as well. At the beginning of the project, the Project Manager will work with the other members of the project management team to identify all the project stakeholders and determine how they would like to be updated on the project. The Project Manager will also determine what information the project needs from the stakeholders. The output of this work is detailed in the Communication Management Strategy. (You'll learn more about the Communication Management Strategy later in this chapter.)

Here are some examples of people who might be stakeholders in the project to build a new hotel for a leisure company:

- A local government agency where the hotel will be sited

- The trade union representative of the builders of the hotel

- The quality assurance manager for the leisure company

- The local tourism office in the city where the hotel will be built

- The leisure company's legal department

The Customer/Supplier Environment

PRINCE2 states that the project will operate in a *customer/supplier environment*, but what does this mean and how does it relate to the three stakeholder interests of business, user, and supplier that I have been discussing in this chapter?

Usually the customer will represent the user and business interests. However there are exceptions to this broad rule. For example, there might be a situation where an organization is developing a new product to sell to a client. In this case the business interest aligns with the supplier and the customer might simply be the users. Where the user interest is external to the organization sponsoring the building of the product, it is good practice to still represent it in some way within the sponsoring organization. For example, the sales or marketing functions might put forward a Senior User. This might be in addition to a Senior User who comes from the customer.

Another complication is in a situation where there is a customer commissioning work from a commercial supplier. From which organization does the Project Manager come? Well, it could be either. Maybe the customer expects the supplier to do all the project management. If this is the case the customer might want to appoint a Project Assurance role that monitors the supplier's project management of the product. Alternatively someone from the customer could act as Project Manager. Usually, unless stated otherwise, PRINCE2 assumes that the Project Manager comes from the customer side.

Communication Management Strategy

The Communication Management Strategy describes how the project management team and the external stakeholders will communicate with each other. In any project, effective communication is vital between all the various parties involved or with an interest in the project. Sitting down at the beginning of the project and thinking about how communication will take place, and then regularly checking that this approach is followed, helps to ensure that everyone has information relevant to them in a timely manner.

Contents

I'll now go through the different sections of the Communication Management Strategy and give you some examples of what they might contain in the project to build a new hotel for a leisure company.

One general comment I have about the Communication Management Strategy is that the way PRINCE2 divides the document into different sections is rather artificial.

Take a sentence such as "The personal assistant to the managing director will chair a daily conference call among the project team to discuss project progress." This piece of information describes how communication will be done on the project, so it should go into the Communication Management Strategy, but in which section does it belong? The sentence contains a procedure (carry out project progress updates), a timing (daily), a technique (conference call), and a responsibility (personal assistant to chair the meetings)! In reality, the Communication Management Strategy might not be subdivided so neatly into the different sections. If this is the case, the Project Manager must still make sure that all the types of information described by the section headings are in the document.

Introduction

The Introduction states the purpose, objectives, and scope of the document and identifies who is responsible for the strategy. For example, the Introduction for the hotel project might say the following:

> This document outlines how the project to build a new hotel in Shanghai will ensure that all stakeholders in the project are informed of all relevant project information. The Executive of this project, the Asian business development manager, is responsible for effective communication.

Communication Procedure

This section contains any communication methods to be used during the project. The best way of thinking about this is that this section will contain "things to do" regarding communication. For example, the Communication Procedure section for the hotel project might say the following:

> All project communication issued to external parties to be checked by the communication department. A copy of all external communication to be filed in the communication folder in the project file.

Tools and Techniques

This section contains specific techniques that might be used in the steps highlighted in the Communication Procedure section. For example, the project might use email, Internet collaboration tools like Yahoo Groups, or stand-up meetings. Here are some examples of Tools and Techniques entries for the hotel project:

> Daily project conference calls to take place to update all teams on the project progress and issues

> Formal press releases to be issued regarding major project milestones

Records

This section states how the project will store information on the communication that has taken place. Here's an example of a Records entry for the hotel project:

> Keep a log of all communication sent to external parties. The log should state who the communication was sent to, the format of the communication, the date issued, and a description of the content of the communication.

Reporting

This section specifies any reports that will be created to track the implementation of the Communication Procedure. Here's an example of a Reporting entry for the hotel project:

> Send a report to the Project Board at the end of each stage detailing all communication that has been sent from the project management team to any external third party.

Timing of Communication Activities

This section specifies when communication activities should take place. For example, the Timing of Communication Activities section for the hotel project might include the following entry:

> The communications department to carry out a performance audit on the way communication has been managed at the end of each stage

Roles and Responsibilities

This section describes who will be responsible for the various steps set out in the process section. For example, the Roles and Responsibilities section for the hotel project might include the following entry:

> Project Support to file all external communication

Stakeholder Analysis

This section contains a list of all parties who have been identified as having an interest in the project. These can include people who are advocates of the project and/or those who are against it. For example, the Stakeholder Analysis section for the hotel project might list the following stakeholders:

- Trade union representative for the building firm
- Global business development director
- Shanghai tourist board

Information Needs for Each Interested Party

This section describes the type of information that needs to be provided to the stakeholders. Stakeholders might be interested in a variety of types of information about the project, such as up-to-date progress information, information on particular project risks or issues, or statistics on how many quality checks on the project's products are passing or failing. It will also show what information the project needs from stakeholders. For example, the hotel project might include the following entry in this section:

> The human resource manager for Asia to be sent details of all risks and issues related to personnel. Please send an extract from the relevant registry entry.

The Life of the Communication Management Strategy

The Project Manager creates the Communication Management Strategy during the Initiating a Project process at the beginning of the project. (The Initiating a Project process was described in Chapter 2, "Starting a Project Successfully with PRINCE2." It contains a set of steps that the Project Manager and the Project Board carry out to plan the project.)

At the end of each stage of the project, the Project Manager should review the Communication Management Strategy to check that it contains all the key stakeholders for the next part of the project. When the Project Manager is planning the end of the project, he should also review the document to check which stakeholders must be informed of the closing of the project.

Other Management Products Used by the Organization Theme

As well as the Communication Management Strategy, the Project Brief and the Project Initiation Documentation are important Organization theme management products.

The Project Brief's Use in the Organization Theme

The Project Manager creates the Project Brief in the Starting up a Project process. Two sections are relevant to the project organization. The project management team structure section describes the various roles of the project and how they interrelate. This may be in the form of an organization chart. The role descriptions section describes the responsibilities for each role.

The Project Initiation Documentation's Use in the Organization Theme

Once the Project Board has authorized the Project Brief described in the previous section, the Project Manager will then create the Project Initiation Documentation. The Project Manager will copy the project management team structure and the roles and responsibilities sections from the Project Brief into the Project Initiation Documentation. During the Initiating a Project process, the Project Manager might have to add more detail to these sections.

The Project Manager also specifies in the Project Initiation Documentation whether a Change Authority will be set up for the project. This information will go into the Configuration Management Strategy.

Summary

This chapter described how the PRINCE2 Organization theme is used to organize the people on a project. The Organization theme ensures that everyone involved in the project—at the decision, management, and delivery levels—understands what is expected of them. It also ensures that all the roles necessary for a project to be successful are covered.

As you learned in this chapter, there are three main perspectives on any project: business, user, and supplier. PRINCE2 calls these the three project interests. These interests are represented on the main decision-making body in a PRINCE2 project: the Project Board. The Executive represents the business interest, the Senior User represents the user interest, and the Senior Supplier represents the supplier interest.

You saw in this chapter that there are four main management levels represented within the PRINCE2 project management team structure. The highest level of authority is corporate or programme management, who triggers the project at the outset. Next is the Project Board, who directs the project and makes key decisions. Below the Project Board is the Project Manager, who manages the project on a day-to-day basis, and under the Project Manager are the teams who deliver the project's products.

You learned that the PRINCE2 project management team is made up of a variety of roles, each with its own set of responsibilities. You also learned that these roles can be taken by people on the customer or the supplier side of the project. PRINCE2 specifies that all projects take place in a customer/supplier environment.

A key management product related to the Organization theme is the Communication Management Strategy. This strategy defines how communication will be managed between the people inside and outside the project management team. It contains a list of people with an interest in the project (stakeholders) and defines how the project team needs to communicate with them.

You saw that the Organization theme is an important part of PRINCE2. Every activity in the process model defines which role should be involved with that activity.

Exam Essentials

Explain the purpose of the Organization theme.   The Organization theme defines and establishes the project's structure of accountability and responsibilities.

Outline the three primary interests on a project.   Know the three primary interests on a project—business, users, and suppliers—and that the Executive, Senior Users, and Senior Supplier represent these interests on the Project Board.

Outline the four levels of management.   Be able to list the four levels of management: corporate and programme management, directing, managing, and delivering.

Know the responsibilities and characteristics of the Project Board.   The Project Board is the main decision-making body on the project and contains three roles: the Executive, the Senior User, and the Senior Supplier. Their work takes place in the Directing a Project process.

List the responsibilities and characteristics of the Executive.   The Executive represents the business perspective on the Project Board. He is the ultimate decision maker, he must secure the funding for the project, and he must ensure that the project provides value for money.

Explain the responsibilities and characteristics of the Senior Users.   The Senior Users represent the user perspective on the Project Board. They must ensure that the project's products are fit for their purpose; they also provide user resources to help specify the products before they are created and then again to review them during and after they are created.

Know the responsibilities and characteristics of the Senior Suppliers.   The Senior Suppliers represent the supplier perspective on the Project Board. They are responsible for providing resources to the project that will create the project's products to the required level of quality.

List the responsibilities and characteristics of Project Assurance.   There are three types of Project Assurance: business, user, and supplier assurance, which align with the Project Board roles of the Executive, Senior Users, and Senior Suppliers, respectively. The role monitors the project to ensure that it meets the needs of their unique perspective on the project. The role may provide guidance to the Project Manager and the Team Managers.

Know the responsibilities and characteristics of the Project Manager.   The Project Manager manages the project on a day-to-day basis on behalf of the Project Board. His work takes place across many of the PRINCE2 processes, including Starting up a Project, Initiating a Project, Managing a Stage Boundary, Controlling a Stage, and Closing a Project.

Be familiar with the responsibilities and characteristics of the Change Authority.   The Change Authority is given authority by the Project Board to authorize some changes to the project's products within certain predefined constraints.

Know the responsibilities and characteristics of the Team Manager.   The Team Manager manages the team's work in designing, creating, and delivering the project's products. His work takes place in the Managing Product Delivery process.

List the responsibilities and characteristics of Project Support.   Project Support provides a range of support activities to the Project Manager, Team Manager, and the team. Their work takes place across many of the PRINCE2 processes, including Starting up a Project, Initiating a Project, Managing a Stage Boundary, Controlling a Stage, Managing Product Delivery, and Closing a Project.

Understand the term *stakeholder*.   Know that the term *stakeholder* means any individual, group or organization that can affect, be affected by, or perceive itself to be affected by an initiative (project, programme, activity, or risk).

Know the purpose and contents of the Communication Management Strategy.   The Communication Management Strategy specifies how the project management team and the stakeholders of the project will communicate with each other. It also describes any analysis that has been done to determine who has a vested interest in the project and what their communication needs are. This strategy is created by the Project Manager during the Initiating a Project process and then updated during the Managing a Stage Boundary process. It is then referred to continually for reporting requirements of the project management team and other stakeholders.

Review Questions

The rest of this chapter contains mock exam questions, first for the Foundation exam and then for the Practitioner exam.

Foundation Exam Questions

1. Which PRINCE2 role is responsible for securing the funding for the project?

   A. Corporate or programme management

   B. Executive

   C. Business Sponsor

   D. Project Manager

2. Which of the following statements represents a PRINCE2 reason why Team Managers might be appointed to the project management team?

   1. A team is sited at a different geographic location from the Project Manager.

   2. A team has been demotivated by micromanagement.

   3. A team is building products using a specialist skill.

   4. A team has many members.

   A. 1, 2, 3

   B. 1, 3, 4

   C. 1, 2, 4

   D. 2, 3, 4

3. According to PRINCE2, which of the following roles might be given some authority to authorize requests for change?

   1. Corporate or programme management

   2. The Project Board

   3. The Project Manager

   4. The Team Manager

   A. 1, 2, 3

   B. 1, 3, 4

   C. 1, 2, 4

   D. 2, 3, 4

4. Which of the following may have responsibilities beyond the end of the project?

   1. Corporate or programme management
   2. Executive
   3. Senior User
   4. Quality Assurance

   A. 1, 2, 3
   B. 1, 3, 4
   C. 1, 2, 4
   D. 2, 3, 4

5. Which PRINCE2 management product contains details of any stakeholder analysis that has been done for the project?

   A. Project Brief
   B. Risk Management Strategy
   C. Communication Management Strategy
   D. Project Approach

6. Who might appoint the Project Manager?

   A. Project Support
   B. Quality Assurance
   C. Project Management Office
   D. Executive

7. Which of the following options represents a good candidate for a Senior User?

   1. Someone who can assess and confirm the viability of the project approach
   2. Someone who will represent those who maintain the project's products in their operational life
   3. Someone who can represent those who will buy the project products once they have been developed
   4. Someone who will be in charge of marketing the project's products once they have been developed

   A. 1, 2, 3
   B. 1, 3, 4
   C. 1, 2, 4
   D. 2, 3, 4

8. Which of the following statements is **NOT** true of Project Assurance?

    A. Project Board members can carry out Project Assurance tasks.

    B. Project Support can be assigned Project Assurance responsibilities.

    C. Project Assurance has three focuses aligned to the three primary interests of the Project Board.

    D. Project Assurance may give advice and guidance to the Project Manager.

9. Which of the following is a purpose of the Organization theme?

    A. Manage uncertainty within the project

    B. Identify what resources will be needed to carry out the project tasks

    C. Ensure there are periodic reviews of project roles to verify they continue to be effective

    D. Establish the quality criteria of the project's products

10. If the project is a small one, it may be appropriate for the Project Manager to also carry out the responsibilities of which of the following roles?

    A. Executive

    B. Project Assurance

    C. Project Support

    D. Quality Assurance

Practitioner Exam Questions

Exam Spotlight

When preparing for the Practitioner exam, the Organization theme is particularly important to study for a couple of reasons. First, one of the nine Practitioner exam questions will be focused on this topic. Second, questions on any of the other syllabus areas might also ask about roles and responsibilities relevant to that question's topic.

The following Practitioner questions are divided into sections by question type and are based on the Practitioner exam scenario that you will find in this book's Introduction.

Section 1: Practitioner Sequence Questions

Column 1 is a list of actions that, according to PRINCE2, need to be carried out in the project. For each action in Column 1, indicate in which order these actions should occur by selecting the appropriate option from Column 2.

Column 1	Column 2
1. Document the stakeholder engagement procedure	A. First
2. Appoint the Executive	B. Second
3. Create the role descriptions for the Senior User	C. Third
4. Appoint the Project Manager	D. Fourth

Section 2: Practitioner Multiple Response Questions

> **Exam Spotlight**
>
> During the Practitioner exam, you will be able to refer to *Managing Successful Projects with PRINCE2* (Stationery Office, 2009). This can be very useful when questions such as those in part B ask which role has which responsibility. You might look in Chapter 5 on the Organization theme for help with answering the question; however, the appendix on roles and responsibilities is a better place to refer to. The information in the appendix is easier to read quickly. For each role, there is a bulleted list of their responsibilities.

The following four questions give five possible candidates supported by *true* statements for a particular PRINCE2 role. In the context of PRINCE2, only two of the candidates along with the supporting statements are appropriate for that role.

1. Which of the following **2** statements give possible alternative candidates for the role of the Executive?

    A. The Marketing Director, because she will fund the project from the marketing budget

    B. The Personal Assistant to the CEO, because she has recently attended a PRINCE2 seminar

    C. The Chief Executive of Quality Furniture, because he is a major shareholder in the company

    D. The IT Manager, because he is responsible for all major IT initiatives within Quality Furniture

    E. The Operations Manager, because he will be impacted by the project if sales increase

2. Which of the following 2 statements give possible alternative candidates for the role of the Senior User?

    A. The CEO, because his position enables him to control the strategic nature of the project

    B. The Marketing Director, because she will focus on realizing benefits from the website

    C. The IT Manager, because he will be responsible for maintaining the website after it is built

    D. The HR Director, because he will be responsible for ensuring project roles align with HR corporate practices

    E. The Operations Director of Digital Design, who will build the software for the website

3. Which of the following 2 statements give possible alternative candidates for the role of Senior Supplier?

    A. The IT Manager, because he will provide resources to maintain the website

    B. The Operations Manager, because he is responsible for supplying furniture to clients

    C. Consultant from FirstTech, because they supplied the recommendations for the project

    D. The Personal Assistant to the CEO, because she is responsible for contracts with third-party suppliers

    E. The Operations Director of Digital Design, who will build the software for the website

4. Which of the following 2 statements give possible alternative candidates for the role of supplier assurance?

    A. FirstTech consultant, because he can provide expertise on the IT products

    B. Quality Furniture's lawyer, because he can inspect the contracts with the IT suppliers to ensure that the delivery aims are realistic

    C. The Operations Manager, because he can ensure quality control of the furniture leaving the factory

    D. Quality Furniture's accountant, because he will check the project's finances to ensure value-for-money

    E. The Marketing Director, because she can check that the website is capable of achieving the forecast increase in sales.

Section 3: Practitioner Matching Questions

Column 1 contains a list of PRINCE2 project roles. Column 2 contains a list of project responsibilities. For each role in Column 1, select from Column 2 the responsibility that the role should carry out. Each selection from Column 2 can be used once, more than once, or not at all.

Column 1	Column 2
1. Executive	A. Ensure that the website is technically feasible.
2. Senior User	B. Delegate work to the third-party supplier designing the website.
3. Senior Supplier	C. Sign the loan secured on the factory premises that will fund the project.
4. Project Manager	D. Determine whether the website has increased sales by 20% one year after the website's completion.

Chapter

4

Business Case Theme

✓ Define outputs, outcomes, benefits, and dis-benefits.

✓ Understand the purpose of the Business Case theme.

✓ Understand the purpose and the content of the Business
   Case management product. Know the processes in which
   it is developed, verified, maintained, and confirmed, and
   which roles are responsible for each.

✓ Understand the purpose and the content of the Benefits
   Review Plan management product. Know the processes
   in which it is developed, used, and reviewed, and which
   roles are responsible for each.

✓ Know the relationship between a programme's Business
   Case and a project's Business Case.

The justification for a project should always be clear. There should be a solid set of reasons that show why the project is being undertaken. These reasons should be valid, not only at the outset, when those involved with the project are putting together an argument to secure financing, but also throughout the life of the project. It is easy for the justification for a project to disappear as things progress. Perhaps costs rise, new competitive forces enter the marketplace, or technologies change. It is also important to check that projects meet the objectives set out in their Business Case. This often can't be evaluated until some time after a project has finished. At this point, those involved with the project will probably have moved on to other things. It is therefore easy to forget to verify that the expected return on the project's investment did actually happen. The Business Case theme helps to overcome these challenges.

What Is the Business Case Theme?

The purpose of the *Business Case theme* is to set up a series of mechanisms to ensure that the project remains desirable, viable, and achievable. It helps to evaluate whether a business justification exists for carrying out the project. It ensures that in all the major decisions taken about the project, such as whether it should start, whether it should go on to the next major part (stage), or whether it should finish, the viability of the project is considered. It also ensures that when the project management team is making decisions on proposed changes or how to deal with risks, the impact on the Business Case will be taken into consideration.

The Business Case theme covers these topics:

- The relationships between outputs, outcomes, benefits, and dis-benefits

- The purpose and contents of two management products: the *Business Case*, which sets out the justification for the project, and the Benefits Review Plan, which plans how to measure the returns from the project

- The activities involved with developing the justification for the project, using the justification to drive decision making, ensuring the project is capable of bringing about its predicted returns, and planning to measure those returns

- The PRINCE2 roles that are responsible for developing the justification for the project

Outputs, Outcomes, and Benefits

In Figure 4.1, you can see the causal relationship between outputs, outcomes, and benefits.

FIGURE 4.1   Outputs, outcomes, and benefits

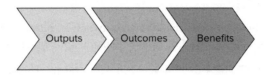

Outputs are the things that the project produces. Maybe your project builds a hotel, designs a new website, or writes a book. All of these are examples of outputs. Sometimes, outputs aren't tangible things you can see and touch. For example, a project might create a new financial process. As you saw in Chapter 1, "Overview of PRINCE2," outputs are also called specialist products. (And as you also saw in Chapter 1, there is another type of product called management products. These are the documents that are created to help manage the project. For example, the Business Case and the Benefits Review Plan, which I discuss later in this chapter, are examples of management products.)

The ultimate aim of projects isn't just to produce outputs. You want to get some *benefit* for your organization out of these outputs. If you just produced an empty hotel that never sold any rooms, the hotel chain wouldn't be too pleased. Although this example sounds ridiculous, it is all too easy to focus on the outputs of the project and forget to measure if the organization benefited in the way you predicted. This is mainly because benefits usually happen some time after the project has finished. For example, it may be months (or even years) before you will know whether online sales justify the investment in a website project.

Before you get to benefits, PRINCE2 introduces an interim step called outcomes. An *outcome* is the result of the change derived from using the project's outputs. So if you build a new hotel, the outcome is the ability to sell rooms in the new location. If you create a new financial process, the outcome might be the ability to process invoices quicker.

A benefit is the measurable improvement that results from the outcome. In the hotel project example, a measurable benefit might be that selling rooms in the new location has increased sales by 20 percent. In the new financial process project example, a measurable benefit might be a $10,000 decrease in administrative costs resulting from processing invoices quicker.

Sometimes, the project might have negative consequences. For example, a project is done to merge two departments together and the morale of the staff decreases. Or if you fund a project to build a new website, there is not enough money to upgrade everyone's laptops. These negative consequences are called *dis-benefits*. Don't confuse dis-benefits with risks. There is uncertainty over whether a risk will occur, whereas a dis-benefit is a definite consequence of the project.

Exam Spotlight

On the exams, you might be asked to distinguish between an output, an outcome, a benefit, and a dis-benefit. Here are some tips to help you spot which is which:

- Memorize the exact PRINCE2 definitions for the four terms. These come from *Managing Successful Projects with PRINCE2* (The Stationery Office, 2009). They are:

    - A project's *output* is any of the project's specialist products.

    - An *outcome* is the result of the change derived from using the project's outputs.

    - A *benefit* is the measurable improvement resulting from an outcome that is perceived as an advantage by one or more stakeholders.

    - A *dis-benefit* is an outcome perceived as negative by one or more stakeholders.

- Although the definition of an output is a product, sometimes it is not a product in the conventional sense (such as a computer or a car). For example, a decision can be a product. The best way to think about outputs is that they are the result of a series of tasks or activities. For example, the project management team might discuss a number of potential approaches to a project (the discussions are activities), and the result of the discussions is a decision on which option to pursue (the decision is a product or an output).

- Don't confuse outcomes and benefits. The definition of an outcome—the result of the change derived from using the project's outputs—sounds like it could be a benefit. But benefits are measurable, whereas outcomes are not.

- Don't confuse dis-benefits with risks. Risks can be potential bad things that result from the project, whereas dis-benefits are actual consequences that will definitely occur.

 Real World Scenario

Business Case in the Pharmaceutical Industry

One of the challenges of applying the Business Case theme is determining whether there was a link between a benefit occurring and a project. For example, my consultancy worked on a web project in the pharmaceutical industry. A new website was created to give doctors information on a range of drugs. One of the forecast benefits of the project was an increase in the number of those drugs prescribed by physicians. But if this occurred, was it due to the website, or was it due to other factors such as more sales activity, an increase in the disease, or a lack of competitor activity? It is better to focus on outcomes that are directly linked to the website, such as the reduction in printing drug information leaflets. So a benefit for the project might be something like "Forecast 40 percent reduction in printing drug information leaflets."

Business Cases Where Money Isn't the Motivation

The term "business case" suggests that all PRINCE2 projects must operate in a business environment. However, this doesn't have to be the case. I have worked on PRINCE2 projects in the public sector, in charities, in the military, and in research and development departments where the focus isn't immediate payback.

For example, I did some work for a trade union's training and development department. Their projects developed their members' job-related skills and encouraged their employers to invest in training. How do you measure whether a project like this has been successful? The answer is by focusing on various success metrics, such as the number of members attending a specific training course, and then compare which projects would achieve this aim for the best value for money. If a website costing $100,000 gets 100 members signed up on a course, it is not as good a value as a $10,000 seminar that signs up 1,000 members.

I often work with NATO and the UK military forces. Once again, they aren't looking for a profit on their new aircraft carriers. They will focus on what level of investment can achieve certain quantifiable military capabilities.

Using the Business Case Theme

There are four main groups of Business Case theme–related activities that are carried out before the project, during the project, and after the project. These are:

Develop   Develop is when the Business Case is created. I describe its composition later in the chapter, but for now, think of it as containing a prediction of the benefits the project will bring and details of the costs, time, and risks of the project.

Verify   At various times, the Business Case is reviewed to see if the project is still a worthwhile initiative. In the verify activity, the project team regularly reviews the predicted benefits to see if they still outweigh the estimated costs, time, and risks that the project needs to take on.

Maintain   As the project progresses, things will change. Costs might rise, new competitors might enter the marketplace, or work might overrun. All of these changes might have an impact on the Business Case. So the Business Case needs to be regularly updated in the maintain activity.

Confirm   The purpose of the confirm activity is to determine whether the benefits predicted were achieved. For example, if the project was to build a hotel, did it reach its predicted target in room sales? Confirming benefits usually takes place post-project.

Figure 4.2 shows a summary of when these groups of activities occur before, during, and after the project.

FIGURE 4.2:   The development path of the Business Case

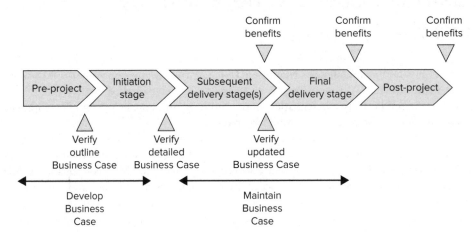

Based on Cabinet Office PRINCE2® material. Reproduced under licence from the Cabinet Office.

Developing the Business Case

The Business Case is developed both before the project starts and during the initiation stage. I talked about how the pre-project and initiation stage are managed both in Chapter 1, "Overview of PRINCE2," and in Chapter 2, "Starting a Project Successfully with PRINCE2."

Before the project starts, corporate or programme management creates a Project Mandate. The mandate contains the reasons for the project. Remember that the Project Mandate can be either high-level or detailed. Whatever form it takes, it should at least have some valid reasons for the project.

Once the Project Mandate has been created, the Starting Up a Project process begins. This is a pre-project process with a set of activities focused on determining whether the project idea is worthwhile and viable. The Executive role (the main decision maker and the representative of the business perspective on the project) creates an outline Business Case based on the information in the Project Mandate.

The next step occurs in the initiation stage. The Initiating a Project process is used to manage this stage. The Project Manager creates the Project Plan. He takes the estimates for time, cost, and potential risks from the Project Plan and uses this information to refine the Business Case. At this point, it becomes the initial Business Case. You can think of it as version 1 of the detailed Business Case.

Maintaining the Business Case

As the project progresses, it is likely that the information in the Business Case will become outdated. Costs will rise, new risks will be identified, and estimates for the project's benefits will change. So it is important to regularly update the Business Case. The Project Manager does this at the end of each delivery stage in the Managing a Stage Boundary process. The Managing a Stage Boundary process sets out how to do this in the "update the Business Case" activity. This is the maintain step of the Business Case development path that you saw earlier in Figure 4.2.

There is one other situation when the Project Manager might maintain the Business Case. In Chapter 5, "Plans Theme," you will learn about Exception Plans. The Project Board might ask the Project Manager to create an Exception Plan to show how the project will recover after a forecast breach in stage or project tolerances. As you will learn in Chapter 5, the Exception Plan is also created in the Managing a Stage Boundary process, and once the plan has been created, the Project Manager will update the Business Case with any new information.

For a more detailed explanation of how the Managing a Stage Boundary process helps the Project Manager manage the end of a delivery stage or an exception situation refer to either Chapter 1, "Overview of PRINCE2," or Chapter 10, "Managing the Middle of a Project Successfully with PRINCE2."

Verifying the Business Case

At the end of each stage (both initiation and delivery stages), the Project Manager must go to the Project Board (the main decision-making body of the project) and ask for authorization to move on to the next stage. Once again, refer to Chapter 1, "Overview of PRINCE2," if you need to remember how this stage-by-stage approach works.

The Business Case is one of the main things that the Project Board considers when giving authorization to move forward. They will want to see that the Business Case is up-to-date and that it presents a valid business argument for continuing with the project. This is the verify step of the Business Case development path that you saw earlier in Figure 4.2.

Confirming the Benefits

The confirming the benefits activities look to see if the benefits were achieved. As I said at the beginning of this section, most benefits will become apparent after the project has finished. If the project is to build a website to sell products, the sales won't happen until after the site is complete. However, there are circumstances when benefits happen before the end of a project. For example, consider a project to build a new block of apartments. Sometimes, building developers sell apartments before they have been built. People buy off the architectural plans. In this case, the benefits, in the form of sales, could accrue before the project ends.

The Benefits Review Plan is used to plan the review of benefits. I will describe its composition in detail later in this chapter. For now, think of it as containing a series of activities necessary to see if the project's benefits have occurred, along with who is responsible for those activities and when they will occur. Most of these activities will be planned for after the project.

The Benefits Review Plan is first created during the initiation stage. It is then updated with any relevant new information at the end of each delivery stage. Finally, it gets updated at the end of the project to ensure all the post-project reviews of benefits are included.

The Senior User has a leading role in confirming the benefits. I talked about the Senior User in Chapter 3, "Organization Theme." Remember that the Senior User is a role within the Project Board, the main decision-making body. There may be a number of people carrying out Senior User roles. They will all be representing some form of use of the project's products. For example, if the project is to build a website to sell a company's products, there might be a Senior User representing the customers, another representing the marketing director who uses the website to sell products, and another representing the product information department, who load details of the company's range of products onto the site.

In PRINCE2, the Senior User has two important responsibilities that are connected to the Business Case theme: first, to forecast the benefits from the project, and second, to demonstrate that the benefits have actually happened (in other words, to confirm the benefits). To see why they have these responsibilities, consider the marketing director in the previous example. He uses the website to create sales. He is thus in the ideal position to forecast how many sales (benefits) the website will bring as well as to track the sales (benefits) after the project, once the website has been built. Therefore fulfilling the Senior User is likely to involve a commitment beyond the project.

Finally, in relation to confirming the benefits, two other roles are important. The Executive is responsible for managing benefits reviews during the project. Corporate or programme management is responsible for managing post-project benefits reviews.

The Business Case Management Product

Rather confusingly as well as being the name for a theme, the Business Case is also the name of a management product. The theme, as you have seen, describes the activities, roles, processes, and management products involved with ensuring that there is business justification for the project. One of the management products that the Business Case theme describes is the Business Case management product!

The Purpose

The purpose of the Business Case is to set out the justification for the project. It provides a compelling argument to show why the project represents value for money and will give a good return on investment. In order to do this, the Business Case balances out the benefits that can be expected from the project against the cost of the initial project and any ongoing costs of operating the project's products. It also takes into account any risks that the project or the organization will be exposed to as a result of this project.

The Business Case is used to drive decision making in the project. For example, when Project Board members are considering whether to authorize the project to start, go on to the next stage, or close, they use the Business Case as an input into their decision. It is also used when the project management team is deciding whether to implement a change to the project's products. In this case, they want to check that the change doesn't have adverse effects on the Business Case.

The Contents of the Business Case

In this section, I use the hotel example to help you understand the type of information that goes into each section of the Business Case. For this exercise, assume you are working for an international hotel chain and need to put together a PRINCE2 Business Case for a new site in Shanghai.

Executive Summary

Every PRINCE2 Business Case should start with a high level summary of the contents of the Business Case. This will be useful for senior stakeholders of the project, such as those at the corporate or programme level.

Reasons

On the PRINCE2 exam, as well as when you're working on an actual PRINCE2 project, you need to know exactly what to put in the reasons section of a Business Case. Although the main reason that you are doing the hotel project may be to make a profit, this would go in the Expected Benefits section of your Business Case. The reasons section of a PRINCE2 Business Case should explain the *background* of the project, such as a challenge you are facing or an opportunity that has arisen. Another way of distinguishing a reason from a benefit is that a reason relates to something that has happened, whereas a benefit is a forecast of something that will happen.

For the hotel project, you might include one of the following statements in the Reasons section:

> Our competitors are opening successful hotels in China's major cities, and to remain competitive, we need to do the same.

Or

> Our market share of the international business market is falling due to our lack of representation in the Asian marketplace.

Business Options

The business options show different ways of responding to the challenges and opportunities set out in the reasons section. In the example, the reason you are doing this hotel project is that you are underrepresented in the Chinese market. In response to this, you might include the following options in your Business Case:

- Build new hotels under your brand in some of the major Chinese business centers.
- Form a partnership with an established chain of Chinese hotels.
- Buy an established chain of Chinese hotels.

Be careful not to confuse these business options (which explain *how* you will meet the business challenge) with the project approach (which explains *how* you will deliver the chosen Business Option). In the example, the business option you might choose is to build a new hotel. The project approach you might use to deliver this option is outsourcing the construction to a building company. This information belongs in the Project Brief and is created in Starting Up a Project.

PRINCE2 suggests you should always consider the "do nothing," "do the minimum," and "do something" options.

A decision on which business option to pursue needs to be made at either the Project Mandate or Starting Up a Project stage. However, it might take some time to do this. Starting Up a Project is supposed to be a relatively quick step in relation to the rest of the project. So how do you deal with this?

In some cases, you might be able to decide quickly which Business Option to choose. Maybe the hotels are renowned for their stylized modern architecture, and it wouldn't make sense to do anything but build new hotels. However, if this is not case, you might consider doing two projects. In the first project, you would conduct a Feasibility Study to review the different Business Options and make a recommendation on which option to pursue; in the second project, you implement that recommendation.

Expected Benefits

The expected benefits are the ultimate aim of the project. As you learned in the "Outcomes, Outputs, and Benefits" section earlier in this chapter, the project creates products, such as a hotel, and then the products produce benefits, such as room sales. Because of the causal link between outputs and benefits, ultimately what products a project creates is determined by what benefits the organization commissioning the project wants. So an expected benefit for the hotel project could be phrased as follows:

Sell $10 million worth of room sales in each of the first 3 years of opening.

Most expected benefits happen after the project has finished; however, there are cases when you might start to receive benefits during the project. Remember the hotel gym example—you first build the gym, open it up, and start selling memberships, and then you build the hotel. You get some benefit from the gym before the project is finished. All benefits should be measurable. Statements such as "increase the competitiveness of the hotel," "increase the morale of workers," or "lower costs" are not benefits. In all these cases, it would be difficult to determine whether they've been achieved. Instead, they need to focus on an objective measurement. For the hotel project, the Benefits section might include the following:

Increase the market share of business travelers from 20 percent to 30 percent in the Asian market.

As I said in the "Reasons" section, don't confuse benefits with reasons. Benefits are forecasted events. Reasons are things that have happened, that have led to the project.

Expected Dis-benefits

PRINCE2 defines a dis-benefit as "an outcome that is perceived as negative by one or more project stakeholders." Be careful not to confuse this with a risk. Risks are uncertain events—

they may or may not happen. Dis-benefits have happened or will happen. They are definite consequences of the project that will impact someone or something in a bad way.

Maybe for the hotel project, one of the consequences of building a hotel in Shanghai is that there are no funds left for the European Division to carry out their hotel expansion plans.

Timescales

Various timescales need to be reviewed. Over what period will the project run? When will the project's benefits occur? Over what period will the benefits from this project be tracked? With the latter, in theory, you could track the benefits over the entire operational life of the hotel, but it might be more reasonable just to track them over the next few years. This could be because this is the period over which the project will recover its costs.

For the hotel project, the Timescales section could read as follows:

> Construction will start on March 2012 and continue until September 2015. Bedroom sales, meeting room sales, and restaurant and bar sales will be received immediately on opening, and these will be tracked for the following 3 years.

Costs

The benefits need to be weighed against the cost of the project and the operational costs of running the products. Also, you need to set out how the project will be funded.

For the hotel project, the Costs section could read as follows:

> The Shanghai hotel is estimated to cost $150 million to build. The annual operational costs of the hotel in the first 3 years are estimated to be $20 million per annum. The project will be funded by the Asia-Pacific Business Expansion Budget.

Major Risks

It is important with any investment decision to weigh the risk. For example, if I had $1,000 in savings, I could invest in the stock market and get a much higher return than investing in a government bond. However, I might decide that the bond is better, since there is very little risk with this investment.

Any project is full of uncertainty. This makes investing in the project risky. So an important part of the Business Case is an evaluation of the risk that will be taken on.

This section details major project risks and the overall risk exposure. PRINCE2 suggests that this information be presented in the form of a Summary Risk Profile like the one in Figure 4.3. In the figure, each of the circles represents an individual risk. Risk number 1 is estimated to have a high probability of happening, and if it does happen, it would have a high impact on the project. An example might be that there is a high likelihood that a competitor will also open a Shanghai hotel, and this will have a large impact on the forecast sales figures. I will discuss risks in more detail in Chapter 7, "Risk Theme."

FIGURE 4.3   Summary Risk Profile

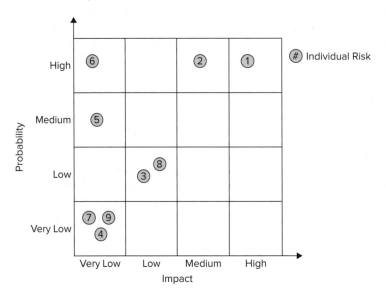

Investment Appraisal

The Investment Appraisal section compares the expected benefits with the project and operational costs over a period of time. There are many ways of doing this. For example, you could state how many years it would take to pay back the original investment. Maybe the hotel will generate $30 million in profit each year, so it will take 5 years to pay back the original $150 million investment. Another approach would be to work out the rate of return the hotel project will give. For the hotel, this would be $30 million profit divided by $150 million investment, which is 20 percent.

PRINCE2 does not prescribe a particular investment appraisal technique—it simply states that some appraisal of the investment should be set out in the Business Case. *Managing Successful Projects with PRINCE2* describes a number of investment appraisal techniques, but they are not part of the accreditation exam syllabus.

Exam Spotlight

Remember that on the Practitioner exam, you can refer to the official PRINCE2 manual: *Managing Successful Projects with PRINCE2*. This is useful if you encounter a question about the contents of a management product. Usually, I suggest that for these sorts of questions, you refer to the PRINCE2 manual's Appendix A. This appendix shows the composition of all the PRINCE2 management products. However, you'll find a better explanation of the contents of the Business Case in *Managing Successful Projects with PRINCE2's* Chapter 4. I suggest you use that instead.

> ### 🌐 Real World Scenario
>
> **Business Cases in the Dot-com Era**
>
> About 10 years ago, I worked for two Internet startups. The Business Cases that justified their projects were very different from ones in more established organizations. Both startup companies were funded by venture capitalists who were willing to take on a lot of risk, given the high forecast benefits. To balance out their risk exposure, they'd fund an entire portfolio of businesses, with the expectation that only a minority would actually succeed.

Analyzing the Impact of Risks and Issues Using the Business Case

Throughout the project, the Project Manager will be regularly reviewing the issue and risk situation. When a new risk or issue is discovered, the Project Manager will review how it will affect the project objectives, including the Business Case. For an issue, this is called carrying out an impact analysis. For a risk, this is called a risk assessment. In both cases, the Business Case will be reviewed.

Programme Business Cases

In some circumstances, the project will be part of a programme. A programme in PRINCE2 is a collection of projects that are managed together. The outcomes of all the projects are connected with each other or contribute to each other in some way. For example, the activities to create the infrastructure for the London 2012 Olympics are collectively considered a programme of work. Multiple projects exist within the programme, such as the project to create the main stadium, another project to promote the event, and so on.

Each project's Business Case will need to align with the programme's Business Case. In some situations, there may be just a programme Business Case and no Business Case at the project level. In other situations, each project's Business Case might be very limited compared to a project run outside of a programme. It might just contain a list of benefits, a budget, and a statement describing how the project is contributing to the overall aims of the programme.

Multiple Business Cases

In any one project, there might be many different parties either working on the project or in some way impacted by it. Consider the hotel project. For example, there might be a leisure company that has commissioned the building of the hotel and will own and run the hotel once it has been built. Then, there might be a construction company that builds the hotel. Each of these parties will have a different Business Case, justifying their involvement in the project. The leisure company's Business Case will focus on the sales of hotel rooms, whereas the construction company's Business Case will focus on the profit they will make in the building of the hotel. When talking about Business Cases in a project, it is important to be clear which one is being referred to.

The Benefits Review Plan

The Benefits Review Plan plans the activities necessary to see whether the expected benefits from the project are achieved. It also includes activities to see how the products have performed in their operational life.

Figure 4.4 shows the composition of the Benefits Review Plan. This is the management product that I talked about previously in the "Confirming the Benefits" section.

FIGURE 4.4   The composition of the Benefits Review Plan

Benefits Review Plan

- scope of the plan showing what benefits will be measured
- who is accountable for the expected benefits
- how to measure expected benefits
- when to measure expected benefits
- what resources are needed to review the benefits
- baseline measures from which improvement can be calculated
- how to review the performance of the project's products.

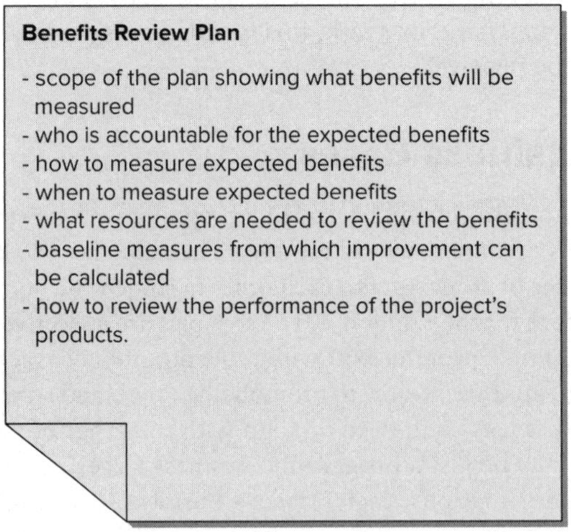

Determining whether a benefit has occurred as a result of a project is not always straightforward. For example, it may be necessary to use accountants to calculate financial benefits such as profit and sales. Or you may need to have a human resources (HR) expert design an employee survey in order to objectively measure a subjective benefit such as increased morale. All this work needs to be scheduled in the Benefits Review Plan.
It needs to be clear that it was the project that led to any benefits, not some other cause. Therefore, any pre-project benefits should be measured and their levels set out in the Benefits Review Plan.

The Project Manager and the Executive should also plan how to review the operation of the project's products. In the hotel example, you could measure the hotel's occupancy rate or the number of times crucial systems like the heating or the accounting software broke down.

Business Case Responsibilities

PRINCE2 assigns a number of responsibilities to the various roles within the project management structure to ensure that the viability of the project is reviewed throughout the project.

Corporate and Programme Management

Using the Project Mandate, corporate or programme management must instigate a project that has a viable Business Case. They must also appoint an Executive who will be responsible for the project's Business Case throughout the life of the project.

After the project, corporate or programme management takes responsibility for the Benefits Review Plan and must ensure that the project's benefits (or lack of them) are reviewed.

Executive

Throughout the life of the project, the Executive is responsible for the Business Case. This includes checking that a Business Case is created during the Starting Up a Project process, refined during the Initiating a Project process, and updated during the Managing a Stage Boundary process. In all the decisions that the Executive makes during the project, he will ensure that the latest Business Case still justifies the continuation of the project.

Most of the project's benefits will occur once the project is completed. However, some might occur during the project. For example, if you are building residential apartments, some might be sold before they are built. The Executive is responsible for ensuring that benefits that occur during the project are reviewed as specified in the Benefits Review Plan.

Once the project is completed, the Executive's role is finished. Any post-project benefits reviews are the responsibility of corporate or programme management.

Senior User

In the "Confirming the Benefits" section earlier in this chapter, you learned that the Senior User is responsible for forecasting the benefits from the project and demonstrating that they actually occur. Refer back to that section if you need to remember why this is.

Don't confuse the Executive responsibility (weighing up the forecast benefits with the costs, time, and risks that need to be taken on) with the Senior User's responsibility (which is purely focused on the benefits side of the Business Case equation).

Project Manager

Although the Executive is responsible for the Business Case, it will be the Project Manager who will create and update it on his behalf. The Project Manager must also ensure that the effects on the project's business objectives are taken into account when assessing risks and issues.

Other Roles

The Senior Supplier may be focused on ensuring that any supplier Business Case (if one exists) is still viable. They are also expected to raise any issues, such as delayed delivery dates or increased costs, which might impact the customer's Business Case.

The Project Assurance role that focuses on business assurance on behalf of the Executive checks that the project remains on target to deliver products that will achieve the expected business benefits and will deliver value for money.

Project Support, if they exist, will be involved in the administration of creating, updating, and tracking the different versions of the Business Case.

Summary

In this chapter, I described the Business Case theme. This theme sets out how PRINCE2 ensures each project has a viable Business Case.

As you learned in this chapter, there is a causal link between the outputs that a project produces, the changes that these outputs make to the environment, and the benefits that might result because of these changes. For example, a project might produce a new accounting procedure. This is a PRINCE2 *output*. The result of the new procedure produces a change, which is that invoices are processed quicker. PRINCE2 calls this change an *outcome*. Finally, if you measure the result of this change, you might find that productivity has increased by 20 percent. In PRINCE2, this measurable result is called a *benefit*.

It could be that a project has undesirable consequences, which PRINCE2 calls *dis-benefits*. PRINCE2 defines a dis-benefit as an outcome that is perceived as negative by one or more stakeholders. For example, if two departments were merged together to lower costs, a negative consequence might be that employee morale decreases.

Some projects are not done for financial payoff, such as military projects. In this case, you need to define the measurable objectives and compare different ways of achieving those objectives. Some options might cost less, take less time, or involve less risk.

Throughout the project, certain steps must be taken to ensure continued business justification. At the beginning of the PRINCE2 process model, in Starting Up a Project, the Executive develops an outline Business Case. Then in Initiating a Project, this is refined by the Project Manager. This more detailed version becomes "version one." At the end of each stage, in Managing a Stage Boundary, the Business Case might get updated to a new version. As you learned in this chapter, the Project Board uses the latest version of the Business Case to determine whether a project should proceed to the next step.

You also learned that the most important management product in this theme is the Business Case. It shows the positive effects of the project and the forecast benefits, and balances those against the project's timescale, costs, and risks. The other important management product is the Benefits Review Plan. This plan specifies when, how, and who will be involved with the reviews to see if the project's benefits have been achieved.

This chapter also described the PRINCE2 roles that have relevant Business Case responsibilities. Corporate or programme management must instigate projects by setting out the business reasons in the Project Mandate. They must also appoint an Executive who will be responsible for the Business Case throughout the life of the project. Post-project, corporate or programme management ensures that the benefits are reviewed. Throughout the life of the project, the Executive has primary responsibility for ensuring that the project is delivering value for money and that the products are capable of achieving the forecast benefits. The Senior User is responsible for forecasting the likely benefits the project can expect and demonstrating that these benefits have been achieved both during and after the project. The Project Manager manages the creation and maintenance of the Business Case and the Benefits Review Plan.

Exam Essentials

Understand the definition of a project output, outcome, benefit, and dis-benefit. A project produces specialist products called outputs, the results of the change derived from these outputs are called an outcome, and the measurable improvement from the outcome is referred to as a benefit. A dis-benefit is an outcome that is perceived as negative by one or more stakeholders.

Know the purpose of the Business Case theme. The purpose of the Business Case theme is to establish mechanisms to judge whether the project is (and remains) desirable, viable, and achievable as a means to support decision making in its continued investment.

Be familiar with the purpose and contents of the PRINCE2 Business Case. Know what information goes into which section of the Business Case and how it is used throughout the project. The purpose of the Business Case is to document the justification for the project.

Be familiar with the purpose and contents of the Benefits Review Plan. Know what information goes into which section of the Benefits Review Plan and how it is used throughout the project. The purpose of the Benefits Review Plan is to show how and when a measurement of the achievement of the project's benefits can be made.

Understand the various activities that ensure continued business justification throughout the PRINCE2 process model and post-project, and which roles are involved. Know the individual activities that are involved in developing the Business Case, maintaining the Business Case, verifying that there is still business justification for the project, and confirming that any benefits have occurred. Understand which processes these activities occur within and which roles are responsible for them.

Understand the relationship between a programme's Business Case and a project's Business Case.   Know that when a project is part of a programme, its Business Case needs to be strongly aligned with the programme's Business Case. Know that in certain circumstances, the project may not have a Business Case and will simply refer to the programme's Business Case.

Review Questions

The rest of this chapter contains mock exam questions, first for the Foundation exam and then for the Practitioner exam.

Foundation Exam Questions

1. Which of the following is responsible for ensuring that post-project benefit reviews are carried out?
   A. Executive
   B. Senior User
   C. Project Manager
   D. Corporate or programme management

2. Which of the following is a purpose of the Benefit Review Plan?
   A. Describe how and when the performance of the project's products can be measured.
   B. Document the justification for the project.
   C. Define the project.
   D. Pass on details of unfinished work and ongoing risks.

3. At what time in the project is the Business Case updated and then reviewed?
   A. When carrying out an impact analysis on an issue
   B. When carrying out a risk assessment
   C. At the end of each management stage
   D. At a post-project benefits review

4. Which product will act as an input into the creation of the outline Business Case?
   A. Project mandate
   B. Project Brief
   C. Project Initiation Documentation
   D. Daily Log

5. Which of the following options represents an example of a PRINCE2 output?
   A. Benefits Review Plan
   B. New computer software
   C. Quicker processing of invoices
   D. 20 percent increase in productivity

6. The reviews of the project's benefits are first planned in which process?
   A. Starting Up a Project
   B. Initiating a Project
   C. Controlling a Stage
   D. Managing a Stage Boundary

7. During which of the following processes is the outline Business Case refined into the detailed Business Case?
   A. Starting Up a Project
   B. Initiating a Project
   C. Managing a Stage Boundary
   D. Directing a Project

8. Which role is responsible for drafting the outline Business Case?
   A. Executive
   B. Project Manager
   C. Project Support
   D. Senior User

9. Which of the following is an example of the Business Case being developed?
   A. The Executive drafting the outline Business Case
   B. A review by the Project Board of the justification of the project
   C. The Senior User providing a statement of the achievement of benefits during a benefit review
   D. The Project Manager updating the Business Case at the end of a stage

10. Which of the following roles is responsible for specifying the benefits and subsequently providing actual versus forecast statements at the benefit reviews.
    A. Senior User
    B. Executive
    C. Senior Supplier
    D. Project Manager

Practitioner Exam Questions

Exam Spotlight

Remember that you will be able to refer to *Managing Successful Projects with PRINCE2* during the Practitioner exam. The seven questions in Section 1 are about recording information in the Business Case. Usually, when you're tackling a question about a management product, you should refer to Appendix A of *Managing Successful Projects with PRINCE2*. The Business Case is the only exception to that rule. There is a better description of the contents of the business case in the Business Case theme chapter of *Managing Successful Projects with PRINCE2*. I recommend that as you read the questions in Section 1, you have the relevant pages open so that you can practice referring to the book while answering a Practitioner-style question.

The Practitioner questions in Section 1 and Section 2 are based on the Practitioner exam scenario described in this book's Introduction and on the following additional information.

Additional Information

The project is in the initiation stage. The Project Manager is in the process of refining the Business Case. By talking to the Chief Executive and the Marketing Director, he has collated the following information.

Quality Furniture has been paying $5,000 per year for the current website. The Chief Executive sees little return from this investment. Its other main marketing activity is posting a catalogue to a mailing list. The Marketing Director estimates that this costs $20,000 per annum. She believes that sales from their catalog have dropped since last year, when a competitor launched a new website.

The Quality Furniture board of directors explored the following alternatives to help meet the marketing challenges:

- Invest in a series of TV and radio advertisements.
- Invest in automated production methods so that Quality Furniture can reduce the price of its furniture.
- Open two new stores.
- Produce an easy-to-use website with an online sales facility.

The Quality Furniture board of directors choose the last option.

Last year, Quality Furniture's sales were $1.2 million. The Marketing Director estimates that the website will increase sales by 20 percent per annum over the next 3 years. She also forecasts that regular mailshot costs could be reduced by $5,000 per annum. She believes the website will open up new international markets and help regain market share lost to their competitor. If the project is successful, the Marketing Director would like to launch another project to promote Quality Furniture on social media sites.

The Chief Executive worries that, because Quality Furniture has little experience in IT projects, it may choose a poor supplier, which might affect the forecast sales.

The project will be funded by a loan secured on Quality Furniture's factory premises.

Section 1: Practitioner Multiple Response Questions

Each of the following seven questions include *true statements* about the web project, but only two statements are appropriate entries for that heading in the project's Business Case.

1. Which two statements should be recorded under the Reasons heading?
    A. Sales are forecast to increase by 20 percent.
    B. An easy-to-use editing function would reduce the issues with out-of-date online information.
    C. A competitor has launched a successful website that is drawing sales away from Quality Furniture.
    D. Sales are $1.2 million for the year.
    E. The current website is providing a poor return on investment.

2. Which two statements should be recorded under the Business Options heading?
    A. Continue with the current website.
    B. Design the website by using a focus group of customers.
    C. Contract the creation of the website to a third-party supplier.
    D. Build an easy-to-use website, which can sell furniture online.
    E. Manage the project using five management stages.

3. Which two statements should be recorded under the Expected Benefits heading?
    A. Increase sales by 20 percent per annum in the next 3 years.
    B. Reduce mailshot costs by 25 percent.
    C. Open up international markets.
    D. Increase market share against competitors.
    E. Increase the website ranking in major Internet search engines.

4. Which two statements should be recorded under the Expected Dis-benefits heading?
    A. If the website crashes, it will reflect poorly on Quality Furniture's reputation.
    B. Selecting the wrong supplier may impact the quality of the website.
    C. This project will involve raising $150,000 in finance.
    D. Financing the web project will mean no funding for the factory extension project.
    E. Staff training on the new website will impact normal operations.

5. Which two statements should be recorded under the Timescale heading?

    A. The project will take 6 months.

    B. Suppliers will be allowed 3 weeks to reply to tenders.

    C. The Social Media project is estimated to take 2 months.

    D. Sales increases will be measured over 3 years.

    E. If the supplier is poor, the project may not be delivered on time.

6. Which two statements should be recorded under the Costs heading?

    A. Social media promotion is estimated to cost $50,000.

    B. Secure a loan of $150,000 using the factory as collateral.

    C. The new website will cost an additional $10,000 per year to maintain.

    D. If requirements aren't stated clearly, the software development company could ask for an increase of $20,000 to fund additional work.

    E. Mailing costs will be reduced by $5,000.

Exam Spotlight

In question 6 of Section 1 of the Practitioner Questions, option C is "The new website will cost an additional $10,000 per year to maintain." This is one of the correct answers. However, this information was not mentioned either in the scenario in this book's Introduction or the Additional Information. This sort of question often confuses students. How can an option be correct when it introduces new information that has not been previously mentioned? To understand the reason why this can be right, you need to carefully read the instructions for this section of questions. At the top of the section, it says "Each of the following seven questions includes *true statements* about the web project." So every option given is a *true statement*. However, many of the options, even though they are correct for this scenario, are not relevant for the section of the Business Case that the question asks about.

Be careful not to miss the words *true statements* in a Practitioner question. It means that the examiner will be introducing new information about the scenario within the body of the question.

---

7. Which two statements should be recorded under the Risks heading?

    A. Because of the lack of IT experience, a poor supplier may be chosen.

    B. The overall exposure of the project to risk is rated as medium.

    C. Funding this project will delay other projects.

    D. Using social media to promote the company may lead to negative online comments about the furniture.

    E. Using a loan to fund the project will increase financing costs.

Section 2: Practitioner Assertion/Reason Questions

This part consists of five questions based on the project scenario in this book's Introduction and the Additional Information provided previously in this Practitioner Questions section.

Exam Spotlight

For further information about how to tackle this type of question, refer to the "Exam Spotlight" under "Section 3: Practitioner Assertion/Reason Questions" in Chapter 2, "Starting a Project Successfully with PRINCE2."

Rows 1 to 5 in the following table consist of an assertion statement and a reason statement. For each line, identify the appropriate option, from options A to E, that applies. Each option can be used once, more than once, or not at all.

A. The assertion is true and the reason is true, *and* the reason explains the assertion.

B. The assertion is true and the reason is true, *but* the reason does not explain the assertion.

C. The assertion is true and the reason is false.

D. The assertion is false and the reason is true.

E. Both the assertion and the reason are false.

Assertion		Reason
1. The current sales of Quality Furniture should be written into the Benefits Review Plan.	BECAUSE	The Benefits Review Plan should include baseline figures against which the improvements will be measured.
2. One of the responsibilities of the Chief Executive's Executive role is to measure the sales figures and report them to corporate or programme management.	BECAUSE	After the project, the Executive is responsible for demonstrating that forecast benefits have been achieved.
3. During the Controlling a Stage process in Stage 3, any authorized changes to the design of the website might involve updates to the Business Case.	BECAUSE	The cost of developing the outputs of the project is an input into the Business Case.
4. At the end of Stage 2, the Project Board will authorize the software supplier's Business Case.	BECAUSE	In a PRINCE2 project, the customer/supplier environment means there might be more than one business case in a project.
5. The achievement of all the project's benefits will be assessed at the final Project Board authorization.	BECAUSE	Before authorizing project closure, the Project Board will be able to review if the project has met all its objectives.

Chapter

5

Plans Theme

PRINCE2 EXAM OBJECTIVES COVERED IN THIS CHAPTER:

✓ **Understand the purpose of the Plans theme.**

✓ **Understand the different levels of plans recommended by PRINCE2.**

- Know that there are three levels of plans recommended by PRINCE2: the Project Plan, Stage Plans, and Team Plans.

- Understand the purpose and interrelationship between the three levels of plans.

- Understand the purpose of the Exception Plan and its interrelationship with the other levels of plans.

✓ **Know the recommended composition of a plan.**

- Know in which processes the different levels of plans are developed, used, and reviewed.

- Know which roles are responsible for developing, using, and reviewing the different levels of plans.

✓ **Know the four tasks of product-based planning.**

- Understand appropriate actions involved with creating the Project Product Description, product breakdown structures, Product Descriptions, and product flow diagrams.

- Know which roles are involved with creating the Project Product Description, product breakdown structures, Product Descriptions, and product flow diagrams.

✓ **Understand the PRINCE2 approach to plans.**

The Plans theme describes an approach that helps you forecast the people, resources, and activities needed in order to create your project's products. It helps the project management team predict how long the project will take and how much it will cost. The Plans theme describes how to document these forecasts into plans, which can then be used to track and monitor your project's progress. The plans help to communicate time, cost, and resource information to the project management team and external stakeholders.

You will see that there are different types of PRINCE2 plans containing different levels of detail. Each type of plan is useful for a different level of management. You will learn what information each of these PRINCE2 plans contains.

This chapter will cover an important PRINCE2 planning philosophy called *product-based planning*. Product-based planning starts with understanding the products that need to be delivered before identifying the work that has to be done.

Along with the theory, as usual there are plenty of tips to help you prepare for the exams and also practice Foundation and Practitioner questions about the Plans theme.

Levels of Plans

In PRINCE2, there are three possible levels of plans that can be created in a project: a Project Plan, Stage Plans, and Team Plans. These are shown in Figure 5.1. Above these levels of plan, there may be a higher-level corporate or programme management plan that the activities of the project need to align to. However, this plan will not be created within the project by the project management team, so it is not considered a PRINCE2 plan level. The corporate or programme plan would be created either by those taking on senior positions within the organization that commissioned the project or by those running a programme that the project is part of.

The Exception Plan that you can see to the right of Figure 5.1 is a special sort of plan. It is not considered to be a PRINCE2 plan level. The Exception Plan shows how the project will recover after there has been a forecast breach in stage or project tolerances. Once it has been approved by the Project Board, it replaces either a Project Plan or a Stage Plan. You'll learn more about the Exception Plan later in this section.

FIGURE 5.1   The PRINCE2 planning levels

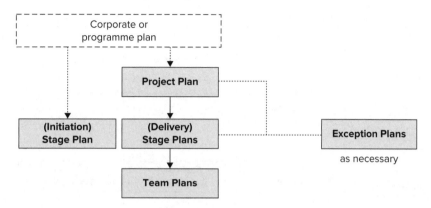

Based on Cabinet Office PRINCE2® material. Reproduced under licence from the Cabinet Office.

The Project Plan

The Project Plan is the top level of plans. The Project Manager creates the Project Plan in the Initiating a Project process. It shows the work that needs to be done from the point after the initiation stage to the end of the project. The Project Plan provides the Business Case with the planned costs and time. It allows the Project Manager to refine the Business Case during the Initiating a Project process.

The Project Plan shows the highest level of detail out of all the three levels of PRINCE2 plans. It describes the main products that are to be delivered in the project and shows broadly the activities and resources that are needed to deliver them. It should indicate how the project will be divided into various management stages.

After the Project Manager creates the Project Plan in the initiation stage, the Project Board reviews its contents and decides whether to authorize the project. They do this review in their Directing a Project process.

Once the project is active, the Project Board uses the Project Plan (once again during Directing a Project) to track and monitor the progress of the project. It provides an appropriate high level of detail for the members of the Project Board, because, given their seniority in the project, it is unlikely they will want to get involved in the day-to-day details.

At the end of each stage during Managing a Stage Boundary, the Project Manager updates the Project Plan with high-level details of what occurred in that stage as well as any new high-level details for the subsequent stages that are now known.

You can see the time that the Project Plan covers in Figure 5.2. The figure shows an example of a four-stage project. The first stage is the initiation stage, and then there are three delivery stages. You can see in this example that in order to manage the project, the project management team has created one Project Plan, four Stage Plans, and eight Team Plans.

FIGURE 5.2 Example plans for a four-stage project

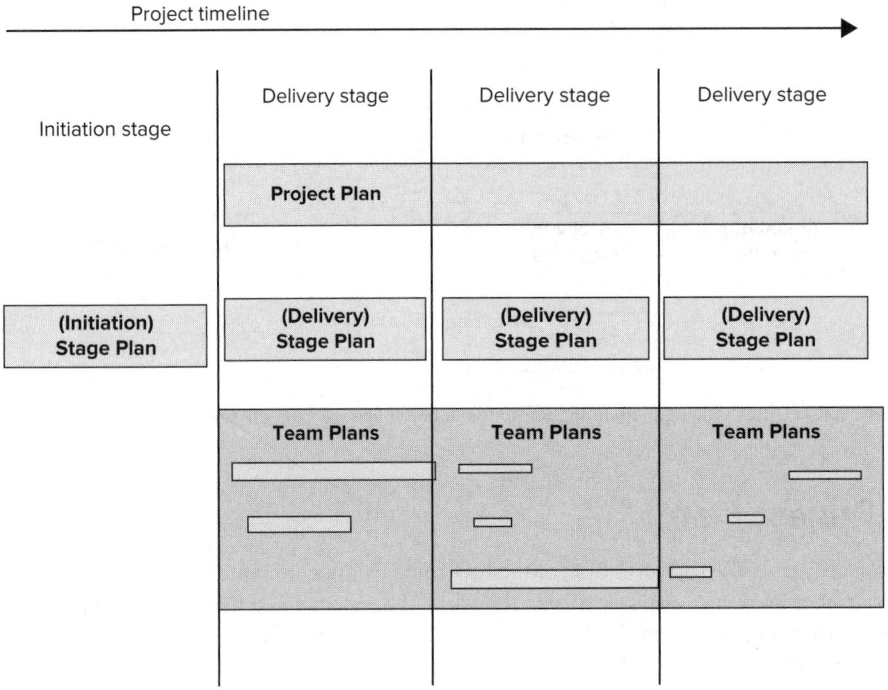

The Stage Plan

After the Project Plan, the next level of plans is the *Stage Plan*. Stage Plans are created by the Project Manager and provide a lower level of detail than the Project Plan. They include enough information to allow the Project Manager to track and control the work done in the stages on a day-to-day basis.

Because the Stage Plans are more detailed than the Project Plan, it is usually difficult to create them until near the time that the work described in the plan will be done. For example, if you are managing a project to build a hotel, it would be difficult to create the Stage Plan for the construction of the building until after the stage in which the architectural plans are created.

There are two processes where the Project Manager might create Stage Plans. The Stage Plan for the initation stage is created in the Starting Up a Project process. This plan shows the work that needs to be done to create the Project Initiation Documentation. The Project Manager updates the Stage Plan for the initiation stage with progress information during the Initiating a Project process as the work of that stage proceeds. All of the other Stage Plans are created in the Managing a Stage Boundary process and show the work for the next delivery stage. The Project Manager updates these plans with progress information during the Controlling a Stage process as the work of the delivery stages is completed and specialist products are delivered.

The Project Board reviews each stage's plan (as part of the Directing a Project process) in order to decide whether to authorize the Project Manager to manage the delivery of that stage.

The Team Plans

Team Plans are the lowest level of plans. These plans contain the necessary level of detail for individual teams to both forecast and then track and control their work. PRINCE2 says that these plans are optional, because there might be enough detail within the Stage Plan and the Work Package for the team to use. Also, since the teams may be working for different organizations that may follow other project approaches, the format and composition of the Team Plans is not specified by PRINCE2.

The Team Manager (or the team members if there is no Team Manager) creates and updates the Team Plans in the Managing Product Delivery process. The Team Plans may be created at the same time that the Project Manager creates a Stage Plan. In fact, the Stage Plan may simply be an amalgamation of the Team Plans that cover that stage's work.

The Exception Plan

Exception Plans are created to show how the project or a stage will recover from a breach in project or stage tolerances. To understand how Exception Plans work, you must understand a little about tolerances and exceptions. Chapter 9, "Progress Theme," includes detailed descriptions of tolerances and exceptions, but for now, the following explanation will be enough.

Remember that there are four levels of management in PRINCE2: corporate or programme management, Project Board, Project Manager, and the Team Manager (or the team members themselves if there is no Team Manager). Each level of management sets out certain constraints within which the level below must work. These constraints are mainly defined in terms of the amount of money and/or time that a level of management must work within. (Constraints could be set around other things as well, such as quality, scope, benefit, and risk.) It might be that the constraints are set with some flexibility. For example, corporate or programme management could tell the Project Board that the objective is to deliver the project within 12 months but it would be acceptable to deliver it 2 months earlier or 1 month later. In PRINCE2, these allowable deviations are called *tolerances*.

There are different levels of these tolerances that align with the levels of management. Corporate or programme management sets project tolerances for the Project Board, the Project Board sets stage tolerances for the Project Manager, and the Project Manager sets Work Package tolerances for the team or Team Manager. Obviously, project tolerances are the largest, and then stage tolerances, and finally, the smallest are Work Package tolerances.

If any level of management realizes they are forecasting to breach the tolerances given to them by the management level above, they are in what PRINCE2 calls an *exception situation*. The exception signals that that level of management has run out of authority and must escalate the situation to the level of management above. As you will see in the following subsections, the exception situation might eventually lead to the creation of an Exception Plan.

Example of Using an Exception Plan to Replace a Stage Plan

In a project to build a hotel, the project has reached the stage where each of the floor's bedrooms is being built. Maybe when building one of the floors, there has been a mistake. Instead of creating 20 double rooms, 10 smaller single rooms and 15 double rooms have been built. The Project Manager consults with the construction manager and finds out that this situation could be handled in one of the following ways:

- Leave the rooms as they are and build five more double rooms and no single rooms in the next floor to be built.
- Rebuild the single rooms as double rooms. Doing so will take an additional 8 weeks of work.

When the Project Manager is given a stage to manage by the Project Board, he agrees to build the products according to their Product Descriptions. However, the Product Description for this floor of rooms says there should be 20 double rooms, which in this case, there aren't.

The Project Manager checks to see if he can authorize work to correct the problem without breaching the stage tolerances he has been given by the Project Board. In this example, he has been given a 2-week time tolerance for this stage. However, the work to correct the problem will take an additional 8 weeks. He cannot correct the problem within the stage time tolerance, so he is in exception and must escalate this situation to the Project Board.

The Project Manager escalates the situation to the Project Board using an Exception Report. The Exception Report describes the various options to deal with the problem and recommends one. In this case, the Project Manager would describe the two options and maybe he would recommend rebuilding the single rooms as double rooms and taking the additional 8 weeks.

On receiving the Exception Report, the Project Board can do a number of things. In the extreme case, they could decide that the problem is so serious that the project needs to be closed prematurely. But that seems unlikely in this situation. Alternatively, in the case of products that have been created incorrectly (called *off-specifications*, which you'll learn about in Chapter 8, "Change Theme"), the Project Board could approve the incorrect products (called *giving a concession*, which you'll also learn about in Chapter 8).

Finally, the Project Board could decide to investigate in more detail the Project Manager's recommended option. They will ask the Project Manager for an Exception Plan that shows what work is involved with rebuilding the single rooms as double rooms. In this situation, the Exception Plan will show the work that needs to be done from the time of the exception to the end of the current stage. Much of the work it details could be exactly the same as the original Stage Plan for this stage, showing the remaining work involved with building all the other floors' bedrooms. However, there will now be some additional tasks to change those incorrect single rooms into double rooms—and of course, the Exception Plan will run 8 weeks longer than the original Stage Plan to allow for this additional work.

The final part to this story is that the Project Board will review the Exception Plan (in their Directing a Project process) and decide whether to authorize it. If they do authorize it, the Exception Plan becomes the new current Stage Plan that the Project Manager will then use to control and monitor the remaining work in that stage plus the new additional corrective work.

You can see this situation as Option 1 in Figure 5.3. One final point to cover is which process the Project Manager uses to create the Exception Plan. Rather bizarrely, the Exception Plan is created in Managing a Stage Boundary. This can sometimes be confusing, because, of course, at the point that the exception occurs (represented by the dotted vertical line in Figure 5.3), the project has not reached the end of the stage. A good way of thinking about this is that because of the breach of tolerances, the project needs an emergency stage boundary. During this emergency stage boundary, the Project Board needs to review a new detailed plan to see how to recover from the exception. Therefore, the Project Manager must use Managing a Stage Boundary in order to prepare to meet with the Project Board. (By the way, "emergency stage boundary" is not a PRINCE2 term—I'm just using it to better explain the situation.)

FIGURE 5.3   Exception Plans

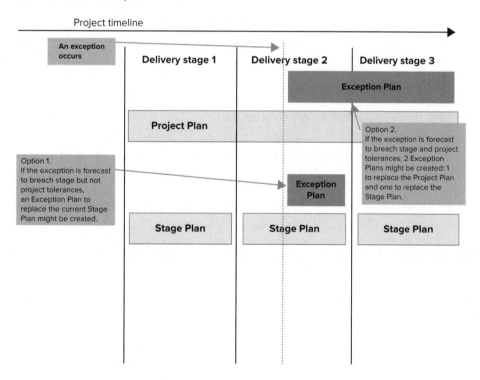

Example of Using an Exception Plan to Replace a Project Plan

In the previous example, the Exception Plan was created at the Stage Plan level. It covered the work from the point of the exception to the end of the current stage. However, in some situations, the Exception Plan might have to cover the work from the point of the exception to the end of the project. In such a case, the Exception Plan would be created at a Project Plan level. You can see this situation as Option 2 in Figure 5.3.

Why would the Project Manager create an Exception Plan at the Project Plan level? It all depends on how badly tolerances are forecast to be affected by whatever problem the project is facing. Imagine that in the last section's situation, the Project Manager once again recommends to the Project Board the option to rebuild the room, and once again this is forecast to take an additional 8 weeks. However, this time the additional 8 weeks will not only breach the stage time tolerances but also breach the project time tolerances.

In this example, corporate or programme management has given the Project Board a 6-week time tolerance within which they must deliver the project. When the Project Manager escalates the problem with the bedrooms to the Project Board, the board realizes that the recommended remedial action will breach their project time tolerances.

In this situation, if the Project Board wants to pursue the Project Manager's recommended option, they will ask for an Exception Plan that not only details the work to finish the stage, but also shows what effect that work will have on subsequent stages. In this example, it looks like the only effect would be that the work in the subsequent stages is delayed, but in another situation, it could be that the work in subsequent stages might change as well.

The Project Manager once again creates this project-level Exception Plan in Managing a Stage Boundary. This time, however, this project-level Exception Plan needs to be approved at the corporate or programme management level. Once it is approved, the Exception Plan becomes the new Project Plan.

Breaches in Work Package Tolerances

In PRINCE2, Exception Plans can replace Stage Plans or Project Plans. They are not used to replace Team Plans. If a Team Manager (or team member if there is no Team Manager) realizes there will be a breach of their Work Package tolerances, they will raise an issue. If the issue does not breach the Project Manager's stage tolerance, the Project Manager can then deal with this problem by amending the Work Package or issuing a new Work Package.

The Plan Management Product

In this section, you will learn about the PRINCE2 recommended format for a plan. Stage Plans, Project Plans, and Exception Plans created at the project or stage level follow this recommended format. Team Plans could follow the recommended format, but this is not obligatory. It could be that the Team Plans are created by a third-party organization that is not following PRINCE2. In this case, they may have different planning standards. Even if this is not the case, the Team Plans could simply be a schedule attached to the Work Package.

A PRINCE2 plan shows the work needed to create and deliver the project's products, what resources and people are needed, and when the work will be done. It also describes the products that are to be delivered. A plan should show not only the activities to create the products, but also all of the supporting activities such as quality control to check the product's fitness for purpose, the controlling and monitoring that the managers do to keep the work on track, configuration management to track the status of the products, and risk management to lower the risk of threat and increase the possible opportunities within the plan.

Exam Spotlight

A Practitioner question might ask about the types of information that belong in different sections of a plan. For example, the question might ask in which section of the plan a Project Manager should write an amount of money that has been set aside to fund risk responses. The answer, if you didn't know it already, is the budgets section.

Remember that you will be allowed to refer to the official PRINCE2 manual, *Managing Successful Projects with PRINCE2* (Stationery Office, 2009) during the Practitioner exam. When the exam asks in which section of a management product various pieces of information should go, Appendix A in the PRINCE2 manual is a good source of information. Appendix A shows the format of all the management products.

One potentially confusing situation when using the PRINCE2 manual is when the exam asks what should go where in a specific sort of plan such as a Project Plan or a Stage Plan. If you look in Appendix A of the PRINCE2 manual, there is no Project Plan or Stage Plan section. This is because there is a generic Plan section, which covers the format of the Project Plan, Stage Plans, and Exception Plans.

When I teach PRINCE2, I have my class write a note next to the Plan section in Appendix A of the PRINCE2 manual that this covers the other types of plans as well. I recommend that you do the same.

Many plans that I have worked with contain only scheduling information, such as who is doing what on a particular date. In addition to containing a schedule, PRINCE2 plans contain a lot more information, such as details on any assumptions that have been made, prerequisites that must be in place before the plan starts, and the Product Descriptions for the products within the scope of the plan.

Figure 5.4 shows the composition of a PRINCE2 plan. This format is used for Project Plans, Stage Plans, and Exception Plans.

FIGURE 5.4 Composition of a plan

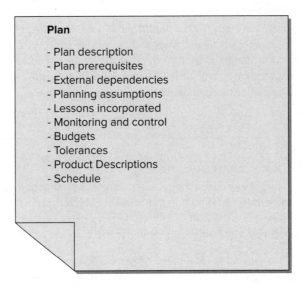

Plan

- Plan description
- Plan prerequisites
- External dependencies
- Planning assumptions
- Lessons incorporated
- Monitoring and control
- Budgets
- Tolerances
- Product Descriptions
- Schedule

The following section describes the type of information that might go into the different sections of a Stage Plan, using the example of a project to build a hotel. Imagine that this plan is for a particular stage in that project where the bedrooms will be decorated and furnished.

Plan Description

The plan description should give the reader an idea of what the work in this plan encompasses and what type of plan this is (Project, Stage, or Exception Plan).

In this case, the plan description might say something like the following:

> This plan covers the work of the stage to decorate and furnish all the bedrooms of the hotel. The work in the plan will install each room's electrics and plumbing, decorate the rooms, and install bathroom suites and the room's furniture.

Plan Prerequisite

A plan *prerequisite* is something that must be in place before the work of the plan can begin and must remain in place for the plan to succeed. For example, a prerequisite for the building of the rooms is that the Health and Safety officer has signed off on the safety of the main hotel building that was built in the previous stage.

Spotting a prerequisite can be difficult in the exam, so have a good look at the related exam spotlight on this subject.

Exam Spotlight

Spotting what is a prerequisite can be tricky. Consider the example of the Stage Plan to decorate and furnish the bedrooms in the project to build a hotel. Here are three possible prerequisites for this Stage Plan, one of which is right, and the other two wrong:

1. The gym building (sited on a plot next to the hotel and built in the previous stage) is completed.

2. The decorators (needed 3 weeks into the stage) are available to paint the rooms.

3. The engineering director of the construction company must sign off on the structural integrity of the hotel building before work can begin on fitting out the interior.

Option 1 looks suspiciously like a prerequisite, but it is not. It is true that the gym building will probably have been completed by the time the project moves on to furnishing and decorating the rooms, but work on furnishing the rooms could begin if the construction of the gym overran. There is no dependency between the gym work and the decorating of the bedrooms in a separate building.

Option 2 again looks suspiciously like a prerequisite, but once again, it is not! Something is a prerequisite only if the plan cannot even start without the prerequisite happening. In this case, the plan could start without the decorators; it is just that work would be delayed if they were still not available by week 3.

Option 3 is of course the correct one. In this case, no work can begin furnishing the rooms until the structural integrity of the outer building has been confirmed. The plan's work cannot even start until this sign-off has occurred.

External Dependencies

External dependencies are products that will be needed for the work described within the plan, but they will be created outside the scope of the plan. In other words, the Project Manager will not delegate work to anyone to create the external dependencies. Another project or group of people could be creating the external dependency products, or maybe those products already exist.

In the project to create a hotel, an example of an external dependency might be the tender responses from potential construction suppliers. These are needed for the stage during which third-party vendors are procured but the Project Manager will not manage the work to create the tender responses.

External dependencies could also be activities that are being done outside the scope of the plan, but need to be done in order to carry out some of the plan's activities.

Planning Assumptions

This section of the plan contains the planning assumptions that have been made when forecasting the work in the plan. For example, in the hotel project, the manager of the electricians might have told the Project Manager they will be available to do their work as long as another job they are currently doing doesn't overrun. When putting the stage plan together, the Project Manager would write in this section that the plan is based on the assumption that the electrician's current work finishes on schedule.

Lessons Incorporated

This section in a plan shows what previous relevant experience has been considered when putting the plan together.

In the hotel project, a lesson might be the following:

> A previous hotel construction project found that it was important to include penalty fees for late delivery in third-party supplier contracts to reduce the risk of delays.

Monitoring and Control

One of the main reasons for having a plan is to use it as a yardstick to continually compare actual versus planned progress so that the Project Manager can quickly tell if the work is behind schedule. If work starts to be delivered late, the Project Manager will have to take corrective action to bring things back on track.

Here are a few examples of how the Stage Plan could be monitored and controlled:

- Review the Stage Plan at the end of each day to compare forecast work against actual work.
- Request a Product Status Account from Project Support to track the progress of the stage's products. (The Product Status Account is a report generated from the project's configuration management system that gives a snapshot of the state of the project's products. You'll learn more about this in Chapter 8, "Change Theme.")
- Produce a Highlight Report every 2 weeks and send it to the Project Board and any other recipients as detailed in the Communication Management Strategy. (A Highlight Report is a type of progress report sent from the Project Manager to the Project Board. You'll learn more about this in Chapter 10, "Managing the Middle of a Project Successfully with PRINCE2.")
- Instruct all teams in their Work Packages to produce a weekly Checkpoint Report updating the Project Manager on the progress of their work. (A Checkpoint Report is a type of progress report sent from the Team Manager to the Project Manager. You'll learn more about this in Chapter 10, "Managing the Middle of a Project Successfully with PRINCE2.")

Budgets

This section contains information about the following:

- The amount of money budgeted for the plan's work.
- The amount of time budgeted for the plan's work.
- The amount of money set aside to fund changes to the plan's products or scope. This is called the change budget. (You'll learn about change budgets in Chapter 8, "Change Theme.")
- The amount of money set aside to fund countermeasures to deal with risks. This is called the risk budget. (You'll learn about risk budgets in Chapter 7, "Risk Theme.")

Here is a sample budget entry for the Stage Plan to decorate and furnish the hotel:

$500,000 has been budgeted for the work to furnish and decorate the bedrooms. Four months has been budgeted to carry out the work. A risk budget of $50,000 has been set aside to fund the hiring of extra contractors should the work overrun. A change budget of $20,000 has been set aside to fund minor changes (up to $500 each) to the specifications of any of the room fittings.

Tolerances

This section describes the plan's time, cost, and scope tolerances. For example, there might be some time tolerance in the Stage Plan. Maybe the objective is to deliver the stage in 4 months, but the Project Board would allow it to overrun by 2 weeks if needed.

Scope tolerance is allowable flexibility on the products that will be delivered within the plan. For example, if there is time, Wi-Fi will be fitted to all the rooms, but it is not essential to do so within this stage.

Product Descriptions

As I mentioned in the introduction to this chapter, product-based planning is an important PRINCE2 concept. A product-based planning approach ensures that the project management team is very clear about what products will be created before they start to plan what activities and resources are needed. To help implement this approach, all PRINCE2 plans contain Product Descriptions for each product that will be delivered within the scope of the plan. The Product Descriptions contain detailed and measurable specifications for a product together with a description of how these specifications will be checked and who should be responsible for signing off on the products.

This section might also contain the Product Descriptions for products that are external dependencies for this plan. (You will find a more detailed explanation of the purpose and composition of Product Descriptions in Chapter 6, "Quality Theme.")

So in the example, the stage plan for the decoration and furnishing of the bedrooms might contain the Product Descriptions for the bedrooms and Product Descriptions for some of the individual components of the bedrooms, such as items of furniture or bathroom fittings.

Schedule

This section shows what activities are needed in order to deliver the products described in the preceding section. It also shows the sequence of those activities, what resources will be needed, which people will carry out the tasks, and what dates the different tasks are forecast to start and finish. As the work in the plan progresses, this section will be updated with what actually happened.

The schedule could be shown in a variety of formats, such as a Gantt chart (a graphical way of showing schedules), a calendar, or simply a list of tasks with dates and peoples' names next to them. One format that PRINCE2 suggests is a product checklist like the one shown in Figure 5.5. The product checklist shows a list of the products to be delivered within the scope of the plan together with relevant key status dates for each product, such as forecast delivery date, actual delivery date, and forecast approval date.

FIGURE 5.5   Product checklist

Product identifier	Product title	Product Description approved		Draft ready		Final quality check completed		Approved		Handed over (if applicable)	
		Plan	Actual	Plan	Actual	Plan	Actual	Plan	Actual	Plan	Actual

Based on Cabinet Office PRINCE2® material. Reproduced under licence from the Cabinet Office.

This section will also contain a product breakdown structure and product flow diagram. (You will learn about these two diagrams in the "Product-Based Planning Technique" section later in this chapter.)

PRINCE2 Approach to Plans

Figure 5.6 shows the seven steps of the PRINCE2 planning procedure. One fundamental planning concept in PRINCE2 is that the project management team should clearly define what products will be delivered before planning the activities and resources necessary to work on those products. This concept is called *product-based planning*. This means that although there might be a certain amount of iteration and repetition of the steps in the planning procedure, Define and analyze the products should be done at least once before going on to the activity-focused steps.

FIGURE 5.6   The PRINCE2 approach to plans

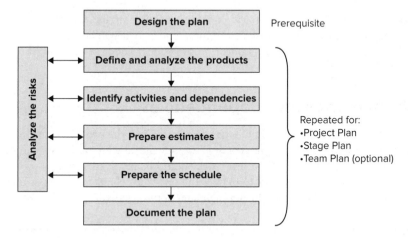

Based on Cabinet Office PRINCE2® material. Reproduced under licence from the Cabinet Office.

Design the Plan

The first step is "Design the plan." The first thing that the project management team must decide is how they would like to present the plans within their project. There is, of course, a variety of plan formats, from Gantt charts, to a list of tasks on a spreadsheet, to a far more basic set of sticky notes on a wall! In this step, the project management team chooses a suitable format for their project.

In addition to deciding on the format of plans, this step is where the project management team decides what estimating techniques to use. There are many ways to estimate how long tasks will take and how much they will cost—for example, reviewing records from similar initiatives, using statistical methods such as three-point estimating, or consensus approaches such as the Delphi technique. For the PRINCE2 exam, it is not necessary to understand any of these approaches to estimating. You just need to know this is when the estimating technique is chosen.

Another area the project management team needs to consider is whether to use any planning tools, such as project software.

Although the planning procedure might be carried out numerous times in any project, this particular step might be done only once. After the project management team has chosen the plans' format, estimating techniques, and planning tools, there is no need to repeat this step.

During the Design the plan step, the project management team may need to review corporate or programme documentation to see if there are any standards for plan formats, estimating approaches, and/or planning tools that they need to follow.

Define and Analyze the Products

The next step is "Define and analyze the products." This is the step where the product-based planning technique is used. You will learn more about this technique later in this chapter. It involves identifying all the products that will be delivered within the plan and then describing them in sufficient detail so that the teams understand what needs to be created and the Project Manager can track and monitor their work. In addition to identifying specialist products, this step lists the management products such as progress reports that will be created.

The main output from this step is a collection of Product Descriptions describing the outputs (and inputs) to this plan.

Identify Activities and Dependencies

The third step is "Identify activities and dependencies." Once the products within the scope of the plan have been identified, the next step is to understand what activities will deliver those products. The teams that will do this work should be involved with this step.

In addition to identifying the work to deliver the products, the plan identifies quality activities to check the products and the management activities involved with controlling and monitoring the work.

Finally, any dependencies between the activities should be described. There are two types of dependencies in PRINCE2: internal or external. Internal dependencies are when one activity cannot start until another activity has finished. An external dependency is when the project management team needs something from outside of the project such as a product or a decision before starting some work detailed in the plan.

Prepare Estimates

During the "Prepare estimates" step, the project management team forecasts how long the tasks will take, how much they will cost, and what effort and resources are required to carry out the activities in the plan. The estimates will inevitably change as more is discovered about the project.

Prepare the Schedule

Now that all the tasks have been identified and the time, effort, and cost of those tasks have been estimated, the next step is "Prepare the schedule," which involves forecasting the dates that the tasks will start and finish. The Project Manager will consider resource and team availability, as well as the availability of the people involved with reviewing and approving the products.

Once the schedule is complete, it can be presented graphically so it is easy for everyone to see what needs to be done and when. It is usual to identify key milestone dates within the schedule showing when key outputs need to be created.

Having assigned people and resources to the various pieces of work, the Project Manager can create a cost budget for the plan. This should include any provision for dealing with risks (risk budget) and changes (change budget) and whether there is any proposed flexibility around the costs targets (cost tolerance). These costs must be authorized by the appropriate level of management: Project Manager for a Team Plan, Project Board for a Stage Plan, and corporate or programme management for a Project Plan.

Analyze the Risks

Because plans are forecast and predicting the future is difficult, all plans contain some element of uncertainty, or in PRINCE2 terms, risk. The "Analyze the risks" step should be carried out in parallel with the other steps in the planning procedure. Any threats or opportunities that are identified are dealt with using the PRINCE2 risk management procedure. (You will learn how PRINCE2 approaches risk management in Chapter 7, "Risk Theme.")

Each plan should be considered a draft until the risks inherent in that plan have been identified and assessed, and countermeasures to deal with the risks have been put into place.

Document the Plan

The last step is "Document the plan." Here, the outputs from preceding steps are put together in a document. This document will probably contain the overall schedule and some narrative areas describing the risks associated with the plan, external dependencies, and planning assumptions.

It might be a good idea to have a number of document formats, such as a higher-level format for senior executives and a more detailed format to use for the day-to-day management of the project.

Product-Based Planning Technique

The product-based planning technique is done in the second step of the planning procedure, Define and analyze the products. The technique includes four steps, as you can see in Figure 5.7.

FIGURE 5.7   The product-based planning technique

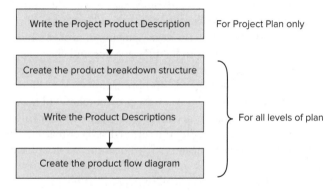

The focus of the product-based planning technique is to identify all the individual products that need to be delivered within the scope of the plan and to understand what characteristics will make these products fit for their purpose.

Write the Project Product Description

The first step is "Write the Project Product Description." This is when the final outputs of the project are documented using a Project Product Description. For example, in the hotel project, the Project Product Description would describe the broad (but measurable) characteristics of the hotel, including the number of bedrooms, the number of floors, and what main components the hotel will contain (such as restaurants, bars, and health centers).

The Project Manager, in consultation with the Senior Users and the Executive, creates the Project Product Description in the Starting Up a Project process. You will find more information about the Project Product Description, such as its recommended composition and how it is used throughout the project to control the quality of the final outputs, in Chapter 6, "Quality Theme."

Create the Product Breakdown Structure

The next step is "Create the product breakdown structure." A *product breakdown structure* is a graphical tool that helps the project management team identify all the products that will be delivered within a plan. It usually has a hierarchical structure rather like an organization chart, although it could be in the format of a mind map or simply an indented list. The project management team can draw the product breakdown structure together, starting by identifying the big components that need to be delivered, and then breaking each of these components into smaller and smaller pieces until they are down to a level where the products at the end of any particular branch of the structure can be individually installed, created, or modified.

The following "Conference Scenario" is taken from *Managing Successful Projects with PRINCE2*. It involves a project to organize a conference.

Conference Scenario

A project is required to organize and run a conference for between 80 and 100 delegates. The date and subject matter are set, and the focus of the conference is to bring members of a particular profession up to date on recent developments in professional procedures and standards. The project team will need to identify a venue and check its availability, facilities, and price before booking it. They will also need to identify suitable speakers and book them, before producing a detailed agenda and programme. A mailing list of delegates is available, and once the venue has been booked, the project team will need to issue a press release based on the agreed programme. Part of the project will involve producing 100 delegate handouts, with a cover reflecting the selected subject matter. These handouts must contain a printed agenda covering the agreed programme, copies of the slides and notes used by the speakers, and a feedback form to capture attendee reviews. Booking arrangements for attending the conference, including details of the programme and venue, must be sent out in the mail shot (a bulk mailing to potential delegates). The team will need to regularly update the attendance list based on responses to the mail shot, and make arrangements to recruit staff to help on the day, based on the final attendance list.

Scenario based on material from *Managing Successful Projects with PRINCE*®. Reproduced under licence from the Cabinet Office.

Product Breakdown Structure for the Conference Project

Figure 5.8 shows the product breakdown structure for the conference scenario. It identifies all the products that need to be delivered. The word "product" can be misleading. Many people imagine a product to be a tangible "thing" that you could see and touch. However, look at some of the "products" in Figure 5.8. "Booked venue" is a product, which is not a tangible thing at all. A good way of thinking about PRINCE2 products is that they are outputs from a series of activities. A series of activities is involved in booking a venue, such as meeting with the owners of the venue, negotiating terms, and signing contracts. The output of these activities is the "booked venue."

FIGURE 5.8 Conference product breakdown structure

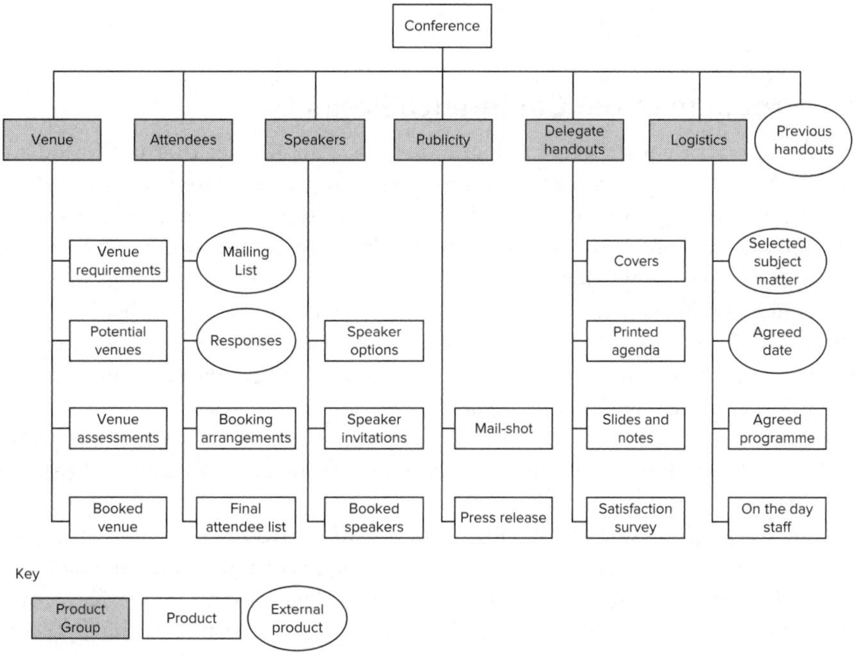

Based on Cabinet Office PRINCE2® material. Reproduced under licence from the Cabinet Office.

One common misconception PRINCE2 exam candidates have about the product breakdown structure is that the diagram shows the sequence in which the products will be delivered. It doesn't! It just shows the products needed for the plan. The fact that the "potential venues" is to the left of the "speaker options" does not necessarily mean that the "potential venues" product needs to be delivered before the "speaker options" product. The sequence of delivery will be shown in the product flow diagram, which you'll learn about in a minute.

You'll see that the diagram has grouped together certain products. This could mean one of two things. They could be a group of similar products, such as the four products under the "venue" box. In this case, the "venue" box is not actually a real product—it is a product grouping. The project team won't deliver a "venue" (i.e., they won't build something like a conference center within the scope of this project). The "venue" box is there just to group together the four products underneath in a neat way. If it weren't there, you'd have to put "venue requirements," "potential venues," "venue assessments," and "booked venue" on the level above. This is fine, but it would make the diagram very wide!

The other sort of grouping shows when one product is physically composed of a collection of other products. You can see an example of this in the conference product breakdown structure. "Delegate handouts" is physically made up of "covers," "printed agenda," "slides and notes," and "satisfaction survey." Unlike in the venue example, this time the product at the top of this branch, "delegate handouts," is a real product. The project team creates "delegate handouts" and they consist of the four products below it in the product breakdown structure.

This product breakdown structure goes down to three levels. However, it could go down to many more levels. For example, the "booked speakers" could be split up into different types of speakers.

External Products in the Conference Project

On the product breakdown structure in Figure 5.8, you can also see that some products are shaped as ellipses. These are *external products*. External products are ones that already exist or are being created or updated outside the scope of the plan, but are required in order to create one or more of the plan's products. They are inputs into the plan's work. For example, the scenario says that the "mailing list" already exists, so this is an external product. It is not within the scope of the project team's work to create the list.

The "responses" from people wishing to attend the conference are another external product. They won't be created or updated by the teams involved with this project, but they are needed in order to deliver the conference.

One way of identifying an external product is to ask yourself, "Will the Project Manager need to delegate the work to create this product to any of the project teams?" If the answer is no, then it is an external product.

One common trap that exam candidates fall into with regard to external products is thinking that these are products created outside of the organization that commissioned the project. Take the "press release" product in the scenario. The scenario says, "The project team will need to issue a press release." This is a product that is created by the project team, and because it is within the scope of work of the plan, it is not external. However, imagine the scenario had said, "An external publicity company will issue a press release for the project team." Does this sentence change the "press release" to an external product?

The answer is no. The fact that a third-party supplier is now creating the "press release" does not make it external. The product is still within the scope of the plan, and the Project Manager will still have to delegate the work to the publicity company. In most current projects, a lot of work will be delegated or outsourced to third-party suppliers, but as long as those products are within the scope of the work of the plan, they are not external.

Because people outside of the project management team create external products (unless, of course, they exist already), there is more uncertainty about whether they will be delivered on time and to the correct specification. PRINCE2 suggests that there should be a corresponding entry in the Risk Register for any external products and that the uncertainty should be managed using the PRINCE2 risk management procedure. It might be useful to create a Product Description for the external product and give this to the people involved with its creation to reduce the risk of the wrong specification being delivered.

Write the Product Descriptions

The third step is "Write the Product Descriptions." Once the product breakdown structure has been used to identify all the products that are needed for a plan, the next step is to gain an understanding of the specifications for those products. A *Product Description* is written for each product. This describes the measurable characteristics of the product, known as *quality criteria*. These can be used to confirm that the right product has been delivered. It also shows any techniques or approaches that will be used to ensure that a product complies with its quality criteria and who is responsible for reviewing and approving that product. (You'll learn more about Product Descriptions in Chapter 6, "Quality Theme.")

The Project Manager creates the Product Descriptions, although it is sensible to include other parties who have specialist knowledge of the products, such as the Senior Users, the Senior Suppliers, and the teams.

Product Descriptions for any product should be started as soon as the need for that product has been identified. At this point, they may be in draft form, and as more is known about the products, the Product Descriptions will become more refined. A product's Product Descriptions should be signed off at the same time as signing off the plan that will be used to deliver it.

In a small project, it may be only necessary to create a Project Product Description. This might contain enough level of detail for the project management team to understand unambiguously what needs to be delivered.

Create the Product Flow Diagram

The final step is "Create the product flow diagram." The *product flow diagram* takes the products identified in the product breakdown structure and puts them in the order that they will be delivered. Creating the product flow diagram allows the project management team to conceptualize the dependencies between the products. The diagram will also be useful in the next step of the planning procedure, when the project management team considers the sequences of activities needed to create the products (during the Identify activities and dependencies process). The final product in the product flow diagram is the final output of that plan.

Figure 5.9 shows the product flow diagram for the conference scenario project that you saw earlier in this section. As you can see, the diagram shows the order in which the products from the product breakdown structure are delivered. It also shows that some of the products are external products, by putting them into ellipses.

FIGURE 5.9 Product flow diagram for the conference project's Project Plan

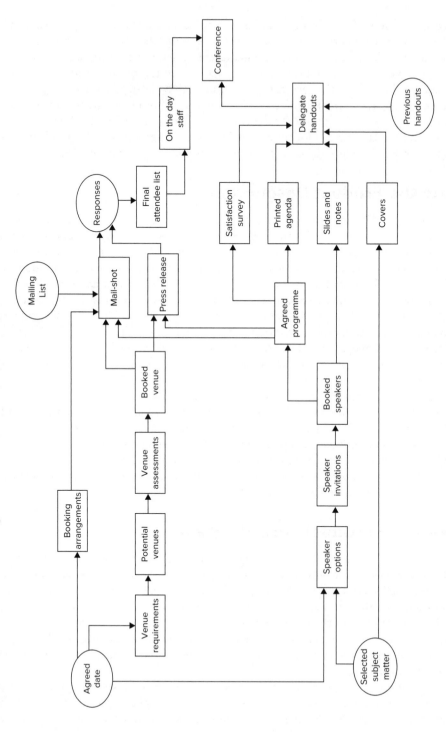

Most of the boxes and circles from the product breakdown structure have been copied across to the product flow diagram. The only exception is the product grouping products from the product breakdown structure, such as "venue" and "speakers." As you learned in the "Create the Product Breakdown Structure" section, these are not real products. The project team will not deliver them. They were only in the product breakdown structure to make the diagram easier to follow by collating similar products in the same place.

Benefits of the Product-Based Planning Technique

There are a number of benefits that the product-based planning technique brings to planning, including the following:

- It helps to clearly define the scope of the plan, and reduces the risk of "scope creep" or the team forgetting essential products.
- It provides clarity over what needs to be delivered.
- If the users are involved with the creation of the Product Descriptions, it reduces the risk of acceptance disputes once the products have been delivered.
- It helps the project management team identify products that will be delivered outside of their project team, so that they can take countermeasures against potential delivery problems.
- It helps provide clarity about who will review and approve products and how this will be done.

Summary

In this chapter, you learned about the PRINCE2 Plans theme. This theme helps define how the products of the project will be delivered. It identifies what activities will be needed and who will do the activities, and helps to estimate the duration and cost of the project.

You saw that there are a number of levels of plan. The highest level created within a project is the Project Plan. This has the broadest level of detail and is used by the Project Board to monitor the progress of the project. Then, for each stage, there will be a more detailed Stage Plan. This helps the Project Manager control the day-to-day activities of a stage. Finally, the lowest and most detailed plan is the Team Plan.

In addition to the different levels of plans, PRINCE2 provides an Exception Plan. This plan is used to show how the project will recover from a breach in tolerances and might replace a Project Plan or a Stage Plan.

In this chapter, you learned that every PRINCE2 plan (whether it is at the project, stage, or team level) should include a number of pieces of information such as a schedule, planning assumptions, lessons learned from previous projects, and Product Descriptions for the products that are within the scope of the plan.

You also learned that PRINCE2 recommends an approach to planning. This approach implements the PRINCE2 concept of product-based planning. First, the products to be delivered are identified and described, and then the activities and the resources needed to create those products are forecast.

The product-based planning technique is one step within the PRINCE2 planning procedure. The technique consists of four parts. In the first part, the overall outputs from the project are described using a Project Product Description. In the second part, the individual products for a particular plan are identified using a product breakdown structure. In the third part, each product is described using Product Descriptions. And in the fourth part, the sequence in which the products will be delivered is shown in a product flow diagram.

Exam Essentials

Understand the purpose of the Plans theme.   The purpose of the Plans theme is to facilitate communication and control by defining the means of delivering the products.

Identify the three levels of plans recommended by PRINCE2.   PRINCE2 recommends three levels of plans: Project Plan, Stage Plans, and Team Plans.

Know the purpose of the Project Plan and understand in which processes the Project Plan is developed, used, and reviewed and which roles are responsible for doing this.   The Project Manager creates the Project Plan during Initiating a Project; the plan covers the work of the entire project after the initiation stage and describes how the major products of the project will be delivered. The Project Board uses the plan to control and monitor the project during Directing a Project.

Know the purpose of the Stage Plans and understand in which processes the Stage Plans are developed, used, and reviewed and which roles are responsible for doing this.   The Project Manager creates the Stage Plans during Managing a Stage Boundary. The plan covers the work of an individual management stage within the project. The Project Manager uses the plan to control and monitor the day-to-day work of the stage during Controlling a Stage.

Know the purpose of the Team Plans and understand in which processes these Plans are developed, used, and reviewed and which roles are responsible for doing this.   The Team Manager or team creates the Team Plans during Managing Product Delivery. The plan covers the work of one or more of a team's Work Packages. The Team Manager or team uses the plan to control and monitor the day-to-day work of delivering one or more Work Packages during Managing Product Delivery.

Know the purpose of the Exception Plans and understand in which processes the Exception Plans are developed, used, and reviewed and which roles are responsible for doing this.   The Exception Plan is prepared by the Project Manager during Managing a Stage Boundary and is at either a project or stage level. The Exception Plan shows the actions required to recover from either a forecast project or forecast stage tolerance deviation. Once the Exception Plan has been approved, it becomes the Project Plan or a Stage Plan.

Understand the interrelationship between the various levels of the PRINCE2 plans. The Project Plan is divided into a number of management stages and each management stage has a corresponding Stage Plan. Each Stage Plan describes how to deliver a number of Work Packages. A more detailed description of the work involved with delivering one or more Work Packages might be described in a Team Plan.

Understand the recommended composition of the PRINCE2 plan. Know the recommended types of information that should appear in a PRINCE2 plan, such as Product Descriptions, schedule, and plan prerequisites.

Know the four tasks involved with the PRINCE2 product-based planning technique and which roles are involved with these actions. The product-based planning technique involves four tasks: writing the Project Product Description, creating the product breakdown structure, writing the Product Descriptions, and creating the product flow diagram. The Project Manager is responsible for these activities when using the product-based planning technique to prepare the Project Plan or the Stage Plan; the Team Manager or team is responsible for these activities when preparing the Team Plan.

Understand the PRINCE2 approach to plans. Know that there are seven steps to the PRINCE2 approach to plans: design the plan, define and analyze the products, identify activities and dependencies, prepare estimates, prepare the schedule, document the plan, and analyze risks.

Review Questions

The rest of this chapter contains mock exam questions, first for the Foundation exam and then for the Practitioner exam.

Foundation Questions

1. Which of the following would **NOT** appear on a Project Plan?

   A. Activities that create the specialist products

   B. Activities that create the management products

   C. Resources to deliver major products

   D. Activities that carry out post-project benefit reviews

2. How does the Plans theme help to implement the "manage by exception" principle?

   A. By stating that all plans should contain a lessons incorporated section

   B. By providing Stage Plans to help the Project Manager manage the day-to-day aspects of a stage

   C. By stating that all plans should contain a tolerance section

   D. By providing the product-based planning technique

3. Which of the following is the only level of plan whose format or composition is not prescribed by PRINCE2?

   A. Project Plan

   B. Stage Plans

   C. Team Plan

   D. Exception Plan

4. Which of the following statements apply to an Exception Plan?

   1. May be created following a forecast breach in stage tolerances levels.

   2. May show actions required to recover from the effect of a forecast breach in project tolerance levels.

   3. Once approved, it becomes either the new baselined Project Plan or Stage Plan.

   4. May show the actions required to recover from the effect of a forecast breach in Work Package tolerance levels.

   A. 1, 2, 3

   B. 1, 2, 4

   C. 1, 3, 4

   D. 2, 3, 4

5. Which of the following options is a fundamental aspect that must be in place and remain in place for a plan to succeed?

   A. Schedule

   B. Plan prerequisite

   C. Planning assumption

   D. Customer quality expectation

6. Which of the following is **NOT** a purpose of the Plans theme?

   A. To help the project management team to think ahead

   B. To establish whether the targets for time and cost are achievable

   C. To provide a baseline against which progress can be measured

   D. To establish mechanisms to judge whether the project is desirable, viable, and achievable

7. Which of the following options does PRINCE2 **NOT** recommend when designing a plan?

   A. Considering the best format for the project plans

   B. Considering any company or programme standards that the project plans need to adhere to

   C. Identifying uncertainties inherent in the plan

   D. Considering whether any planning tools should be used to create the project plans

8. In which of the following steps in the approach to planning does PRINCE2 recommend using the product-based planning technique?

   A. Design the plan

   B. Define and analyze the products

   C. Identify activities and dependencies

   D. Prepare estimates

9. Which of the following product types already exists or is being created outside the scope of the plan?

   A. Quality product

   B. Management product

   C. Specialist product

   D. External product

10. Which of the following is one of the benefits of product-based planning?

   A. Helps to provide clarity regarding product approval responsibilities

   B. Helps to identify the shortest possible completion time of the project

   C. Helps to identify how the performance of the project's products will be reviewed

   D. Helps to define techniques for estimating throughout a project

Practitioner Questions

The following Practitioner questions are divided into two sections by question type and are based on the Practitioner exam scenario described in this book's Introduction.

Section 1: Matching Type

Column 1 lists statements to be included in the Stage Plan for stage 2, and Column 2 lists some of the Stage Plan headings. For each statement in Column 1, select from Column 2 the Stage Plan heading under which it should be recorded. Each selection from Column 2 can be used once, more than once, or not at all.

Column 1	Column 2
1. Quality Furniture's existing standard terms of conditions will be sent to potential suppliers. The Chief Executive is currently revising these in another project.	A. Plan description
2. The Personal Assistant to the Chief Executive said that in her experience, suppliers can take up to a month to respond to a request to tender.	B. Plan prerequisites
3. If no suitable responses are received from the list of potential suppliers given to Quality Furniture by FirstTech, $5,000 has been set aside to fund a request for tender advertisement in the technical press.	C. External dependencies
4. The Project Board must approve the Project Initiation Documentation.	D. Planning assumptions
5. A weekly highlight report will be sent to the Project Board.	E. Lessons incorporated
	F. Monitoring and control
	G. Budgets
	H. Tolerances
	I. Schedule

Section 2: Classic Multiple-Choice Type

The questions in this section are based on the example practitioner scenario described in this book's Introduction and the following "Stage 2 Product Summary Information." After reviewing both of these, answer the questions about the use of the product-based planning technique for stage 2 of the project, which you will find under "Classic Multiple-Choice Questions."

Exam Spotlight

The Practitioner question in Section 2 asks about the application of the product-based planning technique and gives some additional information about the products that will be needed in order to deliver one of the stages of the project. You should first review the additional information and try to spot the products. (You might want to underline or highlight them in the text.)

There are a number of methods you could use to spot the products. First, products will be nouns in the text. For example, "technical requirements" is a noun and is, in fact, a product. Be careful, though—not all the nouns are products; for example, "potential supplier" is a group of people who will be involved with the work of the stage.

Another way to spot the products is to look for inputs to or outputs from an activity or series of activities. For example, maybe the project team is reviewing and selecting a potential web page design for the Quality Furniture website. During the review, they will need to refer to the existing branding standards. What products would be involved in this activity? First, there are the "existing branding standards," which are an input into the activity of reviewing the designs. Then, the output of reviewing the designs is a "selected design."

Thinking of the words "selected design" as a product can sometimes confuse candidates of the PRINCE2 exams. "Selected design" could simply be an email that says, "Let's go for design number two." It isn't a product in the sense that you could box it up and give it to someone. However, it is the output to a series of activities, so it *is* a PRINCE2 product.

You also need to be able to spot the external products. These are products that already exist, such as the "existing branding standards." They could also be products that are created outside the scope of the plan, such as the "tender responses." PRINCE2 recommends that external products be highlighted on the product breakdown structure and the product flow diagram, and suggests putting them into a different shape than the other products, such as an ellipse.

A good test to see if a product is external is to ask yourself whether the Project Manager will need to delegate any work to a team to do anything to that product. If the answer is no, then it is an external product.

Stage 2 Product Summary Information

The following text is a summary of the products that will be needed for the delivery of stage 2.

Using technical requirements that will be created by the Quality Furniture's IT manager and the feasibility study created before this project, the requirements for the upgraded website will be created.

Each potential supplier will be sent a request to tender documents. This will need to comply with the established Quality Furniture procurement standards. The request to tender documents will include a set of due diligence questions to be answered by the potential supplier, Quality Furniture's requirements for the upgraded website, the standard Quality Furniture corporate brochure, and a set of the existing standard terms of conditions that Quality Furniture uses to engage with suppliers. The Personal Assistant to the Chief Executive who usually deals with procurement will send the request to tender documents to a list of suitable software developers that will be compiled during this stage by FirstTech.

Suppliers will need to send Quality Furniture a tender response that will include a completed tender application form, a proposal for how the supplier will meet the website requirements, a copy of their latest accounts, and a list of reference sites that Quality Furniture can contact. The Personal Assistant to the Chief Executive and the Quality Furniture IT manager will review the tender responses and create a short list of potential suppliers. The reference sites of the suppliers on the short list will be checked and one supplier will be selected.

The Chief Executive needs to approve the selected supplier before the final contracts and purchase orders are sent.

Classic Multiple-Choice Questions

Using the Project Scenario in this book's Introduction and the preceding "Stage 2 Product Summary Information" for reference, answer the following seven questions about the plan for stage 2 of the web project.

Decide whether the statements reflect an appropriate application of the product-based planning technique to create the plan for stage 2 and select the response that supports your decision.

1. The Product Description for the "request to tender documents" shows the "procurement standards" as an item under the "derivation" heading.

    A. Yes, because the "procurement standards" are a source product needed to create the "request to tender documents."

    B. Yes, because the "procurement standards" will form part of the "request to tender documents."

    C. No, because the "procurement standards" should be an item under the "composition" heading.

    D. No, because this dependency can be shown on the product flow diagram.

2. The Product Description for the "request to tender documents" shows the "Quality Furniture corporate brochure" as an item under the "composition" heading.

    A. Yes, because the "Quality Furniture corporate brochure" is needed before creating the "request to tender documents."

    B. Yes, because the "Quality Furniture corporate brochure" will be part of the "request to tender documents."

    C. No, because the "Quality Furniture corporate brochure" is an external product.

    D. No, because the "Quality Furniture corporate brochure" should be an item under the "Quality method" heading.

3. The "list of suitable suppliers" has been shown as an external product for stage 2 in the product breakdown structure. Is this an appropriate application of product-based planning for this stage?

    A. Yes, because the personnel of FirstTech are external to Quality Furniture.

    B. Yes, because the "list of suppliers" refers to external suppliers.

    C. No, because the "list of suppliers" will be created within the scope of the plan for stage 2.

    D. No, because the "list of suppliers" will be needed by the Personal Assistant to the Chief Executive.

4. "Tender responses" have been shown on the product flow diagram as an external product for stage 2. Is this an appropriate application of product-based planning for this stage?

    A. Yes, because the potential suppliers are external to Quality Furniture's organization.

    B. Yes, because the Project Manager is not accountable for the creation of "tender responses."

    C. No, because "tender responses" are needed in order to deliver stage 2.

    D. No, because the Project Manager will need to monitor whether any "tender responses" are received.

5. The Project Manager has created an entry in the Risk Register showing the delivery of the "tender responses" as a threat to stage 2. Is this an appropriate application of product-based planning for this stage?

   A. Yes, because external products are risks to the delivery of a plan.

   B. Yes, because all products in a plan should have a corresponding entry in the Risk Register.

   C. No, because risk management should not be done in parallel to planning activities.

   D. No, because this is the role of the Personal Assistant—she deals with potential procurement problems.

6. "Review tender responses" has been shown as a product that precedes the "short list of potential suppliers" in the product flow diagram for stage 2. Is this an appropriate application of product-based planning for this stage?

   A. Yes, because the tender responses will be reviewed before the "short list of potential suppliers" is created.

   B. Yes, because the review of the tender responses happens within the scope of stage 2.

   C. No, because "review tender responses" should only be shown in the "derivation" heading in the Product Description for the "short list of potential suppliers."

   D. No, because "review tender responses" is an activity.

7. "Approved selected supplier" has been shown on the product flow diagram for stage 2 as a product that precedes "final contract." Is this an appropriate application of product-based planning for this stage?

   A. Yes, because this is a product that needs to be delivered before the "final contracts" are sent to the selected supplier.

   B. Yes, because "final contracts" is the final product of the stage.

   C. No, because approving the selecting supplier is an activity.

   D. No, because "approved selected supplier" is not a product.

Chapter

6

Quality Theme

PRINCE2 EXAM OBJECTIVES COVERED IN THIS CHAPTER:

✓ **Know the purpose and scope of the Quality theme.**

✓ **Define the difference between quality planning and quality control.**

✓ **Define the difference between Project Assurance and quality assurance.**

✓ **Understand the quality planning actions that take place within a project and which roles have responsibilities for these actions.**

- ▪ Define the difference between a customer's quality expectations and acceptance criteria.

- ▪ Know that the Project Manager, with the help of the Senior User, documents the customer's quality expectations and the acceptance criteria in the Project Product Description and how these will be verified.

- ▪ Know that the Project Manager describes how the project will be managed with respect to quality in the Quality Management Strategy.

- ▪ Know that the Project Manager, with the help of the Senior User, creates Product Descriptions describing a product's quality criteria and how these will be verified.

✓ **Understand the quality control actions that take place within a project and which roles have responsibilities for these actions.**

- ▪ Know that quality control within a project involves carrying out quality methods, maintaining quality approval and acceptance records, and gaining acceptance for the project's products.

- ▪ Know that the authority defined in a Product Description has the responsibility for carrying out quality methods to verify a product's quality.

✓ **Know that the PRINCE2 approach to quality is known as the quality audit trail.**

✓ **For the following management products, know their purpose, composition, in which processes they are developed, used, and reviewed, and which roles are responsible for each:**

- Project Product Description

- Product Description

- Quality Register

- Quality Management Strategy

✓ **Understand the objectives of the quality review technique, the responsibilities of the various quality review team roles, and the actions that occur throughout the technique.**

This chapter covers the PRINCE2 approach to quality. In it, you will learn how the PRINCE2 processes, roles, and management products are used to ensure the project creates products that are fit for purpose.

All projects are exposed to a number of quality risks. At the end of a project, it is all too common to have disputes about what should have been delivered as well as user dissatisfaction with the end result. The Quality theme helps mitigate these risks by ensuring that project team members are clear about what they are delivering and follow procedures that ensure these products are created.

The Quality theme shows how to describe an approach that ensures that quality products are created on a project. This approach is documented in the Quality Management Strategy. The strategy covers how the project will carry out quality planning activities, such as working with the ultimate users of the products to capture their requirements and then ensuring that these requirements are documented. It covers how the project will approach quality control activities in which the product will be inspected or tested to see if the product has been built correctly. It will also cover how to assign people to assurance roles to check that the approach specified in the strategy is being followed.

In this chapter, you will see how the PRINCE2 Quality theme recommends that quality planning, quality assurance, and quality control activities be carried out.

What Is Quality?

Normally, the word *quality* is almost synonymous with *luxury*. In my dictionary, the definition of this word is "degree or standard of excellence, especially to a high standard." For example, if I tell my friends that I bought a quality suit, they might think I have got a tailor-made garment—maybe even from Saville Row (a street in London that sells very expensive suits, sometimes to royalty). (Unfortunately, unless you get all your colleagues to buy this book, that's a bit beyond my price range!)

In PRINCE2, the word *quality* is used a little differently than its everyday usage—it means fit for purpose. Taking my suit example, if I were to consider what sort of suit would be fit for my purpose, I would think about what I need my suits for. My work requires a lot of travel, so my suits need to be pretty durable. I need a suit to be able to survive being crumpled up in various suitcases and sat on during long plane journeys. I also need a suit that will look good in front of my clients.

The PRINCE2 Quality theme is focused on ensuring that a project creates products that are fit for the purpose for which they will be used. It also focuses on ensuring that the project is managed in a way that is appropriate for the type of project. Therefore, processes as well as products need to be fit for purpose.

The PRINCE2 definition of the word *quality* is a mouthful, but for completeness, Here it is:

> Quality is defined as the totality of features and inherent or assigned characteristic of a product, person process, service and/or system that bear on its ability to show that it meets expectations or satisfies stated needs, requirements or specification.

I don't recommend that you spend time memorizing that long sentence. Just keep in mind that quality is all about making something fit for the purpose it is ultimately needed for.

What Is Scope?

It is important to understand that the terms *scope* and *quality* refer to different concepts. *Scope* defines the number and range of products to be delivered. For example, the scope of the London 2012 Olympics project defines how many stadiums have to be built for all the various types of sports as well as any additional products that must be created, such as websites or upgrades to the transport network. Many projects suffer from *scope creep*, in which more and more things are added to the original project requirements without thought about how these additions might impact project objectives such as quality, costs, and timescales.

Once the scope of the project has been defined, the specifications for each product within that scope must be defined. The specifications that will make any individual product fit for its purpose should be clearly stated in measurable terms. You can think of these specifications as the *quality* of any individual product within the *scope* of the project.

In PRINCE2, you will see the word *scope* used to describe the number of products to be delivered within a particular plan. So PRINCE2 might refer to the scope of a Project Plan, a Stage Plan, or a Team Plan. In each case, this means the number and range of products to be delivered by that plan.

What Is Quality Management?

In PRINCE2, *quality management* is the means by which a project creates products that are fit for their purpose. It involves a set of activities that are focused on understanding what would make the project's products meet the client's needs and then ensuring that these products are built. Quality management consists of four areas:

Quality Management Systems   First, there needs to be a systematic approach to quality in the project. The systematic approach should specify various procedures to follow, roles and responsibilities, and various documents that need to be created and maintained. The aim of the *quality management system* is to ensure that the products that are created are fit for their purpose. PRINCE2 itself is an example of a quality management system.

Quality Assurance   It is all very well having a quality system, but will anyone follow it? *Quality assurance* is the activity of reviewing a project's organization, processes, and/or products to assess independently whether the systematic approach to quality is being followed and is leading to the creation of products that meet the client's needs.

Quality Planning   *Quality planning* is about defining the specification for the project's products. It is also about understanding how the products will be checked to see if they conform to these specifications.

Quality Control   The last area of quality management, *quality control*, involves determining whether the products have been (or are being) built correctly. Products are checked against their specifications.

Quality Assurance and Project Assurance

The term *quality assurance* is used in two ways in PRINCE2:

- As a function or a department within an organization whose responsibility is to establish and/or maintain the quality management system

- As an activity to review the project independently to ensure it is being managed in a way that is appropriate given the objectives that have been set for it and any organizational standards and policies that exist

Quality assurance is done by a group of people who will be independent of the project management team. Maybe these people come from a dedicated Quality Assurance department, whose responsibility is to check the organization's operations on an ongoing basis to ensure that things are being done properly. Now and again, this department is asked to carry out quality assurance activities on particular projects, to independently check that the project is being conducted in an appropriate manner. If no such department exists, corporate or programme management may appoint people to carry out the quality assurance activities for a project or may decide to do the activities themselves.

Do not confuse the term *quality assurance* with Project Assurance. Project Assurance is the responsibility of the Project Board, which checks to see if the project is being conducted properly. Each of the Project Board roles (Executive, Senior User, and Senior Supplier) has an accountability to carry out Project Assurance (business assurance, user assurance, and supplier assurance, respectively).

The activity of quality assurance is similar to the activity of carrying out the responsibilities of Project Assurance. Both involve reviewing the project to determine whether it is being conducted in an appropriate manner. The difference is that whoever is doing Project Assurance reports to the Project Board (or the members of the Project Board might do it themselves), whereas whoever is carrying out quality assurance reports to corporate or programme management. Project Assurance is independent of the Project Manager but is within the project management team, whereas the people doing quality assurance are independent of the project management team.

Figure 6.1 shows where Project Assurance and quality assurance sit within the project management team structure that you learned about in the section "The Four Levels of Management" in Chapter 3, "Organization Theme."

FIGURE 6.1 Quality assurance and Project Assurance

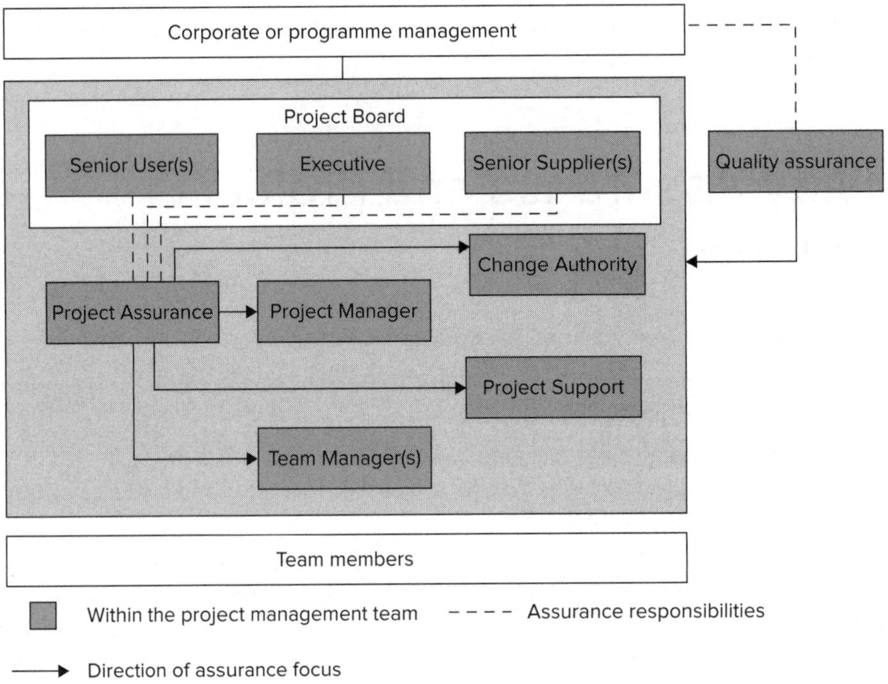

Based on Cabinet Office PRINCE2® material. Reproduced under licence from the Cabinet Office.

Quality Planning

Quality planning involves the following aspects:

- Defining the specification of the project's products
- Understanding how the products will be inspected and reviewed to see if they conform to their specifications and who should have responsibility for this review
- Defining who should have responsibility for final approval of the products

In PRINCE2, the Project Product Description and the Product Descriptions define the specifications of the project's products. The difference between the two is that for any project, there is only one Project Product Description that describes the overall output of the project, whereas there may be many Product Descriptions that describe all the individual components of the overall output.

For example, if you are the Project Manager of a project to build a hotel, you write one Project Product Description that describes the hotel at a high level. This document provides the overall specifications, such as how many rooms the hotel should have of each type (penthouse, double, single, and so on), how many floors it should have, and what the hotel's main parts are (such as the lobby, a restaurant, a gym, or a swimming pool).

Then you write a Product Description for each component of the hotel. For example, you create a Product Description for the swimming pool, the lobby, the penthouses, and so on.

Both the Project Product Description and the Product Descriptions describe specifications in a measurable way so that when the products have been built, there can be no argument over whether the right products have been created. For example, the Product Description of the swimming pool should contain the exact dimensions that the pool needs to conform to. The Product Description also describes how the products are to be reviewed to determine whether they meet their specifications. Finally, the Product Description outlines who is responsible for signing off on the products.

The next two sections describe both the Project Product Description and the Product Descriptions in greater detail.

The Project Product Description

The customer's requirements from the project deliverables are described in the Project Product Description. In this section, you will learn about the purpose of the Project Product Description; where in the PRINCE2 process model it is created, reviewed, and updated; and finally, what it contains.

The Life of the Project Product Description

I am hoping that by now, you have a fairly good grasp of the overall PRINCE2 process model. You're going to need it to follow the information in this section properly. If you feel you haven't, I recommend you reread the section "An End-to-End Walk-through of PRINCE2" in Chapter 1, "Overview of PRINCE2," before tackling this section.

The Project Manager liaises with the Senior Users and the Executive to create the Project Product Description during the Starting up a Project process. At the end of that process, the description is put into the Project Brief. The Starting up a Project process is used to provide information to the Project Board in order for them to decide whether to commission the project. They make this decision by reviewing the Project Brief in their Directing a Project process.

The Starting up a Project process is fairly lightweight, so time isn't wasted on initiatives that aren't taken any further. At this point, the Project Product Description needs to contain only enough detail to enable the Project Board to decide whether to commission the project.

If the Project Board does decide to commission the project, the initiation stage starts. The Project Manager uses the Initiating a Project process to refine the Project Product Description if necessary. This is then put into the Project Plan section of the Project

Initiation Documentation. (In PRINCE2, plans contain descriptions of the products that will be created within the scope of that plan, as you learned in Chapter 5, "Plans Theme.") After the initiation stage, the Project Board reviews the Project Initiation Documentation with its Project Product Description and decides whether to authorize the project to move on to delivering specialist products.

Moving on from the beginning of the project, the Project Product Description is reviewed at the end of each stage by the Project Manager during the Managing a Stage Boundary process. At this point, the Project Product Description may be updated to reflect new information available at that point in the project. If it is updated, this new version needs to be approved by the Project Board while they are approving the next stage.

When products are handed over from the project team to the ultimate clients or those who will operate the products on behalf of the clients, the Project Product Description is used to verify that the correct deliverables have been created. The handing over of the product from the project team will take place at the end of the project during the Closing a Project process, or if the products are handed over in a staged way throughout the project, this will also occur for the interim deliverables during the Managing a Stage Boundary process.

The Composition of the Project Product Description

Figure 6.2 shows the composition of the Project Product Description.

FIGURE 6.2   The composition of the Project Product Description

Project Product Description

- Title
- Purpose
- Composition
- Derivation
- Development skills required
- Customer's quality expectations
- Acceptance criteria
- Project-level quality tolerances
- Acceptance method
- Acceptance responsibilities

As you can see in Figure 6.2, the Project Product Description has 10 sections. Here is a brief description of what each section contains, using the example of a project to build a new hotel in Shanghai aimed at the business traveler for a hotel chain:

Title   The title is the name of the project, which in this example is "Shanghai International Hotel."

Purpose   The purpose describes what function the overall outputs of the project will fulfill and who will use them. In the hotel project example, the purpose for the hotel chain might be to move into the Chinese market and remain competitive in the business traveler market.

Composition   Composition lists the major products that the project will deliver. It basically defines the scope of the project. For the hotel project, this section lists all of the hotel's major parts, including the lobby, the restaurant, the gym, the swimming pool, how many of each type of rooms there will be (such as 10 penthouse suites, 30 luxury double rooms, 50 standard rooms), and so on. In addition, other products, such as an invitation to tender documents, promotional literature, or websites that are part of the scope of the project, may be listed here.

Derivation   This section shows what products are needed before the project starts. For the hotel project, this may be the Project Mandate or architectural plans that were drawn up before the project started.

Development Skills Required   This section presents a broad idea of the sorts of skills required to build the overall outputs of the project. For the hotel, this section may include bricklaying, plumbing, or electrical skills. The section may also indicate where these skills could be sourced, such as recruitment agencies or supplier names.

Customer's Quality Expectations   Customer's quality expectations are the expectations that the customer has about the overall outputs of the project. In the hotel example, the hotel chain may require a luxury hotel, a hotel focused on the needs of the business traveler, or a hotel that complies with certain building regulations. These expectations are often presented in a subjective form. This means it is difficult at the end of the project to prove that products complying with these attributes have been delivered. For example, if the project management team has a different idea of what a luxury hotel means to the client, there could be delivery disputes.

Acceptance Criteria   To overcome potential delivery disputes because of subjective customer quality expectations, the Project Manager should work with the customer to define measurable product attributes that are derived from the quality expectations. These are called acceptance criteria. In the hotel project example, the use of acceptance criteria makes it much easier to prove that the right hotel has been built. The measurable attributes can cover a range of areas about the products, such as ease of use, ease of support or maintenance, appearance, major functions, development or running costs, capacity, availability, reliability, security, accuracy, and/or performance. Acceptance criteria examples for the hotel can include the number of rooms, the size of the hotel, and/or how many hours per day security services will be available.

Project-level Quality Tolerances   This section details any acceptable leeway that the customer will allow around the acceptance criteria. In the hotel project example, the hotel should have 200 bedrooms but 190 would be acceptable.

Acceptance Method   The acceptance method describes how the customer will accept the products once they have been built. In the hotel example, this can be as simple as counting the number of rooms that have been built. For some products, however, it could be complex. For example, if the project was to build a car, one of the acceptance criteria may relate to how many hours of continuous use the car can withstand, and the acceptance method may involve a technical stress test.

Acceptance Responsibilities The acceptance responsibilities section defines who is responsible to sign off on the overall outputs from the project. When the hotel is accepted, it stops being the responsibility of the project team and starts to become the responsibility of the customer or the group of people who will maintain and operate the hotel. It should be clear who has signed off on the product so that there are no disputes over who should fix problems that might arise during the hotel's operation—the project team or the operational team.

 Real World Scenario

The Importance of Being Clear About When Projects End

It is critical to be clear about when the products of a project have been handed over from the project team to either the client or the operations team. I worked for a company that created the computer infrastructure for organizations' websites. The computer infrastructure consisted of large, high-capacity computers on which organizations' website software ran. These computers were sited in datacenters that had high-capacity links to the Internet and all sorts of ways of ensuring that the computers kept running in the event of problems. For example, they had gas generators in case the local electricity supply failed. Once the company built the infrastructure, they operated and maintained it as well on behalf of the client.

When I started working for this company, what tended to happen was that one group of people built the sites and then also supported them. The problem with this arrangement is that the two types of work were very different in nature and needed to be managed in an entirely different way. The building of the infrastructure had to be planned, whereas the support work was far more ad hoc in nature. The result of having one team manage both types of work was that the planned building of infrastructure for new clients was delayed while engineers dealt with support calls from old sites. The team was not set up to manage, prioritize, and deal with the growing amount of support calls that came in every day.

The company overcame this problem by dividing the engineers into two teams. One built the products and the other supported them. This arrangement worked much better. The project teams could focus on building infrastructure for new clients and could more easily plan out their work, without the constant interruptions of support calls.

The support team set up systems that collected all the support calls that were coming in, prioritized them, and dealt with them in a timely manner. They also created a new sign-off process. They only took on the responsibility of supporting a new client's infrastructure once the other team had created support documentation and ensured the products they had created complied with standards defined by the support team.

The result of splitting the team into two was that the building work was done in a more timely manner, support calls were dealt with more effectively, and the standards that the infrastructure was built to improved.

Product Descriptions

In this section, you will learn about the purpose of Product Descriptions; where in the PRINCE2 process model they are created, reviewed, and updated; and what they contain.

The Purpose of Product Descriptions

Product Descriptions specify each of the project's products. They set out measurable criteria that the finished product can be compared against to see if the right product has been created. However, Product Descriptions are more than just specifications. They also give information on the skills required to develop, review, and approve the products; who will use the product when it is complete and for what purpose; and what method will be used to ensure that the product has been created properly.

The Life of the Product Descriptions

During the life of a project, increasingly detailed descriptions of the project's outputs are needed in order to plan the work to create those products. As you saw in the previous section, the Project Manager creates the overall Project Product Description in the Starting up a Project process. In the hotel project example, this management product describes the attributes of the hotel at a high level, such as the number of rooms it will have and its main components (the lobby, restaurant, and so on).

However, the broad descriptions in the Project Product Description won't be detailed enough to manage the building of all the individual components of the hotel, so the project uses Product Descriptions to describe the project's outputs in more granular detail. During the Initiating a Project process, the Project Manager creates the Project Plan. The plan specifies, at a high level, how the major products of the project will be delivered. At this point, the Project Manager also creates Product Descriptions for these major products. He does this in consultation with the Senior Users, the Senior Suppliers, and perhaps the teams who will be involved in these products' creation. So at this point in the hotel project, Product Descriptions for things like the lobby, the swimming pool, and the types of bedrooms are created.

Now imagine that the project has moved on to a point when, during the next stage, the work to furnish the guest rooms will be done. The Project Manager must create a Stage Plan for this work. The Stage Plan shows what products will need to be created or procured in order to furnish the rooms—the beds, the baths, the desks in the rooms, and so on. The Project Manager (again with the help of the Senior Users, the Senior Supplier, and maybe the teams) creates Product Descriptions for these products so that the teams involved will understand the work they need to do. These more granular Product Descriptions are created during the Managing a Stage Boundary process alongside the creation of the Stage Plan.

Finally, perhaps the teams need even more detailed Product Descriptions in order to do their work to furnish the bedrooms. For example, say the plumbers require a detailed description of the types of faucets that will be fitted to the bath. In this case, they can include even more detailed Product Descriptions for things like the faucets when they are creating their Team Plans. It is the responsibility of the Team Managers to do this during the Managing Product Delivery process.

Each of these even more detailed Product Descriptions must, of course, align and be consistent with the higher-level Product Descriptions and also the very high-level Project Product Description. In each case, the Project Manager has to liaise with the members of the Project Board, Project Assurance, and the teams in order to create the Product Descriptions. This is especially the case when the products are of a technical nature and the Project Manager does not have expertise in that area.

The Product Descriptions are then used after the product has been created to check that the right output has been created. Basically, the product that has been created is compared with the measurable specification in the product's Product Description (in the quality criteria section) to see if they match. This is done in the Managing Product Delivery process. The Product Descriptions define who is responsible for reviewing the products as well as who is responsible for final approval of the products. This is called the appraisal approach to quality control. The Product Descriptions may also be used throughout the building of the products to perform a continual check that the products being created are heading in the right direction. This is considered the in-process to quality control. These two approaches to quality control will be described in more detail later in this chapter.

The Composition of a Product Description

Figure 6.3 shows the composition of a Product Description.

FIGURE 6.3   The composition of the Product Description

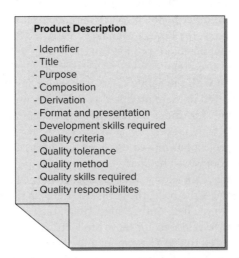

As you can see in Figure 6.3, the Product Description has 12 sections. Here is a brief description of what each section should include, using as an example the Product Description of a penthouse room in the hotel chain project:

Identifier   Every product in a PRINCE2 project is assigned a unique identifier. This identifier helps the Project Manager track and monitor all the project's products. Chapter 8,

"Change Theme," describes the PRINCE2 approach to configuration management, which is all about tracking, monitoring, and protecting the project's products.

Title   The title in our example is "Penthouse Suite."

Purpose   This section defines the product's purpose and who will use it. Some products are ends in themselves, whereas others are created as a means to an end. For example, the purpose of the foundations is to hold up the rest of the hotel, whereas the purpose of the penthouse is to fulfill the needs of the high-end business traveler.

Composition   This section lists the main components that this product contains. In the penthouse example, this can include items such as the bedroom, lobby, bathroom, and furniture.

Derivation   This section lists other products that are needed in order to create this product. For the penthouse example, maybe the project team needs to create the design of the rooms before they begin building them.

Format and Presentation   If the product is a document or a report, this section shows the characteristics of how this product will be presented.

Development Skills Required   This section specifies the sorts of skills needed to create the products. It may also indicate where these skills can be sourced. It will not contain the actual names of people—those will go into the relevant Stage Plan or the Team Plan that plans the work to create this product. For the penthouse, this may include a list of relevant skills such as carpentry, plumbing, or decorating.

Quality Criteria   The *quality criteria* describes the measurable specifications that the product must comply with. The end product can then be compared against these specifications to see if the right thing has been created. For the penthouse, these criteria may specify the dimensions of the room, the color of the walls, the type of materials that will be used, and so on.

Quality Tolerance   This section describes any leeway that the client will allow for the quality criteria. For example, a king-sized bed has been specified for the penthouse, but a queen-sized one would be acceptable.

Quality Method   The *quality method* describes how the product will be checked to see if it meets its quality criteria. Sometimes, this can be as simple as using a measuring tape to check the dimensions of the room. Other times, the quality method might be more complicated, such as using a decibel meter to check that the soundproofing in the walls is providing the necessary noise insulation.

Quality Skills Required   This section describes the skills required to carry out the quality methods and indicates where the skills can be sourced. It will not contain the names of people—these are entered in the relevant Stage or Team Plan where the quality activities are planned. For the penthouse, perhaps there is a specialist company that checks buildings for soundproofing qualities.

Quality Responsibilities   This section contains the names of the producer, the reviewers, and the approvers of the product. The approvers of the product have the ultimate sign-off for the penthouse.

Exam Spotlight

As discussed in previous chapters, you will be able to refer to the official PRINCE2 manual, *Managing Successful Projects with PRINCE2* (Stationery Office, 2009), during the Practitioner exam. This is particularly useful if you are asked a question about the contents of one of the management products such as either the Project Product Description or the Product Descriptions. Appendix A of *Managing Successful Projects with PRINCE2* shows the information that all 26 management products should contain. It would take a far better memory than mine to remember all the nuances of what goes where in each document, so when you are asked a question about the composition of a management product in the exam, make it easy on yourself and refer to Appendix A.

However, if you are asked a question about either the Project Product Description or the Product Description, be careful not to refer to the wrong one. When I give candidates mock questions on the Project Product Description or Product Descriptions in my classes, I can confidently predict that at least half the class will refer to the wrong management product in Appendix A. The Project Product Description and the Product Description are similar products, but they are *not* the same. Don't confuse them in the exam.

Quality Control

Quality control is the fourth area of quality management that was introduced in the "What Is Quality Management?" section earlier in this chapter. This area involves checking that the products meet the quality criteria described in their Product Descriptions by carrying out the quality methods (also described in the Product Descriptions).

A number of levels of quality control exist in PRINCE2:

- A series of *quality checks* may be carried out on each product. For example, the penthouse described in the preceding section might require a quality check of the dimensions of the room, a quality check of the soundproofing of the walls, a quality check testing the fire safety of the room, and so on. The quality checks will use the approaches described in the Product Description's quality methods section. Once each check has passed, a quality record should be kept to provide evidence that the product has been reviewed. Project Support will file these *quality records*.

- Once each product has passed all its quality checks, it is ready for *approval*. This is the official signing off on the product. The product will be signed off by the person or people defined in the quality responsibilities section in the Product Description. An *approval record* should be kept to provide evidence of this signing off. Project Support will file the approval records.

- Once a group of products is ready to be delivered to the final customer, the client must accept them. *Acceptance* is where the final output(s) of the project, such as the hotel, are "handed over" to the customer. In many projects, this might take place only at the end. For example, once the hotel has been built, it will be "handed over" from the ownership of the project management team to the group who will operate and maintain the hotel on behalf of the hotel chain. However, many projects will hand over interim deliverables. For example, the hotel project might first build the hotel gym and deliver it to the hotel chain for them to open and operate before the rest of the hotel is finished. The Project Product Description describes who is responsible for providing acceptances (acceptance responsibilities section), how they will do this (acceptance method section), and what measurable characteristics the products need to comply with in order for them to be acceptable (acceptance criteria). *Acceptance records* are kept to provide evidence of these acceptances. Project Support will file these acceptance records.

Using the Quality Register

The Project Manager creates the Quality Register during the Initiating a Project process. It is used to track all the quality checks carried out on the project's products. The composition of the Quality Register is shown in Figure 6.4.

FIGURE 6.4   The composition of the Quality Register

To illustrate, the following paragraphs describe how the Quality Register is used to check the quality of the penthouse product for the hotel project.

First, the Project Manager plans the stage in which the penthouse rooms will be built and quality-checked. Working with the Team Managers and the Senior Suppliers, the Project Manager produces the Stage Plan for that stage. This Stage Plan includes the Product Descriptions for the penthouse as well as the activities that create the penthouses and quality-check them. This planning work is done in the Managing a Stage Boundary process.

Once the Stage Plan is created, the Project Manager reviews the plan to find all the quality activities. This is also done in the Managing a Stage Boundary process. For each quality check activity that he finds, the Project Manager creates a corresponding entry in the Quality Register. At this point in the project, the Quality Register entries show only the planned details. So for a quality check to verify the dimensions of the penthouse rooms, the Project Manager fills out the following details:

Quality Identifier   For example, if this is the 23rd check on the project, the Project Manger enters **23** here.

Product Identifier(s)   The Project Manager takes this ID from the product's Product Description.

Product Title(s)   In this example, the Project Manager enters **Penthouse** here.

Method   This is the quality method that has been specified in the Product Description. This entry might be as simple as **Use a measuring tape** for the penthouse example.

Roles and Responsibilities   These are the names of the people specified in the Stage Plan for this quality activity. In the penthouse example, this includes the name of the person or team creating the rooms, the people responsible for reviewing the rooms, and the person responsible for signing off this quality check—all of which are found in the Product Description.

Planned Date of Quality Check   For this section, the Project Manager refers to the Stage Plan and writes in the date for which the quality check has been planned.

Planned Date of Sign-off of Quality Check   For this section as well, the Project Manager refers to the Stage Plan and writes in the date when the quality check is scheduled to be signed off.

Figure 6.5 shows the Quality Register entry for the quality check to verify the dimensions of the penthouse rooms as it will look during the planning of the stage.

FIGURE 6.5   Example of a Quality Register entry during stage planning

Quality identifier	Product identifier(s)	Product title(s)	Method	Roles and responsibilities	Planned date of quality check	Planned date of sign-off of quality check	Actual date of quality check	Actual date of sign-off of quality check	Result	Quality records
23	121	Penthouse	Measuring	Simon-producer Jack-reviewer Jane-approver	08-Feb	10-Feb				

Once the Stage Plan is authorized, the Project Manager manages the work in that stage using the Controlling a Stage process. At some point, the Project Manager authorizes the work to build and then quality-check the penthouse rooms by giving a Work Package to the relevant team or Team Manager.

The work of building and checking the quality of the penthouse rooms takes place in the Managing Product Delivery and is the responsibility of the Team Manager or the team. Once the quality checks have been done, the Quality Register is updated with the results. The Work Package describes who should update the Quality Register with the results. At this point, the entry in the Quality Register for the quality check that verifies the dimensions of the penthouse rooms would look like Figure 6.6.

FIGURE 6.6   Example of a Quality Register entry after a quality check

Quality identifier	Product identifier(s)	Product title(s)	Method	Roles and responsibilities	Planned date of quality check	Planned date of sign-off of quality check	Actual date of quality check	Actual date of sign-off of quality check	Result	Quality records
23	121	Penthouse	Measuring	Simon-producer Jack-reviewer Jane-approver	08-Feb	10-Feb	11-Feb	11-Feb	Pass	

If a product fails its quality check and has to be resubmitted for a new quality check after some remedial work has been done, a new entry in the Quality Register is created that refers to this resubmission quality check.

Types of Quality Methods

Remember that quality methods are used to check whether products conform to their quality criteria. The quality methods for each product are described in their Product Description. PRINCE2 has two types of quality methods:

In-process Methods   In-process methods are checks that are done during the creation of the product. They might involve interim checks during the build of the product. Or they might involve a special way of building a product that ensures that it conforms to its quality criteria—for example, a car manufacturing line using robots to build the parts of the car.

Appraisal Methods   Appraisal methods are checks that are done on the product after it has been finished. There are two types: testing, whereby an objective criterion is measured to indicate whether it meets its quality criteria, and quality inspection, whereby some sort of judgment needs to be reached. For example, a software product is appraised to determine if it is "easy to use." This rather ambiguous statement can be tested in a rigorous way by using industry standards and carrying out a predetermined system of checks.

Using the PRINCE2 Quality Approach

If you use the PRINCE2 quality approach, you should be pragmatic about how you implement it. Do you really need to create lots of separate Product Descriptions for every product created, or can you somehow combine a lot of this information? The point of the Product Descriptions is to define the measurable criteria for each product so the creators of the products know what they are aiming for. If there were separate Product Descriptions for all the products, this could create a lot of documentation. Also, some of the information in the Quality Register replicates information in the Product Descriptions, such as the responsibilities and the quality methods.

A number of PRINCE2 software tools are available that can help you create these PRINCE2 management products. The tools provide templates and replicate information between different products to avoid double entry. If you are going to use PRINCE2 in a detailed way, you'll find it useful to look at these tools.

One of the ways to tailor PRINCE2 is by cutting down on the amount of management documentation when it is not necessary. You will learn more in Chapter 12, "Tailoring PRINCE2 to the Project Environment".

Application of the Quality Theme in a Project

This section pulls together the quality approaches discussed in the preceding sections of this chapter. I will take you through the project to build a hotel for a hotel chain and describe how the PRINCE2 quality approach is applied.

Figure 6.7 shows what PRINCE2 calls the quality audit trail. As you can see, there are six major steps in the PRINCE2 quality approach to a project, and these steps produce auditable records. In the following sections, you will learn what is involved in each of these six steps.

FIGURE 6.7 The quality audit trail

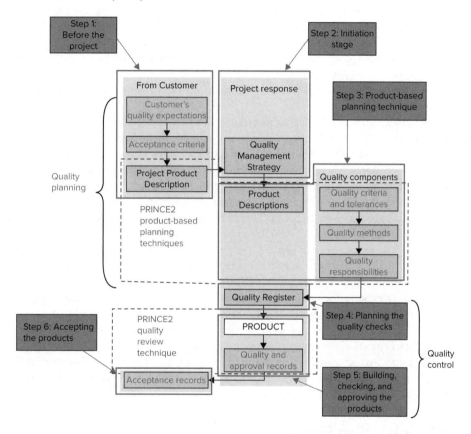

Before tackling the following sections, you should have a basic understanding of how the PRINCE2 process model fits together, at least at a high level. If you don't know this yet, go back to Chapter 1, "Overview of PRINCE2," and read the section "An End-to-End Walk-through of PRINCE2."

Step 1: Before the Project

The first step in the PRINCE2 quality approach is to understand what the customer's quality expectations are regarding the outputs of the project. These might be rather ambiguous (such as the customer asking for a luxury hotel or one aimed at the business traveler), so from these subjective customer's quality expectations, objective acceptance criteria are derived.

For example, if the customer's quality expectations of the hotel are that it will be suitable for the business traveler, some relevant acceptance criteria could be that each room will have laundry service, each television will have news channels in all main business languages, and room service will be available on a 24-hour basis.

When corporate or programme management creates the Project Mandate that triggers the start of PRINCE2, it will contain at the very least a good idea of the customer's quality expectations. It may also contain the acceptance criteria, although it may be left to the project management team to derive these criteria in the Starting up a Project process.

In the hotel example, corporate or programme management could be the hotel chain's board of directors. They decide that they would like to open a luxury hotel aimed at the business traveler in Shanghai. They create a Project Mandate outlining this customer's quality expectations.

Once the Project Mandate has been created, the Starting up a Project process starts. The Executive and the Project Manager design and appoint the project management team, including the Senior Users. The Senior Users are responsible for establishing the requirements for the project's products. There may be a number of perspectives on how the products will be used, and therefore, a number of Senior Users. In the hotel example, Senior Users may represent the marketing team of the hotel, who will use the hotel as a tool to create sales for the hotel chain. There may also be Senior Users who represent actual customers of the hotel, such as a market research company who are experts on the business traveler.

During the Starting up a Project process, the Senior Users are responsible for ensuring that the customer's quality expectations and the acceptance criteria correctly define products that are fit for their purpose. They work with the Project Manager to document the customer's quality expectations and acceptance criteria in the Project Product Description. It is the responsibility of the Project Manager to create the Project Product Description.

After the Starting up a Project process, the Project Board reviews the Project Brief. The Project Brief contains the Project Product Description along with other outputs from Starting up a Project, such as the outline Business Case. The Project Board uses the information in the Project Brief to decide whether to commission the project. They make this decision in the Directing a Project process.

Step 2: Initiation Stage

During the initiation stage, the Project Manager is responsible for the activities in the Initiating a Project process. One of these activities is to prepare the Quality Management Strategy. The Quality Management Strategy sets out how the project will be managed to ensure that the outputs meet the customer's needs. The next section of this chapter, "The Quality Management Strategy," describes this management product in more detail, but for now, all you need to know is that it establishes how quality planning, quality control, and quality assurance are to be carried out during the project. It also describes the various documents (such as the Quality Register), roles, and reports that have to be created in order to manage the quality of the products effectively.

During the initiation stage, the Project Product Description is reviewed and refined if necessary.

Step 3: Product-Based Planning Technique

As the project progresses, the specification details contained in the Project Product Description will probably be too broad to plan the building of all the individual components that the project will create. To resolve this problem, the Project Manager creates Product Descriptions that describe all the components of the main outputs from the project. In the hotel example, the Project Manager might create Product Descriptions for the hotel's lobby, the different types of bedrooms, the restaurant, and so on.

A product's description is created at the same time as the plan that shows the activities needed to create it. For example, the Project Plan shows how to create the major products of the project and also contains the Product Descriptions for these major products. In the hotel example, these major products might be things like the hotel lobby and the different types of rooms. The Project Manager creates the Project Plan and the accompanying Product Descriptions in the Initiating a Project process.

The Initiating a Project process may not be the only place where Product Descriptions are created in the PRINCE2 process model. When the Project Manager develops the Stage Plans, he can create more detailed Product Descriptions or refine old ones to aid in the planning of that stage. When Team Managers create Team Plans, they might also create even more detailed Product Descriptions.

In the hotel example, imagine that the Project Manager is planning the stage during which the swimming pool will be constructed. He does this planning during the Managing a Stage Boundary process. First, the Project Manager creates a Product Description for the swimming pool (unless it has already been created). This Product Description describes the measurable quality criteria for the pool, such as the dimensions, the materials that will be used to construct it, and the type of heating system that will be used. It also defines what quality methods will be used after the pool's construction to test the product's compliance with the quality criteria. For example, perhaps safety tests can be applied to check the pool. Finally, the Product Description describes the quality responsibilities, such as who is responsible for producing the pool, reviewing it, and finally approving it.

Step 4: Planning the Quality Checks

When the Project Manager is planning the work for creating the products in any stage, he also plans the quality control activities needed to confirm that the right product has been built. For each quality check planned, the Project Manager creates a corresponding entry in the Quality Register, just as you saw in the "Using the Quality Register" section earlier. So for the swimming pool example, the Project Manager may make separate Quality Register entries for the dimension quality check, the safety test quality check, and a test of the swimming pool's heating system.

Step 5: Building, Checking, and Approving the Products

During the fifth step, the swimming pool is built. The Project Manager authorizes a Team Manager or a team to carry out this work by creating a Work Package in the Controlling a Stage process. The Work Package contains the Product Descriptions of all the products that the team needs to create, such as the Product Description for the swimming pool. The team accepts the responsibility for creating the pool in their Managing Product Delivery process. They review the planned quality checks of the pool shown in the Quality Register with Project Assurance to see if any further reviewers are necessary. If so, they update the Quality Register with the names of these additional reviewers.

Then the pool is created and its quality checked by the people indicated in the pool's Product Description. This occurs during the Managing Product Delivery process. At this time, the pool is measured, the heating system is checked, and so on.

The Work Package that the Team Manager received details the procedure for updating the Quality Register with the results of the quality checks. It is the responsibility of the Team Manager (or the team if there is no Team Manager) to ensure that the Quality Register is updated with the results of the quality checks. The Project Manager reviews this updated Quality Register when reviewing the Work Package status during the Controlling a Stage process.

Finally, after the pool has passed all of its quality checks, it is approved. PRINCE2 reserves the word "approval" for signing off on an individual product of the project (as opposed to acceptance, which is another type of sign-off, as you'll see in a moment). The Product Description of the swimming pool describes who should approve the product. It is the responsibility of the Team Manager (or the team if there is no Team Manager) to obtain evidence that the project has passed all of its quality checks (by obtaining quality records) and that the project has been approved (by obtaining approval records). These records are referenced in the Quality Register and sent to Project Support for filing.

Step 6: Accepting the Products

The final step is getting acceptances for the project's products. Acceptance in PRINCE2 is different from approval. Acceptance of the project's products is the ultimate approval. It is when the products transfer from the ownership of the project team to the customer or the group that will maintain or operate the products for the customer.

In all projects, a handover takes place of the products to the final client (or their operational representatives) at the end of the project. For example, at the end of the hotel project, the hotel is handed over to the operational team, who need to give their acceptance. It is the Project Manager's responsibility to obtain this acceptance during the Closing a Project process.

In some projects, there may also be some interim products delivered during the project. For example, in the hotel project, perhaps the gym is built and delivered before the end of the project. The gym's operational team needs to give the project management team a formal acceptance that they have taken ownership of the gym. It is the Project Manager's responsibility to obtain this acceptance. These interim acceptances are obtained during the Managing a Stage Boundary process.

In both cases, PRINCE2 states that records of the acceptance should be kept. As you learned earlier in this chapter in the "Quality Control" section, these are called acceptance records.

The Quality Management Strategy

The Project Manager creates the Quality Management Strategy in the Initiating a Project process. This strategy defines how the project will be managed to ensure that products of the right quality will be created. Figure 6.8 shows the composition of the Quality Management Strategy.

FIGURE 6.8 The composition of the Quality Management Strategy

As you can see in Figure 6.8, the Quality Management Strategy has seven sections. The following descriptions use the hotel project example to give you an idea of what sort of information should be included in each section.

Introduction

The introduction establishes the purpose and objectives of the Quality Management Strategy. The purpose in the hotel example is to ensure that the project creates a hotel that meets the acceptance criteria defined in the Project Product Description and that the project complies with all relevant construction and safety standards. It also states who is responsible for the Quality Management Strategy. In the hotel example, this may be the Project Board.

Quality Management Procedure

This section sets out the variety of steps, activities, and templates (such as Product Descriptions) that will be used to ensure the correct products are built. It covers the following three quality management areas:

Quality Planning   This section addresses the steps that will be taken throughout the project to define the specifications for the overall products in the Project Product Description and the individual products in the Product Descriptions. In the hotel project, this may include defining the steps that will be taken to specify the designs of the hotel, such as working with architects to create prototype models, then moving on to detailed computer-aided design drawings.

Quality Control   This section addresses the steps that will be taken throughout the project to verify that the correct products are being or have been built. It defines quality standards to be followed, such as building or construction standards. It provides templates or forms, including the Quality Register or quality records (such as sign-off forms). There may be a certain set of quality methods that will be used repeatedly throughout the project. In the hotel project example, a fire and safety test may be required on the entire building. Such standard types of quality methods are defined here. Finally, in some cases, certain metrics are used to help determine whether the products comply with their specifications. In the hotel example, the rooms may be checked for soundproofing using the decibel range. The quality control section specifies that decibels will be used and defines threshold levels the rooms must comply to.

Quality Assurance   Throughout the project, one area of quality assurance activities may be to carry out a number of compliance audits. For example, in the hotel project, the hotel chain wants to check that the construction company is following engineering and health and safety standards. This section shows how these compliance audits are to be carried out.

There may already be a number of procedures for quality management defined at a corporate level, in which case these procedures do not have to be repeated—the Quality Management Strategy can simply refer to them. For example, there may be a procedure that is used before the opening of a new hotel, to check that all the systems are working correctly and the hotel is ready for its first customers.

In the hotel project, the construction work will probably have been outsourced to a construction company. This construction company will follow many industry-defined standards such as health and safety and engineering standards. This section of the Quality Management Strategy can refer to these supplier standards.

Tools and Techniques

In any project, there may be specific tools or techniques used during various parts of the quality management procedure. For example, in the construction of the hotel, a variety of tools are typically used to check the safe construction of the hotel, such as a fire safety check. Or there may be a special technique for checking the soundproofing of rooms.

Records

This chapter has covered a variety of quality records that should be kept to prove that products have been signed off correctly. There may be records to show that a product has passed a variety of quality checks, records to show that products have been approved (approval records), and records to show that products have been passed over to the clients or the operational teams (acceptance records). This section defines the format of these records, where they will be stored, and how they will be used.

This section also describes the composition and format of the Quality Register.

Reporting

This section describes any quality management reports, what their purposes are, their timing, and who they should go to.

In the hotel project example, the Project Board wants to see a variety of information about quality in the End Stage Report:

- The quality activities that took place during the stage and their results
- The products that were approved during this stage
- The off-specifications that were approved (products that did not comply with their Product Descriptions but were approved anyway)
- The acceptances that occurred during the stage

Timing of Quality Management Activities

This section states when formal quality management activities will take place. In the hotel project example, a health and safety compliance audit of the construction work may take place at the end of each stage.

Roles and Responsibilities

This section describes the roles and responsibilities for quality management activities. For example, the Senior Users are responsible for checking the Product Descriptions to see whether they meet their expectations, and the Project Manager is responsible for checking that each Stage Plan contains quality checks for all the products to be created and that there is an entry for these quality checks in the Quality Register.

The Quality Review Technique

The *quality review technique* is a way of checking the compliance of a product with its Product Description. It is primarily designed to assess products that take the form of a document or something similar, such as a presentation. However, it could be used for any type of appropriate product.

The quality review technique entails three steps:

Step 1—Preparation   First, a *chair* is appointed, who will run the quality review technique process. A *presenter* is then appointed, who will represent the producer of the product under review. The presenter sends the product and its Product Description to a number of *reviewers*, who will perform a quality check on the product to see whether it complies with its Product Description. If the reviewers spot any small grammatical or typing errors, they can write directly on the document. If the reviewers spot any larger errors, they start creating a question list for the presenter. An *administrator* is also appointed to help out with . . . guess what . . . administration!

Step 2—Review Meeting   A meeting is held to review the product and is attended by all the quality review technique roles. During this meeting, the attendees discuss the questions that the reviewers have about the product. The outcome of the meeting is one of the following: the product is deemed complete and signed off; it is deemed conditionally complete, and the presenter has a number of actions to remedy a few quality problems; or the product is deemed incomplete. In the latter case, the whole quality review technique will have to be repeated at a later date, after the problems with the product have been dealt with.

Step 3—Review Follow-up   If there were follow-up actions to remedy problems with the product, these are coordinated by the presenter and then signed off by the reviewers. The chair then signs off that the product is complete.

If the quality review technique is used, it is done in the Managing Product Delivery process. The quality review technique roles can more or less be carried out by anyone, as long as there is no conflict of interest such as someone producing a product and then reviewing it. The product's Product Descriptions specify who will carry out the various quality review technique roles for its review.

After a document-based product has gone through the quality review technique, and it has been signed off, no changes should be made to it. It is in a state that PRINCE2 calls baselined. (You'll learn more about baselines in Chapter 8, "Change Theme.") If someone wants to make changes, they must create a new version of the product and make their changes to that version.

The quality review technique is useful for involving key interested parties in the product and getting them to buy into the product. Sometimes at the end of a project, disputes arise about whether a product is correct. However, if the people disputing the quality of the product were involved with signing off the product, it is more difficult for them to complain!

Roles Involved with the Quality Theme

This chapter described the various roles that are involved with the Quality theme. Here is a quick review of these roles to help you prepare for the exams:

Corporate or Programme Management   Provides a quality assurance function.

Executive   Approves all the main quality management products, such as the Project Product Description and the Quality Management Strategy, and confirms the acceptance of the main outputs of the project.

Senior User(s)   Involved with specifying the project's products in the Project Product Description and the Product Descriptions, providing resources to verify that the correct products have been created and accepted, and approving the key products.

Senior Supplier(s)   Involved with reviewing the specifications for the products set out in the Project Product Description and the Product Descriptions to verify that they are feasible to deliver. They approve the quality methods, tools, and techniques that are set out in the Quality Management Strategy and the Product Descriptions to confirm that they will create the products to a necessary level of quality.

Project Manager   Creates all the major quality management products, such as the Quality Management Strategy, Project Product Description, Product Descriptions, and Quality Register. He liaises closely with the Senior Users, Senior Suppliers, Executive, and the Team Manager (or the teams if there is no Team Manager) in order to do so. When he authorizes work to the teams, he ensures that the correct quality control work is carried out.

Team Manager   Creates the products to comply with his Product Descriptions, ensuring that the correct quality control is carried out and that there is evidence of the quality activities with quality records. He reviews the Quality Register to ensure that it is updated with the results of quality activities. If there is no Team Manager, then these responsibilities are taken on by the team members.

Project Assurance   Assures the Project Board that the Quality Management Strategy is implemented correctly. Provides advice and guidance to the Project Manager, Team Managers, or the team members if there are no Team Managers, and those involved with quality activities on the application of the Quality Management Strategy and the suitability of quality reviewers and approvers.

Project Support   Provides administrative support and assistance; maintains the Quality Register and the quality records.

Summary

In this chapter, you learned about the PRINCE2 Quality theme. The Quality theme ensures that a project creates products that are fit for their purpose.

The first thing you learned in this chapter was the PRINCE2 meaning of the word *quality*. In everyday speech, *quality* is often used to mean luxury. However, in PRINCE2, quality means fit for purpose. Quality management is the means by which a project ensures that products that are fit for purpose are created. There are four components to quality management: a quality system, which defines an approach to quality; a quality assurance function, which checks that the quality system is being implemented; quality planning, where the specifications of the products are defined; and quality control, which is a set of activities to verify that the right products have been or are being built.

Two important management products are involved with quality planning: the Project Product Description and the Product Descriptions. The Project Product Description describes the overall characteristics of the major output(s) of the project. Product Descriptions provide lower-level specifications for each of the components that the major outputs consist of.

You saw that there is one important management product used for quality control: the Quality Register. This register is used to track all the quality checks that are carried out on the project's products. It contains information about when the check took place, who was involved, and whether the check passed or failed.

The Quality Management Strategy defines how the project will approach the four aspects of quality management. The Project Manager creates the Quality Management Strategy during the initiation stage of the project.

The final part of the Quality theme that you learned about in this chapter is the quality review technique. This gives a particular approach for reviewing paper-based documents and verifying whether they have been created in accordance with their Product Description.

Exam Essentials

Know the purpose and scope of the Quality theme. The purpose of the quality theme is to ensure that products that are fit for their purpose are produced by the project. The Quality theme covers the four areas of quality management: quality systems, quality assurance, quality planning, and quality control.

Define the difference between quality planning and quality control. Quality planning defines the characteristics of the project's products that will make them fit for their purpose and shows how these characteristics will be verified. Quality control is the activity of verifying that the project's products have been created according to their Product Descriptions.

Define the difference between Project Assurance and quality assurance. Quality assurance is the responsibility of corporate or programme management and involves independently monitoring the project's organization, processes, and products to assess whether the quality requirements will be met. Project Assurance is the responsibility of the Project Board and involves monitoring that the project is being conducted properly.

Define the difference between a customer's quality expectations and acceptance criteria. The customer's quality expectations describe the overall level of quality expected of the project's products and the standards and processes that must be applied to achieve that quality. Acceptance criteria are a prioritized list of measurable criteria that the project's products must meet before the customer will accept them.

Understand the quality planning activities that take place using the Project Product Description and which roles are responsible for these actions.   The Project Manager, with the help of the Senior User and the Executive, creates the Project Product Description that outlines the customer's quality expectations and the acceptance criteria. The Project Product Description describes the acceptance method, showing how the product will be checked for compliance with its acceptance criteria and who is responsible for accepting the products.

Understand that quality planning involves describing how the project will be managed with respect to quality and which roles are responsible for these actions.   The Project Manager creates the Quality Management Strategy that describes how the project will be managed with respect to quality.

Understand the quality planning activities that take place using the Product Descriptions and which roles are responsible for these actions.   The Project Manager, with the help of the Senior User, creates Product Descriptions that contain the quality criteria for each product. The Product Descriptions describe the quality methods to be used to verify that the products comply with their quality criteria and who is responsible for carrying out the quality methods and approving the products.

Understand the quality control actions that take place in a project and know which roles are responsible for these actions.   The person indicated in a product's Product Description carries out quality control actions to verify that the product matches its quality criteria and that quality and approval records should be kept as evidence that the product has been checked and approved. The person specified in the Project Product Description carries out the ultimate approval of a product, and acceptance records should be kept as evidence of a product's ultimate approval.

Understand how to carry out quality methods.   Each product's completeness is verified by using quality methods defined in that product's Product Description.

Know that the PRINCE2 approach to quality is also called the quality audit trail.   Throughout a PRINCE2 project, a series of auditable records are created as evidence that quality planning and control activities have taken place.

Know the purpose and composition of the Project Product Description and in which processes it is developed, used, and reviewed, and which roles are responsible for each.   The purpose of the Project Product Description is to describe the customer's quality expectations and acceptance criteria, to outline the method and responsibilities for the project, and to gain agreement with the user on the project's scope and requirements. The Project Manager creates the Project Product Description during Starting up a Project, refines it in Initiating a Project, and may update it during Managing a Stage Boundary.

Know the purpose and composition of the Product Description and in which processes it is developed, used, and reviewed, and which roles are responsible for each.   The purpose of the Product Description is to understand the nature, purpose, function, and appearance of the product. It contains the product's quality criteria, the quality methods, and the quality responsibilities. The Project Manager creates Product Descriptions during Initiating a Project when creating the Project Plan and during Managing a Stage Boundary when creating a Stage or Exception Plan. The Team Manager creates Product Descriptions when creating the Team Plans during Managing Product Delivery.

Know the purpose and composition of the Quality Register and in which processes it is developed, used, and reviewed, and which roles are responsible for each.   The Quality Register is used to summarize all the project's quality management activities and provide information for the End Stage Reports and End Project Reports. The Project Manager creates the Quality Register in Initiating a Project and updates it when planning a stage during Managing a Stage Boundary with the details of planned quality checks. The authority defined in the Work Package updates the Quality Register with the results of quality checks during the Managing Product Delivery process.

Know the purpose and composition of the Quality Management Strategy and in which processes it is developed, used, and reviewed, and which roles are responsible for each.   The purpose of the Quality Management Strategy is to describe how the project will be managed with respect to quality. The Project Manager creates the Quality Management Strategy during Initiating a Project.

Understand the objectives of the quality review technique.   The objectives of the quality review technique are to assess the conformity of a product with its quality criteria, to involve key interested parties, and to baseline a product for change control.

Understand the responsibilities of the various quality review technique roles.   The chair has overall responsibility for the quality review technique, the reviewers review the product, the presenter represents the producer of the product, and the administrator provides support.

Be familiar with the actions that take place in the quality review technique.   The three main stages of the quality review technique are review preparation, review meeting, and review follow-up.

Review Questions

The rest of this chapter contains mock exam questions, first for the Foundation exam and then for the Practitioner exam.

Foundation Questions

1. Which of the following roles is responsible for creating Product Descriptions during a project?
    - **A.** Executive
    - **B.** Senior User
    - **C.** Senior Supplier
    - **D.** Project Manager

2. Which of these is **NOT** a recommended quality review team role?
    - **A.** Scribe
    - **B.** Chair
    - **C.** Presenter
    - **D.** Administrator

3. Which of the following statements are true of both Project Assurance and Quality Assurance?
    - **1.** They provide assurance that the project is being run to corporate standards.
    - **2.** They are independent of the managing level of the project management team.
    - **3.** The role is carried out on behalf of the business, user, and supplier perspectives of the Project Board.
    - **4.** They check that adequate quality planning and control processes are in place.
    - **A.** 1, 2, 3
    - **B.** 1, 2, 4
    - **C.** 1, 3, 4
    - **D.** 2, 3, 4

4. Which of the following is an objective of the quality review technique?
    - **A.** To provide quality feedback to the producer during the creation of a product
    - **B.** To determine a customer's quality expectations of a product
    - **C.** To carry out a series of quality activities that will prepare a product so that it is ready for approval
    - **D.** To define a range of standard quality methods appropriate for the project

5. Identify the missing word(s) in the following sentence:

    [?] is achieved by implementing, monitoring, and recording the quality methods of the project.

    A. Quality planning

    B. Quality control

    C. Quality assurance

    D. Project assurance

6. Which of the following is a purpose of the Project Product Description?

    A. To gain agreement from the user on the project's scope and requirements

    B. To define how the project will be managed in order to deliver products that are fit for their purpose

    C. To define how the project will control uncertainty

    D. To define how the project will track, protect, and control the project's products

7. Which of the following is **NOT** a quality planning activity?

    A. Creating Product Descriptions to understand what is required of a product

    B. Scheduling the development activities of a product so that it will match its Product Description

    C. Deriving acceptance criteria from a customer's quality expectations

    D. Defining the quality methods that will be used to check that a product conforms to its quality criteria

8. Which of the following provides evidence that the quality checks referred to in the Quality Register have been carried out?

    A. Product Description

    B. Configuration Item Record

    C. Quality records

    D. Sign-off forms

9. When describing a car to be produced for a project, which of the following options is an example of acceptance criteria?

    A. Produce an environmentally friendly car.

    B. Produce a car that can run for 100 miles per gallon.

    C. Produce a luxury car.

    D. Produce a car with an attractive metallic finish.

10. Which management product should the Team Manager check for the procedure to update the Quality Register?

    A. Checkpoint Report

    B. Quality Management Strategy

    C. Work Package

    D. Project Initiation Documentation

Practitioner Questions

The Practitioner questions in Sections 1, 2, and 3 are based on the Practitioner exam scenario that you will find in the Introduction to this book.

Section 1: Multiple Response Questions

Answer the following two questions about the processes in which the Quality Register is developed, used, and reviewed, and which roles are responsible for each. Remember to limit your answers to the number of selections requested in each question.

1. During which of the following two activities is the Quality Register updated?

   A. Starting up a Project, when preparing the Project Product Description

   B. Managing a Stage Boundary, when planning the next stage

   C. Controlling a Stage, when reviewing the Work Package status

   D. Managing Product Delivery, when accepting a Work Package

   E. Closing a Project, when handing over products

2. Which two roles are responsible for updating the Quality Register?

   A. Executive

   B. Senior User

   C. Project Manager

   D. Team Manager

   E. Project Assurance

Section 2: Sequence Type

Column 1 in the following table lists quality activities that might be performed related to the request for tender document that will be sent to potential web design companies. For each activity in Column 1, decide whether it was an appropriate application of PRINCE2, and if so, select the order in which it should have been performed from Column 2. Note that not all of the answers in Column 2 might be used.

Column 1	Column 2
1. Create a Project Product Description identifying the request for tender document in the composition section.	A. First
2. Use the quality review technique to check that the request for tender document is of the required standard.	B. Second
3. Create a Product Description for the request for tender document, defining its composition and how it will comply with Quality Furniture standards.	C. Third

(continued)

Column 1	Column 2
4. Identify the quality review technique as a standard quality method in the quality management procedure section of the Quality Management Strategy.	D. Fourth
5. Obtain an acceptance record from the Project Board for the request for tender document at the end of Stage 2 during the end stage assessment meeting.	E. Fifth
6. Obtain an approval record from the person identified in the request for tender document's Product Description as the approver.	F. Sixth
	G. Not appropriate

Section 3: Multiple Response Type

In addition to being based on the example practitioner scenario described in the Introduction to this Study Guide, this section is based on the following "Quality Notes from the Daily Log" and the Quality Register. After reviewing all of this information, answer the questions about the use of the Quality Register during stage 3 of the project, which you will find under "Multiple Response Questions."

Quality Notes from the Daily Log

Digital Design will create designs for each type of page on the website. The designs describe the format and layout of each web page and the type of information they will hold. Quality Furniture's marketing director and IT manager will review the web page designs and approve them using the PRINCE2 quality review technique. The IT manager will check that the designs comply with international standards on web page accessibility for the visually impaired. The chief executive will give approval to all the web page designs once they have all gone through a quality check.

Quality Furniture's marketing department, led by the marketing director, will create a plan for the website content, specifying the information each page on the website is to contain. The chief executive, who has taken on the Executive role in the project, wants to review this plan and approve it using the PRINCE2 quality review technique. The information must be checked for compliance against Quality Furniture's branding standards.

The IT manager will create a technical design indicating the computer and networking hardware needed to run the new website. It will also show how the website will link to the Quality Furniture sales system. This technical design will need to comply with Quality Furniture's IT standards. Digital Design will need to review and approve this technical design to check that it is compatible with their standards for building websites. The IT manager's assistant will check the technical design using Quality Furniture's standard technical review process.

As the Senior Supplier assurance representative, the Firsttech consultant will provide advice and guidance on the quality activities to review the stage 3 products.

During the review of the plan for the website content, the chief executive found that it did not conform to the branding standards and rejected the product. However, the marketing director amended the plan for the website content within the delivery schedule, and another quality review took place a few days later. This time, the chief executive signed off on the plan.

During the review of the technical design, the IT manager's assistant noticed that there was an error in the specification for the link to the sales system. The IT manager amended this and resubmitted the plan for another a quality review. The plan passed the second quality review.

The following image shows draft Quality Register entries that were made during stage 3. This draft contains errors, which you will be asked about in the following "Multiple Response Questions."

Quality Register (contains errors)

Quality Identifier	01	02	03	04
Product Identifier	WEBPAGE01	PRODPAGE01	CONTENTPLAN01	TECHDESIGN
Product Title	Design for the Website Home Page	Design for the Website Product Page	Plan for the Website Content	Technical Design
Quality Method	Quality Review Technique	Quality Review Technique Use software to create the design.	Quality Review Technique	Quality Review Technique
Roles and Responsibilities (People are from Quality Furniture, unless otherwise specified.)	Presenter: IT Manager Reviewer: Marketing Director Chair: Project Manager	Presenter: Digital Design's Operations Manager Reviewer: IT Manager, Marketing Director Chair: Marketing Director	Presenter: Marketing Assistant Reviewer: Chief Executive	Reviewer: Digital Design's Operations Manager, IT Manager's Assistant
Target Review Date	June 10	June 14	June 11	June 15
Target Sign-off Date	June 11	June 15	June 11	June 16
Actual Review Date	June 10	June 16	June 11	June 15
Actual Sign-off Date	June 10	June 20	June 11	June 16
Result	Pass	Pass	Pass	Pass
Quality Records	NONE	Acceptance record in the form of signatures from reviewers	An initial quality review found that the plan did not conform to branding standards. The Marketing Director was tasked to correct this. The plan was amended and passed during a second quality review.	Quality Furniture IT Standards

Multiple Response Questions

Answer the following four questions about the use of the Quality Register during stage 3 of the project. Remember to limit your answers to the number of selections requested in each question.

1. Which two statements apply to the entry from the Quality Register with quality identifier 01?

   A. Delete the information about the quality method, because the quality review technique is only appropriate for management products.

   B. Move the Quality Furniture's IT manager to the reviewer role, because someone from Digital Design would be more suitable as a presenter.

   C. Amend the chair role to be the operations manager of Quality Furniture, because only someone independent of the project management team should take on this role.

   D. Amend the actual sign-off date, because it is before the target sign-off date.

   E. Add a reference to the international standards for web pages that will be used during the quality inspection of the quality records.

2. Which two statements apply to the entry from the Quality Register with quality identifier 02?

   A. Delete the information in the quality method row about using the software to create the design, because this is a development approach.

   B. Amend the person taking on the chair role to the Project Manager, because one person cannot be a chair and a reviewer.

   C. Add the Chief Executive as an approver in the roles and responsibilities section.

   D. Amend the target review date to correspond to the target sign-off date, because products must be signed off during their review.

   E. Delete the information against the quality records, because acceptance records are only obtained for the ultimate approval of the project's products.

3. Which two statements apply to the entry from the Quality Register with quality identifier 03?

   A. Amend the person taking on the reviewer role to the marketing director, because the Executive of a PRINCE2 project cannot take on a reviewer role.

   B. Amend the person taking on the presenter role to the marketing director, because the marketing assistant is too inexperienced for this role.

   C. Amend the result as "fail," because another separate entry in the Quality Register needs to be created for the second quality review that signed off the plan.

   D. Amend the quality record information, because it should not contain details of how to correct errors found in the product.

   E. Amend the quality record information, because it should not contain details of another quality review event.

4. Which two statements apply to the entry from the Quality Register with quality identifier 04?

A. Amend the quality method used to the Quality Furniture standard technical review process.

B. Delete the reference to the Digital Design operations manager taking on the reviewer role, because external suppliers cannot review the project's products.

C. Add a suitable person to take on the chair role, because all quality checks must include a chair role.

D. Change the result to "fail," because another separate Quality Register entry should be created for the reassessment of the designs.

E. Delete the reference to the Quality Furniture IT standards in the quality records section, because this entry should only include a reference to evidence that the product has been signed off.

Chapter

7

Risk Theme

PRINCE2 EXAM OBJECTIVES COVERED IN THIS CHAPTER:

- ✓ Know the PRINCE2 definition of a risk and understand the difference between a threat and an opportunity.

- ✓ Understand the purpose of the Risk theme.

- ✓ Understand the risk management procedure.

- ✓ Understand how to define a risk using cause, effect, and objectives.

- ✓ Understand how to measure a risk's probability, impact, and proximity.

- ✓ Define risk response types and understand which are used to respond to a threat or an opportunity.

- ✓ Know the difference between a Risk Owner and a Risk Actionee.

- ✓ Know the purpose of a Risk Management Strategy, its recommended composition, in which processes it is used, and which roles are responsible for it.

- ✓ Know the purpose of a Risk Register, its recommended composition, in which processes it is used, and which roles are responsible for it.

- ✓ Understand the concept of inherent, secondary, and residual risks.

- ✓ Understand the concept of risk appetite and risk tolerance.

- ✓ Know how to use a risk budget.

- ✓ Understand risk responsibilities.

- ✓ Link risk management with the other elements of PRINCE2.

Because of the unique nature of projects, you will face many potential threats and opportunities when managing them. Rather than passively waiting for threats or opportunities to materialize, you use risk management to deal with them proactively. The PRINCE2 Risk theme provides a simple but effective procedure for managing risks. The approach includes steps that help you identify, assess, and control potential risks in your project, as well as effectively communicate the risk situation to the project stakeholders. The Risk theme helps you increase the likelihood of delivering the benefits from a project by managing the uncertainty associated with the initiative.

Why Are Projects So Risky?

One of the challenges that you face when managing a project is uncertainty. This varies from project to project. Imagine you were managing the Apollo missions to send a man to the moon—it would be difficult for you to predict exactly how things would turn out. At the other extreme, imagine you are working for a hotel business and your job is to manage building new sites. When you're ready to build a new hotel, even though it might be at a new location, with a different design and some new personnel, it will be far easier for you to predict things.

The amount of uncertainty therefore depends on how familiar the project situation is to those involved with the initiative, and this is a key indicator of your likely overall exposure to risk. Basically, when you are unclear as to how things might turn out, all sorts of things could go wrong!

Now let's compare this uncertainty with the amount of risk you face in nonproject or business-as-usual work. Here, there is little uniqueness or uncertainty—what you do one week is probably pretty similar to what you did the week before. For example, once you've built the hotel and it is open for business, every week will be a cycle of cleaning rooms, cooking for guests, checking them in and out, and so on. You can far more easily predict potential problems, so there is far less risk.

The PRINCE2 Approach to Risk

Given the fact that all projects contain an amount of risk, how does PRINCE2 deal with this? Basically, it disciplines everyone involved with the project to regularly ask the following questions:

- What could potentially go wrong?
- What could the team do (or plan to do) that would reduce the effects of these threats on the project?
- What potential opportunities could occur?
- What could the team do to enhance the effects of these opportunities on the project?

One interesting thing to note is that PRINCE2 uses the word *risk* to cover potential opportunities as well as threats (more on this in the next section). Once you have asked these questions, PRINCE2 ensures that you carry out your responses to the risks.

How does PRINCE2 implement risk management? There are various parts to it, which I've set out here. Don't worry—we'll go through all of these in more depth throughout this chapter.

Risk Management Strategy   At the outset, you write a Risk Management Strategy, which specifies how you are going to manage risk on the project.

Risk Responsibilities   All the PRINCE2 roles have risk management responsibilities.

Risk Management Procedure   The PRINCE2 risk management procedure involves a number of general risk management steps, or "things to do." You must ensure these happen regularly throughout the project.

Risk Management Products   PRINCE2 gives you a number of management products (usually documents) where you can store risk-related information, such as the Risk Register and the Risk Management Strategy.

PRINCE2's risk management approach should reduce the effect of risk on your project and thus increase the likelihood of its success. This is basically the purpose of the Risk theme.

How Does PRINCE2 Use the Word *Risk*?

Normally, when you talk about facing risk, you think of it as a negative thing. My dictionary defines risk as "the possibility of incurring misfortune or loss." For example, it might rain, which would slow down the building of your hotel. However, PRINCE2 also thinks of risk as the possibility of good things occurring. For example, the price of concrete might fall and reduce your construction costs.

The definition of risk according to *Managing Successful Projects with PRINCE2* (Stationery Office, 2009) is "An uncertain event or set of events that, should it occur, will have an effect on the achievement of objectives." There are two types of uncertain events:

Threats   *Threats* are events that, if they occur, would have a negative effect on the project.

Opportunities   *Opportunities* are events that, if they occur, would have a positive effect on the project.

Planning How to Manage Risk on the Project

In PRINCE2, you set out how you will manage risk in the Risk Management Strategy. In this section, I will explain why you should have such a strategy and describe what it should contain.

An Example of a Risk Management Approach

How does a Project Manager lower the project's exposure to risk? Let me give you an example. The Project Manager decides on a simple approach. First, every Monday morning at 9:00 a.m., he chairs a risk management workshop with all members of the project management team. During the workshop, the Project Manager ensures that the following activities are covered:

- Attempt to spot any new project threats or opportunities. The Project Manager decides to facilitate the group using a "brainstorming" technique. He asks each individual to write down as many new risks as they can think of on sticky notes. Then the group puts all the sticky notes on a whiteboard and eliminates any duplicates. Seeing everyone else's risks may spur people to think of new ones.

- The group then decides how to respond to these new risks.

- Finally, the group reviews previously identified risks. Are they getting worse or better? Is the way the project management team is responding to those risks helping? Is there anything else the team can do to mitigate these risks?

After the workshop, the Project Manager has several other responsibilities:

- He must record all information about each risk in a central Risk Register.

- He must make sure that the team's decisions on risk responses are carried out.

- He must report on the current risk situation in his weekly progress reports.

- He must ensure that Project Assurance is aware of this approach to risk management and that they audit it on a regular basis.

This example is a repeatable approach that the Project Manager can use throughout the project to lower the exposure to threats and increase the exposure to opportunities. It is basically what PRINCE2 calls a Risk Management Strategy. It may be simple, but in my experience, even this approach is a more robust way of managing risk than the one many large-scale projects use!

Using the Risk Management Strategy

In Figure 7.1, you can see the composition of the Risk Management Strategy. This is the management product that the Project Manager in the preceding example uses to document his approach to risk during the project. Over the next few pages, I will show you what information he would put in each section.

FIGURE 7.1   Composition of the Risk Management Strategy

Risk Management Strategy

- Introduction
- Risk management procedure
- Tools and techniques
- Records
- Reporting
- Timing of risk management activities
- Roles and responsibilites
- Scales
- Proximity
- Risk categories
- Risk response categories
- Early warning indicators
- Risk tolerance
- Risk budget

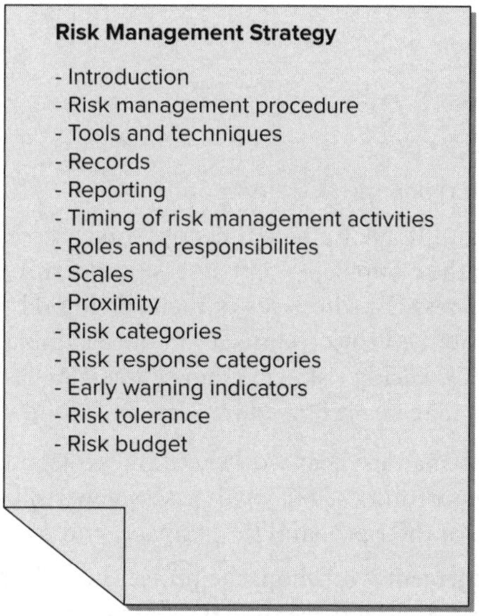

Exam Spotlight

Remember that during the Practitioner exam, you will be able to refer to *Managing Successful Projects with PRINCE2*. This is particularly useful for questions about management products such as the Risk Management Strategy. Appendix A of *Managing Successful Projects with PRINCE2* sets out the composition of the Risk Management Strategy and gives brief notes on what should be in each section. This means that you don't need to memorize all the sections of all the management products for the Practitioner exam.

One interesting point to note about the Risk Management Strategy is that six of the headings are the same ones that you find in the other strategy management products: Procedure, Tools and Techniques, Records, Reporting, Timing, and Roles and Responsibilities. The other strategy management products are the Quality Management Strategy, which I cover in Chapter 6, "Quality Theme," the Configuration Management Strategy, which I cover in Chapter 8, "Change Theme," and the Communication Management Strategy, which I cover in Chapter 3, "Organization Theme."

Risk Management Procedure

This section contains the generic steps that the Project Manager regularly performs to deal with risk. PRINCE2 recommends that whatever process the Project Manager chooses, it should cover the following five basic areas of risk management:

- Identifying risks
- Assessing risks
- Planning your responses to risks
- Implementing your responses
- Communicating to everyone the risk situation

Looking at the steps that PRINCE2 recommends, you can see that the Project Manager has covered all of them in the example, except assessing risks. As you will see later, PRINCE2 allows you to assess risks in terms of their likelihood, impact, and proximity (when they might occur). So the Project Manager in our example will add a step that includes another aim for the weekly risk workshops: assessing risks. The Project Manager can then write the Risk Management Procedure section as follows:

> During the weekly risk management workshop, the project management team will spot any new threats or opportunities. They will assess new risks and reassess previously spotted risks in terms of their probabilities, impact, and potential timings.

> During the risk management workshop, the project management team will also plan responses to any threats that will lessen their effect on the project, and plan responses to any opportunities that will increase their effect on the project.

> After the meeting, the responses will be put into action and monitored and tracked to ensure they are implemented.

> A weekly review of risks will be included in the weekly project progress report.

Tools and Techniques

In this section, the Project Manager describes any risk management tools or techniques. These can include techniques for carrying out any part of the risk management procedure, such as how to identify risks or how to estimate a risk's probability or impact. In the example, the Project Manager uses a "brainstorming" technique for identifying risks. The Tools and Techniques section describes the risk technique as follows:

> During the risk management workshops, use a brainstorming technique to spot threats and opportunities. The brainstorming technique involves the following steps:
>
> 1. Each member of the project management team should individually write down at least 20 new risks on separate sticky notes.
>
> 2. The Project Manager puts the sticky notes on a whiteboard, removing any duplicates.
>
> 3. The team reviews the sticky notes to see if they prompt any new risk ideas and removes any that don't make sense.

Exam Spotlight

In the example, the Project Manager has set out a brainstorming risk identification technique. There are quite a number of other techniques that he could have used. *Managing Successful Projects with PRINCE2* lists four more in the Risk theme chapter: review lessons, risk checklists, risk prompt lists, and risk breakdown structure. *Managing Successful Projects with PRINCE2* also gives a range of risk estimation techniques such as probability trees, expected value, Pareto analysis, and probability impact grid. However, you won't be tested on how any of these techniques work—you just need to know that these approaches would be described in the Tools and Techniques section of the Risk Management Strategy.

Records

In this section, the Project Manager describes how he plans to store the information on all the individual risks. Our example was a bit sketchy on this; it just stated that all the risks should be recorded in a central register. So in this section, the Project Manager needs to describe the format and composition of that central register.

Figure 7.2 shows the PRINCE2 recommended composition of a Risk Register. The Project Manager may decide to follow this and store the information in a spreadsheet. The Records section will then read as follows:

> The project's Risk Register will follow the PRINCE2's recommendaed composition. It will be stored in the spreadsheet called `Risk_Register` under the `Project` folder.

FIGURE 7.2   Composition of the Risk Register

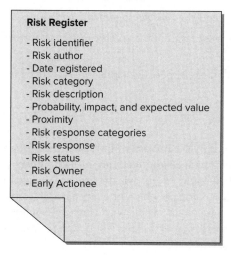

Risk Register

- Risk identifier
- Risk author
- Date registered
- Risk category
- Risk description
- Probability, impact, and expected value
- Proximity
- Risk response categories
- Risk response
- Risk status
- Risk Owner
- Early Actionee

Reporting

In this section, the Project Manager describes how the project is going to communicate the risk situation to all the project stakeholders. It shows which reports on risk will be sent out, their purpose, when they will be sent, and who will receive them. The Reporting section may read as follows:

> In the weekly progress reports, include a risk situation section. This should include the top five risks to the project as well as an overall indicator of the risk exposure as Red, Amber, or Green. This weekly report will go to all the project management team members and all the project stakeholders identified in the Communication Management Strategy.

Timings

The Timings section indicates when risk management activities will occur. It can refer to a time of the week, such as Monday morning at 9:00 a.m., or to a regular time in the PRINCE2 model, such as at the end of a stage. The Timings section may read as follows:

> Carry out the risk management workshop as described in the Procedure section each week on Monday morning at 9:00 a.m.

> Report on the risk situation when sending out the weekly progress report on Friday afternoon.

Roles and Responsibilities

This section specifies who has risk management responsibilities. For example, the Roles and Responsibilities section can look like this:

- The Project Manager chairs the risk management workshop.
- All Team Managers attend the risk management workshop.
- The Project Manager must ensure that all risk responses agreed to in the workshop are implemented.
- The Project Board will make timely decisions on risk situations escalated to them during the project.

Scales

The Scales section describes how the project will measure the probability and impact of risks. Most people use broad scales such as low, medium, or high; others try to be more specific and use percentages. When it comes to impact, the Project Manager might need to consider different ways of scaling depending on which of the project objectives the risk might affect. For example, if it affects the timelines, the Project Manager can measure it in weeks, or if it affects the budget, he can measure it in dollars. The Scales section describes how the various aspects of risk can be measured as follows:

Categorize each risk as having high, medium, or low probability.

Review the impact of each risk in terms of its impact on time, cost, quality, scope, benefits, and the risk situation. For each one, rate the impact as high, medium, or low.

Proximity

The *proximity* of a risk is another way of saying when the risk might happen. It also gives an indication of how the risk's probability or impact might vary over time. During the project, each risk needs to be assigned a proximity category, which will indicate when it might occur. It is in this section that the Project Manager indicates which categories will be used. In our example, the Project Manager can set out the Proximity section as follows:

The timings of each risk should be categorized as: imminent, within the stage, within the project, or beyond the project.

More on Proximity

Proximity indicates when a risk might occur. It also indicates how the probability of a risk (or the impact on the project if it occurs) might vary over time. For example, if you are building a house, a risk to the project might be inclement weather. The probability of this risk will increase in the winter months and decrease in the summer months.

Risk Categories

Categorizing risks is useful for two reasons. First, it gives you some structure when you are trying to identify potential risk. Rather than start with a blank piece of paper, you can focus on a range of areas where risk can occur, which should increase the chances of spotting more potential problems. One standard set of categories is PESTLE. It stands for Political, Economic, Social (such as a managerial risk; for example, a poorly trained manager might not control his team well and thus produce poor-quality products), Technological, Legal, and Environmental (such as a risk arising because the project is within the public sector environment, such as a long and meticulous procurement process that would slow down the project).

The other reason that risk categories are useful is that they help the project management team audit how broad their risk focus is. A quick review of the Risk Register might reveal to the project management team that they are very good at spotting technological risks but poor at spotting legal risks. If this is the case, they might want to get legal experts involved in the risk identification workshops.

The Risk Categories section could read as follows:

Hardware, software, third-party suppliers, contractual

Risk Response Categories

It's useful to have some generic approaches on how to respond to risks; otherwise, you might employ the same techniques time and time again. Here are two common threat responses:

Avoid In the *avoid* response, the project management team does something that either stops the risk occurring or, if it does occur, ensures it doesn't affect the project.

Reduce In the *reduce* response, the project management team does something that lowers the probability of the risk occurring or lowers its impact on the project.

As you will see in the "Plan" section of the risk management procedure later in this chapter, PRINCE2 suggests a number of generic approaches for tackling both threats and opportunities. But for now, here's a simple example of what the Risk Response Categories section might say for the example project:

> For all threats to the project, first try to prevent them. If this is not possible, try to reduce their likelihood or impact on the project. As a last resort, escalate the risk to the Project Board and closely monitor it.

Early Warning Indicators

A number of things might indicate to the Project Manager that all is not well with the project. For example, the project may fall behind schedule by a certain number of days, or the customers may keep changing their minds. It is useful to set some thresholds in a number of areas that, if they are breached, indicate that the project might be at greater risk.

The Early Warning Indicators section could read as follows:

> If any of the following thresholds are breached, notify all project stakeholders and allow Project Assurance to carry out a full risk review:
>
> - The project schedule falls behind by more than one month.
> - The number of requests for change exceeds 20.
> - The number of issues recorded in the issue register as severe exceeds 10.

Risk Tolerance

Risk tolerance is the threshold level of risk that, if exceeded, needs to be escalated to the next level of management. This section sets the risk tolerance at the project and stage levels. In effect, it tells the Project Manager and the Project Board when they need to escalate the risk situation.

There are two ways of setting this threshold. An overall figure could be set—for example, the risk tolerance for the project is that the expected impact of all project risks is below $1 million. Alternatively, the project management team could say that if certain types of risks appear, such as risks that could result in operational failure, they need to be escalated.

The Project Manager in the example might set out the Risk Tolerance section as follows:

> All risks that have a high probability and high impact must be escalated to the Project Board.

Risk Budget

The project management team may decide to set aside some of the project budget to fund various risk responses. This is called a *risk budget*. The money might be reserved for dealing with a particular set of named risks, or it might be a more general fund. In this section, the Project Manager states if the project management team is going to set up a risk budget and how it will be used.

In the example, the Project Manager might set out the Risk Budget section as follows:

"$10,000 to be used to fund responses to any risks that have high probability and impact"

The Risk Management Procedure

Figure 7.3 shows the five steps of the PRINCE2 risk management procedure.

FIGURE 7.3 Risk management procedure

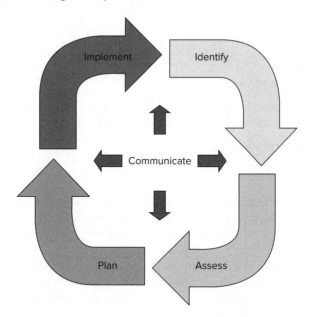

Based on Cabinet Office PRINCE2® material. Reproduced under licence from the Cabinet Office.

Here's a simple example of how to use this procedure. Say you are going to an important meeting tomorrow morning. To get there, you will travel by train, but there's a risk you might be late. How can you use PRINCE2's risk management procedure to help you?

1. **Identify.** A few days before your trip, you try to think of all the things that might go wrong. The alarm clock might not ring. The train might be late. The taxi to get to the train station might not arrive.

2. **Assess.** Now you measure these risks in terms of their likelihood and impact. Doing so will show you which ones you need to tackle. How likely is it that the alarm clock might not ring? It's a battered old thing, so pretty high! Without it ringing, you'll oversleep and miss the meeting. That would have a high impact. High impact, high probability—this sounds like a risk, so you should do something about it!

3. **Plan.** In this step, you consider what to do about the high risks. You could:

    - Buy a new alarm clock.

    - Buy several alarm clocks and set them all before you go to bed.

    - Travel to the location the day before and stay in a nearby hotel.

4. **Implement.** Now you put your risk response plans into action. You buy several new alarm clocks and stay in a rather nice hotel.

5. **Communicate.** You need to ensure that everyone involved in the project is aware of the risk situation and that all new potential risks are being identified and fed back to the Project Manager. In the example, this doesn't make sense (unless you want to talk to yourself).

So you see, the PRINCE2 risk management procedure is just common sense. You probably use it every day to get around life's potential potholes. Now let's look at each of these steps in more detail.

Identify

The Identify step has two focuses:

- Identify the risk context by looking at the general characteristics of the project and the environment it sits within to decide how risky it might be.

- Identify individual risks to the project.

Identify Context

In this step, the project management team will decide how risky the situation is by looking at the characteristics of the project and the environment it will operate within. Using this information, they can then formulate an approach to manage risk for the project. This approach is detailed in the Risk Management Strategy.

In certain projects, some objectives are more at risk than others. For example, if a city is hosting the Olympics, the stadium must be ready for the event. Therefore, there is probably more risk involved in delivering the project on time than delivering to the other objectives of cost, scope, quality, risks, and benefits.

Certain general characteristics make projects riskier. For example:

- Projects involving many stakeholders

- Projects involving third-party suppliers

- International projects

Risk management will be more rigorous for projects with these sorts of characteristics.

How a project team manages uncertainty is also determined by the commissioning organization's attitude to risk. Some organizations have a high *risk appetite*, such as a venture capital–funded company. Other organizations have a low risk appetite, such as a publicly funded government department. A project management team will probably be much bolder with risks in an environment with a high risk appetite.

Using this knowledge of the risk context, the project management team can then determine a relevant approach to managing risk in the Risk Management Strategy.

 Real World Scenario

Adapting the Risk Management Approach to the Risk Context

Two projects I was involved with last year looked identical at first glance. Both were to deliver an organization's public information over a website. Could I take the project management approach from one project, and apply it without change to the second? When I considered the risk context, I saw that the environments were very different. One was for an insurance company in a highly competitive market, looking to take risks to get ahead; the other was for a tightly regulated pharmaceutical company, where the impact of getting information wrong could be stiff government penalties. Being clear about this difference helped me develop and follow a far more rigorous approach to risk management in the drug company project.

Identify Risks

Throughout the life of a project, the Project Manager must ensure that potential threats and opportunities are identified and recorded in the Risk Register. Remember that there are two types of risks: threats, which are uncertain events that would have a negative effect on the project objectives, and opportunities, which are uncertain events that would have a favorable effect on the project objectives. Note the emphasis on doing this activity *throughout* the project. In my experience, this step is done very well at the beginning of most projects and then is forgotten about as things progress.

PRINCE2 recommends that the Project Manager identify each risk's cause, the event that might follow, and the potential effect on the project. Let me give you an example. If you had a risk of being late for a meeting, what would be its risk cause, risk event, and potential effect?

Risk Cause *Risk cause* is the source of the risk. It is sometimes called the risk driver. In the example, this could be the alarm clock not ringing.

Risk Event *Risk event* is the uncertain event that might follow the risk cause. If the alarm doesn't ring, you might oversleep and be late for the meeting.

Risk Effect   Given the risk event, *risk effect* is how the project objectives might be affected. (Remember that the project objectives are time, cost, quality, scope, risk, and benefits.) In this case, the effect of oversleeping is that you don't sign an important client, which would affect sales figures (benefits).

Some risks might have multiple causes. You might be late for the meeting because the train broke down.

Assess

The Assess step has two focuses:

- *Estimate* each individual risk's probability of occurring, impact, and proximity.
- *Evaluate* the overall risk exposure of the project.

Estimate

During the Estimate step, the Project Manager needs to measure each risk. This helps him decide which are the worst threats and the best opportunities to focus on. It also helps him determine whether he has breached any risk tolerance levels, which would mean escalating to the next higher level of management.

In the beginning of this section, I discussed assessing individual risks in terms of their probability and impact. The Project Manager should also measure a risk's proximity, such as when it is likely to occur and whether the probability and/or impact of a risk might vary over time.

Here's another example. Say you are a Project Manager on a project to build a new hotel and there is a threat that a competitor hotel might open before yours and reduce your sales as a result. You could estimate this risk as follows:

1. You measure its probability. There are several techniques you could use to estimate a risk's probability, such as a Monte Carlo analysis or even a simple guesstimate. Exactly how you do this is out of the scope of PRINCE2; however, you should try to be consistent in your approach. During the Initiation Stage of your project, specify the probability estimating technique you will use throughout the project. This goes in the Tools and Techniques section of your Risk Management Strategy.

    In the hotel example, you might consider a number of things in order to estimate the probability of the competitor hotel opening before yours, such as the average time the competitor has taken to build other hotels and how far ahead they are with their plans. This will give you a rough idea of the likelihood of your competitor opening their hotel before yours. You then assign the risk a likelihood using the probability scales specified in the Scales section of the Risk Management Strategy. Maybe it's as simple as defining the risk as low, medium, or high likelihood.

2. You measure the impact of this risk. Any risk, if it occurs, could potentially affect any of the six project objectives: cost, time, scope, quality, risk, and benefits. In the Scales

section of the Risk Management Strategy, you specify the impact scale you will use for each objective type. For example, for cost impacts, you could use scales such as "Under $1000," "$1000–$10,000," and "Above $10,000." In the example, you might decide that this risk would affect your forecast sales (benefits) and say the potential impact would be to decrease room sales by $200,000 in the first three years.

3. You measure the risk's proximity. This is the time factor of the risk, when it might materialize, and how its impact and/or probability might vary over time. Once again, you should use the scales specified in the Risk Management Strategy, which this time are found in the Proximity section. Example scales might be "Imminent," "In the next month," "In the next 6 months," and so on. For your hotel risk, you might believe this threat is Imminent.

Exam Spotlight

PRINCE2 provides a number of risk estimation techniques such as probability trees, expected value, Pareto analysis, and the probability impact grid. It also offers two risk evaluation techniques: using risk models or an expected monetary value technique. You will not be tested on any of these. In fact, the only two techniques that you might be tested on are the quality review technique in the Quality theme and the product-based planning technique in the Plans theme. If you want further information on the risk techniques, refer to the Risk theme chapter in *Managing a Successful Project with PRINCE2*.

Evaluate

At various times, the Project Manager will want to gauge the project's overall exposure to risk. There are many ways to do so. He can simply count how many risks appear in the Risk Register. Or he can use the expected value technique illustrated in Table 7.1.

TABLE 7.1 Expected value risk evaluation technique

Risk ID	Probability (%)	Impact ($)	Expected value ($) (probability multiplied by impact)
01	20%	$10,000	$2,000
02	50%	$30,000	$15,000
03	30%	$100,000	$30,000
		Expected Overall Value:	**$47,000**

The project management team should specify the standard approach to measuring overall risk exposure in the Tools and Techniques section of the Risk Management Strategy. The Project Manager will gauge the overall risk situation throughout the project, particularly at stage boundaries. The Executive uses this information to assess whether the Business Case is still valid and determines whether to authorize the next stage.

Plan

The next step in the risk management procedure is planning one or more responses to the risks the project management team have spotted. PRINCE2 suggests a number of standard countermeasures to risks, as listed in Table 7.2.

TABLE 7.2   Threat and opportunity responses

Threat responses	Opportunity responses
Avoid	Exploit
Reduce (probability and/or impact)	Enhance
Fallback (reduces impact only)	
Transfer (reduces the financial impact only)	
Share	Share
Accept	Reject

Planning Risk Responses to Threats

Here's another example to help you understand the standard approaches to responding to threats. During the project to build a new hotel that you're project managing, the operations manager has come to you worried that if it snows, it will delay construction, potentially raise costs, and affect the quality of the building. You can respond to this risk using any of the following approaches:

Avoid   You can respond in such a way that the probability of the threat occurring and/or its impact reduces to zero. In the example, you can avoid the risk by building over the summer when there is no likelihood of snow.

Reduce   You can do something that reduces either the probability or the impact of the risk. In the example, you can fit snow tires to the construction vehicles, allowing them to work more easily in icy conditions.

Fallback   *Fallback* is a reactive response. You wait for the risk to occur, and then carry out a previously planned action. In the example, if it snows, you book the construction workers into a nearby hotel so that they won't find it difficult to get to work.

Transfer   In the *Transfer* response, you pass on some of the potential impact of a risk to a third party. Examples of this approach are taking out insurance or specifying penalty clauses in case a third party doesn't deliver as planned. In the example, you can ask the construction company to sign a contract that makes them financially liable for late delivery.

Accept   The *Accept* response involves making a conscious decision to retain the threat. The project team should continue to monitor the risk. (If you never spotted the risk or ignored it hoping it would go away, that's not considered an Accept response!) You would do this when the cost of doing something about the risk is outweighed by its potential impact and/or probability. For example, if you spotted a risk that a meteorite might crash into the construction site, the probability is clearly ludicrously low, so investing in a bank of missiles to shoot down any rogue visitors from outer space probably wouldn't make sense!

Share   *Share* is a special response because it applies to a situation that could turn into an opportunity or a threat. There are always two parties involved. Let me give you an example. Say the hotel is going to be very luxurious and all the penthouses will have gold fittings. Normally, if the price of gold goes up, the fittings supplier would raise their prices by an equivalent amount. However, if the price of gold falls, they might not pass on the whole reduction and therefore increase their profit margins. If you choose a Share response, you would write a contract with the fittings supplier to ensure that both parties equally share the costs of the threat and the benefits from the opportunity. Maybe the cost of the fittings is tied somehow to the price of gold.

 Real World Scenario

Using PRINCE2 Risk Management in the Corporate World

I consulted on a project to deliver a software system to a major corporate client. Early in the project, I identified a risk that the company's procurement department could take a long time to sign off contracts with new suppliers. This could be a problem because we were planning to outsource the construction of the software to a third party. To mitigate the threat to the project timeline, we considered several approaches. We could try to reduce the risk by either engaging the procurement department earlier or allowing the company's IT department to do more of the work. In the end, we avoided the risk. Because we already had an existing contract with this client, their procurement department allowed us to quickly amend that contract to state that we would deliver the software. Then we signed a corresponding contract with a software supplier to deliver the software to us.

Planning Risk Responses to Opportunities

PRINCE2 suggests four possible ways of responding to a potential opportunity for a project:

Exploit   The *Exploit* response ensures that the opportunity will happen and that it will have a favorable impact on the project.

Enhance The *Enhance* response increases the likelihood that the opportunity will happen and/or increases the favorable impact on the project if it does.

Share This is the same response that I described earlier in the "Planning Risk Responses to Threats" section.

Reject With the *Reject* response, a deliberate decision is made not to try to enhance or exploit the opportunity.

To help explain this, here's an example. In the hotel construction project, the Project Manager spots an opportunity. He remembers that on a similar project last year, he used a good electrical contractor who was very quick at doing her work. If he can use her again, he may be able to deliver parts of the project earlier. When he investigates the electrical contractor's availability, he discovers she is busy on another project. How can he use the PRINCE2 opportunity responses described to respond to this potential opportunity?

Exploit The Project Manager delays the start date of the project until after the electrical contractor's current work has finished, and then ties her into a contract to do the work.

Enhance The Project Manager offers the electrical contractor more money to persuade her to finish her current work early and start work on the hotel project.

Reject The Project Manager recruits another electrical contractor who is available.

Share This response wouldn't apply to this situation. For a full discussion on the Share countermeasure, refer to the section "Planning Risk Responses to Threats" earlier in this chapter.

Exam Spotlight

Make sure that you learn the names for the various types of risk responses. Some of them are not intuitive. For example, the thought of rejecting an opportunity can sound like a strange thing to do, but it is a viable PRINCE2 response. It is important for a candidate taking the certification exams to understand the PRINCE2 meanings for words, especially when those words are used in a different way in everyday speech.

Implement

In the implement step of the risk management procedure, the Project Manager takes all the good ideas that have been generated to respond to risks and puts them into action. For the hotel construction example, snow tires are fitted to the vehicles so the team can continue working if it snows. For the meeting example, where you were worried you might be late, you bought several alarm clocks to ensure you wake up on time. The Project Manager is ultimately responsible for instigating, tracking, and monitoring the risk response plans, with the aid of the Risk Owners and Actionees, as described in the next section.

Risk Owners and Risk Actionees

A *Risk Owner* should be allocated to each risk. His role is to monitor a risk and manage any countermeasures. He should have relevant expertise. For example, a legal risk might be owned by the company lawyer. The Risk Owners don't necessarily have to be part of the project management team.

Risk Actionees are those who actually perform the countermeasures. An example of a *Risk Actionee* is someone who fits snow tires to the hotel construction equipment to mitigate against bad weather.

Every entry in the Risk Register should identify that risk's Risk Owner and Risk Actionee. It is the responsibility of the Project Manager to add this information.

Risk Budget

The risk budget is used to fund risk responses. In the hotel construction example, this is how the Project Manager will fund the purchase of all those snow tires to help in bad weather.

Table 7.3 shows how the Project Manager might calculate a risk budget. At the outset of the project, he spots as many potential threats and opportunities as possible. He then estimates their likely monetary impact and the potential cost of implementing countermeasures. Multiplying these two costs by the percentage likelihood gives a weighted cost for each risk, the sum of which gives a forecasted risk budget. As the project progresses, the Project Manager will spot other risks, so it would be prudent to set aside more than the $67,000 calculated in Table 7.3.

TABLE 7.3 Calculating a risk budget

Risk ID	Impact costs	Response costs	Total costs	Likelihood	Weighted cost
1	$30,000	$4,000	$34,000	30%	$10,200
2	$10,000	$1,000	$11,000	5%	$550
3	$45,000	$20,000	$65,000	50%	$32,500
4	$80,000	$15,000	$95,000	25%	$23,750
				Total Weighted Cost:	**$67,000**

Whether a risk budget will be established and how it will be used is described in the Risk Management Strategy. The value of the risk budget is described in the project's plans.

Exam Spotlight

Always spend the right budget in the right situation. For example, avoid the temptation of spending the risk budget if you need to fund a change to a product and there is no change budget left.

Inherent, Residual, and Secondary Risks

If the project management team applies a risk response to an *inherent risk* (the risk it starts off with), it might not necessarily remove the potential problem, thus leaving some *residual risk*. The countermeasure might even introduce a new *secondary risk*. The relationship between these three types of risk is shown in Figure 7.4.

FIGURE 7.4 Types of risk

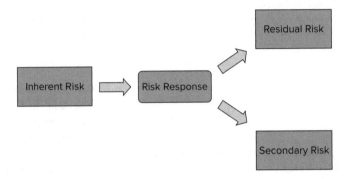

Consider this example. You are building a hotel and there is a threat of heavy rain. In response to this risk, you erect scaffolding with a tarpaulin top. There is still some residual risk left, though, because although the construction site will stay dry, the rain might affect deliveries. You have also introduced a secondary risk: The scaffolding might collapse, injuring some of the workforce.

Communicate

Good communication is vital in order for a project management team to effectively manage risk. If you refer back to Figure 7.3, you can see that PRINCE2 shows this by putting the Communicate step of the risk management procedure in the center of the other steps. The Project Manager must ensure a broad and balanced perspective when identifying and assessing risks and then planning responses to those risks. This will mean asking the opinions of all the project management team and other stakeholders. Also, for the Project Manager to be effective at monitoring and controlling the work to respond to risks, he will need to closely communicate with those involved.

Exam Spotlight

In the Practitioner exam, you may be asked which of the PRINCE2 reports have a section for risk reporting. Check this by looking at the management product descriptions for Highlight Report, Checkpoint Report, End Stage Report, Lessons Report, and End Project Report in Appendix A of *Managing Successful Projects with PRINCE2*.

Roles Involved with the Risk Theme

Exam Spotlight

If a Practitioner exam question asks you about risk responsibilities, there is a handy table at the back of the Risk theme chapter in *Managing Successful Projects with PRINCE2* that explains what each role does. In fact, for any question about responsibilities related to any of the seven themes, there is a similar table at the end of each "Theme" chapter in *Managing Successful Projects with PRINCE2*.

Let's now look at what the PRINCE2 project roles do when managing risk. First, consider the senior roles. A generic project Risk Management Strategy might already exist for the programme or organization, in which case corporate or programme management will instruct the Project Board to follow it.

All of the Project Board roles consider the risk situation from their own perspective, and ensure that potential threats or opportunities are identified, assessed, and controlled. For example, the Senior Users must take into account whether there are any threats to correctly defining product requirements, the Senior Suppliers must ensure that there are no threats to delivering the products by the deadline date, and the Executive must be looking for opportunities to increase the return-on-investment of the project.

The Executive also has a broader risk management role. He is responsible for ensuring that a Risk Management Strategy exists and is being followed. PRINCE2 (and the general business world) sees the effective controlling of risk as a necessary condition to delivering value-for-money benefits.

Although the Executive is responsible for ensuring the Risk Management Strategy exists, it will probably fall on the Project Manager to create it. The Project Manager also ensures that the project continually identifies, assesses, and controls risks. This doesn't mean that, for example, he has to sit in a room on his own and identify all the potential threats to the project! Rather, through activities such as risk management workshops, he facilitates the project management team to continually assess the risk situation. He must ensure that an up-to-date record of information exists on all the project's threats and opportunities in the Risk Register. The Project Manager may be lucky enough to have Project Support help him with information recording and filing.

The Team Managers and their teams are in the best position to spot technical, implementation, and practical risks to the project. Therefore, it is essential to include them in the process of identifying, assessing, and controlling risks.

The Project Assurance role will be checking that risk management is being done in line with the Risk Management Strategy. If not, they will need to escalate to the Executive.

Exam Spotlight

Be careful with exam questions that ask who does what. Sometimes, there are a number of roles that do very similar things. For example, the Executive is responsible for the Risk Management Strategy (he ensures that one exists, and through his assurance role, check to see it is being followed). However, it is the Project Manager's role to create the Risk Management Strategy and perform the management tasks set out in it.

Summary

In this chapter, you learned about the Risk theme, which describes how to deal with potential threats to and opportunities for the project.

The first thing you need to understand is that the word *risk* means a slightly different thing in PRINCE2 than in everyday speech. You may be used to thinking of a risk as a potential problem, but in PRINCE2, it could also be a potential opportunity. Either way, it might affect how you deliver project objectives.

Project situations are riskier than business as usual. This is because projects are unique endeavors, and all sorts of unforeseen threats or opportunities might arise.

PRINCE2 sets out a clear procedure to deal with risk. It involves five steps: Identify, Assess, Plan, Implement, and Communicate.

PRINCE2 recommends a number of standard countermeasures to a threat: avoid the threat so it will not occur, reduce the threat so that it is less likely to occur or its impact will be diminished, plan a fallback action to reduce the impact should the risk occur, transfer the financial effect of the risk to a third party, or make a conscious decision to accept the risk.

In this chapter, you learned that there are a number of PRINCE2 standard responses for opportunities: exploit the opportunity so it definitely occurs; enhance the opportunity so it is more likely to happen, or its favorable impacts are increased; or reject the opportunity, making a conscious decision not to pursue it. In some situations, a risk can turn out to be a threat or an opportunity. In this case, PRINCE2 recommends applying a Share response that allows two parties to share the costs if the situation turns into a threat and the benefits if the situation becomes an opportunity. You also learned that each risk should be assigned a Risk Owner who will monitor, manage, and control that risk. The Risk Owner might be aided by various Risk Actionees who carry out risk countermeasure tasks.

Exam Essentials

Be able to define a risk using cause, event, and effect. Every risk should be described in a clear and unambiguous way. PRINCE2 states that you should consider three things about a risk: what could cause it, the uncertain event that might follow the cause, and the effect on the project objectives if the event does occur.

Understand how to define a project's approach to risk management using the Risk Management Strategy. Be familiar with defining the project's risk management approach using the sections of the Risk Management Strategy such as procedure, timings, responsibilities, records, reporting, and tools.

Understand how to use the Risk Register to record information on individual risks. Be familiar with the format of the Risk Register and understand the types of information that are held on each risk.

Know that effective risk management is a prerequisite for continued business justification. Know that there is a strong relationship between risk management and delivery of the Business Case.

Understand all the steps of the risk management procedure. Know the five steps of the risk management procedure: Identify, Assess, Plan, Implement, and Communicate. Be clear what happens in each step.

Know who is responsible for the various areas of risk management. The Project Manager is responsible for ensuring that all risks are identified, assessed, and controlled. The Executive is responsible for ensuring that effective risk management is carried out. Understand the various other risk responsibilities for the rest of the project management team.

Review Questions

The rest of this chapter contains mock exam questions, first for the Foundation exam and then for the Practitioner exam.

Foundation Exam Questions

1. Which of the following options is **NOT** part of the PRINCE2 risk management procedure?

   A. Implement

   B. Impact Analysis

   C. Communicate

   D. Identify

2. Which principle does the Risk theme primarily support?

   A. Focus on products

   B. Learn from experience

   C. Management by stages

   D. Continued business justification

3. In which PRINCE2 management product should the Project Manager specify the amount of risk that the team is allowed to take on?

   A. Work Package

   B. Risk Management Strategy

   C. Risk Register

   D. Project Initiation Documentation

4. The output of which step of the risk management procedure is a prerequisite for the creation of the Risk Management Strategy?

   A. Evaluate

   B. Identify Risks

   C. Estimate

   D. Identify Context

5. How would a Team Manager escalate a risk to the Project Manager?

   A. Checkpoint Report

   B. Risk Report

   C. Raise an issue

   D. Exception Report

6. You are a Project Manager and are buying a major input for the project from Japan. If the yen were to appreciate, it would mean a big increase in the project costs. You decide to buy some yen futures, which, if the currency did increase, would give a financial payout. What sort of PRINCE2 risk response is this?

   A. Transfer

   B. Share

   C. Fallback

   D. Avoid

7. When calculating how much of a risk budget to set aside for the project, which information would **NOT** be helpful?

   A. Cost of running weekly risk workshops

   B. Forecast cost of responding to three major risks

   C. Likelihood of a risk

   D. Financial impact of a major risk

8. "The current overall exposure of the project to risk stands at Red" is an example of the Project Manager _____ the risk situation.

   A. Evaluating

   B. Estimating

   C. Implementing

   D. Identifying

9. Categorizing each of the risks spotted helps the Project Manager:

   A. Sort the risks in the Risk Register more easily

   B. Decide who is responsible for funding each risk's response

   C. See areas of the project that need more focus in terms of identifying risks

   D. Allocate responsibilities for risk ownership

10. A suitable Risk Owner for a strategic risk would be the:

   A. Senior User

   B. Executive

   C. Project Manager

   D. Project Support

Practitioner Exam Questions

The following Practitioner questions are divided into sections by question type and are based on the Practitioner exam scenario that you will find in this book's Introduction.

Section 1: Practitioner Multiple Response Questions

Exam Spotlight

Remember that you will be able to refer to *Managing Successful Projects with PRINCE2* during the Practitioner exam. This is particularly useful when questions, such as the six questions in this section, refer to one of the PRINCE2 management products. Always use the management product descriptions in Appendix A of *Managing Successful Projects with PRINCE2* to help you. For example, in question 1, check the Risk Management Strategy to see exactly what sort of information should be in the Procedure section. You can also refer to the "Using the Risk Management Strategy" section in this chapter, but unfortunately, you can't take this book into the exam.

Each of the following questions includes a list of statements, but according to PRINCE2, only two statements are appropriate entries for that heading in the project's Risk Management Strategy. Remember to limit your answers to the number of selections requested in each question.

1. Which two statements should be recorded under the Risk Management Procedure heading?
    A. Run a risk management workshop consisting of two steps: identification of risks and planning responses.
    B. Identify all products that will be tracked using the company's product tracking system.
    C. At the end of each stage, send out an overall evaluation of project risk to the Project Board.
    D. Monitor and control all risk response plans.
    E. Each Highlight Report should show details of all high risks and an overall evaluation of risk.

2. Which two statements should be recorded under the Records heading?
    A. Each End Stage Report should include a risk profile for the project.
    B. The Project_Risks spreadsheet in the Project folder is to be used to store information on any threats or opportunities identified.
    C. The project's Risk Register should contain information on the probability, impact, and proximity of each risk.
    D. All changes to a product's status are to be recorded in its Configuration Item Record.
    E. If the number of risks in the Project_Risks spreadsheet is more than 30, escalate the situation to Project Assurance.

3. Which two statements should be recorded under the Reporting heading?

    A. The selected software development supplier should include in their weekly Checkpoint Reports any potential opportunities to save development time.

    B. Highlight Reports should be sent to Quality Furniture's major investors and include any threats to the project's Business Case.

    C. After the risk management workshop, enter all new risks into the Risk Register.

    D. The number of off-specifications is to be reported to the Project Board on a weekly basis using the Highlight Report.

    E. The software developer's Project Manager is to be responsible for sending out weekly progress reports

4. Which two statements should be recorded under the Roles and Responsibilities heading?

    A. At the end of each stage, the overall risk situation will be reported to the Project Board.

    B. Software risks, hardware risks, business risks.

    C. The Project Manager will carry out an impact analysis on all formal issues.

    D. The Project Manager will chair the weekly risk workshop.

    E. The Executive will review the project for any strategic or business risks.

5. Which two statements should be recorded under the Scales heading?

    A. Proximity will be allocated to one of the following scales: imminent, within the stage, within the project, or beyond the project.

    B. The probability that the chosen software supplier will be unsuitable is scaled as medium.

    C. The probability of risks will be categorized as low, medium, or high.

    D. The risk that a competitor will launch their website before ours is scaled as having high impact.

    E. The cost impact of risks will be defined in terms of expected value in dollars.

6. Which two statements should be recorded under the risk tolerance heading?

    A. Any issue that is forecast to exceed this stage's cost tolerance must be escalated to the Project Board.

    B. The project's risk budget is $10,000, but there is an extra $2,000 to spend in mitigating any large unforeseen risk.

    C. If the software supplier identifies any risk with high probability and impact, they must escalate this to the Project Manager immediately.

    D. Quality Furniture's Board would like to know if any risk is identified that might impede the normal running of the sales system.

    E. Any opportunity that would increase sales by more than the forecast 20 percent should be referred to the Board of Directors.

Section 2: Practitioner Matching Questions

The project is in Stage 2, and the request for tender has been sent out to a number of software suppliers. The Executive is concerned that because of Quality Furniture's lack of experience in IT and the Internet, there is a risk that they will choose an inappropriate or poor supplier for the work. If this happens, a number of the project's objectives, such as the timeline, costs, and the anticipated benefits, could be impacted.

Column 1 contains a list of risk responses identified by the Project Manager following an assessment of this risk. Column 2 contains a list of threat response types. For each risk response in Column 1, select from Column 2 the type of response it represents. Each option from Column 2 can be used once, more than once, or not at all.

Column 1	Column 2
1. Add a clause in the supplier contract that makes the supplier financially liable if certain cost, quality, and time criteria are not met.	A. Avoid
2. Recruit a specialist in IT procurement and give him the role of supplier assurance on the project.	B. Reduce
3. Decide that the risk of choosing the wrong supplier is too high, cancel the project, and continue to use the old website.	C. Fallback
4. Wait for the software development stage and if the supplier starts to deliver poor quality, terminate the supplier's contract and use a recommended IT contractor to finish the work.	D. Transfer
5. Decide that the cost of mitigating this risk does not outweigh the benefit of doing so.	E. Accept
6. Decide to split the tender into several parts and allocate the work to several different suppliers.	F. Share

Chapter

8

Change Theme

PRINCE2 EXAM OBJECTIVES COVERED IN THIS CHAPTER:

✓ **Understand the purpose of the Change theme.**

✓ **Understand the meaning of baselines, releases, and configuration items.**

✓ **Know the three types of issues.**

✓ **Understand the change budget and the Change Authority.**

  ▪ Understand the purpose of the change budget.

  ▪ Understand the responsibilities of the Change Authority.

  ▪ Know in which processes the change budget and Change Authority are agreed to and which roles are responsible.

✓ **Understand the issue and change control procedure.**

  ▪ Know the five steps involved with the issue and change control procedure and the activities involved.

  ▪ Know the roles and processes involved with the issue and change control procedure.

✓ **Understand the configuration management procedure.**

  ▪ Know the five steps involved with the configuration management procedure and the activities involved.

  ▪ Know the roles and processes involved with the issue and configuration management procedure.

✓ **For the following management products, know their purpose and composition; in which processes they are developed, used, and reviewed; and which roles are responsible for each:**

  ▪ Configuration Management Strategy

  ▪ Configuration Item Record

  ▪ Issue Report

  ▪ Issue Register

  ▪ Product Status Account

In this chapter, you will learn how PRINCE2 deals with change. Change in a project is inevitable. There are many areas that might be subject to change: clients might change their minds about the products they require, new technology might become available, the business environment might change, and so on.

The Change theme does not prevent change; instead, it describes an approach that ensures that the decision about whether to implement changes is made at the right level of authority and only after the impact of the change has been considered.

The Change theme also looks at configuration management. Configuration management covers how to distinguish each product using a coding system, how to track the status of the products, and how to protect the products from unauthorized changes. Configuration management is an essential prerequisite for effective change management.

Change Theme Terminology

This section defines some common terms that PRINCE2 uses with regard to the Change theme.

Baselines

The PRINCE2 definition for a *baseline* is "a snapshot of a release, product and any component products, frozen at a point in time for a particular purpose." What this means is that when a product is baselined, it is stored and protected from any unauthorized changes. A product might be baselined because it has just been approved. Changes to a baselined product can only be authorized using the *issue and change control procedure*. The issue and change control procedure ensures that the impact of these changes is considered and then authorized at an appropriate level of management. You will learn more about the issue and change control procedure later in this chapter.

If changes are authorized for a document-based product that has been baselined, a new version will be created and the changes will be made to that new version. Some of the PRINCE2 management products will be baselined and may go through multiple versions during the life of the project. Here is a list of these baseline management products:

- Benefits Review Plan
- Business Case

- Communication Management Strategy
- Configuration Management Strategy
- Plan (Project, Stage, and Team)
- Product Description
- Project Brief
- Project Initiation Documentation
- Project Product Description
- Quality Management Strategy
- Risk Management Strategy
- Work Package

Releases

A *release* is a "complete and consistent set of products that are managed, tested and deployed as a single entity to be handed over to the user(s)." A release is a group of products that work together as a unit. For example, imagine you are writing a technical book. You could think of the chapters of the book as individual products. Maybe each chapter refers to information in the other chapters (a bit like this book). When all the chapters are finished and the book is ready to be published, the set of products (or chapters) is a release.

Configuration Item

A *configuration item* is "an entity that may be a product, a component of a product or a set of products that form a release." Each of the configuration items in a project will be configuration-managed. This means the Project Manager will have identified that entity as being something that he needs to track the status of, control changes to, and protect once it has reached a certain state and needs to be baselined.

Often, a configuration item will simply be a product in the project. For example, in the book project introduced in the last section, the configuration items will be the chapters of the book. If the project was to build a car, as Project Manager, you might want to track the progress of creating all the parts of the car such as the engine, the wheels, the seats, and the body framework. All of these car parts are examples of configuration items.

Types of Issues

There are three types of PRINCE2 issues: *request for change*, *off-specification*, and a *problem/concern*. Anyone with an interest in the project can raise an issue. If they want to do so, they should contact the Project Manager, who will then document the issue in the

Issue Register (if it is a formal issue) or the Daily Log (if it is an informal issue). The Project Manager will then deal with the issue using the issue and change control procedure that you will learn about later in this chapter.

Request for Change

A request for change occurs when someone asks that a change to one of the baselined products be considered.

For example, in a project to build a new hotel in Shanghai for a hotel chain, the following are examples of request for changes:

- The hotel chain's head of business development asks to change the approved architectural designs to include a gym.

- The operations director of the construction company asks to change the approved specification of the building materials to take account of changes in building standards.

- The Executive asks to change the latest version of the Project Initiation Documentation because the forecast sales for the hotel have increased.

When a request for change has been authorized, two things might need to be changed: the product itself and its Product Description. For example, say the hotel's gym has been built according to its Product Description with red walls. Then a request for change is authorized to paint the walls blue. First, the Project Manager will create a new version of the gym's Product Description that states that the walls should be blue. Next, he will authorize a Work Package for the painters to paint the walls blue. Obviously, if the project hasn't gotten to the point of painting the gym's walls, then only one thing needs to change: the Product Description.

You will learn about who can authorize a request for change in the "Change Authority" section later in this chapter.

Off-Specification

PRINCE2's definition of an off-specification is "something that should be provided by the project, but currently is not (or is forecast not to be) provided. This might be a missing product or a product not meeting its specification."

An off-specification is a product or set of products that either has or definitely will be delivered incorrectly. This could happen in one of the following two situations:

- Each product needs to be delivered so that it complies with its quality criteria. These quality criteria are measurable characteristics or specifications for that product. The quality criteria are contained within each product's Product Description. If a product has been (or will be) delivered and does not (or will not) comply with its quality criteria, then it is an off-specification.

- Each plan describes the products that need to be delivered. This is known as the scope of the plan. If one or more of these products is (or will be) missing, this situation is also an off-specification.

For example, in a project to build a new hotel in Shanghai for a hotel chain, the following are examples of an off-specification:

- A quality inspection on the swimming pool finds that it does not comply with the health and safety standards outlined in its Product Description.

- As the gym is being constructed, the building company realizes that a mistake was made when the site was surveyed. There is not enough space on the plot of land to create the building specified in the gym's Product Description.

- The promotional website for the new hotel has been delivered, but due to technical problems, a specified part of the site that allows online users to check room availability and book online reservations does not work.

When a product is off-specification, the Project Board may choose to accept the product, even though it is wrong. This is called giving a *concession*. As you'll learn later in this chapter, the Project Board might have delegated this type of decision to a Change Authority.

If no concession is given, then the product needs to be corrected. In this case, the Project Manager might be able to authorize some corrective work. However, sometimes, the work to correct the off-specification might lead to a breach in the cost and time tolerances given to the Project Manager by the Project Board. In this case, the Project Manager needs to escalate this situation to the Project Board. (You will learn more about tolerances and exceptions in Chapter 9, "Progress Theme.")

Problem/Concern

The final type of issue is a problem or a concern. PRINCE2 defines this as "any other issue that the Project Manager needs to resolve or escalate." Obviously, the previously described issues are problems and concerns as well, but the problem/concern category is reserved for things that cannot be categorized as either requests for change or off-specifications.

For example, in a project to build a new hotel in Shanghai for a hotel chain, the following are examples of problems or concerns:

- Notification that the Chinese authorities are taking longer than expected to grant work permits to some of the construction staff. This will delay the construction stage by over a month.

- The specifications for the electrical systems need to be rewritten in order to comply with the Chinese system.

- The Project Manager has been taken to the hospital with appendicitis, and he will be off work for at least a week.

Change Authority

It is the Project Board's responsibility to approve requests for change or concessions in response to an off-specification. The only caveat to this is when the project is part of a programme, but you'll learn about that in a moment.

In a project where there might be a lot of requests for change, the Project Board might not have time to review them all. In this case, they can delegate some authority to approve changes and off-specifications to a person or group called the *Change Authority*. The Project Board will place certain constraints on the authority of the Change Authority, such as the following:

- The authority to sign off only changes that cost less than a prearranged limit
- The authority to sign off only changes that impact the project or stage timescales by less than a prearranged limit
- The authority to sign off only changes that won't affect the broader characteristics of the final outputs of the project described in the Project Product Description
- The authority to sign off only changes that won't affect the current operational ability of the organization

There could be a number of levels of Change Authority. For example, the Project Board authorizes large changes, a separate body of people called the Change Authority authorizes medium-sized changes, and the Project Manager authorizes small changes.

The Project Board decides how many levels of Change Authority there should be within the project, and what constraints will be placed on each level's authority. This is done in the initiation stage, and the decision is documented in the Configuration Management Strategy. A Change Authority might consist of people from the project management team, including Project Assurance. It is sensible to ensure that business, user, and supplier perspectives are all represented on the Change Authority.

If the project is part of a programme, it is up to programme management to define what level of Change Authority the Project Board will have within the project. Corporate or programme management may also take on some responsibility for approving changes within the project, in which case, they are likely to be involved with authorizing the most severe and highest-priority changes.

Figure 8.1 shows the different levels of Change Authority.

FIGURE 8.1 Change Authority levels

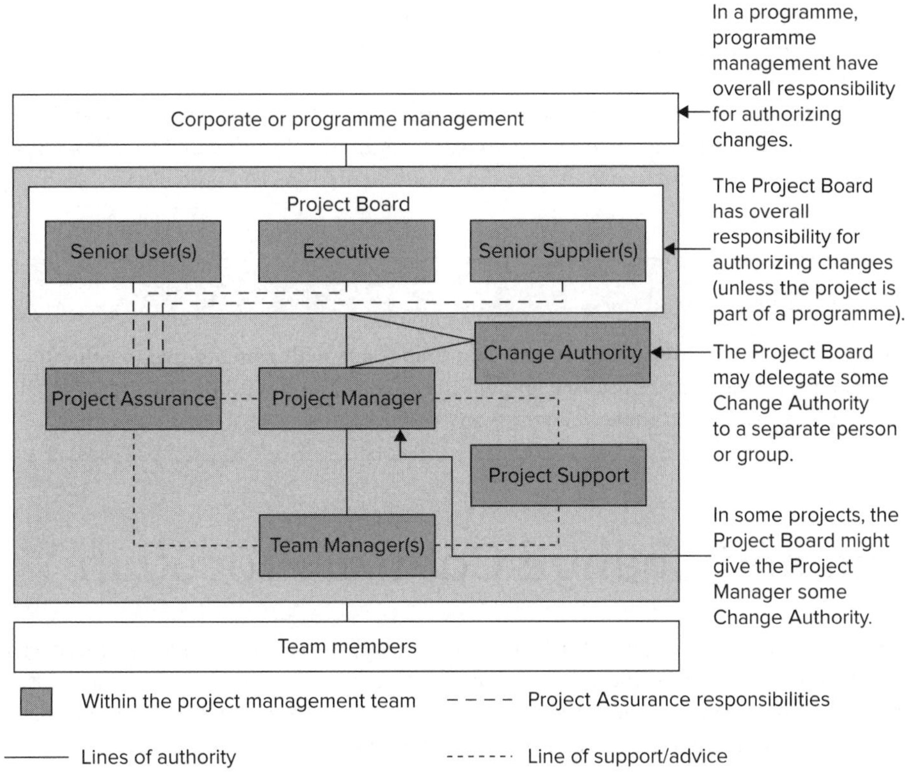

In a programme, programme management have overall responsibility for authorizing changes.

The Project Board has overall responsibility for authorizing changes (unless the project is part of a programme).

The Project Board may delegate some Change Authority to a separate person or group.

In some projects, the Project Board might give the Project Manager some Change Authority.

Based on Cabinet Office PRINCE2® material. Reproduced under licence from the Cabinet Office.

Change Budget

The *change budget* is a sum of money that funds the implementation of authorized requests for changes. It could also be used to pay for the initial investigation work to understand the potential impacts on the project of implementing the request for changes.

In the project to build a hotel, if the Marketing Director requests that 10 more penthouse suites be added, both investigating the impact of adding these additional rooms and then, once they are authorized, building them, would be funded from the change budget.

Change budgets are useful when there are likely to be many changes in a project. They avoid the necessity to continually refer to the next higher level of authority for every change that is requested. There are many examples of projects that might involve lots of changes, such as in the information technology industry, where rapid technological advances take place.

The Project Board might authorize the use of some of the change budget to one of the lower levels of Change Authority, in which case, they might want to set some constraints on how the money can be spent. Typical constraints might include limiting the expenditure on any single change or limiting the overall spending within a particular stage, without reference to the Project Board.

A change budget might be allocated to the entire project, in which case, it would be documented in the Project Plan. A change budget might also be allocated to a particular stage in the project, in which case, it would be documented in the Stage Plan.

Exam Spotlight

It is important not to confuse when to use cost tolerances with when to use the change budget. Cost tolerances do not fund changes; the change budget funds changes. A cost tolerance is used when the costs of a stage or a project unexpectedly overrun.

Issue and Change Control Procedure

The three types of issues (request for change, off-specification, and problems or concerns) are managed using the issue and change control procedure. As you can see in Figure 8.2, this procedure is made up of five activities: capture, examine, propose, decide, and implement. You will learn what happens in each activity in the following subsections.

FIGURE 8.2 Issue and change control procedure

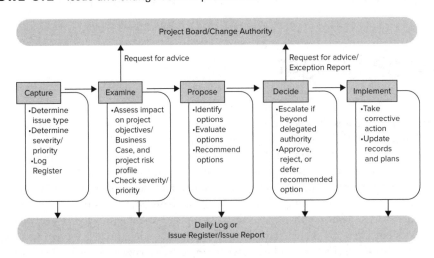

Based on Cabinet Office PRINCE2® material. Reproduced under licence from the Cabinet Office.

For any project, the project management team will need to decide how to tailor the PRINCE2 issue and change control procedure for their project. The Project Manager will document this tailored procedure in the Configuration Management Strategy during the initiation stage. You will learn more about the Configuration Management Strategy later in this chapter.

Capture

The Project Manager captures the issue by documenting it. Formal issues are captured in the issue register and informal issues go into the Daily Log. It is the Project Manager who must decide whether the issue should be treated formally or informally. The Configuration Management Strategy will define the authority the Project Manager has to decide which issues he can treat as informally and also the approach to scaling the severity and priority of issues. An informal issue might be something like getting a new security pass for one of the workers or dealing with someone being out sick for the day. These sorts of things can go into the Daily Log that only the Project Manager tracks. (You learned about the Daily Log back in Chapter 2, "Starting a Project Successfully with PRINCE2." The Project Manager uses the Daily Log as a diary or personal action list.)

For formal issues, the Project Manager creates an entry in the Issue Register. You can see sample Issue Register entries in Figure 8.3.

FIGURE 8.3 Issue Register entries

Issue identifier	Issue type	Date raised	Raised by	Issue Report author	Issue description	Priority	Severity	Status	Closure date
23	RFC	08-Feb	John Smith—Head of Business Development	John Smith—Head of Business Development	Competitor is building a hotel with gym nearby—request to change architectural designs to include gym	High	High	Raised	
24	OS	11-Feb	Louise Newman	Tim Taylor	Swimming pool has not passed the health and safety review due to defects in the build	High	High	Impact analysis	
25	P/C	14-Feb	Taj Rehal	Jon Billimore	Project Manager has food poisoning and will probably be sick for at least one week	High	Med	Raised	

For each issue listed in the Issue Register, the Project Manager creates an accompanying *Issue Report*. However, the Project Manager might ask the person who raised the issue to draft the first version of the Issue Report. Figure 8.4 shows an example of an Issue Report.

FIGURE 8.4 Issue Report

Issue Identifier: 24	Issue Type: Off-specification	Issue Report Author: Tim Taylor
Date Raised: 11th Feb	Raised By: Louise Newman	
Issue Description: During the health and safety check, a number of defects to the swimming pool were discovered. There are no slip stones around the pool and there is no guard rail. Both of these should have been delivered according to the baselined product description for the pool.		
Impact Analysis: An impact analysis to correct the pool defects has been done. The work to add the missing features will take an extra 5 days and will be funded by the swimming pool construction firm.		
Recommendation: Proceed with the remedial work. This needs to be authorized by the Project Board because there is no remaining time tolerance for the stage.		
Priority: High	Severity: High	Decision Date:
Decision:		
Approved By:		Closure Date:

The Project Manager captures issues in the Capture and examine issues and risks activity during the Controlling a Stage process. You will learn more about this process in Chapter 10, "Managing the Middle of a Project Successfully with PRINCE2."

Examine

The Project Manager is now responsible for examining the issue. This involves considering the potential impact of implementing a request for change or investigating the impact of correcting an off-specification (or the impact of authorizing a concession). Sometimes, for less severe issues, the Project Manager can decide it is not worth the cost and time to do a full formal impact analysis.

The *impact analysis* must consider the following:

- What impact the issue has or will have on the six aspects of project performance: cost, time, scope, quality, benefits, and risk.

- What impact the issue has or will have on the wider environment outside of the project. For example, if the project is part of a programme, what impact could the issue have on the other projects within the programme?

- What impact the issue has or will have on the business, user, and supplier perspective on the project.

The Project Manager examines issues in the Capture and examine issues and risks activity during the Controlling a Stage process. The information from the results of the impact analysis should be documented in both the Issue Register and the Issue Report.

Propose

The Project Manager now needs to propose how to deal with the issue. He will involve relevant people who understand the problem and weigh the benefits of implementing potential options against the time, cost, and risks that might be involved.

For example, maybe the issue under review is the off-specification you saw earlier. As the gym is being constructed, the building company realizes that a mistake was made when the site was surveyed. There is not enough space on the plot of land to create the building specified in the gym's Product Description.

The Project Manager canvasses the opinion of the building company and the architects on how a smaller gym might be created. He asks them for cost and time forecasts for this smaller gym. He asks the marketing director what effect a smaller gym would have on the forecast sales for the hotel. He also investigates the potential for buying adjacent land to create the original-sized gym. After investigation, he proposes two options:

- Create a smaller gym. This might have little effect on the construction costs and schedule but introduce the business risk that it might have a detrimental effect on possible gym membership sales and room sales.

- Create the original-sized gym on a plot of land that is 50 yards away from the main hotel. This would increase costs and delay construction. The marketing director may decide that whereas this wouldn't affect sales of gym memberships to nonresidents at the hotel, it might put people off staying at the hotel due to the distance the gym would be from the main building.

The Project Manager must describe the two options in the Issue Report and show the benefits of each option and the effects on the project's objectives (time, cost, quality, scope, benefits, and risks).

If either of these two options would breach the project or stage tolerances, the Project Manager should consider creating an Exception Report.

Decide

The next step involves making a decision on which option to pursue to deal with the issue. Either the Project Manager has the authority to deal with the issue or will have to escalate the issue.

The Project Manager has the authority to deal with issues in the following circumstances:

- The Project Manager has been allocated enough cost or time tolerance to tackle the problem or concern.
- The Project Manager has been allocated enough cost or time tolerance to correct the off-specification.
- The Project Manager has the Change Authority to authorize a particular request for change and the change budget to fund it.

If the Project Manager has the authority to deal with the issue, he will pick an option from the previous propose step. This is done in the Take corrective action activity during the Controlling a Stage process.

If the Project Manager does not have the authority to deal with the issue, he will escalate the situation to either the Project Board or the relevant Change Authority using an *Exception Report*. Before creating the Exception Report, the Project Manager would send the Project Board or Change Authority a copy of the Issue Report, as early warning of the issue. An Exception Report describes the issue, specifies the options to deal with it, and recommends one of the options. (You will learn more about the Exception Report in Chapter 9, "Progress Theme.") This will be done in the Escalate issues and risks activity during the Controlling a Stage process.

The Project Board's or Change Authority's response will depend on the type of issue. For example:

- If the issue is a request for change, the Project Board or Change Authority might approve it, reject it, or defer it for a later decision. They might also ask for more information.
- If the issue is an off-specification, the Project Board or Change Authority might grant a concession, instruct that the off-specification be resolved using one of the options proposed, defer the decision, or request more information.
- If the issue is a problem or concern, the Project Board or Change Authority might provide some guidance.

The Project Board or Change Authority will probably ask the Project Manager to produce an Exception Plan before any work is done to deal with the issue. The Exception Plan will plan out the work to implement the option that deals with the issue.

Implement

The final step in the issue and change control procedure is implement. If the Project Manager has the authority to deal with the issue, he will implement the option he has chosen. Otherwise, he will create an Exception Plan for approval by the Project Board. The Project Manager creates the Exception Plan in Managing a Stage Boundary and it is approved by the Project Board during Directing a Project. (Exception Plans were covered in detail in Chapter 5, "Plans Theme.")

The Project Manager then updates the Issue Register and Issue Report with details of the decision and informs any interested parties. Once the issue has been closed, he updates the Issue Register and Issue Report for a final time.

Configuration Management Procedure

The purpose of configuration management is to identify all the things that the project will need to deliver (configuration items), track the current status of each of these things as they are being worked on, and protect them from anyone making unauthorized changes to them, especially after they have been approved. Configuration management helps a project manage changes to products.

Configuration management consists of five core activities: planning, identification, control, status accounting, and verification and audit. The best way to explain what happens in each of these activities is through an example.

Imagine you and some of your work colleagues have been asked to create and document a project management method for the organization where you work. You have decided it will be a tailored version of PRINCE2 called PRINCE2PLUS. You are going to be the Project Manager. The following sections explain how you would perform configuration management.

Planning

The first step is planning how you will carry out the configuration management on the project. To do so, you will need to make the following decisions:

- To what level of detail will you track the project's products? The main output of the PRINCE2PLUS project might be a document with a chapter on how to do each area of project management. Throughout the project, you could track the status of every single page. This would mean that every time someone finishes a page, you would need to update your records with the new page's status. This level of control is probably unnecessary. Instead, you might decide to track the progress of each chapter.

- Where will the information on the current status of the products be stored? Also, where will the actual products be stored? Maybe in the PRINCE2PLUS project, you decide to store the status information in a spreadsheet and the chapters of the book as text files on a central computer. On a different type of project, where more physical things are being created, you would need to decide where to store all of these things. For example, on a project to build a car, you would need to decide where to store the car parts.

- What security technique will you use to protect the products from unauthorized changes? For example, in the PRINCE2PLUS project, the text files for each chapter might be password-protected. In the car project, there might be a padlock on the room that stores the parts.

- Who will be responsible for maintaining and reporting on the current status information on the products? (This is the sort of responsibility that might be allocated to anyone doing the Project Support role.)

The Project Manager will document the answers to these sorts of questions in the Configuration Management Strategy during the initiation stage of the project.

Identification

The project management team now needs to identify all the things that the project will deliver and that they want to track. Say that in the previous planning activity for the PRINCE2PLUS project, you decided to track the project's products to the chapter level. You now need to identify what chapters will be created. Maybe there will be one chapter on risk management, another on quality management, and so on. Maybe you also want to track the progress of some other things that are being delivered, such as a training pack for staff and a new information page on project management for the company website. You identify all the individual outputs you want to track. These outputs are called the configuration items.

For each configuration item, you need to create a Configuration Item Record. This is a set of information about the configuration item, such as what state it is currently in, what its latest version is, who is working on it, and so on. It is the responsibility of Project Support to maintain the Configuration Item Records throughout the project. You can see PRINCE2's recommended composition of a Configuration Item Record in Figure 8.5.

FIGURE 8.5   Configuration Item Record

Most of the headings in the Configuration Item Record are self-explanatory, but a few of them are worth further discussion:

Project identifier, Item Identifier, and Current Version   These first three headings form a unique identifier for that configuration item. For example, the chapter on risk management for the PRINCE2PLUS project might be *P2PLUS,RISK,v1*. Using those three pieces of information, that chapter can be identified among all the other documents being created by the organization. This coding system enables you to uniquely identify each product.

Owner   This is the person or group who will take ownership of that product when it is finished and handed over to the users, clients, or those who will operate or maintain that product. For example, in the PRINCE2PLUS project, the owner might be someone in charge of the project management office for your organization.

Copy Holders   This is only relevant for a document-based product. Maybe there are several people writing different chapters of the PRINCE2PLUS document, but all the chapters need to refer to each other in a consistent manner. Therefore, each author needs to be aware of the latest version of everyone else's chapters. The Configuration Item Record for each chapter would need to list all the other chapter authors who should be sent the latest copy of that chapter.

Item Type   This section refers to whether this record holds information on a product, component, or a release.

Item Attributes   This section can be used to specify a certain category of configuration items, such as ones produced in a certain stage or ones that are management or specialist products. Reports can then be created that include information on just one of these categories.

Product State   Some products go through defined states during their creation and delivery. For example, a machine might be disassembled, moved, and then reassembled. This section specifies the state that the product is currently in.

Variant   This section shows the possible variants of the product. For example, a document might be available in several different languages.

Source   This section shows the original source of the product—for example, an in-house or third-party supplier.

The information in the Configuration Item Record will be updated during the life of the product as it moves through its creation and delivery processes. Every time the project management team identifies a new product that needs to be delivered, they create a Product Description for that product and an accompanying Configuration Item Record to track that product's status.

Control

The control activity does the following things:

- Stores, protects, and retrieves the information on the configuration items
- Stores, protects, and retrieves the products themselves
- Makes sure that only the right people are working on the products at the right time
- Makes sure that only authorized changes are made to products that have been baselined

In the PRINCE2PLUS project, this activity will involve ensuring that the person working on each chapter is updating the correct version; that once each chapter has been quality-checked and approved, it is protected from unauthorized changes (maybe by putting a password on the computer document file); and that when chapters are finished, the authors notify Project Support so they can update the chapter's Configuration Item Record with the change of status.

Status Accounting

From time to time, as Project Manager, you will want to learn the current status of all or some of the products. For example, if you are running the PRINCE2PLUS project, you might have been asked to create a progress report or maybe an End Stage Report, in which case, you need up-to-date information on the state of the project's products. You could get this information by scanning through the information in every one of the Configuration Item Records. However, it would be a lot easier if you could create a report that summarizes the information on either all or a category of the Configuration Item Records. In PRINCE2, this report is called a *Product Status Account*.

Figure 8.6 shows a Product Status Account being run against a subset of the Configuration Item Records in the project.

FIGURE 8.6 Product Status Account

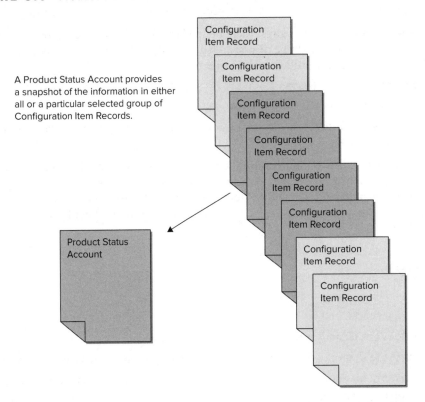

The Project Manager can request a Product Status Account at any of the following stages in a project:

- When preparing a Highlight Report during the Controlling a Stage process
- When reviewing the stage status during the Controlling a Stage process
- When preparing an End Stage Report during the Managing a Stage Boundary process
- When preparing for a planned or premature close during the Closing a Project process

It is Project Support's responsibility to create the Product Status Account.

Verification and Audit

There are two parts to the core activity of Verification and Audit. The first part involves checking that the information in the Configuration Item Records is correct by comparing the status information with the state of the actual products. The second part involves checking that the project management team has been following the configuration management approach described in the Configuration Management Strategy. Typically, this step is carried out at the end of the stage and at the end of the project. The Configuration Management Strategy describes how regularly these configuration audits should be done and who should be involved. Project Assurance will want to play a role in this activity.

 Real World Scenario

Real-World Examples of Configuration Management

One example of a configuration management tool is a document management system. This system might have a variety of features, such as safely storing multiple versions of a document, allowing the user to "roll back" to previous versions; reporting on the history of changes to the document and who made them; and allowing different levels of access to certain documents such as read/write or read-only.

Another example is using configuration management to help manage software development projects. On a large software project, each developer might create a small part of the product. Each part might consist of thousands of lines of code and go through many versions until it is ready for release. A software developer must ensure that their part of the product works consistently with all the other parts being developed, because mistakenly changing one line of code might cause the product to fail.

On a frequent basis, all the different parts will be combined to see if they work together. With thousands (and in some cases, millions) of ways through the different logical paths of the computer code, it takes a lot of hard work and discipline to create the many individual parts that work together properly.

What all this means is that it is essential to keep track of the status of each part of the product, who is working on it, and what its latest version is. It is also essential to be able to go back to older versions, in case a new version breaks the code base. Finally, it is critical to protect the parts of the code that have been approved, in case anyone mistakenly makes unauthorized changes to the software that prevent it from working correctly. All of these activities are configuration management. In the world of computer programming, many software tools are available that carry out these tasks—identifying, tracking, and protecting all the parts of the code.

Configuration Management Strategy

The Project Manager creates the Configuration Management Strategy during the initiation stage of the Initiating a Project process. It identifies how the project's products will be controlled and protected. It answers the question, "How will the project management team manage issue and change control and configuration management?"

The Configuration Management Strategy includes the following sections:

Configuration Management Procedure   This section describes the steps that will be repeated throughout the project to identify, protect, and track the project's products. It covers the five core activities of configuration management described in the previous section (planning, identification, control, status accounting, and verification and audit). The control activity includes how the products will be stored and retrieved, what security will be placed around the products, and how the products will be handed over to those who will operate or maintain them in their operational life.

Issue and Change Control Procedure   This section describes the steps that will be repeated throughout the project to control issues and changes and authorize them at a relevant level of authority. This procedure should cover the core activities of change and issue control described in the previous section (capturing, examining, proposing, deciding, and implementing).

Tools and Techniques   This section describes tools and/or techniques that will be used to control change or carry out configuration management. An example of a configuration tool is a software system that tracks and stores all the information on the products.

Records   This section describes the composition and format of the Issue Register and the Configuration Item Records.

Reporting   This section describes the various reports that will be created in issue, change, and configuration management, such as the Product Status Accounts and the Issue Reports.

Timing of Configuration Management and Issue and Change Control Activities   This section includes the timings of activities such as configuration audits.

Roles and Responsibilities   This section describes who will be responsible for the various activities involved with issue, change, or configuration management, including whether a Change Authority and change budget will be set up.

Scales for Priority and Severity   This section describes the scales that will be used to grade the priority and severity of issues—for example, low, medium, or high or one to five.

Roles Involved with the Change Theme

This chapter described the change-related responsibilities for the various PRINCE2 roles. Here is a quick review of these responsibilities to help you prepare for the exams:

Corporate or Programme Management   Might be the highest level of Change Authority in a project.

Project Board   During the initiation of the project, the Project Board authorizes the Configuration Management Strategy that has been prepared by the Project Manager. In particular, they will need to decide whether to use a Change Authority and, if so, agree on the level of authority to be delegated. They will also set the scales for issue severity and priority.

During the project, they will approve all changes (unless delegated to a Change Authority) and make decisions on escalated issues. Finally, they will approve Exception Plans when stage-level tolerances are forecast to be exceeded.

The Senior Users, Executive, and Senior Suppliers should make their decisions on issues by taking into account their perspective on the project (user, business, and supplier perspective, respectively).

Project Manager   During the initiation of the project, the Project Manager prepares the Configuration Management Strategy and creates the Issue Register.

During the project, the Project Manager creates Issue Reports and Exception Reports and maintains the Issue Register. He manages the issue and change control procedure and ensures that the project management team follows the approach outlined in the Configuration Management Strategy.

Team Manager   The Team Manager must escalate any issues associated with his Work Package to the Project Manager and help in the preparation of any necessary Exception Plans. He also needs to manage any issues as directed by the Project Manager and assist the Project Manager in examining the impact of an issue and options to deal with it.

Project Assurance   Project Assurance must review issues and changes by assessing their impact on the business, user, or supplier perspective on the project. Project Assurance should monitor the project management team's adherence to the project's approach to issue and change control as well as the configuration management that is described in the Configuration Management Strategy. Project Assurance should also be involved in configuration audits.

Project Support   Project Support should establish document control procedures for the project and assist with the creation and maintenance of documents such as Issue Reports, Exception Reports, Configuration Item Records, and the Issue Register as directed by the Project Manager. Project Support administers the configuration management procedure.

Summary

In this chapter, you learned about the Change theme. The Change theme helps to control and manage changes to the project's products. It ensures that the right level of authority authorizes changes. The theme also covers the closely connected topic of configuration management, which helps to identify, track, and protect the project's products.

First, the chapter defined some Change theme terminology: baselines, release, and configuration items. A baseline is a product that is frozen at a point in time for a particular reason. It may be frozen for all sorts of reasons, such as because it is ready for review or because it has been approved. Releases are a set of products that work together as a group in a consistent and coherent manner. A release might describe a group of products that will be handed over to the client. Finally, a configuration item could be a group of products, a single product, or even a part of a product. It is the status of these configuration items that the Project Manager will track during the project.

You then learned that there are three types of issues in PRINCE2. The first is a request for change. The second is called an off-specification. This is when a product is (or will be) missing or a product doesn't (or won't) match its specification. The final type of issue is a problem or concern. The problem or concern could be about all sorts of things, such as spending too much money, a key member of the staff being ill, or a supplier going bankrupt.

The chapter also described the Change Authority. This is a person or a group of people who have been given authority to approve changes to the project's products. The Change Authority might have a change budget that would be used to fund the changes.

You then saw how all issues and changes in a PRINCE2 project are handled by the issue and change control procedure. There are five core activities to this procedure: (1) capturing or documenting the issue; (2) examining the issue and thinking about what sort of impact it will have on the project; (3) proposing a set of options to deal with the issue; (4) making a decision on what option to pursue; and (5) implementing the decision.

In addition to describing the issue and change control procedure, the Change theme describes the configuration management procedure. You saw that this also has five core activities: (1) planning how configuration management will be approached in the project; (2) identifying all the configuration items that will be tracked and protected within the project; (3) controlling those configuration items so the right people are working on them at the right time; (4) on a regular basis, reporting on the current status of the configuration items; and (5) checking that all the records that are held on the configuration items are up-to-date and correct.

The final topic that this chapter covered was the Configuration Management Strategy. This management product documents how change control and configuration management will be done on the project. The Project Manager creates the Configuration Management Strategy near the beginning of the project, during the initiation stage.

Exam Essentials

Understand the purpose of the Change theme.   The purpose of the Change theme is to identify, assess, and control any potential and approved changes to the baseline.

Define a baseline.   A baseline is a snapshot of a release, product, and any component products, frozen at a point in time for a particular purpose.

Define a release.   A release is a complete and consistent set of products that are managed, tested, and deployed as a single entity to be handed over to the user(s).

Define a configuration item.   A configuration item is an entity that is subject to configuration management. The entity may be a component of a product, a product, or a set of products that form a release.

Know the three types of issues.   The three types of issues in PRINCE2 are request for change, off-specification, and problem or concern.

Understand the purpose of the change budget, in which processes it is agreed to, and which roles are involved.   The change budget is used to fund the work to implement requests for change and possibly the analysis work looking at the impact of the change. Know that the use of a change budget will be authorized by the Project Board or corporate or programme management and will be agreed to when a plan is authorized during Directing a Project.

Understand the responsibilities of the Change Authority. Know in which processes the Change Authority is agreed to and which roles are responsible.   The Change Authority is a person or group given authorization by the Project Board to approve changes. The Project Board decides whether to use a Change Authority and what constraints to place on their authority during the Initiating a Project process when the Configuration Management Strategy is prepared.

Know the five core activities of the issue and change control procedure and which roles and processes are involved.   The five core activities to the issue and change control procedure are capture, examine, propose, decide, and implement. The Project Manager carries out most of the five activities during the Controlling a Stage process, although if a breach in tolerances is forecast, the Project Manager might need to create an Exception Plan as part of the Managing a Stage Boundary process and decisions might need to be made by the Project Board during the Directing a Project process.

Know the five core activities of the configuration management procedure and which roles and processes are involved.   The five core activities of the configuration management procedure are planning (carried out by the Project Manager when preparing the Configuration Management Strategy during Initiating a Project); identification (carried out by the Project Manager when preparing Project Plans during the Initiating a Project process or preparing Stage or Exception Plans during the Managing a Stage Boundary process); control (carried out by the Project Manager mainly during the Controlling a Stage process); status accounting (carried out at various times by the Project Manager such as during Controlling a Stage, Managing a Stage Boundary, or Closing a Project); and finally, verification and audit (carried out by the Project Manager and Project Assurance, usually at the end of a stage in Managing a Stage Boundary and the end of the project in Closing a Project).

Know the purpose and composition of a Configuration Management Strategy; in which processes it is developed, used, and reviewed; and which roles are responsible.   The purpose of the Configuration Management Strategy is to document how change control and configuration management will be carried out during the project. The strategy is created by the Project Manager during Initiating a Project, and it is used and reviewed by the Project

Manager and Project Assurance throughout the project to ensure that the project is following the correct approach to configuration and change management.

Know the purpose and composition of a Configuration Item Record; in which processes it is developed, used, and reviewed; and which roles are responsible. The purpose of a Configuration Item Record is to track information relevant to a particular configuration item. It is created as soon as the need for that configuration item is identified and then updated throughout the life of the configuration item. Project Support is responsible for maintaining the Configuration Item Records.

Know the purpose and composition of an Issue Register; in which processes it is developed, used, and reviewed; and which roles are responsible. The purpose of the Issue Register is to track information regarding all the issues in the project. The Project Manager creates the Issue Register during the Initiating a Project process, and it will then be updated with new issue information throughout the project by Project Support.

Know the purpose and composition of an Issue Report; in which processes it is developed, used, and reviewed; and which roles are responsible. The purpose of the Issue Report is to track information regarding a particular issue in the project. The Project Manager is responsible for the creation of the Issue Report during the Controlling a Stage process, and it will then be updated throughout the life of that issue by the Project Manager.

Know the purpose and composition of a Product Status Account; in which processes it is developed, used, and reviewed; and which roles are responsible. The purpose of the Product Status Account is to provide information to the Project Manager regarding the status of all or a subset of the configuration items. The Project Manager might ask Project Support to create a Product Status Account at various times throughout the project, such as when preparing a Highlight Report or reviewing stage status during the Controlling a Stage process, when preparing the End Stage Report during the Managing a Stage Boundary process, or when preparing to close the project during the Closing a Project process.

Review Questions

The rest of this chapter contains mock exam questions, first for the Foundation exam and then for the Practitioner exam.

Foundation Questions

1. Which one of the following is an off-specification?
   1. A missing product
   2. A product not meeting its specification
   3. A product delivered late
   4. A product that is forecast not to be provided
   A. 1, 2, 3
   B. 1, 2, 4
   C. 1, 3, 4
   D. 2, 3, 4

2. In which of the typical core activities of the configuration management procedure would a coding system be developed for each configuration item?
   A. Planning
   B. Identification
   C. Control
   D. Status accounting

3. Which of the following options might be funded by a change budget?
   A. Assessing threats to the project
   B. Analyzing the impact of a request for change
   C. Reducing the probability of a threat
   D. Implementing actions following a quality review

4. Which of the following is a purpose of the Configuration Management Strategy?
   1. Describes how the project's products will be stored
   2. Describes how changes to the products will be controlled
   3. Describes how products will be identified
   4. Describes how to achieve each product's required level of quality
   A. 1, 2, 3
   B. 1, 2, 4
   C. 1, 3, 4
   D. 2, 3, 4

5. Which role is responsible for maintaining information on the status of each configuration item?

   A. Project Support

   B. Project Manager

   C. Change Authority

   D. Project Assurance

6. When might the Project Manager call for a Product Status Account?

   1. When preparing the Configuration Management Strategy

   2. When preparing a progress report for the Project Board

   3. At the end of the project

   4. Toward the end of a stage

   A. 1, 2, 3

   B. 1, 2, 4

   C. 1, 3, 4

   D. 2, 3, 4

7. Which management product is used to track all products that do not meet their specifications?

   A. Configuration Management Strategy

   B. Issue Report

   C. Issue Register

   D. Configuration Item Record

8. If the Project Board decides to accept an off-specification, what is this called?

   A. Concession

   B. Threat

   C. Issue

   D. Quality issue

9. Which of the following could **NOT** be a candidate for a Change Authority?

   A. Corporate or programme management

   B. Project Board

   C. Project Manager

   D. Project Support

10. Which of the following could **NOT** be a configuration item?

    A. A component of a product

    B. A management product

    C. A request for change

    D. A specialist product

Practitioner Questions

The following Practitioner questions are divided into three sections by question type and are based on the Practitioner exam scenario that you will find in this book's Introduction.

Section 1: Classic Multiple Choice Type

Answer the following two questions about the Configuration Management Strategy.

1. What information should be recorded under the configuration management procedure heading?

    A. Information on any document security corporate standards to be followed

    B. How to capture requests for change to the project's products

    C. How to assess uncertainties related to the project's products

    D. When configuration audits should be carried out throughout the project

2. What information should be recorded under the issue and change control procedure heading?

    A. Information on how to hand over the website to the operational team

    B. A reference to Quality Furniture's standard impact analysis procedure

    C. The format of the Issue Register

    D. Any metrics to be employed in order to verify the product's fitness for purpose

Section 2: Sequence Type

Read the following information regarding a request for change in the Quality Furniture project and then answer the sequence question.

Additional Information for Section 2

The project is in stage 4, and the website for Quality Furniture is being built. The Chief Executive recently saw a competitor's website that had a facility to view the furniture from many different angles (3D View). He would like this facility in the new website. Currently, this is not specified in the baseline designs for the site. Stage 4 has a change budget of $5,000, a cost tolerance of $8,000, and a time tolerance of 1 week.

Sequence Question for Section 2

Column 1 in the following table lists activities that might be carried out while handling this request for change from the Chief Executive. For each activity in Column 1, decide whether it was an appropriate application of PRINCE2, and if so, select the order in which it should have been performed from Column 2. Note that not all of the answers in Column 2 might be used.

Column 1	Column 2
1. The Project Manager escalates the request for change to the Project Board, showing the potential impacts and the options to implement 3D View.	A. First
2. The Project Manager chairs a meeting with the project team to look at the possible benefits of 3D View, the costs of creating it, and the time it will take. The results are that the cost of 3D View will be an additional $6,000, add 3 more days to the schedule, and potentially increase online sales by a further 10%.	B. Second
3. The Project Board asks for an Exception Plan.	C. Third
4. The Project Manager details the change control procedure that will be used to manage the 3D View request for change in the Configuration Management Strategy.	D. Fourth
5. The Project Manager asks the Chief Executive if he could draft an Issue Report detailing his ideas on 3D View.	E. Fifth
6. Using the cost tolerance, the Project Manager implements the request for change.	F. Sixth
	G. Not appropriate

Section 3: Assertion/Reason Type

Using the following additional information, answer the four assertion/reason questions about the preparation of the Configuration Management Strategy.

Additional Information for Section 3

The following text is a memo regarding project document management that has been sent from Quality Furniture's Administration Manager to the Project Manager:

> All project documentation should be stored in Quality Furniture's document management software system. This will keep both new and old versions of each document. After each document has been approved, it will be password-protected, and only the Project Manager and the Administration Manager should have read/write access.

A document information list will be kept in a spreadsheet called DOCINFO. Each row of the spreadsheet will relate to a project document giving current status and other relevant information. Quality Furniture's Administration Assistant will keep the spreadsheet up-to-date. Each document should be given a unique identifier.

At the end of each stage, the Quality Furniture Administration Manager will verify that the information in the DOCINFO spreadsheet is accurate.

Assertion/Reason Questions for Section 3

Rows 1 to 4 in the following table consist of an assertion statement and a reason statement. For each line, identify the appropriate option, from options A to E, that applies. Each option can be used once, more than once, or not at all.

A. The assertion is true and the reason is true, *and* the reason explains the assertion.

B. The assertion is true and the reason is true, *but* the reason does not explain the assertion.

C. The assertion is true and the reason is false.

D. The assertion is false and the reason is true.

E. Both the assertion and the reason are false.

Assertion		Reason
1. "Quality Furniture's document management system will be used to track and control all project documentation" should be recorded in the "configuration management procedure."	BECAUSE	The configuration management procedure should cover activities to control the project's products, including storage and retrieval.
2. The composition and format of the DOCINFO spreadsheet should be recorded under the "records" section.	BECAUSE	The "records" section shows how to store information regarding off-specifications that occur in the project.
3. "A review of the accuracy of the information in the DOCINFO spreadsheet will take place at the end of each stage" should be recorded under the "timings" section.	BECAUSE	Configuration audits are part of the verification and audit activity in the configuration management procedure.
4. "The Administration Assistant will maintain the information in the DOCINFO spreadsheet" should be recorded in the Quality Management Strategy rather than the Configuration Management Strategy.	BECAUSE	Maintaining the quality of the information about the project's configuration items is a quality activity.

Chapter

9

Progress Theme

PRINCE2 EXAM OBJECTIVES COVERED IN THIS CHAPTER:

✓ Understand the purpose of the Progress theme.

✓ Understand the concepts of tolerances and exceptions.

 ▪ Know when and how tolerances are set.

 ▪ Know in which management products tolerances are documented.

 ▪ Know when and how exceptions are reported.

 ▪ Understand the different levels of tolerance and how they relate to the application of management by exception by the different levels of management.

✓ Understand the lines of authority and the four levels of management within the project management team.

✓ Understand the purpose of the Daily Log.

✓ Know the difference between event-driven and time-driven controls.

✓ Know the factors to consider when dividing a project into management stages.

✓ Understand the concept of management stages and what differentiates them from technical stages.

✓ For the following management products, know their purpose, composition; in which processes they are developed, used, and reviewed; and which roles are responsible for each:

 ▪ Work Package

 ▪ Lessons Log

 ▪ Lessons Report

 ▪ Exception Report

The scope of the Progress theme can be difficult to understand. The project management area covered by the other themes is far more obvious. For example, it's easy to understand that the Organization theme describes the people who are involved in a project and what they should do, and the Risk theme describes how to deal with potential problems. But it isn't obvious what the Progress theme covers.

In the previous version of PRINCE2, the Progress theme was called the Control component. (In the previous version, a component was pretty much the same thing as a theme.) I think Control was a better name, because the Progress theme is all about *controlling* all the activities and the people in the project so that the objectives that have been set are achieved. There are lots of parts of PRINCE2 that help *control* what is happening on a project, many of which you have already read about in other chapters. For example, the Product Descriptions that you learned about in the Quality theme help to define what is to be delivered, and so help control the creation of the products. So in addition to introducing a few new topics, the Progress theme also reviews the whole of PRINCE2 to see how the parts of the model help *control* what is happening.

To learn more about how the Progress theme controls a project, read on.

Purpose of the Progress Theme

As mentioned in the introduction to this chapter, the Progress theme is focused on controlling the project so that it achieves its objectives. There are a number of general things that need to be done in order to control a project. First, the project management team must decide what they want the project to accomplish. They do so by setting objectives in terms of time, cost, scope, quality, risk, and benefits. These objectives are described in various management products, including the project's plans and various parts of the Project Initiation Documentation such as the Business Case, the strategies, and the Project Product Description. All of these management products help control the project, because the project management team can use them to compare what is actually happening on the project with what they would like to happen. These products act as a measuring stick to see how well the project is progressing.

The second part of controlling a project is to work out how the project management team will constantly review what is happening in the project against what they would like to happen. There are various parts of PRINCE2 that help you do this. For instance, progress reports such as the Highlight Reports, Checkpoint Reports, the End Stage Reports, and the End Project Report show the project management team how the project is progressing against its objectives. There are also the various logs and registers, which help the Project Manager track things such as issues, risks, lessons, and personal actions. Finally, there are the stages. At the end of each stage, the project management team comes together and reviews the performance of the previous stage.

The last part of controlling the project is making timely decisions at the right level of management, either about whether some piece of work should proceed or how to handle problems in the project. PRINCE2 enables the Project Board to decide, one stage at a time, whether to proceed with the project, and enables the Project Manager to decide when to authorize the team to do the work. Both of these decisions help control the progress of the project by releasing resources a bit at a time. As you will learn in this chapter, the concepts of tolerance and exceptions ensure that the right level of management gets involved in decisions about how to deal with problems when the project is going off track.

As you can see, the Progress theme is quite a collection of different aspects of PRINCE2, some of which have already been covered in other chapters of this book. But in this theme, PRINCE2 reviews these areas and asks the question, "How does this part of PRINCE2 control where the project is going?" The Progress theme also introduces the concepts of tolerances, exceptions, and stages. (These concepts have been mentioned in other chapters, but they're described in more detail in this chapter.)

The Progress theme primarily helps implement two PRINCE2 principles: manage by stages and manage by exception.

Tolerances and Exceptions

The definition of tolerances in *Managing Successful Projects with PRINCE2* (Stationery Office, 2009) is as follows:

> Tolerances are the permissible deviation above and below a plan's target for time and cost without escalating the deviation to the next level of management. There may also be tolerance levels for quality, scope, benefit and risk.

In other words, tolerances enable one management level to specify certain constraints on the authority of the management level below them. For example, when the Project Board delegates the management of each stage to the Project Manager, they define how much time the Project Manager is allowed to use. This time target might have some allowable flexibility. For example, the Project Board might say to the Project Manager, "Deliver this stage in the next six months, although in certain circumstances, we will allow a two-week late delivery." These additional two weeks are an example of a time tolerance.

The Project Board might also set cost tolerances for the Project Manager to deliver the stage. For example, they might say to the Project Manager, "We will give you $50,000 for the next stage, with an allowable overspend of up to $5,000 and an allowable underspend of up to $10,000."

In addition to cost and time tolerances, there could also be scope, quality, benefit, and risk tolerances. You will learn about these later in this chapter.

The definition of exception in *Managing Successful Projects with PRINCE2* is as follows:

> An exception is a situation where it can be forecast that there will be a deviation beyond the agreed tolerance levels.

In the previous example, an exception would occur if the Project Manager forecasts that the stage will be delivered later than the two-week tolerance set by the Project Board. When an exception occurs, it must immediately be reported to the management level above; so in this case, the Project Manager must escalate the situation to the Project Board. In effect, the Project Manager does not have authority to handle the situation and must refer to the Project Board for them to make a decision on how to deal with the delay.

One question that students often ask is, "What is the point of a negative tolerance?" In the previous example, the Project Board has asked the Project Manager to escalate any situation where there might be an underspend of more than $10,000. But isn't spending less than $40,000 a good thing that does not need to be escalated?

There are two main reasons that the Project Board might want the Project Manager to report forecast underspends. First, they might be concerned about the quality of the products, and second, they might be able to reallocate the money to another project or another part of the organization.

One other important point regarding exceptions is that they occur when it can be *forecast* that a tolerance level will be breached, not when the level is actually breached. So in the previous example, the Project Manager is in exception when he forecasts that the stage will spend over $55,000, not when the stage actually does spend over $55,000.

Levels of Tolerance

Figure 9.1 shows cost tolerances being set at three different levels: project, stage, and Work Package. On the left side of the figure, you can see which level of management sets which level of tolerance. Corporate or programme management sets the overall project budget and any tolerances around this budget. These project tolerances are given to the Project Board and define their level of authority. In this case, you can see in Figure 9.1 that the Project Board is given a project budget of $300,000 and must escalate to corporate or programme management if they believe they will overspend on that budget by more than $100,000 or underspend on it by more than $200,000. (Project tolerances therefore are plus $100,000/minus $200,000.) Similarly, for each stage, the Project Board sets a stage budget with tolerances for the Project Manager to work within. Figure 9.1 shows that for one stage in this project, the Project Manager was given a stage budget of $100,000 with tolerances of plus $50,000 and minus $70,000. Finally, for each Work Package, the Project Manager will allocate a Work Package budget with tolerances that the Team Manager or team need to work within. Figure 9.1 shows that for one Work Package in this project, the teams were given a budget of $50,000 with tolerances of plus $20,000 and minus $30,000.

FIGURE 9.1   Levels of cost tolerance

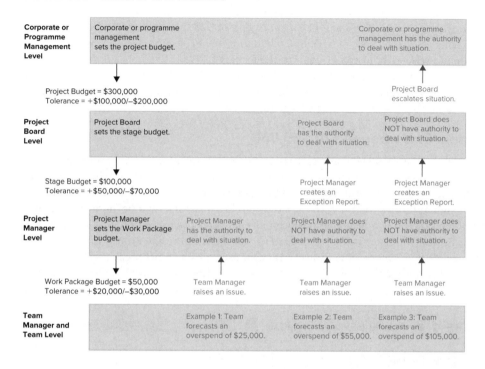

The example in Figure 9.1 shows the setting of three different levels of cost tolerances. Time, scope, and risk tolerances can also be set the same way at a project, stage, and Work Package level. However, the other two types of tolerances—benefit and quality—are not set at these three different levels. Benefit tolerance is only set at the project level. Quality is set at an overall project level and then at a product level. (You'll learn more about benefit and quality tolerances later in this chapter.)

On the right side of the diagram are three examples that show what happens when there is a forecast deviation beyond the Work Package tolerance, then the stage tolerance, and finally, the project tolerance.

Example 1: Overspend of $25,000

In Example 1, the Team Manager realizes he will spend $25,000 more than the $50,000 he has been allocated by the Project Manager. In this case, the Project Manager has set Work Package tolerances to be +$20,000 and −$30,000, so the forecast overspend will breach the Work Package tolerances. An exception has occurred that the Team Manager must escalate immediately to the Project Manager.

In the PRINCE2 model, the Team Manager escalates forecast breaches in Work Package tolerances to the Project Manager by raising an issue in the way that has been agreed to in the Work Package. This might involve simply phoning the Project Manager or perhaps filling out an issue report form and emailing it to the Project Manager.

When the Project Manager receives the issue, he first checks that he has the authority to handle this situation. He can handle overspends as long as they do not breach the stage tolerances. In this case, there will be an overspend of $25,000, but the Project Manager has been given a stage tolerance of $50,000. Therefore, the Project Manager can handle this situation himself, without escalating it to the Project Board.

All of this is based on the assumption that no other Work Packages have overspent their budgets. If they have, this might mean that the cumulative effects of all the overspends would breach the Project Manager's stage tolerances.

Example 2: Overspend of $55,000

In Example 2, the Team Manager forecasts that he will spend $55,000 more than the $50,000 he has been allocated. As in Example 1, he will need to escalate this situation by raising an issue to the Project Manager. However, this time, the Project Manager does not have enough authority to deal with the situation, because there will be an overspend of $55,000 and the Project Manager has been given a stage tolerance of $50,000. This means that the Project Manager will have to escalate this situation to the Project Board.

In the PRINCE2 model, the Project Manager escalates forecast breaches in stage tolerances by sending the Project Board an Exception Report. Figure 9.2 shows an example Exception Report.

FIGURE 9.2 Example Exception Report

Exception Title: *Increase in the price of haulage.*
Cause of the Exception: *Since estimating the costs of haulage of the materials for the hotel to the construction site, the price of oil has doubled. This has caused a substantial increase in the price of transport. The Work Package of the haulage company was forecast to cost $50,000. The haulage company is now predicting there will be an overspend of $55,000, taking the total cost of haulage up to $105,000.*
Consequences of the Deviation: *The consequence of the deviation is that there is not enough money in the stage budget to pay the haulage company. If the materials are not transported to the site, the construction on the hotel cannot start.*
Options: *Increase the budget for the haulage company or procure the services of a less expensive haulage company.*
Recommendation: *It seems that all haulage companies have increased their costs, so we recommend to simply increase the current haulage company's budget.*
Lessons: *A fixed price contract with the haulage company would have limited our exposure to the risk of the oil price increasing.*

The Project Board will then review the predicted overspend and compare it against the project tolerances they have been given by corporate or programme management to see if they have the authority to deal with this situation. In this case, the overspend is $55,000 and the Project Board has a project cost tolerance of $100,000, so they can handle this situation without referring to corporate or programme management.

Example 3: Overspend of $105,000

In Example 3, there is a much more serious overspend. The Team Manager forecasts that he will spend $105,000 more than he has been allocated. As you can see in the figure, first the Team Manager escalates this to the Project Manager by raising the issue. Then the Project Manager escalates it to the Project Board by sending them an Exception Report. Finally, the Project Board realizes that they don't have enough project cost tolerance to deal with this situation, and they refer it to corporate or programme management. So with this situation, only corporate or programme management has the authority to make a decision on how to handle the overspend.

Further Notes on Levels of Tolerance

There are a few things that you need to remember when it comes to levels of tolerance. First, as you saw in the examples, when there is a breach in the level of tolerance, it is escalated to the next level of management only. So if the Team Manager realizes that the breach of tolerance is so severe that it actually breaches the project level of tolerance (as in Example 3), he doesn't escalate this directly to corporate or programme management—he only escalates it to the Project Manager. (As you have just seen in the previous subsection, the Project Manager will then escalate the breach of tolerance to the Project Board, who then in turn escalate it to corporate or programme management.)

Also remember who sets the various levels of tolerance. Corporate or programme management sets the project level of tolerance. They do this at the beginning of the project when they write the project mandate, but they may adjust the tolerance levels throughout the project, especially when the Project Brief or Project Initiation Documentation is authorized.

The Project Board sets the stage level of tolerances during the Directing a Project process, when they authorize the Project Manager to deliver a management stage.

Finally, the Project Manager sets the Work Package level of tolerance when he authorizes a team to work on a Work Package during the Controlling a Stage process.

Types of Tolerance

The six types of tolerance are time and cost (which are known as the standard types of tolerance), scope, risk, quality, and benefit.

Time Tolerance

An example of a time tolerance is "Deliver this project within six months, although an early delivery of one month or late delivery of two weeks would be allowed." Time tolerances can be set at the project, stage, or Work Package level and are described in the Project Plan, Stage Plan, or Work Package, respectively.

Cost Tolerance

An example of a cost tolerance is "The budget for this Work Package is $1,000 plus or minus 10 percent." Cost tolerances can be set at the project, stage, or Work Package level and are described in the Project Plan, Stage Plan, or Work Package, respectively.

Scope Tolerance

Scope tolerance describes any flexibility around the number or range of products that will be delivered. For example, the client for a website project might prioritize the list of features that they want on the website. Some features will be mandatory; others might be "good to have"; and finally, there might be some features that aren't essential to the project and are just "nice to have."

Scope tolerances can be set at the project, stage, or Work Package level and are described in the Project Plan, Stage Plan, or Work Package, respectively.

Risk Tolerance

Risk tolerance defines a threshold level of risk that, if exceeded, needs to be escalated to the next level of management. To be able to set a risk tolerance, the project management team must decide how to measure the level of risk on the project at any one time. One way of doing this is to simply count how many risks are currently listed in the Risk Register. A more sophisticated method is to use the expected value risk evaluation approach you learned about in Chapter 7, "Risk Theme." Table 9.1 is a duplicate of the table used to explain this method in Chapter 7.

TABLE 9.1   Expected value risk evaluation technique

Risk ID	Probability (%)	Impact ($)	Expected value ($) (probability multiplied by impact)
01	20%	$10,000	$2,000
02	50%	$30,000	$15,000
03	30%	$100,000	$30,000
	Expected Overall Value:		**$47,000**

As you can see, each risk is given a percentage that shows the likelihood of that risk and a predicted cost impact. By multiplying the probability of each risk by its forecast cost impact, an expected value for that risk is calculated. Then, an overall value is calculated by adding all the expected values together.

This expected overall figure is the likely amount of money that risks will cost the project. It indicates the level of risk on the project and can be used to set a risk tolerance level. For example, the Project Board might say to the Project Manager, "Escalate the risk situation to us if the overall expected impact of risks rises above $50,000."

There are many other ways of defining an overall risk tolerance for the project. One method worth mentioning is using the risk profile diagram that you first saw in the section "The Contents of the Business Case" in Chapter 4, "Business Case Theme." Figure 9.3 shows that risk profile diagram again, with the addition of a risk tolerance line. If any risk is identified that is above this line, in effect a risk with a high impact and probability, then this situation should be escalated to the relevant level of authority.

FIGURE 9.3   Risk Profile Diagram showing a risk tolerance line

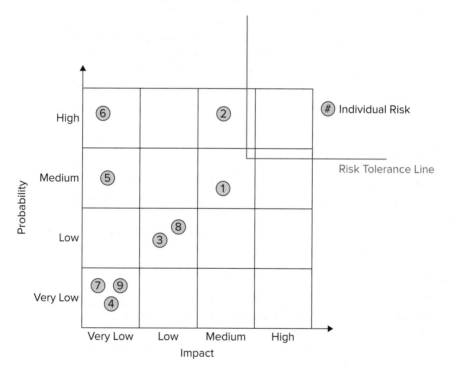

Another way of setting risk tolerances is to define certain types of risks that, if spotted, must be escalated. For example, the Project Board will want to be immediately informed about risks that might threaten their business-as-usual operations.

Risk tolerances can be set at the project, stage, or Work Package level and are written into the Risk Management Strategy, Stage Plan, or Work Package, respectively.

Quality Tolerance

Quality tolerances are allowable flexibility around the specifications of products. They can be set at both a high level in the Project Product Description and at a lower level in the Product Descriptions.

In Chapter 6, "Quality Theme," you learned that the main project outputs are described in the Project Product Description at the beginning of the project. The Project Product Description contains acceptance criteria, which are measurable specifications for the products. For example, in the project to build a hotel, an acceptance criterion might be that the hotel should be able to service 400 guests at one time. If some flexibility in the hotel's capacity was specified, that would be an example of a quality tolerance.

You also learned in Chapter 6, "Quality Theme," that as the project progresses, the project management team needs to create more detailed specifications for the products that are described in the Product Descriptions. For example, in the hotel project, Product Descriptions might be written for the swimming pool, the bedrooms, and/or the lobby. These Product Descriptions should contain quality criteria for each product, which are the measurable attributes of that product. For example, a Product Description for a bedroom might say that the room needs to be 20 square meters. If the specification included some flexibility, such as that the room could be anywhere between 18 to 20 square meters, this would be another example of a quality tolerance.

In summary, quality tolerances at a broad level are described in the Project Product Description, and quality tolerances at an individual product level are described in the Product Descriptions. Remember that the Project Manager creates the Project Product Description and Product Descriptions with any associated tolerances with the help of the Senior Users, the Senior Suppliers, and the teams. The Project Board will sign off on both management products.

Benefit Tolerance

Benefit tolerances are allowable deviations related to the forecast benefits of the project. In the hotel project, here's an example of a benefit tolerance: "Sales for the hotel are forecast to be $20 million, although a figure of $18 million would be acceptable to the board."

Benefit tolerances are set only at the project level and are described in the Business Case. The Project Board authorizes them.

Summary of Tolerance Types

Figure 9.4 summarizes the tolerance types and where they are documented.

FIGURE 9.4 Tolerance types

Tolerance Area	Project Level	Stage Level	Work Package Level	Product Level
Time	Project Plan	Stage Plan	Work Package	not applicable
Cost	Project Plan	Stage Plan	Work Package	not applicable
Scope	Project Plan	Stage Plan	Work Package	not applicable
Risk	Risk Mgt Strategy	Stage Plan	Work Package	not applicable
Quality	Project Product Description	not applicable	not applicable	Product Description
Benefit	Business Case	not applicable	not applicable	not applicable

Based on Cabinet Office PRINCE2® material. Reproduced under licence from the Cabinet Office.

PRINCE2 Controls

As mentioned earlier, there are many parts of PRINCE2 that help control the progress of a project. You already learned about many of these parts in previous chapters, but this section specifically describes what role they play in project control.

Project Board Controls

PRINCE2 enables the Project Board to control the project without the need to attend regular progress and decision-making meetings. This helps reduce the amount of management time the Project Board members need to dedicate to the project. The control mechanisms provided for the Project Board are described in this section.

Figure 9.5 is a simplified version of the diagram that you saw in Chapter 1, "Overview of PRINCE2." This diagram provides an overview of the process model. Using the diagram and the explanation that follows, you will see that the Project Board has three main ways to control the progress of the project: by using authorizations, by monitoring progress, and by putting in place mechanisms to deal effectively with problems and changes.

FIGURE 9.5 Project Board controls

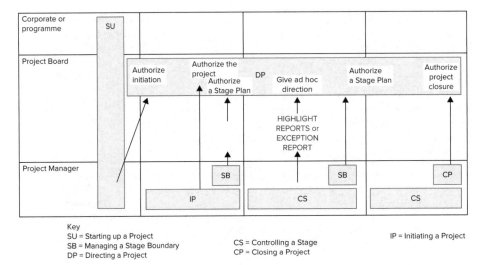

Key
SU = Starting up a Project
SB = Managing a Stage Boundary
DP = Directing a Project

CS = Controlling a Stage
CP = Closing a Project

IP = Initiating a Project

Based on Cabinet Office PRINCE2® material. Reproduced under licence from the Cabinet Office.

Controlling the Project Using Authorizations

First, the Project Board can use the Directing a Project authorizations to control the progress of the project. These authorizations act as gates, which the project has to go through in order to proceed. The Project Board controls access to these gates and thus controls the progress of the project. These authorizations are used at various times in the project, as described here:

- After the Project Manager has finished the work of the Starting up a Project process and created the Project Brief and the Stage Plan for the initiation stage, the project cannot proceed any further until the Project Board authorizes initiation.

- After the Project Manager has finished the work of the Initiating a Project process and created the Project Initiation Documentation, the project cannot proceed any further until the Project Board authorizes the project.

- After the Project Manager has created the next Stage Plan, the project cannot proceed any further until the Project Board authorizes the next stage. This authorization could also be used to authorize an Exception Plan.

- Finally, the project cannot finish until the Project Board has authorized closure.

Controlling the Project by Monitoring Progress

An important part of controlling a project is keeping up-to-date on the progress of the project. Without progress updates, it is impossible to know when to do tasks such as decision making or releasing resources.

The Project Board monitors the progress of the project using Highlight Reports and *End Stage Reports*. You will learn about the composition of these management products in Chapter 10, "Managing the Middle of a Project Successfully with PRINCE2." For now, just think of them as regular progress reports, showing what has happened in the previous period and what is planned to happen in the next period. The Project Board might also use Project Assurance to monitor progress.

Controlling the Project in Exception and Change Situations

Even in a well-managed project, it's inevitable that things will not go according to plan and that people will change their minds about what they require. With PRINCE2, the Project Board can be reassured that major problems and changes will be escalated to them, whereas smaller ones can be dealt with at a lower level of management. The Project Board can use the tolerances that they set for the Project Manager to define the size of problems and changes that they wish to be involved with. If the Project Manager realizes that the tolerances he has been given will be breached, he must escalate this situation to the Project Board using an Exception Report. The Project Board can then decide what action to take.

As you learned in Chapter 8, "Change Theme," the Project Board can also delegate an amount of change authority either to a separate body (called the Change Authority) or to the Project Manager. The Project Board can set certain constraints on the ability to authorize change; for example, the Project Manager might only be allowed to authorize changes up to a certain amount of money. In the same way that the tolerances are used by the Project Board to define the size of the problems they wish to be involved with, the constraints on the Change Authority help the Project Board to define the size of the changes they wish to make decisions about.

Project Manager Controls

The Project Manager uses various parts of PRINCE2 to ensure that each stage he has been given to manage by the Project Board is kept on track and delivers what is expected. There are three main ways that the Project Manager controls each stage: by using Work Packages to delegate work to the teams, by monitoring the progress of the stage, and by putting in place mechanisms to deal effectively with problems and changes.

Controlling the Stage Using Work Packages

The teams are not allowed to start their work until the Project Manager has authorized a Work Package. The Work Package is agreed upon by the team (or the Team Manager acting on the team's behalf) and the Project Manager. It details all the relevant information about the team's work, such as what products they need to deliver, how much time and money they have to do the work, and so on.

A Sample Work Package

To understand how a Work Package is used, consider once again the scenario where a hotel chain has commissioned a project to build a new hotel. Imagine that the Project Manager needs to delegate some work to the procurement team, because they are responsible for creating a request for tender document that will be sent to building construction companies. The Work Package that the Project Manager creates for the procurement team might contain the following information:

Date   This section contains the date that the Work Package was agreed upon between the Project Manager and the Team Manager (or the team members if there is no Team Manager).

Team Manager or Person Authorized   This section contains the name of the person authorized to do the work. In this case, it is the name of the person leading the procurement team who will compile the request for tender document.

Work Package Description   This section describes the work to be done. In this case, it describes the type of information that should be included in the request for tender document and what is involved in putting this document together.

Techniques, Processes, and Procedures   This section describes any special approaches that should be used to deliver the specialist products. In this case, it may refer to any company procurement standards.

Development Interfaces   This section specifies the people with whom the delivery team will need to liaise during the delivery of the Work Package, which PRINCE2 refers to as development interfaces. In this case, the procurement team needs to get the hotel designs from the architects.

Operations and Maintenance Interfaces   This section describes any operations and maintenance interfaces, which are other products that the products delivered by the Work Package will have to work with or connect to in their operational life. The request for tender document won't go into operational life, so this section is not relevant in this example. However, imagine if the work was to create a website where clients could book hotel rooms online. The online booking website would need to connect with the hotel's sales system, so that sales system would be included in this section as an operations interface.

Configuration Management Requirements   As you learned in Chapter 8, "Change Theme," configuration management helps you track, protect, and identify the project's products. This section might cover a number of configuration management aspects related to the work, such as how to store and place security around different versions of the products being created, how to obtain copies of other products, and who to advise of any status changes to the products (because they may need to update the configuration management system). Maybe in this case, the hotel chain's document management system will be used to store all the different versions of the request for tender document.

Joint Agreements   This section specifies the cost, time, and effort that the Project Manager and the team have agreed will be required to complete the work. It may also specify any key milestone dates when certain interim deliverables will be finished. Maybe in this case, the procurement manager and the Project Manager have agreed the work will take two weeks and the procurement team will charge the project $500.

Tolerances   This section specifies the time-, cost-, scope-, and risk-level tolerances that the Project Manager has given the team for the work. Maybe in this case, the Project Manager will allow a three-day tolerance if the procurement department is delayed due to other work.

Constraints   Some work will have to follow certain general constraints, such as health and safety rules or security constraints. In this request for tender document example, there might be a constraint that no company documents can be taken off site and that all documents must be regularly scanned for computer viruses.

Reporting Arrangements   In this section, the Project Manager defines how often the teams report to him as well as the type of information that he expects to see in a progress report. This is effectively defining the composition of the Checkpoint Reports. (You will learn about the PRINCE2 recommended composition of the Checkpoint Reports in Chapter 10, "Managing the Middle of the Project Successfully with PRINCE2.") In this case, maybe the Project Manager asks for a status update at the end of the first week of the work.

Problem Handling and Escalation   This section describes how the team must escalate problems and issues. In this example, the procurement team may be required to call the Project Manager immediately if a problem occurs and then send a written report regarding the matter within 24 hours.

Extracts or References   This section specifies other important documents that the team might need. For example, the Stage Plan is a useful reference because it shows the team how their work fits in with the rest of the activities in the stage. Another important set of documents is the Product Descriptions because they show what needs to be delivered. In this request for tender document example, a necessary reference is the Product Description.

Approval Method   This section describes the approval method to be used for this Work Package, which includes the person or group who will sign off on the work from the Work Package and how the Project Manager should be advised of this. In the example, this section might specify that the head of procurement is responsible for signing off on the request for tender document.

Exam Questions about Work Packages

The Practitioner exam might ask you detailed questions about what each section of the Work Package should contain. It is difficult to remember all the information about what should go where in a PRINCE2 management product. However, don't forget that in the Practitioner exam, you can refer to *Managing Successful Projects with PRINCE2*. This is especially useful for questions about management products like the Work Package, because Appendix A shows you exactly what each of the management products should contain.

Controlling the Stage by Monitoring Progress

Just as it's important for the Project Board to monitor the progress of the project using Highlight Reports and End Stage Reports, it is important for the Project Manager to monitor the progress of a stage using Checkpoint Reports. Checkpoint Reports are created by the Team Managers (or team members if there isn't a Team Manager) and sent to the

Project Manager on a regular basis. They update the Project Manager on the progress of the team's work. As you saw in the previous section, the Project Manager defines the composition and the frequency of the Checkpoint Reports in the Work Package.

Controlling the Stage in Exception and Change Situations

The last way that the Project Manager controls the stage is by using the PRINCE2 logs and registers to review progress and identify any issues or risks that need to be resolved. Anyone can raise an issue or a risk in PRINCE2. When they do so, they should inform the Project Manager so that it can be logged in the appropriate log or register. (Informal issues are put in the Daily Log; formal issues, problems or concerns, requests for change, and off-specifications go in the Issue Register; and risks are put in the Risk Register.) The Project Manager then uses these logs and registers to review the progress of the stage and checks to see whether there are any pressing issues, risks, or actions that might throw the stage off track. For more information about the Risk Register, see Chapter 7, "Risk Theme"; for more on the Issue Register, see Chapter 8, "Change Theme."

The Project Manager creates the Daily Log in Starting up a Project. It is basically the Project Manager's notebook and/or personal action list. It is sometimes known as the Project Manager's diary. It is a useful tool that allows the Project Manager to track the progress of a variety of things that would not be covered in the more formal management product such as the Issue Register or the Stage Plan. It allows the Project Manager to control his day-to-day activities.

When the Project Manager delegates work, he sets tolerances for the teams. If the teams believe they will breach these Work Package tolerances, they must escalate the situation to the Project Manager. Their Work Package will show them how to escalate situations to the Project Manager. This allows the Project Manager to define the sorts of problems he wishes to be involved with and which ones he would prefer the teams to sort out on their own.

Event-Driven vs. Time-Driven Controls

In the last few sections, you have seen how many different areas of PRINCE2 help control the project. For example, the Work Package helps the Project Manager control the team, and the authorizations help the Project Board control the progress of the project. All of these different areas are known as *controls*. PRINCE2 splits up controls into two types: event-driven or time-driven.

Event-driven controls occur after some sort of event, such as the end of the stage or the end of the project. For example, the End Stage Report is an event-driven control and is driven by the end of the stage occurring. Another example is the Exception Report that is driven by a forecast breach of stage tolerances.

The other type are called *time-driven controls*. These controls are not driven by anything in particular happening—they just occur at regular intervals. For example, it is Monday morning and it is time to write the weekly Highlight Report. Another example of a time-driven control is the team writing a regular Checkpoint Report.

Controlling the Capturing and Reporting of Lessons

Students always find the fact that the Lessons Log and the *Lessons Report* are covered in a theme about tracking and controlling progress rather unusual. It does seem a rather awkward admission to this area of PRINCE2, but I will attempt to explain why it is here.

As you have seen already, one of the key principles of PRINCE2 is to "learn from experience." In Starting up a Project, the Project Manager creates the Lessons Log. The Lessons Log is used for two purposes. First, it is used as a repository of experience from previous initiatives that might be useful in the management of this project. Second, it is used to record lessons that are being learned on the current project that might be useful for others. The Lessons Log is therefore a way of controlling the flow of lessons and experience in the project. You can see the composition of the Lessons Log in Figure 9.6.

FIGURE 9.6   Composition of the Lessons Log

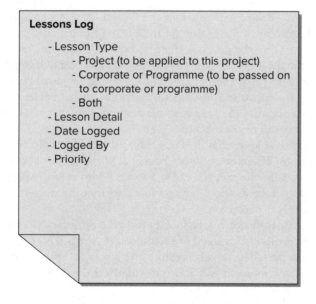

Lessons are passed on to other parts of the organization using a Lessons Report. A Lessons Report could be created at any time in the project, but typically it is created at the end of a stage or the project and is included in the End Stage Report or the End Project Report, respectively. The recipient(s) of the Lessons Report should be in a position to use the experience to improve the programme or the organization. Those in charge of the organization's quality management system would be one typical recipient.

Using Stages to Control a Project

You have already seen that an important principle in PRINCE2 is the ability to manage the project by stages. In this section, you will learn the benefits this brings to how a project is managed and the factors you should consider when dividing a project into stages. You will also see that there are two types of stages in PRINCE2—*management stages* and *technical stages*—and what differentiates one from the other.

Benefits of Stages

The Project Board gives authority to the Project Manager to manage only one stage at a time. At the end of each stage, the Project Manager must report back to the Project Board and ask for permission to move on to the next stage. The end of each stage acts as a review and decision point for the Project Board and enables them to control the project without needing to dedicate much time to the initiative.

In Chapter 5, "Plans Theme," you saw how the Project Manager creates a high-level Project Plan at the beginning of the project (in Initiating a Project) and then only plans the work for each stage when the previous stage is about to finish (in Managing a Stage Boundary). Planning in detail as the project progresses, rather than doing it all at the beginning, helps overcome the planning horizon problem. In the hotel example, it is impossible to plan in detail how to construct the hotel until it has been designed. As such, it would be sensible to organize the project so the design work occurs in one stage and the construction work occurs in the next stage.

You saw earlier in this chapter that the Project Board sets stage tolerances for the Project Manager to work within. Therefore, another benefit of stages is they help the Project Board manage the Project Manager by exception. The Project Board needs to get involved in the activities of a stage only if the Project Manager forecasts that the stage tolerances will be breached and the stage is in exception.

Finally, the Project Board has a role to look beyond the project environment and see what might affect the project. At the end of each stage, they can report back to the project on these external influences. The stages therefore give a way to ensure that the project considers the external environment and how it might affect the project.

Factors to Consider When Dividing the Project into Stages

During Initiating a Project, the Project Manager creates the Project Plan. At this early stage in the initiative, particularly for longer projects, it might be difficult to forecast all the activities that will need to be done. Because of this, the Project Plan will probably be quite high-level. However, at this point, the Project Manager together with the Project Board must use this limited information to decide how to divide the project into stages. How do they do this? PRINCE2 recommends taking the following factors into account:

How far ahead in the project is it sensible to plan?   In the hotel example, it is difficult to plan in detail the construction of the building until the hotel has been designed. So it would be sensible to place the design work in one stage and the construction work in a subsequent stage.

Where are the key decision points going to be?   The Project Board will probably need to be involved in the key decisions, so it would be sensible to make these decisions at the end of a stage, when they meet to decide whether to continue with the project.

How risky is the project?   If projects are riskier, the Project Board will probably want to have more control. The Project Board gains more control by having a project with more short stages rather than fewer but longer stages. This will mean the Project Manager has to report back to the Project Board more frequently at the end of each of the short stages.

How confident is the project management team about the project?   If the Project Board and the Project Manager are not confident about the initiative, they will probably want to have more stages and therefore more review points.

If the project is part of a programme, how might this affect the placement of stage boundaries?   It might be sensible to align project review points with programme review points.

Management Stages vs. Technical Stages

There are two types of stages in PRINCE2: management stages and technical stages. In this section, you will learn the difference between the two.

The first point to understand is that management stages are simply the stages you have learned about throughout this book. They are the section of the project that the Project Manager is managing on behalf of the Project Board at any one time. As you've learned, the Project Board authorizes the Project Manager to manage the project one (management) stage at a time, and at the end of that (management) stage, the Project Manager can go no further without a new authorization from the Project Board. According to *Managing Successful Projects with PRINCE2*, the definition of a *management stage* is as follows:

> Management stages equate to commitment of resources and authority
> to spend.

In essence, the Project Board releases resources and budget to the Project Manager on a management stage–by–management stage basis. Remember that the first management stage is called the initiation (management) stage. This is where the Project Manager manages the work to create the Project Initiation Documentation. Every management stage after this is a delivery (management) stage, where the Project Manager will be managing the work to create specialist products.

If management stages are simply the stages you have been reading about all along, what are technical stages? I always think that the term "technical stage" is rather confusing. Personally, I wouldn't have called them stages at all! They are really a group of activities that are done by people with the same sort of skills. That group of activities might stretch across one or more management stages. For example, in some projects, there is design work to be done, building work to be done, and testing work to be done, so in PRINCE2 terminology, there will be a design technical stage, a build technical stage, and a test technical stage.

According to *Managing Successful Projects with PRINCE2*, the definition of a *technical stage* is as follows:

> Technical stages are typified by the use of a particular set of specialist skills.

The following subsection provides an example that further explains the difference between management and technical stages.

Dividing Technical Stages into Management Stages

I'm going to use the following set of diagrams and text to explain the difference between management stages and technical stages in more detail and how they relate to each other. There is a bit of preamble here, but bear with it as the students I have taught find this a useful example to understand stages.

Take a look at Figure 9.7. Here you can see a high-level Project Plan put together at the beginning of a project. All the project team knows at this stage is that the project will involve five major pieces of work: specifying, designing, building, training, and commissioning. This is not so unrealistic—sometimes at the outset of a project, the project team can only give a high-level forecast of the work to be done

FIGURE 9.7 High-level Project Plan

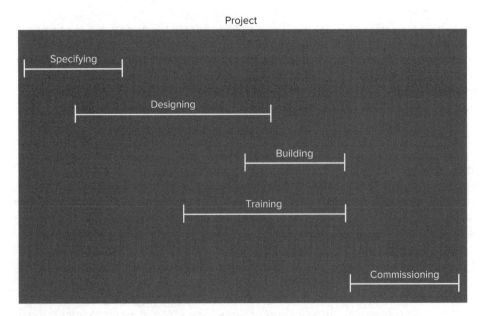

Based on Cabinet Office PRINCE2® material. Reproduced under licence from the Cabinet Office.

As you saw in the previous section, the challenge at the outset of the project is how to divide a high-level Project Plan into various management stages. Figure 9.8 shows how the project team has decided to divide their project into management stages. The first management stage involves doing the specifying work and the first part of the designing work; the second management stage involves doing most of the rest of the designing work and starting the training work; and so on.

FIGURE 9.8   High-level Project Plan divided into management stages

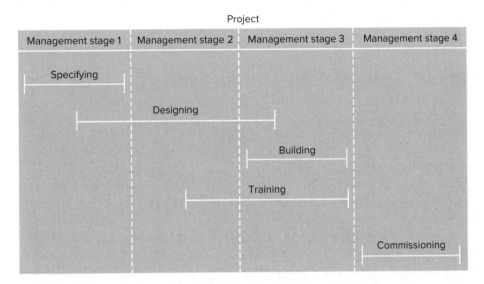

Based on Cabinet Office PRINCE2® material. Reproduced under licence from the Cabinet Office.

There is one problem with the Project Plan in Figure 9.8. A primary benefit of management stages is that they provide a review and decision point for the Project Board. However, at the end of management stage 1, it may be difficult to review the designing work because it has only just started. Similarly, at the end of management stage 2, it may be difficult to review the progress of the designing and training work, because it hasn't finished yet. The only way to review the progress of these pieces of work is to give a percentage-complete figure, which is often quite subjective. One person's 80 percent complete is another's 50 percent. People are overly optimistic about the work that remains or they forget about all the little things that need to be done at the end, which, when they are added together, become one big thing!

Contrast this with reviewing the progress of the specifying work at the end of stage 1. The specifying work has either finished or not finished. The project team can be completely objective when they report on the progress of this work as they can also be with the designing, building, and training work at the end of stage 3 and the commissioning work at the end of stage 4.

A solution to the problem of reviewing work that spans multiple management stages is shown in Figure 9.9. Here, the big pieces of work have been split up so they fit into the management stages. So, for example, the designing piece of work is now done in three parts: the overall design is done in management stage 1, the detailed design is done in management stage 2, and the peripheral design is done in management stage 3. Now it is easier to be more objective when the progress of the designing work is reviewed at the end of stages 1, 2, and 3. For example, at the end of management stage 1, the Project Manager can (hopefully) report to the Project Board that the overall designs have been finished.

FIGURE 9.9   Work stream divided across management stages

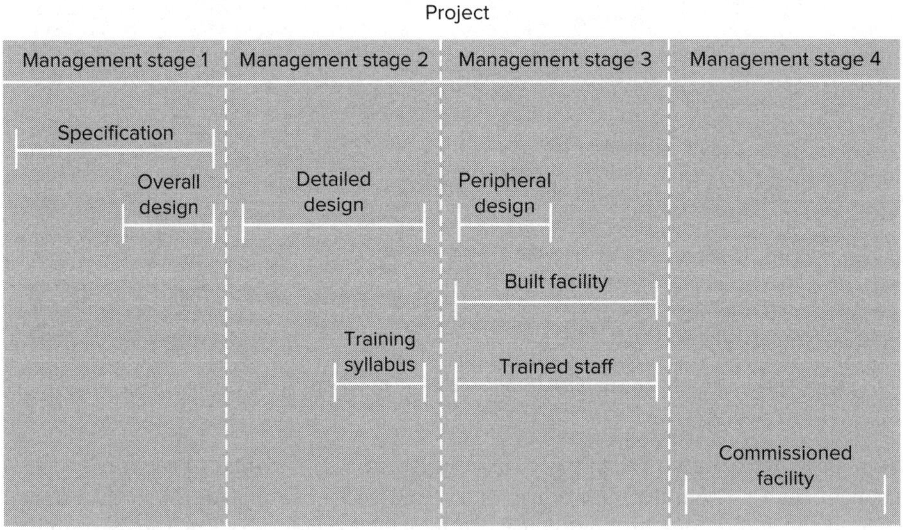

Based on Cabinet Office PRINCE2® material. Reproduced under licence from the Cabinet Office.

Anyway, what does all this have to do with technical stages? If you go back to Figure 9.7, the big pieces of work such as specifying, designing, building, training, and commissioning are technical stages. As I said in the previous section, it can be confusing when PRINCE2 uses the word *stages* to refer to technical stages—they're really just big pieces of work that involve people with the same sort of skills. So, for example, people with design skills do (rather obviously) designing work and people with building skills do (yes, you've guessed it) building work.

In PRINCE2 terms, the challenge in Figure 9.7, Figure 9.8, and Figure 9.9 is to work out how to divide the technical stages into the management stages. The solution in this example is shown in Figure 9.9, where a number of the technical stages have been subdivided so that they fit into the management stages.

Don't be confused here, though. In Figure 9.9, the overall design, detailed design, and peripheral design combine together to form just one technical stage: the designing technical stage. This is because each of those three pieces of work involves the same set of specialist skills: designers.

Exam Spotlight

In the Foundation exam, there are often questions relating to the difference between technical and management stages. They can be quite confusing. The best approach is to keep remembering that technical stages are just big pieces of work that will involve people with similar skills. Those big pieces of work might take place across one or many management stages. Here are some questions to test how well you understand the differences between technical and management stages:

1. Do technical stages and management stages always end at the same time?

    If you look at Figure 9.8, you can see that the answer to this is no. The designing technical stage ends before the management stage 3.

2. Can management stages overlap?

    You can see from Figure 9.8 (and maybe you knew this already) that the answer is no.

3. Can technical stages overlap?

    You can see from Figure 9.8 that the answer to this is yes. For example, at the beginning of stage 3, the designing, building, and training technical stages are all running concurrently.

4. Can you have more than one technical stage running over one management stage?

    You can see from Figure 9.8 that there are three technical stages—designing, building, and training—running across management stage 3. So the answer to this question is yes.

5. Can you have more than one management stage running over one technical stage?

    You can see from Figure 9.8 that the designing technical stage runs over three management stages. So the answer to this question is yes.

Real World Scenario

Technical Stages in the Software Industry

Every industry's projects have different technical stages. For example, in software engineering, the order of events in a project might be as follows: First, the software business experts gather the client's requirements for the software. Next, the software experts design the software. Then, the software is built by software engineers, tested by the testing team, and finally installed by consultants. Each one of these steps is a technical stage.

If the software project is using PRINCE2, the project management team needs to decide how they are going to control the project using the management stages. One way would be to simply align the management stages with the technical stages. So, at the end of the requirements gathering, there is a meeting with the Project Board during which they review the requirements and decide whether to authorize the project to proceed to the designing stage.

However, if one of the technical stages is very long—for example, perhaps building the software takes a year—the Project Board might not be comfortable committing resources for this length of time. In this case, the team could see if the software could be built in a number of modules, each of which is created within its own management stage.

The software project I've just described uses what is called the waterfall approach. The first set of activities defines the requirements, and then the software is designed, built, tested, and commissioned. It is used throughout the software industry but has one big disadvantage. Clients find it difficult to specify what they want in the unfamiliar world of software engineering, even with the help of experts. Also, there are often difficulties in communication between technical people and business people. Unfortunately, with the waterfall approach, the first time you can tell for sure whether the correct requirements have been defined is after all the work to design, build, test, and commission the product has been done and the client has finally received the product.

To reduce the risk of collecting incorrect requirements, the software team could follow another approach. The project team might decide to quickly gather an initial set of requirements from the client and then quickly build a working prototype. They can then show this to the client to get some early feedback. Using this early feedback, they can quickly build another new prototype. By going through this process a number of times, the team gains a better understanding of the client's needs. After several iterations, they then design, build, and test the real product just as they did in the first example.

How does this approach relate to the PRINCE2 management and technical stages? Well, the last piece of the project—the designing, building, and testing of the real product—can be divided into management stages in the same way as the waterfall project. What is more difficult is the prototyping work. In each iteration of the prototyping work, a number of technical stages are involved: gathering initial requirements, designing the prototype, building the prototype, and maybe some quick testing of the prototype. In each iteration, there are multiple concurrent technical stages. How does the project team divide this work into management stages?

One approach is to run each prototype iteration in a management stage. At the end of each iteration, the Project Board can then decide whether to move on to the next iteration during their end-stage assessment.

One of the main ideas related to management stages in PRINCE2 is that their placement shouldn't be dictated by the specialist work. Obviously, the specialist work will be a factor in the decision about where to place the management stages. It may be useful to finish a management stage at the end of a major technical stage so that the Project Board can review its output. However, the ultimate decision about the placement of management stages should be driven by an understanding of how to control the project, not by the specialist work.

Roles Involved with the Progress Theme

This chapter described the progress-related responsibilities for the various PRINCE2 roles. Here is a quick review of these responsibilities to help you prepare for the exams:

Corporate or Programme Management   Corporate or programme management sets project tolerances and documents them in the Project Mandate. They will also make decisions regarding forecast breaches in project-level tolerances.

Project Board   The Project Board sets stage-level tolerances for the Project Manager. They will make decisions regarding forecast breaches in stage-level tolerances. The Project Board controls progress by authorizing the project on a management stage–by–management stage basis.

Project Manager   The Project Manager will control the progress of a stage by authorizing teams to deliver specialist products using Work Packages. The Project Manager sets Work Package–level tolerances for the Team Manager and the teams. He will make decisions regarding forecast breaches in Work Package–level tolerances. The Project Manager will use the Stage Plan to monitor the progress of the stage, manage the production of progress reports such as the Highlight Report and the End Stage Report, and control issues and risks using the Issue Register and the Risk Register.

Team Manager   The teams (and the Team Manager if there is one) agree on the Work Packages with the Project Manager. They must escalate any forecast breach in Work Package tolerances to the Project Manager and regularly report progress using Checkpoint Reports.

Project Assurance   Project Assurance monitors the project to ensure that forecast progress will not exceed project-, stage-, or Work Package–level tolerances. Business assurance will have a particular focus on verifying that there are no new risks to the Business Case of the project.

Project Support   Project Support assists the Project Manager with the creation of progress reports and the maintenance of the project's issues and logs.

Summary

In this chapter, you learned about the Progress theme. The Progress theme covers the various ways that PRINCE2 controls the activities, resources, and people on a project to ensure that the project's objectives are achieved.

The first topic you learned about was tolerances. A tolerance is an allowable deviation of the cost and time targets that have been given to one level of management by the management level above. You saw that tolerances can also be set for the specifications of a product (quality tolerances), the number of products to be delivered (scope tolerances), the level of acceptable uncertainty (risk tolerances), and the benefits that the project's products will bring to the organization (benefit tolerances).

You saw that the time, cost, scope, and risk tolerances might be set at three different levels. Corporate or programme management sets project tolerances for the Project Board, the Project Board sets stage tolerances for the Project Manager, and the Project Manager sets Work Package tolerances for the team. Quality tolerances are established either at a project level or at a product level, and benefit tolerances are set only at a project level.

In this chapter, you learned that the tolerances help one management level manage the one below by exception. If one management level realizes that the tolerances they have been set are forecast to be breached, they are in a situation called an exception. They must then immediately escalate the situation to the management level above for a decision on how to proceed.

This chapter also showed you how the Project Board uses various parts of PRINCE2 to control the project's progress. First, they use the authorization activities in the Directing a Project process to authorize one stage of the project at a time. Second, they need to keep up-to-date on the latest progress of the project in order to control it and so receive progress reports in the form of the Highlight Reports and the End Stage Reports. Finally, the Project Board controls change and issue situations by defining what sorts of situations they want to be involved in and what sort of situations can be resolved by lower levels of management. This is done by setting tolerances and constraints on change authority for lower levels of management.

In addition, you saw how the Project Manager controls the progress of a stage. The Project Manager uses the Work Package to delegate work to the teams and Checkpoint Reports to monitor the team's work and the various logs and registers to control the actions, threats, opportunities, and issues of the project.

You also learned that all the parts of PRINCE2 used to control the project are called controls. There are two types of controls: event-driven and time-driven. Event-driven controls occur after a particular thing has happened. For example, after an exception, the Project Manager creates an Exception Report. Time-driven controls occur on a regular basis, such as the regular sending of Highlight Reports or Checkpoint Reports.

Finally, you learned about stages. There are two types of stages in PRINCE2: management stages and technical stages. Management stages equate to commitment of resources and authority to spend. They provide an important way to help the Project Board control the project. At the end of each stage, the Project Board can review the project and decide whether to commit resources to the next stage. Technical stages are typified by the use of specialist skills and can be thought of as large pieces of work done by people with similar skills.

Exam Essentials

Understand the purpose of the Progress theme.   The purpose of the Progress theme is to establish mechanisms to monitor and compare the actual achievements against those planned; provide a forecast for the project objectives and the project's continued viability; and control any unacceptable deviations.

Understand the concept of tolerances and exceptions.   A tolerance is a permissible deviation above and below a plan's target for time and cost without escalating the deviation to the next level of management. There may also be tolerances for quality, scope, benefit, and risk. An exception is a situation where it can be forecast that there will be a deviation beyond the agreed tolerance levels.

Know when and how tolerances are set.   Corporate or programme management sets project tolerances at the beginning of the project, the Project Board sets stage tolerances at the beginning of each stage, and the Project Manager sets Work Package tolerances when a Work Package is delegated to the team.

Know in which management products tolerances are documented.   Cost, time, and scope tolerances are documented at a project, stage, and Work Package level in the Project Plan, Stage Plan, and Work Package, respectively. Risk tolerances are documented at a project and stage level in the Risk Management Strategy and at a Work Package level in the Work Package. Risk tolerance at a stage and Work Package level may also be documented in a Stage or Team Plan respectively. Quality tolerances are documented in the Project Product Description or the Product Descriptions, and benefit tolerances are documented in the Business Case.

Know when and how exceptions are reported.   The Team Manager reports Work Package–level exceptions by raising an issue to the Project Manager, the Project Manager reports stage-level exceptions by escalating an Issue Report or an Exception Report to the

Project Board, and the Project Board reports project-level exceptions by notifying corporate or programme management.

Understand the different levels of tolerance and how they relate to the application of management by exception by the different levels of management.   Time, cost, risk, and scope tolerances can be set at three different levels—project, stage, and Work Package—and these levels are set by corporate or programme management, the Project Board, and the Project Manager, respectively. When a management level forecasts a breach in the tolerances that have been set by the management level above, they need to escalate the situation to that higher management level.

Understand the purpose and composition of the Exception Report and know in which processes it is developed, used, and reviewed, and which roles are responsible for this.   The Project Manager creates the Exception Report during Controlling a Stage if he is forecasting his stage tolerance will be breached. It provides information about the exception to the Project Board, including options that have been considered to deal with the exception, and allows the Project Board to make a decision on the situation in Directing a Project.

Understand the lines of authority and the four levels of management.   The four levels of management are corporate or programme management, Project Board, Project Manager, and the Team Manager or team. The highest level of authority within the project management team structure is corporate or programme management, followed by the Project Board, then the Project Manager, and finally the Team Manager.

Understand the purpose and composition of the Work Package and know in which processes it is developed, used, and reviewed, and which roles are responsible for this.   The Project Manager creates the Work Package in Controlling a Stage in order to define the information that the Team Manager or team needs to deliver one or more products. Once the Team Manager or team member has accepted the Work Package in Managing Product Delivery, he is responsible for delivering the products that it described.

Understand the purpose of the Daily Log.   The Daily Log is used to record informal issues, required actions, or significant events not caught by the other PRINCE2 registers and logs. It acts as the project diary for the Project Manager.

Understand the difference between event-driven and time-driven controls.   Event-driven controls are used to control a particular event that has occurred, such as the end of a stage or an exception. Time-driven controls do not respond to an event but occur at a regular frequency, such as the creation of Highlight Reports or Checkpoint Reports.

Understand the purpose and composition of the Lessons Log and know in which processes it is developed, used, and reviewed, and which roles are responsible for this.   The Project Manager creates the Lessons Log in Starting up a Project and updates it throughout the project. The Project Manager uses it to collate lessons learned from previous initiatives that would be useful for the current project and also to collate experience from the current project that might be useful for future initiatives.

Understand the purpose and composition of the Lessons Report and know in which processes it is developed, used, and reviewed, and which roles are responsible for this. The Project Manager creates the Lessons Report to pass on lessons from the project to those who might usefully employ them. The Lessons Report can be created at any time in the project, but it is typically created during Managing a Stage Boundary and becomes part of the End Stage Report, or during Closing a Project, when it becomes part of the End Project Report.

Understand the factors you must consider when dividing a project into management stages. PRINCE2 recommends five factors to consider when dividing a project into stages: how far ahead it is sensible to plan, where the key decision points are in a project, the amount of risk in a project, the balancing of too many short management stages (giving lots of management overhead) against too few length ones (giving little control), and finally, how confident the project management team is in proceeding.

Understand the concept of management stages and know what differentiates them from technical stages. Management stages equate to commitment of resources and authority to spend, and technical stages are typified by the use of a particular set of specialist skills.

Review Questions

The rest of this chapter contains mock exam questions, first for the Foundation exam and then for the Practitioner exam.

Foundation Questions

1. When does the Project Manager allocate tolerances to the Team Manager or team?
    A. When planning the stage
    B. When authorizing the stage
    C. When authorizing a Work Package
    D. When approving a Product Description

2. Which of the following information is recorded in the Daily Log?
    1. A risk identified in Starting up a Project
    2. A request for change
    3. An informal issue
    4. A personnel action point for the Project Manager
    A. 1, 2, 3
    B. 1, 2, 4
    C. 1, 3, 4
    D. 2, 3, 4

3. Which management product is used to collate experience that may be useful for input into the project's strategies and plans?
    A. Lessons Log
    B. Exception Report
    C. Issue Register
    D. Project Initiation Documentation

4. Which of the following is NOT a benefit of using management stages?
    A. Allows clarification of the impacts of external influences
    B. Provides review and decision points for the project
    C. Allows project control to be driven by the specialist work
    D. Facilitates the principle of manage by exception

5. Which management products would be used to document any flexibility on what will be delivered?

1. Quality Register

2. Project Plan

3. Stage Plan

4. Work Package

A. 1, 2, 3

B. 1, 2, 4

C. 1, 3, 4

D. 2, 3, 4

6. Which of the following statements is **NOT** true of stages?

A. There are two types of stages: technical and management.

B. Technical stages are a major project control.

C. Management stages might contain more than one technical stage.

D. Technical stages might contain more than one management stage.

7. Which management product does a Team Manager refer to in order to understand any standards regarding the version control and storage of the products that need to be delivered?

A. Configuration Management Strategy

B. Work Package

C. Configuration Item Record

D. Quality Register

8. Who might use the information in a Lessons Report to refine, change, and improve an organization's corporate standards?

A. Team Manager

B. Project Manager

C. Change Authority

D. Quality assurance

9. Which of the following is **NOT** a Project Board control?

A. Regular progress meetings

B. Authorizations of the stages

C. Highlight Report

D. Exception Report

10. "Opportunities that are very likely to occur and would have a major favorable impact on the project should be escalated to the Project Board" is an example of which of the following?

   A. Exception Report

   B. Risk tolerance

   C. Exception

   D. Issue

Practitioner Questions

The following Practitioner questions are divided into two sections by question type and are based on the Practitioner exam scenario in this book's Introduction.

Section 1: Multiple Response Type

Using the following meeting minutes and the extract from the draft Work Package provided as additional information for this section, answer the following six questions about the contents of the Work Package.

Meeting Minutes of the Discussion between the IT Manager and the Project Manager Regarding Digital Design

The following minutes refer to a meeting about controlling and monitoring Digital Design's work to create the website designs.

The design work should start on May 20. The Marketing Director and the IT Manager should carry out an initial review of the designs on June 20. After the first review, there may need to be some reworking of the designs. The final review and approval of the designs should take place on June 30. We will allow a one-week tolerance in case a major rework of the designs is needed. We have budgeted $10,000 for the work with a tolerance of $3,000 if there needs to be a major rework of the designs.

Digital Design should be made aware that the designs must follow recognized standards for web page accessibility for the visually impaired and also comply with Quality Furniture branding standards. The designs should be created using the Quality Furniture design software.

Digital Design should liaise with the IT Manager to ensure that their designs are compatible with the Quality Furniture sales system that the final website will need to link to.

The Marketing Director is leading a team who will be creating a plan to show what information each web page on the new site will contain. Digital Design needs to liaise with the Marketing Director to ensure that their designs are compatible with her information plan.

The Quality Furniture photographer has a stock of furniture photographs. These will be used for the website. Digital Design must check with the photographer that their designs are a good fit with the photographs.

All the designs should be stored in the Quality Furniture document control system that is administered by Quality Furniture's head of administration. Access to the designs should be restricted to the authorized Digital Design personnel and the Marketing Director. Any change to a design's status should be reported to the head of administration.

Digital Design is expected to send a weekly Checkpoint Report to the Project Manager. Any problems should be escalated to the Project Manager by telephone and an impact assessment should follow by email within 24 hours.

The Marketing Director and the IT Manager will give final approval for the designs. Once the designs have been approved, the Project Manager should be notified by email.

Extract from Draft Work Package (may contain errors)

Techniques, processes, and procedures	1. The designs should be created using the Quality Furniture design software.
	2. The work should be managed using the Controlling a Stage process.
	3. Designs must comply with accessibility standards for the visually impaired.
Development interfaces	4. The Marketing Director wants to regularly review the designs.
	5. The IT Manager will ensure that the designs are consistent with the sales system.
Configuration management requirements	6. The Marketing Director will approve the completed designs.
	7. Use the Quality Furniture document control system to store and track the status of the designs.
	8. Restrict access to the designs to authorized personnel at Digital Design only.
	9. Report status changes to any of the designs to the head of administration.
Joint agreements	10. Cost—$10,000.
	11. Designs should be started on May 20 and must be reviewed and approved by the first week of July at the latest.
Reporting requirements	12. Checkpoint Reports are to be sent to the Project Board on a weekly basis.
	13. Digital Design should notify the Project Manager of any issues immediately by telephone.
	14. Checkpoint Reports should follow the standard PRINCE2 format.
Approval method	15. Use the PRINCE2 quality review technique to review the designs.
	16. The designs should be approved by the Marketing Director and the IT Manager.
	17. When the designs have been approved, notify the Project Manager by email.

Multiple Response Questions

Remember to limit your answers to the number of selections requested in each question.

1. Which two statements apply to the "Techniques, processes, and procedures" section?

    A. Delete entry 1, because the design software is a product that the design needs to interface with and therefore should be placed in the "Operations and maintenance interfaces" section.

    B. Delete entry 2, because Controlling a Stage is a PRINCE2 process that the Project Manager will use to manage the whole stage.

    C. Move entry 3 to the "Constraints" section, because it is a set of rules that need to be followed.

    D. Add "Designs should comply with Quality Furniture branding standards."

    E. Add "Liaise with Marketing Director when creating the designs."

2. Which two statements apply to the "Development interfaces" section?

    A. No change to entry 4, because the Marketing Director is someone to whom Digital Design will need to provide information while developing the designs.

    B. Delete entry 4, because the Marketing Director can use Checkpoint Reports to monitor progress.

    C. Move entry 5 to the "Operations and maintenance interfaces" section, because the IT Manager will be in charge of maintaining the website.

    D. Add "Quality Furniture photographer, because he has knowledge of the photographs to be used for the site."

    E. Add Quality Furniture design software, because it will be used to view the designs.

3. Which two statements apply to the "Configuration management requirements" section?

    A. Move entry 6 to "Approval method," because this indicates the person who will approve the products in the Work Package.

    B. Move entry 7 to "Techniques, processes, and procedures," because this describes a tool to be used in the creation of the specialist products.

    C. Amend entry 8 to state that the Marketing Director should also be allowed access to the designs.

    D. Move entry 9 to "Reporting arrangements," because this is about reporting.

    E. Move entry 9 to "Development interfaces," because this is a person who needs to be liaised with during the creation of the specialist products.

4. Which two statements apply to the "Joint agreements" section?

    A. Amend entry 10 to include the $3,000 that will be set aside in case the designs need to be reworked.

    B. No change to entry 11, because this is the time schedule that should be agreed on.

    C. Amend entry 11 to state the designs should be reviewed and approved by June 30, because the information in this section should not include any tolerances agreed to.

    D. Add that the designs should be initially reviewed on June 20, because this is a key milestone in the delivery of the work.

    E. Add that Digital Design and Quality Furniture have jointly agreed to use PRINCE2 as the management method.

5. Which two statements apply to the "Reporting arrangements" section?

    A. Amend entry 12 to Highlight Reports, because these are the types of reports that are sent to the Project Board.

    B. Amend entry 12 to say that the reports should be sent to the Project Manager, because the Team Manager reports to the Project Manager, not the Project Board.

    C. No change to entry 13, because this states how issues will be reported.

    D. Move entry 13 to "Problem handling and escalation," because this refers to the procedure for raising issues.

    E. Amend entry 14 to state that the format of the Checkpoint Reports is described in the Communication Management Strategy.

6. Which two statements apply to the "Approval method" section?

    A. No change to entry 15, because this shows how the designs will be checked to ensure they are fit for their purpose.

    B. Move entry 15 to the Product Descriptions of the designs, because this shows the quality method to be used to verify the designs.

    C. No change to entry 16, because this shows the people who will approve the completed products.

    D. Delete entry 16, because this shows who should approve the completed products, not how they will be checked.

    E. Move entry 17 to "Reporting arrangements," because this deals with how the completion of the designs will be reported.

Section 2: Assertion/Reason Type

Using the meeting minutes provided in the preceding section, answer the following six assertion/reason questions.

Rows 1 to 6 in the following table consist of an assertion statement and a reason statement. For each line, identify the appropriate option, from options A to E, that applies. Each option can be used once, more than once, or not at all.

- **A.** The assertion is true and the reason is true, *and* the reason explains the assertion.
- **B.** The assertion is true and the reason is true, *but* the reason does not explain the assertion.
- **C.** The assertion is true and the reason is false.
- **D.** The assertion is false and the reason is true.
- **E.** Both the assertion and the reason are false.

Assertion		Reason
1. The Work Package for the web page designs must also contain the information plan being created by the marketing department.	Because	The Project Manager controls all the work of a particular management stage in one Work Package.
2. The Work Package for the web page designs may take the form of a legally binding contract.	Because	Consideration should be given in the Project Initiation Documentation on how to tailor PRINCE2 to any commercial customer supplier environment.
3. If Digital Design realizes they cannot complete the designs until the end of July, they should escalate this situation in the next Checkpoint Report.	Because	Checkpoint Reports are a time-driven control.
4. The Project Manager should only authorize the Work Package for the marketing department to create the information plan after the Work Package for the designs is complete.	Because	Technical stages should not overlap.
5. Digital Design should use the Product Description contained in the Work Package to understand the quality expectations for the designs.	Because	Product Descriptions contain quality criteria for the products.
6. The Work Package will show Digital Design who they will need to liaise with during the creation of the designs.	Because	The Work Package contains the techniques, processes, and procedures that will be used to create the specialist products.

Chapter

10

Managing the Middle of a Project Successfully with PRINCE2

PRINCE2 EXAM OBJECTIVES COVERED IN THIS CHAPTER:

✓ **Understand the purpose, objectives, and context of the Controlling a Stage process.**

✓ **Understand the following eight activities of the Controlling a Stage process and know which role has responsibilities within each activity:**

- Authorize Work Packages.

- Review Work Package status.

- Receive completed Work Packages.

- Review the stage status.

- Report highlights.

- Capture and examine issues and risks.

- Escalate issues and risks.

- Take corrective action.

✓ **Understand the purpose, objectives, and context of the Managing Product Delivery process.**

✓ **Understand the following three activities of the Managing Product Delivery process and know which role has responsibilities within each activity:**

- Accept a Work Package.

- Execute a Work Package.

- Deliver a Work Package.

✓ **Understand the purpose, objectives, and context of the Managing a Stage Boundary process.**

✓ **Understand the following five activities of the Managing a Stage Boundary process and know which role has responsibilities within each activity:**

  ▪ Plan the next stage.

  ▪ Update the Project Plan.

  ▪ Update the Business Case.

  ▪ Report stage end.

  ▪ Produce an Exception Plan.

✓ **Understand how the seven themes may be applied within the Controlling a Stage, Managing Product Delivery, and Managing a Stage Boundary processes.**

✓ **For the following management products, know their purpose and composition; in which processes they are developed, used, and reviewed; and which roles are responsible for each:**

  ▪ Highlight Report

  ▪ Checkpoint Report

  ▪ End Stage Report

In this chapter, you will learn how PRINCE2 is used to manage the middle of a project. In PRINCE2, the middle of the project starts on completion of the initiation stage and ends when the Project Manager starts to prepare for the end of the project in the Closing a Project process.

The main focus of the middle of the project is to deliver specialist products (although some management products such as the End Stage Report are also delivered). For example, if the project team were building a new hotel, in the middle of the project, they would deliver specialist products such as the swimming pool, the restaurant, the furniture, and the sales systems. Before and after the middle of the project, only management products such as the Project Initiation Documentation and the End Project Report are delivered.

The middle of the project could last for a few days, weeks, months, or sometimes even years. The Project Manager manages the middle of the project on behalf of the Project Board, one delivery stage at a time. At the end of each delivery stage (apart from the final one), the Project Manager will ask the Project Board for authorization to move on to the next delivery stage.

In this chapter, you will learn how the Project Manager uses the Controlling a Stage process to manage each delivery stage. The Controlling a Stage process covers how the Project Manager delegates work to the teams, deals with reporting, and handles problems and issues.

This chapter also covers how the teams and Team Managers use the Managing Product Delivery process to control the delivery of their work. This includes activities such as negotiating for resources and time with the Project Manager, ensuring that the delivery of their work follows quality standards, and reporting to the Project Manager.

Finally, this chapter will cover how the end of each of the stages is handled using the Managing a Stage Boundary process. At this point, the Project Manager needs to plan the work for the succeeding stage and ask the Project Board for permission to proceed to that stage.

Overview of the Middle of a PRINCE2 Project

In the section "An End-to-End Walk-through of PRINCE2" in Chapter 1, "Overview of PRINCE2," you saw an overview of the process model. I recommend that you review that section again, in particular the "Activities in the Middle of the Project" subsection, before continuing with this chapter. This will help you understand how the three processes discussed in this chapter (Controlling a Stage, Managing Product Delivery, and Managing a Stage Boundary) fit into the overall method.

Figure 10.1 is taken from the section "An End-to-End Walk-through of PRINCE2" in Chapter 1, "Overview of PRINCE2." I have highlighted the part of the model you will learn about in this chapter.

FIGURE 10.1 Middle of the project

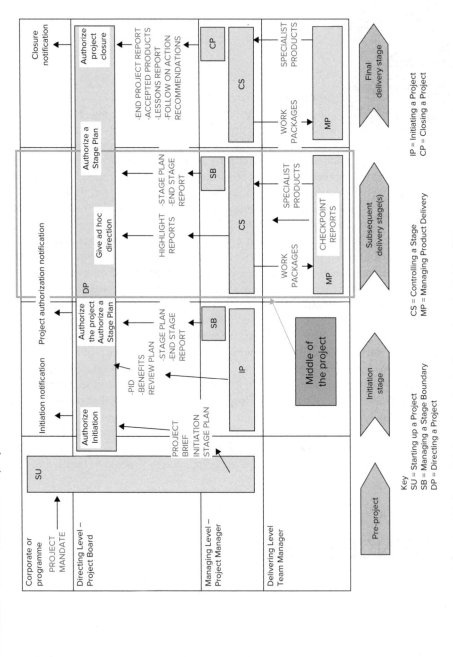

Based on Cabinet Office PRINCE2® material. Reproduced under licence from the Cabinet Office.

The Controlling a Stage and Managing Product Delivery Processes

The Project Manager uses the activities in the Controlling a Stage process to manage each delivery stage. Figure 10.2 illustrates the eight activities of Controlling a Stage. During each delivery stage, the teams will be working on creating the specialist products. The teams use the activities in the Managing Product Delivery process. As you can see in the figure, the Managing Product Delivery process involves three activities.

FIGURE 10.2   Controlling a Stage and Managing Product Delivery

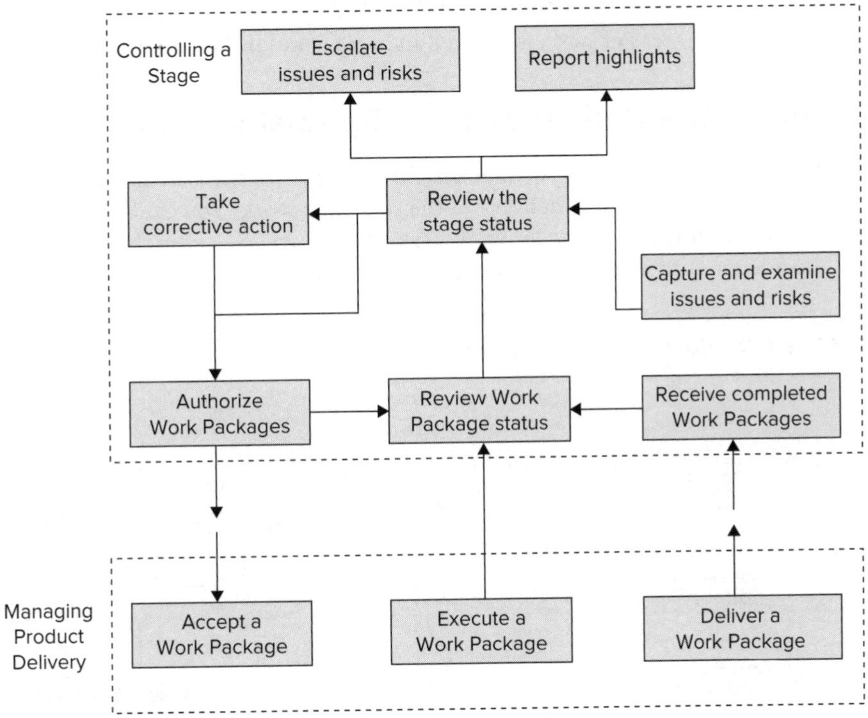

Based on Cabinet Office PRINCE2® material. Reproduced under licence from the Cabinet Office.

The activities in Controlling a Stage and Managing Product Delivery cover four main areas of work:

Controlling the Delivery of the Specialist Work   The Project Manager uses the activities in Controlling a Stage to delegate the work to the teams, review their progress, and accept the work once it is finished. The teams use the activities in Managing Product Delivery to formally accept work from the Project Manager, to deliver the products to relevant quality standards, to ensure quality control activities are carried out, and finally, to understand how to notify the Project Manager when the work is finished.

Reporting on the Progress of the Stage The Project Manager uses the activities in Controlling a Stage to regularly report on the progress of the stage to the Project Board and any other relevant stakeholders. The teams use the activities in Managing Product Delivery to report regularly to the Project Manager.

Dealing with Issues and Risks during a Stage The Project Manager uses the activities in Controlling a Stage to capture and examine issues and risks and ensure that appropriate decisions and actions are made regarding them.

Deciding What to Do Next in a Stage The Project Manager uses the activities in Controlling a Stage to decide what to do next out of options such as authorize new work, write a report, finish the stage, or finish the project.

Each of these four areas of work is covered in more detail in the following sections.

Controlling the Delivery of the Specialist Work

Figure 10.3 shows the Controlling a Stage and Managing Product Delivery activities that are involved with controlling the delivery of the specialist work. You can see that all three of the Managing Product Delivery activities are involved, whereas only three of the eight Controlling a Stage activities are concerned with this area.

FIGURE 10.3 Controlling the delivery of specialist work

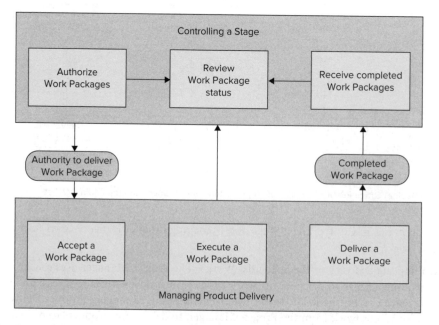

Based on Cabinet Office PRINCE2® material. Reproduced under licence from the Cabinet Office.

Authorize Work Packages

The Controlling a Stage activity of Authorize Work Packages is where the Project Manager hands over the responsibility to deliver one or more specialist products to a team. This is done by creating and agreeing to a Work Package with that team. You learned about the Work Package in Chapter 9, "Progress Theme." Remember that it contains information such as what products need to be created, how much time and money the team is being given to deliver the products, how often to report back to the Project Manager, and who should approve the products once they have been created. Figure 10.4 shows the composition of the Work Package.

FIGURE 10.4   Composition of the Work Package

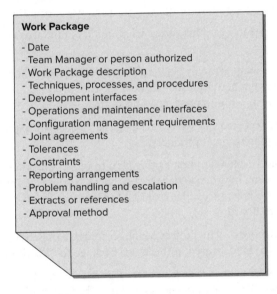

Work Package

- Date
- Team Manager or person authorized
- Work Package description
- Techniques, processes, and procedures
- Development interfaces
- Operations and maintenance interfaces
- Configuration management requirements
- Joint agreements
- Tolerances
- Constraints
- Reporting arrangements
- Problem handling and escalation
- Extracts or references
- Approval method

In a project to build a new hotel, the Project Manager would need to authorize several Work Packages with many teams. For example, the Project Manager would authorize one Work Package for the electrical contractor to wire the rooms, another Work Package for the plumbing contractor to fit the water pipes, another Work Package for the decorator to paint the rooms, and so on.

No team is allowed to start their work until a Work Package has been authorized by the Project Manager. This prevents teams from starting work at the wrong time or doing work that is unnecessary for the project. One Work Package might cover the creation of a number of products.

The Project Manager decides when it is time to authorize a new Work Package by monitoring the progress of the stage using the Stage Plan. Sometimes, the Project Manager might need to authorize a previously unplanned Work Package in response to an issue or a risk. This is possible to do as long as the work doesn't cause a forecast breach in the stage tolerances. (If it will cause a forecast breach in stage tolerances, the Project Manager will have to refer to the Project Board for a decision.)

Before authorizing a new Work Package, the Project Manager should review the following management products in order to understand what information the Work Package should contain:

Stage Plan   This tells the Project Manager what products need to be produced; what time, cost, and effort to be used; and what tolerances are available.

Project Controls Section of the Project Initiation Documentation   This shows the Project Manager whether there are any project standards for controlling the team's work. For example, there might be a standard progress report required from the teams.

Quality Management Strategy   This shows what quality standards need to be followed by the team.

Configuration Management Strategy   This shows how the team should carry out configuration management activities such as how to store products, obtain copies of documents, place security around products, and so on.

Once the team has accepted the Work Package, the Project Manager might have to update the following management products:

Stage Plan   The Project Manager updates this plan to reflect any changes to the schedule that the team is proposing in order to deliver their work. If these changes would take the stage beyond its forecast tolerances, the Project Manager would have to escalate this situation to the Project Board.

Configuration Item Records   The Project Manager updates these records to amend the status of the products to be delivered in the Work Package to "Work in progress."

Quality Register   The Project Manager updates this register to show any changes to planned quality checks. These quality checks will have been initially planned when the Project Manager created the Stage Plan, but at this point, some amendments such as extra reviewers might be needed.

Issue Register and the Risk Register   The Project Manager updates these registers to show information on any new issues or risks that the Work Package will introduce. The Project Manager should discuss the issues and risks that might affect the Work Package with the teams.

Accept a Work Package

As you can see in Figure 10.3, the Accept a Work Package activity belongs to the Managing Product Delivery process. The team and the Team Manager (if there is one) carry out this activity.

The Accept a Work Package activity is simply the reverse side of the Controlling a Stage activity, Authorize Work Packages. It is where the team or Team Manager takes responsibility for delivering the Work Package's products. The team might not accept the initial information in the Work Package. They may need to negotiate with the Project Manager for things such as more time or resources to carry out the work.

The teams will agree with the Project Manager to deliver the Work Package within certain tolerances. As you learned in Chapter 9, "Progress Theme," tolerances are an allowable flexibility for factors like the time and cost. So, for example, the Project Manager might agree that the team has three weeks to deliver the Work Package but in certain circumstances will allow a two-day-late delivery. This means that the team has authority to proceed with the work as long as they are not forecasting that they will go over their schedule by more than two days. If they are, then they must immediately escalate the situation to the Project Manager by raising an issue. The procedure for raising an issue is described in the Work Package.

The Work Package contains the Product Descriptions for the products to be delivered. In Chapter 6, "Quality Theme," you learned about Product Descriptions. As you recall, they contain the product specification and explain how to check and approve the product. The teams use this information in order to understand what to deliver and what quality activities to plan. It might be appropriate for the teams to check with Project Assurance to ensure that the quality activities are still suitable and that no extra reviewers are needed.

The team or the Team Manager should create a Team Plan to show how the Work Package will be delivered within the agreed-to constraints. They should consult with the supplier-side Project Assurance to ensure that the Team Plan follows any relevant supplier standards. The Project Manager might want to review this Team Plan to reassure himself on the viability of the Work Package, although of course, this might not be appropriate in a commercial customer/supplier environment. If the latter is the case, the Project Manager might still ask to review a set of key milestones showing when interim products for the Work Package will be delivered.

One point to note is that the teams might have already created the Team Plan when the Project Manager was creating the Stage Plan. If you think about it, in order to create a plan for the stage, the Project Manager should talk to the teams involved, ask them for their Team Plans, and then use that information to create the Stage Plan. The Project Manager creates Stage Plans in the Managing a Stage Boundary activity, Plan the next stage. If the teams are creating Team Plans in order to help the Project Manager create the Stage Plan, they would be using the Managing Product Delivery activity, Accept a Work Package—even though at this point, the teams are not accepting the Work Package! I know this is a bit confusing, but just think of it as a PRINCE2 glitch!

Execute a Work Package

As you can see in Figure 10.3, the Execute a Work Package activity belongs to the Managing Product Delivery process. The team and the Team Manager (if there is one) carry out this activity. This is where the specialist products are developed. So, in the project to build a new hotel, this is the activity where all sorts of specialist work will be done, such as designing architectural plans, creating tender documents, creating the building, fitting the bedrooms, and so on. You can think of this activity as where the "real work" is done rather than the management stuff like creating plans and the Project Initiation Documentation.

Of course, the first focus for the teams in this activity is the production of the specialist products, but as you will see in this section, they also need to ensure that quality management, configuration management, and reporting are carried out as well.

The teams will develop the specialist products so that they match the specifications described in the products' Product Descriptions. They may have agreed with the Project Manager to use certain techniques, processes, or procedures when they create the products. For example, if the Project Manager delegated some work to create a tender document, the team may have agreed to follow the organizational standards. Any standards to be followed are described in the Work Package.

During the creation of the products, the teams might need to liaise with other people. For example, if the electrical contractors are wiring up the bedrooms, they will want to coordinate with the plumbers to ensure their work doesn't conflict with each other. The "development interfaces" section of the Work Package will describe anyone the teams might need to liaise with.

The specialist products might have to connect with other products during their operational life. For example, the telephone system might need to connect to the booking system. The "operations and maintenance interface" section of the Work Package will describe any specialist products that the products being delivered will need to interface with in their operational life.

The teams (and also Project Assurance) need to ensure that quality control activities to check the products are carried out by the relevant people. As you learned in Chapter 6, "Quality Theme," quality control is all about checking that products are "fit for purpose." The Product Descriptions will specify what quality methods must be used to check the products and also who should be involved with the review and approval of the products. The teams should ensure that quality and approval records are kept to show proof that the quality activities have been done and the products are approved. The teams should ensure that the Quality Register is updated with the results of quality checks.

The teams will need to adhere to any configuration management approaches described in the Work Package. These could cover areas such as where the products need to be stored, how different versions of the product should be identified, or who needs to be updated if a product is completed (because this person will update the product's Configuration Item Record with a new status).

Finally, the teams should regularly update the Project Manager on their progress by sending a Checkpoint Report. The Work Package will describe the format and frequency of the Checkpoint Report. Figure 10.5 shows the PRINCE2-recommended composition of the Checkpoint Report.

FIGURE 10.5   Composition of the Checkpoint Report

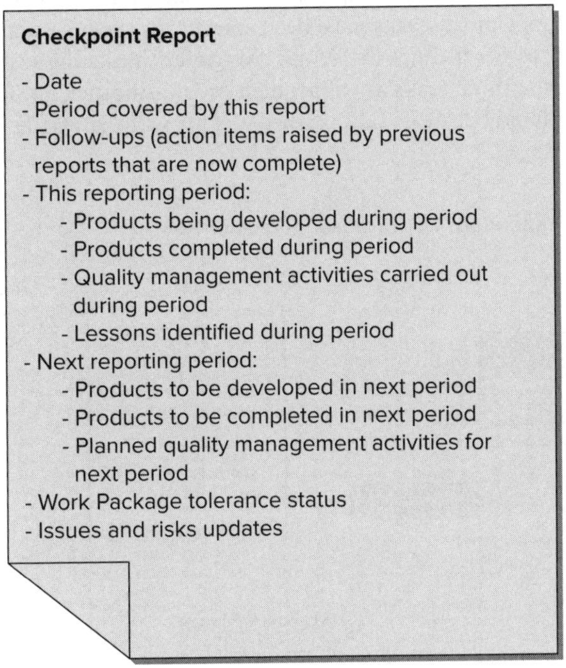

Checkpoint Report

- Date
- Period covered by this report
- Follow-ups (action items raised by previous reports that are now complete)
- This reporting period:
    - Products being developed during period
    - Products completed during period
    - Quality management activities carried out during period
    - Lessons identified during period
- Next reporting period:
    - Products to be developed in next period
    - Products to be completed in next period
    - Planned quality management activities for next period
- Work Package tolerance status
- Issues and risks updates

Review Work Package Status

As you can see in Figure 10.3, the activity Review Work Package status belongs to the Controlling a Stage process. The Project Manager carries out this activity.

On a regular basis, while managing a stage, the Project Manager reviews the progress of all the Work Packages being delivered. If they aren't too far away, the Project Manager could just go and see the teams and review the work they are delivering. However, there are a number of PRINCE2 ways to review the specialist work:

- By reviewing the Checkpoint Reports that the teams send to the Project Manager
- By reviewing the Quality Register to see how quality checks are progressing
- By reviewing the configuration management system to see the current status of the products within the Work Package

The Project Manager will want to assess the overall progress of the Work Package and reassure himself that the work will finish in the time and cost agreed. The Project Manager will use this information to update the Stage Plan with actual progress. The Project Manager will constantly update the Stage Plan with progress information throughout a stage. Figure 10.6 and Figure 10.7 show an example of this. Figure 10.6 shows a simple Stage Plan with three tasks. At this point, none of the tasks have been started, so the information in Figure 10.6 shows the planned or forecast times the Project Manager thinks the tasks will start and end. As you can see, the three tasks are dependent on one another, so, for example, Task 1 must be completed before Task 2 is started. This is the state the plan would be in at the beginning of the stage.

FIGURE 10.6 Stage Plan with forecast details only

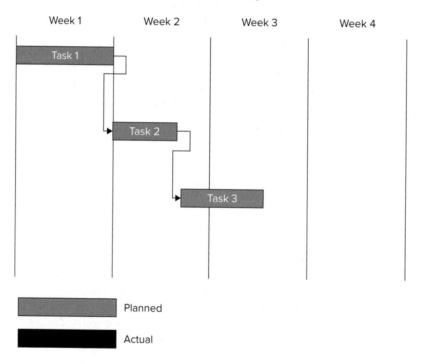

Figure 10.7 shows the situation a couple of weeks into the stage. As you can see, Task 1 has overrun—it should have taken one week, but in fact, it has taken two weeks. The Project Manager has updated the plan with the actual information for the duration of Task 1 and has also updated the forecast start and end dates for Task 2 and Task 3. In any stage, the Project Manager will be constantly updating the Stage Plan in this manner. This updating of the Stage Plan is done in the activity, Review Work Package status.

FIGURE 10.7 Updated Stage Plan with to-date actuals, forecasts, and adjustments

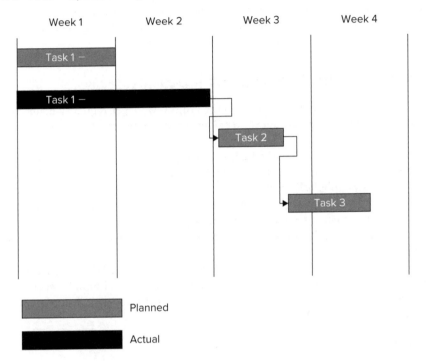

Deliver a Work Package

As you can see in Figure 10.3, the Deliver a Work Package activity belongs to the Managing Product Delivery process. The team and the Team Manager (if there is one) carry out this activity.

At this point, the products that the team has been working on should be complete. The team should ensure they have approval records to prove the relevant people have signed off on the products. (The relevant people are described in the Product Descriptions as approvers.) The team will also check the Quality Register to see if all the necessary quality checks have been done.

Some products might be going straight into an operational environment. If this is the case, the Work Package shows the delivery team what processes to follow to hand over the products to the operations team.

Finally, the team or the Team Manager must notify the Project Manager that the work in the Work Package is complete.

Receive Completed Work Packages

As you can see in Figure 10.3, the activity Receive completed Work Packages belongs to the Controlling a Stage process. The Project Manager carries out this activity.

This activity is simply the reverse side of the Managing Product Delivery activity Deliver a Work Package that was described in the previous subsection. To ensure that the work has been carried out correctly, during this activity, the Project Manager checks approval records, the Quality Register, and Configuration Item Records.

Reporting on the Progress of a Stage

One important part of controlling a stage is the Project Manager regularly updating the Project Board and any other relevant stakeholders on the progress of the work by sending them Highlight Reports.

As you can see in Figure 10.2, the Report highlights activity is part of the Controlling a Stage process and so is carried out by the Project Manager. In this activity, the Project Manager creates a Highlight Report and sends it to the Project Board and any other stakeholders who want to be regularly apprised of progress. The Communication Management Strategy (which was created back in the initiation stage and shows how the project team will communicate during the project) describes the format, frequency, and recipients of the Highlight Report.

Figure 10.8 shows the PRINCE2-recommended format for the Highlight Report. The Project Manager uses many sources of information to create the Highlight Report—for example, information in the registers, the logs, Checkpoint Reports, the configuration management system, and so on.

FIGURE 10.8 Composition of the Highlight Report

Highlight Report

- Date
- Period covered by this report
- Overview of the stage's current status
- This reporting period:
    - Status of Work Packages
    - Products completed during period
    - Products still to be completed
    - Corrective actions taken in period
- Next reporting period:
    - Work Packages to be worked on next period
    - Products to be completed in next period
    - Corrective actions planned for next period
- Project and stage tolerance status
- Request for change—raised, approved/rejected, and pending
- Key issues and risks updates
- Lessons Report

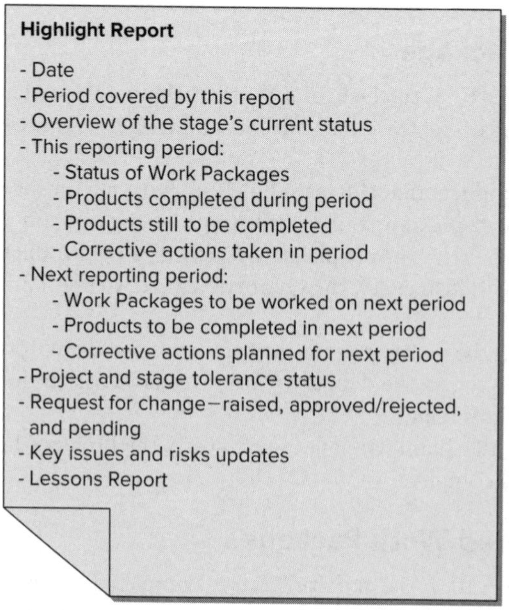

Dealing with Issues and Risks during a Stage

Throughout the stage, the Project Manager will probably be faced with many ad hoc problems and issues. For example, people might ask for a change to a product's specification, a product might be delivered incorrectly, or someone might spot a new threat to the project. There are three Controlling a Stage activities that the Project Manager uses to handle these sorts of situations:

- Capture and examine issues and risks

- Take corrective action

- Escalate issues and risks

Capture and Examine Issues and Risks

Any stakeholder can raise an issue or a risk. The Project Manager should be notified immediately of new issues and risks. He then ensures that they are properly recorded in the relevant log or register. He also ensures that the risk or issue's impact on the project is analyzed.

As you learned in Chapter 8, "Change Theme," there are three types of issues:

Request for Change   Someone wants to change a product or a product's Product Description.

Off-specification   A product(s) has or will be delivered incorrectly.

Problem or Concern   All other issues.

You also saw in Chapter 8, "Change Theme," how all issues and changes are handled using the issue and change control procedure. The procedure has five steps: capture, examine, propose, decide, and implement. The Project Manager does the first two steps—capture and examine—in the Controlling a Stage activity Capture and examine issues and risks.

You learned in Chapter 8, "Change Theme," that formal issues are recorded in the Issue Register and each entry in the Issue Register has an accompanying Issue Report. Informal issues are recorded in the Daily Log.

After the issue has been *captured*, it is then *examined*. You saw in Chapter 8, "Change Theme," that during the *examine* step, the Project Manager works with the rest of the project management team to consider what impact the issue will have on factors such as the cost and time of the project, the wider environment outside of the project, and the interests of the main stakeholder groups such as the suppliers, users, and the business.

The Project Manager should check the Communication Management Strategy to see if there are any stakeholders who need to be informed of this new issue.

In addition to dealing with issues in this activity, the Project Manager captures and examines risks. You learned about risks in Chapter 7, "Risk Theme." You saw in that chapter that a risk is an uncertain event that might affect the project for good or bad. The good ones are called opportunities—for example, there might be the opportunity of recruiting an experienced contractor to work on the new hotel. The bad ones are called threats—for instance, there might be a threat that bad weather could delay the building of the hotel.

You also saw in Chapter 7, "Risk Theme," that the risk management procedure is used to manage risks. The procedure consists of five steps: identify, assess, plan, implement, and communicate. During the Controlling a Stage activity Capture and examine issues and risks, a number of the risk management procedure steps might be carried out. One of the project's stakeholders might tell the Project Manager of a new risk. The Project Manager would log it in the Risk Register (the identify step). The Project Manager would then ensure that the risk is assessed in terms of its probability, impact, and proximity and that countermeasures are planned (the assess and plan steps). The Project Manager should communicate information about the risk to anyone identified in the Communication Management Strategy (the communicate step).

If because of the issue or risk, the Project Manager will take corrective action or escalate the situation to the Project Board, the Project Manager should first use the activity Review stage status to see the full picture of the situation.

Take Corrective Action

In this activity, the Project Manager takes some action to resolve deviations from the Stage Plan caused by an issue. The Project Manager is only able to take corrective action if it does not cause a forecast breach in the stage's tolerances.

One example is authorizing the teams to correct an off-specification. Another is authorizing more resources to work on a product that is behind schedule. The Project Manager should work with the teams to consider the best action to take. Once the option has been chosen, the Project Manager should update any relevant management products such as the Issue Register, Issue Report, Risk Register, Configuration Item Record, or Stage Plan with the option's details. Finally, the Project Manager will then complete the Authorize a Work Package activity to instruct the teams to carry out the corrective action.

Escalate Issues and Risks

There may be situations when an issue or a risk (or the aggregation of a number of issues and risks) cannot be resolved without causing a forecast breach of a stage's tolerances. In this case, the Project Manager must escalate the situation to the Project Board.

The Project Manager uses an Exception Report to escalate issues and risks. As you learned in Chapter 9, "Progress Theme," the Exception Report describes the problem, gives possible options to resolve the issue or risk, and recommends a way forward.

Because it could take some time to put together an Exception Report, PRINCE2 recommends that the Project Manager first alert the Project Board by sending them a copy of the Issue Report.

The Project Board might make a number of responses to the Exception Report, depending on the type of issue:

- They might request more information or time to consider the problem.
- They might approve, defer, or reject a request for change.
- For an off-specification, they might grant a concession, or reject one or defer one.
- They might increase the tolerances of the stage.

- They might instruct the Project Manager to create an Exception Plan showing the Project Board more details of how the recommended option from the Exception Report will be carried out.
- They might even instruct the Project Manager to close the project prematurely.

Once the Project Manager has received the Project Board's response, he should then execute their decision.

Deciding What to Do Next in a Stage

You have now learned about seven of the eight Controlling a Stage activities. As you've seen, they involve delegating work to teams, reviewing progress, dealing with issues, and writing Highlight Reports. In a typical week, the Project Manager will be juggling his time between all of these seven activities.

The final activity, Review stage status, is a bit different from the other seven activities of Controlling a Stage. It is the one in which the Project Manager pauses, reviews the whole situation of the stage, and then decides what to do next.

The Project Manager might use a number of sources of information to review the stage's status. For example, he might refer to Checkpoint Reports, the Stage Plan, the configuration management system, or any of the logs or registers.

After reviewing the status, the Project Manager decides which activity is appropriate to do next. The Project Manager might move on to do another one of the Controlling a Stage activities such as escalating an issue or writing a Highlight Report. Or the Project Manager might realize that the stage is coming to an end and start to do the activities in the Managing a Stage Boundary process, or if this is the last stage of the project, do the activities of Closing a Project.

One other focus for the Project Manager in this activity is to review the Benefits Review Plan to check whether any benefit reviews are due. Remember that the Benefits Review Plan is created in the initiation stage and plans how the benefits from the project will be reviewed. Most benefits from a project usually occur after the project has finished. However, in some projects, benefits might arise during the project itself. For example, if the project is to build a block of apartments, some of the apartments might be sold "off plan" before they have been completed. The Project Manager should ensure that these benefit reviews are executed.

Key Facts for Controlling a Stage and Managing Product Delivery

For the examinations, you do not need to memorize all the details of the Controlling a Stage and Managing Product Delivery activities that you learned about in the preceding section. The Foundation exam won't test you on all the intricate details, and in the case of the Practitioner exam, you will have *Managing Successful Projects with PRINCE2* (Stationery Office, 2009) as a reference.

I recommend that you read through the preceding sections to make sure you understand the details of the processes, and then learn only the key facts for Controlling a Stage and Managing Product Delivery that I've provided for you in Table 10.1 and Table 10.2.

 You might also want to reread the Exam Spotlight in Chapter 2, "Starting a Project Successfully with PRINCE2," which discusses how to approach the PRINCE2 processes when preparing for the exam and how to use *Managing Successful Projects with PRINCE2* to answer process questions in the Practitioner exam.

TABLE 10.1   Controlling a Stage—key process facts

Activity	Key facts
Authorize Work Packages	The Project Manager creates a Work Package that provides the teams and/or the Team Manager with all the information that they will need in order to deliver a set of specialist products.
Review Work Package status	The Project Manager reviews the status of all the Work Packages currently being worked on.
	The Project Manager uses Checkpoint Reports, Configuration Items Records, Product Status Accounts, and the Quality Register to review the team's progress.
	The Project Manager updates the Stage Plan with information on the progress of the Work Packages.
Receive completed Work Packages	The Project Manager receives notification from the teams that a Work Package has been completed. The Project Manager checks the work and ensures that all the products have been approved. The Project Manager updates the Stage Plan to show the Work Package as completed.
Report highlights	The Project Manager creates a Highlight Report and sends it to the Project Board and to any other stakeholders who wish to be kept up-to-date on the project as identified in the Communication Management Strategy. The Highlight Report describes the stage's progress.
Capture and examine issues and risks	The Project Manager documents new formal issues in the Issue Register and creates an accompanying Issue Report. The Project Manager documents informal issues in the Daily Log and risks in the Risk Register.
	The Project Manager ensures that an impact analysis is carried out on issues and that a risk assessment is carried out on risks. New risk countermeasures are planned.
Take corrective action	The Project Manager deals with risks and issues that can be resolved without a forecast breach in stage tolerances.

Activity	Key facts
Escalate issues and risks	The Project Manager escalates risks and issues that cannot be resolved without a forecast breach in stage tolerances. The Project Manager escalates the situation to the Project Board by sending them an Exception Report. The Project Manager carries out the decision made by the Project Board.
Review stage status	The Project Manager reviews the stage and decides what to do next. The next action could be any of the Controlling a Stage activities, or the Managing a Stage Boundary process if the stage is nearing completion, or the Closing a Project process if the whole project is nearing completion.

TABLE 10.2 Managing Product Delivery—key process facts

Activity	Key facts
Accept a Work Package	The team or the Team Manager receives a Work Package from the Project Manager and agrees to carry out the work. The team creates a Team Plan for the work and checks with Project Assurance that the reviewers in the Quality Register are appropriate.
Execute a Work Package	The specialist products are created and delivered by the teams. The teams ensure that quality activities defined in the products' Product Descriptions and the Quality Register are carried out and that products are approved. The team collects quality and approval records as evidence that the quality activities have occurred. The team follows any configuration management procedure detailed in the Work Package to protect, track, and control the products. The team regularly updates the Project Manager about the Work Package's progress by sending a Checkpoint Report.
Deliver a Work Package	The teams notify the Project Manager that the products from a Work Package have been delivered. The teams ensure that all the relevant quality activities have been carried out and that the relevant reviewers have approved the products.

The Managing a Stage Boundary Process

The Managing a Stage Boundary process is done in one of two places: either at the end of the stage (except the final stage, when Closing a Project is used instead) or to create an Exception Plan. In either case, the Project Manager does most of the work in the activities of the Managing a Stage Boundary process.

If the Managing a Stage Boundary process is being used at the end of a stage, the activities help the Project Manager to do three things:

- Review the work of the stage and create an End Stage Report.

- Look ahead to the work of the next stage and create a Stage Plan for it.

- Review the overall project situation and update the Project Plan, the Business Case, and the overall risk situation.

As you learned in the section "The Exception Plan" in Chapter 5, "Plans Theme," the Managing a Stage Boundary process is also used to create an Exception Plan. In that chapter, you learned that although the Project Manager is using the activities of Managing a Stage Boundary to create the Exception Plan, the project might not be at the end of the stage at all. In this situation, there will have been forecast breach of stage or project tolerances, which the Project Manager will have escalated to the Project Board. In response, the Project Board will have asked the Project Manager to create an Exception Plan showing how the project will respond to forecast breach in tolerances. This request for an Exception Plan could occur at any time in a stage, depending on when the exception has occurred. As I said back in Chapter 5, "Plans Theme," one way of thinking about this is that the project needs an emergency stage boundary to deal with the breach in tolerances.

Figure 10.9 shows the activities of the Managing a Stage Boundary process. There are two routes into the process. The visit to Managing a Stage Boundary could be because the end of the stage is approaching, in which case the Project Manager uses the Plan the next stage activity to create the next Stage Plan. Alternatively, the visit to Managing a Stage Boundary might be in response to the Project Board's request for an Exception Plan, in which case the Project Manager uses the Produce an Exception Plan activity to create an Exception Plan. Then, the Project Manager does the other three activities: Update the Project Plan, Update the Business Case, and Report stage end.

FIGURE 10.9 Activities of the Managing a Stage Boundary process

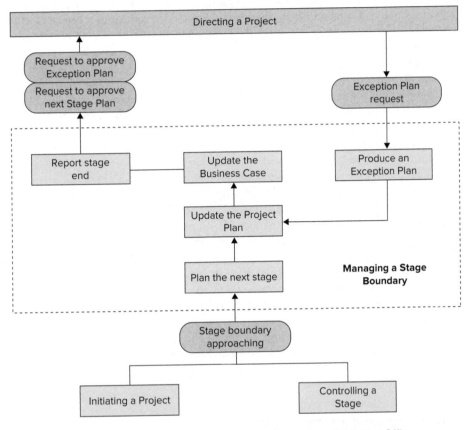

Based on Cabinet Office PRINCE2® material. Reproduced under licence from the Cabinet Office.

Plan the Next Stage

In this activity, the Project Manager creates the Stage Plan for the next management stage. As you learned in Chapter 5, "Plans Theme," the Project Manager creates a broad Project Plan at the beginning of the project, and then just before starting a new stage, the Project Manager creates a more detailed Stage Plan for the upcoming stage. This is in line with the PRINCE2 principle of "manage by stage."

The Project Manager will want to involve as many relevant people as possible to ensure that an accurate Stage Plan is created. He may consult with the teams who will deliver the specialist work, the Senior Suppliers, as well as Project Assurance.

The Project Manager will need to ensure that the Stage Plan takes account of risk, quality, change, configuration, and communication approaches described in the project's strategies. He will also want to ensure that the Stage Plan is aligned with the Project Plan created at the beginning of the project.

During the stage-planning process, the Project Manager may need to create new Product Descriptions. As you learned in Chapter 6, "Quality Theme," the Project Manager (with the help of the Senior Users) will first create broad Product Descriptions when producing the Project Plan. Then, during stage planning, the Project Manager might need to create more detailed Product Descriptions for the products to be delivered in the next stage. For example, in the project to build a new hotel, imagine that the next stage will furnish the hotel rooms. The Project Plan created at the beginning of the project might have contained overall Product Descriptions for each type of room. When planning the stage, more detailed Product Descriptions will be created for components of the rooms such as the furniture, the bath fixtures, and the electrical equipment.

When new Product Descriptions are created, an associated Configuration Item Record will also be created to track the status of that product.

If the Stage Plan is for the final stage of the project, the plan also needs to cover the management activities that will take place during the Closing a Project process to close the project. For example, if you look back at Figure 10.1, you'll see that the Project Manager will plan the closure activities during the second visit to Managing a Stage Boundary during that particular project. If the Stage Plan is *not* for the final stage of the project, the plan will also need to cover the management activities that will take place during the Managing Stage Boundary activities that will take place at the end of that stage.

If new people will be involved in the next stage, the Project Manager will need to update the project management team structure and the roles and responsibilities section in the Project Initiation Documentation.

Finally, the Project Manager may need to update the Quality Register with details of the quality checks planned for the stage, the Issue Register with new issues spotted for the stage, and the Risk Register to describe new threats and/or opportunities associated with the stage.

Produce an Exception Plan

In this activity, the Project Manager will create an Exception Plan. The work within this activity will be very similar to the work done in the Plan the next stage activity that you just learned about. The Project Manager will create a new plan and perhaps some new Product Descriptions and Configuration Item Records. The Project Manager will also need to update a range of associated management products such as the registers, project management team structure, and roles and responsibilities. However, in this case, the plan created shows the Project Board how the project can recover from a forecast breach in tolerances. For example, if the forecast breach is at the stage level, the Exception Plan would be at the Stage Plan level, or if the forecast breach is at the project level, the Exception Plan would be at the Project Plan level.

Another point to note is that the Exception Plan might contain many of the original activities from the Stage Plan or the Project Plan that it will replace (after authorization from the Project Board). The difference is that it also contains a variety of other activities to deal with the forecast breach in tolerance.

Update the Project Plan

The Project Manager will update the Project Plan as follows:

- Update the section of the Project Plan that refers to the current stage with the high-level details of what has actually occurred.

- Update the section of the Project Plan that refers to the next stage with any changes to the forecast work made during creating the next Stage Plan.

The Project Manager should also review the Project Product Description to make sure it still reflects the overall outputs that will be created given the fact that more granular Product Descriptions have been created in the stage-planning process. Any changes to the Project Product Description would need to be referred to the Project Board for a decision.

Exam Spotlight

In the modern project management world, many of us use software tools to create and update project plans. Usually, these tools allow us to see multiple views on a plan, such as a detailed view that the Project Manager can use to track and control work (the equivalent of a PRINCE2 Stage Plan) and a broader "milestone" view that the Project Manager can show to senior stakeholders (the equivalent of a PRINCE2 Project Plan). This means that as we update the plan with the progress of the work, both views are updated simultaneously.

The scenario described in the previous paragraph does not translate to the PRINCE2 process model. As you have learned, in the Controlling a Stage process, the Project Manager updates the Stage Plan with the progress of the work and then later on, in the Managing a Stage Boundary process, updates the Project Plan with a broader, higher-level view of the progress of the work.

Remember this for the exam: PRINCE2 considers the Stage Plan and the Project Plan as two separate (but aligned) plans that get updated at different times.

Update the Business Case

As you saw back in Chapter 1, "Overview of PRINCE2," one of the principles of PRINCE2 is "continued business justification." As the project progresses, one common project management pitfall is not updating and reviewing the original Business Case that justified the start of the initiative. Many things might change during the project that would invalidate the project's justification: costs might rise, schedules get delayed, new competitors arrive, technology changes, and so on. As a result of these potential changes, PRINCE2 states that at the end of each stage, the Business Case needs to be updated. It is this updated Business Case that the Project Board will review when it decides whether to authorize the project to continue on to the next stage.

In this activity, the Project Manager and the Executive review all the sections of the Business Case and update them if necessary. They will use the information created from the previous activities of Managing a Stage Boundary such as the new Stage Plan or Exception Plan and updated logs and registers. The Executive should also consider how changes in the outside environment such as new technologies or new competitors might change the forecast benefits.

The Project Manager should consult with the Executive to consider whether any of the organizations involved with the project have changed their outlook on risk appetite. As you learned in Chapter 7, "Risk Theme," *risk appetite* is the amount of risk that an individual or an organization is willing to take on. Sometimes, for example, an organization might start a risky project, but as time progresses, the outside economic environment deteriorates and they find they are no longer in a position to make riskier investments. If an organization lowers its risk appetite, they may either want to close a project or change the Risk Management Strategy to allow for a more rigorous risk management approach.

With regard to risk, the Project Manager should consult with the Executive to reevaluate the overall risk situation to ensure that it remains within the project risk tolerances and to ensure that the main risks to the project are being managed correctly.

The Project Manager and Executive should review the Benefits Review Plan to check that it has been updated with the results of any benefit reviews that took place in the previous stage and compare these results with the expected results. They should also ensure that any new planned benefit reviews are in the Stage and Project Plans.

Report Stage End

In this activity, the Project Manager creates an End Stage Report that the Project Board will review, along with the other outputs of Managing a Stage Boundary, to decide whether to move on with the next stage of the project. Figure 10.10 shows the composition of the End Stage Report.

FIGURE 10.10 The End Stage Report

End Stage Report

- Summary of stage performance
- Business Case review
- Review of current achievement against project objectives
- Review of achievement against stage objectives
- Review of team performance
- Review of product delivery and quality activities
- Follow-on Action Recommendations for products handed over to operations
- Lessons Report
- Summary of issue and risk situation
- Current forecasts for project objectives
- Forecasts for the next stage

The one caveat to this is when the Project Manager is using the Managing a Stage Boundary process to create an Exception Plan. The previous stage boundary may have only just occurred, so there is little new information to report. In this situation, the Project Manager should ask the Project Board if an End Stage Report is necessary.

Some projects might hand over interim deliverables to the client or an operational team at the end of some of the stages. The Project Manager needs to ensure that the relevant people such as the Senior Users or members of the operational team sign off on the products by giving their acceptances. The Project Manager should also ensure that any relevant Follow-on Action Recommendations associated with those products (such as requests for unauthorized changes or off-specifications that were given concessions) are handed over to the client or operational team.

At this point, the Project Manager might create a Lessons Report. On shorter projects, a Lessons Report might be created only at the end of the project, but on longer ones, it might be useful to pass on experience to relevant people at the end of each stage.

The main recipients of the End Stage Report will be the Project Board, but the Project Manager should check the Communication Management Strategy to see if any other stakeholders should also be sent this document.

The final part of this activity is to seek approval from the Project Board to move on to the next stage of the project.

After Managing a Stage Boundary

Once the Managing a Stage Boundary activities are complete, the Project Board (together with Project Assurance) will review whether to authorize the Project Manager to manage the next stage or the Exception Plan. The Project Board carries out this review in their Directing a Project process. The Project Board will use all the outputs of the Managing a Stage Boundary process in order to make this decision. If Managing a Stage Boundary was used to create an Exception Plan due to a forecast breach in project tolerances, corporate or programme management will also need to be involved with this decision.

One particular focus for the Project Board is to ensure that the updated Business Case still forecasts a worthwhile and viable project. This should be one of the main drivers in their decision whether to continue with the project.

After considering all the previously described factors, the Project Board will do one of the following:

- Approve the Stage Plan or Exception Plan and the associated Product Descriptions. If this is the case, the Project Board will set the tolerances for the new plan and obtain or commit the resources needed for the plan. In addition, the Project Board should approve the updated Benefits Review Plan, Business Case, and Project Plan as well as any other amended sections of the Project Initiation Documentation.

- Ask the Project Manager to make revisions to the plan and give guidance on what changes are needed.

- Instruct the Project Manager to initiate a premature closure of the project.

Finally, the Project Board should communicate the status of the project to any interested parties (as defined in the Communication Management Strategy), especially corporate or programme management.

Key Facts for Managing a Stage Boundary

Just as with the other processes, I recommend that you take some time to familiarize yourself with the information in the preceding section on the Managing a Stage Boundary activities, but it is only necessary to memorize the key facts in Table 10.3 when preparing for the accreditation exams. If any more detailed questions arise in the Practitioner exam, you will be able to refer to *Managing Successful Project with PRINCE2* to find the information.

TABLE 10.3   Managing a Stage Boundary—key process facts

Activity	Key facts
Plan the next stage	The Project Manager creates the next Stage Plan and any associated Product Descriptions and Configuration Item Records. If new people will take on new roles and responsibilities for the next stage, the Project Manager updates the project management team.
Produce an Exception Plan	The Project Manager creates an Exception Plan and any associated Product Descriptions and Configuration Item Records. If new people will take on new roles and responsibilities for the Exception Plan, the Project Manager updates the project management team.
Update the Project Plan	The Project Manager updates the Project Plan with the progress from the previous stage and any new forecast information for the next stage.
Update the Business Case	The Project Manager consults with the Executive and then updates the Business Case with any new information and reviews the overall risk profile and major risks to the project. The Benefits Review Plan is updated with results from benefits reviews from the previous stage and new reviews planned for subsequent stages and post-project.
Report stage end	The Project Manager creates the End Stage Report. The Project Manager ensures that acceptances are obtained for any interim deliverables that are being handed over to the client or the operational team. The Project Manager creates a list of Follow-on Action Recommendations for products being handed over to the operational teams as well as a Lessons Report if necessary.

Themes Used to Manage the Middle of the Project

All of the seven themes are used throughout the activities in the middle of the project. It is important for you to understand how the themes link to the activities of the Controlling a Stage, Managing Product Delivery, and Managing a Stage Boundary processes, because this is a common question topic in PRINCE2 exams.

Business Case Theme

As you learned in Chapter 4, "Business Case Theme," the Business Case theme describes how to ensure that the project is desirable, viable, and achievable throughout the project's life. It shows how to write the project's Business Case, assigns a variety of business-related responsibilities to the roles within the project management team, and shows where in the process model the major business-related activities should occur.

When the Project Manager is reviewing the stage status during Controlling a Stage, he will review the Benefits Review Plan to check whether any benefit reviews are due. Also during Controlling a Stage, the Project Manager will ensure that the impact on the Business Case of new issues and risks is considered.

The Project Manager and the Executive will update the Business Case during the Managing a Stage Boundary process. The Project Board will then use the updated Business Case as a key driver in deciding whether to authorize the next stage of the project during the Directing a Project process.

Organization Theme

As you learned in Chapter 3, "Organization Theme," the Organization theme describes the project management team structure, the project roles, and the project responsibilities. During the Controlling a Stage process, the Project Manager is responsible for managing the stage on behalf of the Project Board. The Project Manager delegates Work Packages to the team or the Team Manager who will be responsible for delivering that work using the Managing Product Delivery process.

During the Managing a Stage Boundary process, when the Project Manager is planning the next stage or the Exception Plan, he may discover that the project management team needs to be updated as new people will become involved with the project or old ones are disengaging from the work. If this is the case, the Project Manager updates the project management team structure and/or roles and responsibilities sections of the Project Initiation Documentation. The Project Board reviews these updates when they are deciding whether to authorize the next stage.

Quality Theme

In Chapter 6, "Quality Theme," you saw that the Quality theme shows how a project should be managed to ensure that it creates the right products. It covers how to do quality planning where the product's specifications are created, how to do quality control where the products are checked to see if they meet their specifications, and how to do quality assurance where quality management aspects of the project are independently monitored.

In the Managing a Stage Boundary process, the Project Manager creates the next Stage Plan or the Exception Plan. This might involve creating new Product Descriptions for the specialist products to be delivered or using Product Descriptions created previously when preparing the Project Plan.

The Stage Plan and Exception Plans created during Managing a Stage Boundary include activities that check the quality of the products. The Project Manager refers to the Quality Management Strategy to see if there are any standards that these quality checks should follow. The Project Manager also refers to the Product Descriptions to see who should review and approve each product. The Project Manager updates the Quality Register with the planned details of these quality checks.

During the Controlling a Stage process, the Project Manager delegates work to the teams by assigning Work Packages. These Work Packages contain Product Descriptions that show the team the quality expectations for the products to be delivered and how they should be checked. Later, when the Project Manager receives the completed Work Packages, he will want to see evidence that the products have been checked and approved by the relevant people described in that product's Product Description.

In the Managing Product Delivery process, the teams deliver the specialist products according to the specifications described in the Product Descriptions. The teams also ensure that the relevant people carry out quality checks on the products and that the Quality Register is updated with the results of the quality checks.

Plans Theme

As you learned in Chapter 5, "Plans Theme," the Plans theme shows how to use various levels of plans (Project Plan, Stage Plan, and Team Plan) to plan the work of the project, what roles are involved with each plan, and what steps are needed to create a plan.

The Project Manager creates a Stage Plan in the Managing a Stage Boundary process as well as updating the overall Project Plan with details from the previous stage and new forecasts for the upcoming stage. The Project Manager uses the Stage Plan during the Controlling a Stage process to track and monitor the work of the teams.

The team or Team Manager may create a Team Plan during the Managing Product Delivery process, which they can then use to track and monitor their work. However, the Team Plan is optional, and the Stage Plan alone may provide enough detail for the team.

If there has been a forecast breach in stage or project tolerances, the Project Board may ask the Project Manager to create an Exception Plan. The Exception Plan shows how the project will recover from the deviation caused by the exception. The Project Manager creates the Exception Plan in the Managing a Stage Boundary process, and after it is approved by the Project Board, the Exception Plan replaces either the Stage Plan or the Project Plan.

Risk Theme

Chapter 7, "Risk Theme," showed you that the Risk theme identifies, assesses, and controls the potential threats and opportunities of the project, and thus improves the likelihood of project success.

During the Controlling a Stage activity Capture and examine issues and risks, the Project Manager records identified risks in the Risk Register. The Project Manager works with the project management team to assess the impact and probability of those risks and plan countermeasures to them. The Project Manager checks the Communication Management Strategy to see if he needs to inform anyone of the risk.

In the Controlling a Stage process, the Project Manager produces regular Highlight Reports for the Project Board and other relevant stakeholders. The Highlight Reports should update the recipients on the current status of risk within the project. Similarly, the teams or Team Manager create regular Checkpoint Reports for the Project Manager that should also include a section on the current risks, this time focused on the risks to the Work Package that the team is delivering.

Finally, when the Project Manager creates the Stage Plan or the Exception Plan, he should ensure that he understands the risks associated with the plan and that there are adequate countermeasures planned for each one.

Change Theme

As you learned in Chapter 8, "Change Theme," the Change theme covers two aspects of project management: how to track and control all of the project's products (configuration management), and how to control changes to the project's products (change management).

During the Controlling a Stage process, the Project Manager captures and examines issues. Issues could be requests for changes, off-specifications, or problems or concerns. The Project Manager can deal with issues if they do not cause a forecast breach in stage tolerances or if the request for change is within the constraints of any change authority he has. If this is the case, he takes corrective action. Otherwise, the Project Manager will need to escalate the issues using an Exception Report.

The Project Board might ask the Project Manager to create an Exception Plan in response to an issue. The Project Manager would create the Exception Plan during the Managing a Stage Boundary process, and it would be approved by the Project Board in the Directing a Project process.

The teams or the Team Manager need to ensure that any issues that would cause a forecast breach to Work Package tolerances are escalated to the Project Manager. The teams must also ensure that the products they deliver are tracked, stored, and protected according the configuration management procedures detailed in the Work Package. The Project Manager uses the configuration system to review the latest status of the products being delivered in the stage.

Progress Theme

As you learned in Chapter 9, "Progress Theme," the Progress theme describes how PRINCE2 controls the work of the project using tolerances to delegate authority, stages that allow the Project Board to control the progress of the project, a variety of reports to monitor the progress of the project, and a number of other controls such as Work Packages and Product Descriptions to constrain the work that is carried out.

The Managing a Stage Boundary process plans out each stage and provides the Project Board with enough information to decide what tolerances to set for each stage and whether to authorize the work. The Controlling a Stage process describes the activities necessary for the Project Manager to manage and control the work of each stage. The Controlling a Stage process allows the Project Manager to delegate work using Work Packages to the teams and set Work Package tolerances.

All the management products used throughout the middle of the project help to monitor or control the work being delivered.

Using the PRINCE2 Principles to Successfully Manage the Middle of a Project

The seven PRINCE2 principles used during the middle of the project are as follows:

Continued Business Justification   The Project Manager updates the Business Case at the end of each stage. The Project Board uses the updated Business Case to drive their decision about whether to authorize the next stage of the project. The Project Manager considers the impact on the Business Case of new issues or risks.

Learn from Experience   Previous experience is always considered when carrying out any of the activities of Controlling a Stage, Managing a Stage Boundary, and Managing Product Delivery. If appropriate, the Project Manager includes a Lessons Report with Highlight Reports and End Stage Reports.

Defined Roles and Responsibilities   The Project Manager ensures that the roles and responsibilities for the project management team are up-to-date for each stage in the Managing a Stage Boundary process.

Manage by Stage   The Project Board authorizes the Project Manager to manage the project one stage at a time. The Project Manager uses the Managing a Stage Boundary process to prepare information for the Project Board to decide whether to authorize the next stage and the Controlling a Stage process to manage each stage once authorized.

Manage by Exception   The Project Board defines stage tolerances within which the Project Manager must manage each delivery stage. The Project Manager has authority to manage each stage unless he forecasts that these stage tolerances will be breached, in which case he must escalate the situation to the Project Board. In a similar way, the Project Manager sets the teams' Work Package tolerances that they must work within.

Focus on Products   The Project Manager creates Stage Plans and Exception Plans using a product-based planning approach to ensure that there are Product Descriptions for each product to be delivered in the stage. The Project Manager gives the teams Product Descriptions to ensure that they deliver products to the correct specifications.

Tailor to Suit the Project Environment   The Project Manager considers whether there is any new tailoring that needs to be applied to the PRINCE2 method when he is planning each stage during the Managing a Stage Boundary process.

Summary

In this chapter, you learned how the activities in the PRINCE2 processes of Controlling a Stage, Managing Product Delivery, Managing a Stage Boundary, and Directing a Project work together to manage the middle part of the project.

More specifically, you learned how the Project Manager uses the Controlling a Stage process to manage the day-to-day activities of a stage on behalf of the Project Board. During this process, the Project Manager delegates work to the delivery teams, continually monitors the activities of the stage, regularly reports progress to the Project Board, and deals with issues and risks.

You also learned about the Managing Product Delivery process. The delivery teams use this process to create the specialist products of the project.

This chapter looked at the Managing a Stage Boundary process. This is a set of activities that the Project Manager will use at the end of a stage in order to prepare to meet up with the Project Board for an end-stage assessment. You also saw that the Managing a Stage Boundary process is used when there is a forecast breach in stage or project tolerances and the Project Board has asked for an Exception Plan.

You saw how Directing a Project is used in the middle of the project. The Project Board uses the Authorize the stage activity at the end of each management stage to decide whether to authorize the next stage. As an input to this decision, they use the work that the Project Manager has prepared in the Managing a Stage Boundary process, such as the next stage plan and the End Stage Report. The Project Board can also give the Project Manager informal advice using the Give ad hoc direction activity and keep track of the progress of the stage by reading the Project Manager's Highlight Reports and Exception Reports.

Finally, you saw how the themes and the principles are used throughout the middle of the project.

Exam Essentials

Understand the purpose of the Controlling a Stage process.   The purpose of the Controlling a Stage process is for the Project Manager to assign work to be done, monitor such work, deal with issues, report progress to the Project Board, and take corrective actions to ensure that the stage remains within tolerance.

Know the objectives of the Controlling a Stage process.   The objectives of the Controlling a Stage process are to focus attention on the delivery of the stage's products so as to avoid scope creep and deliver the correct level of quality in the agreed-to time and cost tolerances, keep issues and risks under control, and keep the Business Case under review.

Understand the context of the Controlling a Stage process.   The Controlling a Stage process is used to manage each of the delivery stages of the project.

Be familiar with the eight activities of the Controlling a Stage process and know which role has responsibilities within each activity.   The Project Manager is responsible for all eight activities in the Controlling a Stage process. There are four categories of activities: managing the work of the teams using the Authorize Work Packages, Review Work Package status, and Receive completed Work Packages activities, managing risks and issues using the Capture and examine issues and risks, Take corrective action, and Escalate issues and risks activities; reporting progress using the Report highlights activity; and reviewing the stage and deciding what to do next in the Review stage status activity.

Know the purpose of the Managing Product Delivery process.   The purpose of the Managing Product Delivery process is to control the link between the Project Manager and the Team Manager(s) by placing formal requirements on accepting, executing, and delivering project work and for the Team Manager(s) to coordinate work to deliver one or more of the project's products.

Know the objectives of the Managing Product Delivery process.   The objectives of the Managing Product Delivery process are to ensure that the team's work is authorized and agreed to; the teams understand what is to be produced and what is the expected effort, cost, and timescales; products are delivered to expectations and within tolerances; and accurate progress information is provided to the Project Manager.

Understand the context of the Managing Product Delivery process.   The teams and/or Team Manager(s) use the Managing Product Delivery process to deliver Work Packages during a delivery stage. It is initiated by the Project Manager during the Authorize a Work Package activity in the Controlling a Stage process.

Understand the three activities of the Managing Product Delivery process and which role has responsibilities within each activity.   The Team Manager and/or the teams are responsible for all three activities in the Managing Product Delivery process. The work is accepted from the Project Manager in Accept a Work Package, created and delivered in Execute a Work Package, and handed back to the Project Manager in Deliver a Work Package.

Know the purpose of the Managing a Stage Boundary process. The purpose of the Managing a Stage Boundary process is for the Project Manager to provide sufficient information for the Project Board to decide whether to authorize the project to move on to its next stage. A secondary purpose of the Managing a Stage Boundary process is to provide an Exception Report to show the Project Board how the project can recover from a stage- or project-level exception. Lastly, another purpose of the process is to review the success of the stage that is just about to finish.

Know the objectives of the Managing a Stage Boundary process. The objectives of the Managing a Stage Boundary process are to assure the Project Board that all of a stage's products have been approved, prepare the Stage Plan for the next stage, review and, if necessary, update the Project Initiation Documentation (in particular, the Business Case, the Project Plan, the project management team, and the overall risk situation), and request authorization to start the next stage. In an exception situation, the objective of the Managing a Stage Boundary process is to prepare an Exception Plan and seek approval to replace either the Project Plan or the Stage Plan with the Exception Plan.

Understand the context of the Managing a Stage Boundary process. The Managing a Stage Boundary process is used at the end of each stage in order to prepare for the work of subsequent stages. It is also used after an exception situation when the Project Board has requested an Exception Plan.

Know the activities of the Managing a Stage Boundary process and which role has responsibilities within each activity. The Project Manager is responsible for the five activities of the Managing a Stage Boundary process. The Project Manager will either create the next Stage Plan using the Plan the next stage activity or create an Exception Plan in the Produce an Exception Plan activity, and will then update the Project Initiation Documentation in the Update the Project Plan and Update the Business Case activities. He will finally create an End Stage Report in the Report stage end activity.

Know how to apply the seven themes within the Controlling a Stage, Managing Product Delivery, and Managing a Stage Boundary processes. The seven themes are used throughout the middle of the project in order to provide continued business justification, learn from experience, manage by stage and exception, focus on products, define roles and responsibilities, and tailor PRINCE2 to the project environment.

Understand the purpose and composition of the Highlight Report; know in which processes it is developed, used, and reviewed; and know which roles are responsible for this. The purpose of the Highlight Report is to provide the Project Board and other relevant stakeholders with regular updates on the progress of the stage. Know that the Project Manager creates the Highlight Report in the Controlling a Stage process and the Project Board reviews the Highlight Report in the Directing a Project process.

Understand the purpose and composition of the Checkpoint Report; know in which processes it is developed, used, and reviewed; and know which roles are responsible for this. The purpose of the Checkpoint Report is to provide the Project Manager with regular updates on the progress of the Work Package. The Team Manager and/or the teams create the Checkpoint Report in the Managing Product Delivery process and the Project Manager reviews the Checkpoint Report in the Controlling a Stage process.

Understand the purpose and composition of the End Stage Report; know in which processes it is developed, used, and reviewed; and know which roles are responsible for this.   The purpose of the End Stage Report is to provide the Project Board with a report on the success or failure of a stage. The Project Manager creates the End Stage Report in the Managing a Stage Boundary process, and the Project Board reviews the End Stage Report in the Directing a Project process.

Review Questions

The rest of this chapter contains mock exam questions, first for the Foundation exam and then for the Practitioner exam.

Foundation Exam Questions

1. Identify the missing words in the following sentence:

A purpose of the Managing a Stage Boundary process is to provide the Project Board with sufficient information so that it can _____.

   1. Review the success of the current stage

   2. Assess whether to commission the project

   3. Confirm continued business justification of the project

   4. Confirm acceptability of the project's risks

   A. 1, 2, 3

   B. 1, 3, 4

   C. 1, 2, 4

   D. 2, 3, 4

2. Which of the following is **NOT** an objective of the Controlling a Stage process?

   A. Produce an End Stage Report

   B. Deliver the agreed products to stated quality standards

   C. Control threats to the stage and project

   D. Keep the Business Case under review

3. Which of the following roles is primarily involved with carrying out the activities of the Managing a Stage Boundary process?

   A. Senior User

   B. Executive

   C. Project Manager

   D. Team Manager

4. Which management product does the Project Manager use to review the progress of Work Packages?

    1. Checkpoint Reports

    2. Quality Register

    3. Lessons Log

    4. Configuration Item Records

    A. 1, 2, 3

    B. 1, 3, 4

    C. 1, 2, 4

    D. 2, 3, 4

5. Which of the following is **NOT** a purpose of the Managing Product Delivery process?

    A. Control the link between the Project Manager and the Team Manager

    B. Place formal requirements on accepting, executing, and delivering the project work

    C. Take corrective action to ensure the stage remains within tolerance

    D. Coordinate work to deliver one or more of the project's products

6. Which of the following is **NOT** a purpose of the Controlling a Stage process?

    A. Hand over the responsibility to deliver Work Packages to the teams

    B. Review the progress of the work to deliver specialist products

    C. Manage the issue and change control process

    D. Provide information that enables the Project Board to decide whether to authorize the next stage

7. Which of the following is an objective of the Managing Product Delivery process?

    A. Ensure that the Team Manager and the teams understand the expected effort, time, and cost needed to deliver the products

    B. Ensure that the various ways to deliver the project are evaluated

    C. Define how quality management will be carried out during the project

    D. Request authorization to start the next stage of the project

8. When the teams (or the Team Manager if there is one) accept a Work Package, which management product may need to be updated with details of extra product reviewers?

    A. Work Package

    B. Quality Register

    C. Checkpoint Report

    D. Configuration Item Record

9. Which of the following is an objective of the Managing a Stage Boundary process?

    A. Ensure that there is business justification for initiating the project

    B. Approve all the products from the current stage

    C. Assure the Project Board that all products in the current stage have been approved

    D. Communicate breaches in project tolerance to corporate or programme management

10. Which management product does the Project Manager use to escalate an issue to the Project Board?

    A. Highlight Report

    B. Lessons Report

    C. End Stage Report

    D. Exception Report

Practitioner Questions

The following Practitioner questions are divided into three sections by question type and are based on the Practitioner exam scenario described in this book's Introduction.

Section 1: Matching Events with Themes

Column 1 contains a list of events that occurred in stage 4 of the Quality Furniture website project. For each event in Column 1, select from Column 2 the appropriate PRINCE2 theme that should have been used to deal with it. Each selection from Column 2 can be used once, more than once, or not at all.

Column 1	Column 2
1. The website development contractor, Digital Design, needs official instructions from the Project Manager to start their work.	A. Business Case
2. One of the software developers who is working remotely has lost his copy of the requirements document. He needs a new copy.	B. Organization
3. The website development contractor, Digital Design, has spotted a new technology that may save the project some time. The Project Manager needs to assess this possibility.	C. Quality
4. The home page of the website has been finished and is ready for review.	D. Plans E. Risk F. Change G. Progress

Section 2: Matching Actions with Controlling a Stage Activities

Column 1 contains a list of actions that the Project Manager will carry out in stage 4 of the Quality Furniture website project. For each action in Column 1, select from Column 2 the Controlling a Stage activity during which the Project Manager should carry out this action. Each selection from Column 2 can be used once, more than once, or not at all.

Column 1	Column 2
1. Give Digital Design official instructions to start their work.	A. The Project Manager authorizes teams to carry out their work in the "Authorize a Work Package" activity.
2. Send a report on the progress of stage 4 to key Quality Furniture shareholders as indicated in the Communication Management Strategy.	B. Review Work Package status
3. Receive an email from the Marketing Director that asks for a previously unspecified ability for the website to be "smartphone"-compatible to be considered.	C. Receive completed Work Packages
4. In order to deal with a delay, ask for further resources from the Project Board over and above the resources that were originally authorized for the stage.	D. Review stage status
	E. Report highlights
	F. Capture and examine issues and risks
	G. Escalate issues and risks
	H. Take corrective action

Section 3: Classic Multiple Choice Questions

The Quality Furniture web project is in stage 4 and the web development company, Digital Design, is building the website. The Chief Executive of Quality Furniture, who has taken on the role of the Executive for the project, has asked his personal assistant to carry out a PRINCE2 compliance audit of the project. The personal assistant has some limited knowledge of PRINCE2 gained from attending a project management conference. The personal assistant has made the following observations about the management of the project. Decide if each observation is an appropriate application of PRINCE2 for this project and select the option that supports your decision.

1. During the Managing a Stage Boundary process at the end of stage 3, the Project Manager worked with Digital Design to create a Stage Plan for stage 4. The Project Manager then created Work Packages for Digital Design and authorized them do their work. Finally, the Project Manager requested authorization for the Stage Plan from the Project Board.

    A. Yes, the Project Manager is responsible for authorizing all Work Packages.

    B. Yes, the Project Manager needs to confirm that the Work Packages for a stage can be delivered before requesting authorization for the Stage Plan that contains those Work Packages.

    C. No, the Project Board should authorize the Stage Plan before the Project Manager authorizes Work Packages for the delivery of work within that stage.

    D. No, the Project Board makes all authorizations within the project, so they should authorize the Work Packages.

2. The First Tech Consultant is carrying out a Project Assurance role on the project. The Digital Design Team Manager consulted with the First Tech Consultant when accepting the Work Package. The First Tech Consultant recommended that some additional reviewers be added to some of the stage's quality checks.

    A. Yes, when accepting a Work Package, the Team Manager should consult with Project Assurance to find out if any extra reviewers are required.

    B. Yes, because Project Assurance is responsible for approving the products within each stage, so they must ensure that appropriate reviewers are allocated to each quality check.

    C. No, all reviewers should be allocated to a stage's quality checks when the Stage Plan is created during Managing a Stage Boundary.

    D. No, the Managing Product Delivery process is focused on the work of the teams, so Project Assurance should not be involved during the Accepting a Work Package activity.

3. During stage 4, the Marketing Director has asked for a change to the baselined home page design. This would be a small change to the tones of blue that are used to more closely match Quality Furniture's brand colors. Because this is a minor change and the Marketing Director is responsible for all outward communication for the company, the Project Manager amends the home page Work Package and instructs the teams to implement the change.

    A. Yes, the Project Manager can authorize small changes to the project's products.

    B. Yes, because the Marketing Director is responsible for communication at Quality Furniture, she would have the authority to instigate this change.

    C. No, once a product has been baselined, it cannot be changed.

    D. No, requests to change baselined products should be recorded in the Issue Register and be subject to an impact analysis before being authorized by the appropriate Change Authority.

4. During the preparation of the End Stage Report for stage 4, the Project Manager realized that the Quality Furniture team had gained some valuable experience in how to deal with third-party IT contractors. The Project Manager thought that this experience might be useful for another project that was currently being run at Quality Furniture to install a new financial software package. The Project Manager created a Lessons Report detailing the experience and appended it to the End Stage Report.

   A. Yes, because Lessons Reports are only created at the end of each stage during the Managing a Stage Boundary process.

   B. Yes, because the Project Manager should pass on any useful experience learned during a stage within the End Stage Report.

   C. No, the Project Manager uses the Lessons Log to pass on experience to relevant people.

   D. No, the Lessons Report is a management product that is only created at the end of the project during the Closing a Project process.

Chapter

11

Managing the End of a Project Successfully with PRINCE2

PRINCE2 EXAM OBJECTIVES COVERED IN THIS CHAPTER:

✓ **Understand the purpose, objectives, and context of the Closing a Project process.**

✓ **Understand the following five activities of the Closing a Project process and know which role has responsibilities within each activity:**

- Prepare planned closure.

- Prepare premature closure.

- Hand over products.

- Evaluate the project.

- Recommend project closure.

✓ **Understand how the seven themes may be applied within the Closing a Project process.**

✓ **Know the purpose and composition of the End Project Report and understand in which processes it is developed, used, and reviewed, and which roles are responsible for this.**

In this chapter, you will learn how to manage the end of a project using PRINCE2. The close of a project can bring various challenges. For example, some projects suffer because there is no clear end to the initiative. This can create a number of problems. The project's products have not been officially passed to the group who will maintain them in their operational life, but the project team believe they have finished working on them. If there are problems with the products, it is not clear whether the project or the operational team should fix them.

Another problem when there is no clear end is that there has been no official review of the project against its original objectives. This can cause longer-term problems for the organization, as unbeknownst to them, they may be continually running projects that do not meet their business aims.

In this chapter, you will see how PRINCE2 aims to reduce the risks of these problems occurring. You will see that the Closing a Project process ensures that there is point in time where all of the project's products need to be accepted by the customers and the operational teams. The Closing a Project process also ensures that the project is reviewed against its original objectives.

Overview of the End of a PRINCE2 Project

Figure 11.1 is taken from the section "An End-to-End Walk-through of PRINCE2" in Chapter 1, "Overview of PRINCE2." If you haven't read that section yet, I recommend that you do so before reading this chapter, as it gives a high-level overview of the whole PRINCE2 process model. You will then be able to understand the context of the Closing a Project process discussed in this chapter.

FIGURE 11.1 End of the project

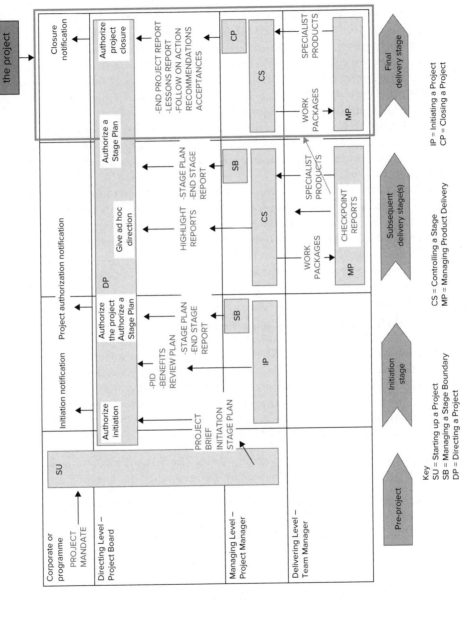

Based on Cabinet Office PRINCE2® material. Reproduced under licence from the Cabinet Office.

In Figure 11.1, I have highlighted the final delivery stage of the project. The first thing to understand is that in *most* ways, the final delivery stage is managed in a similar way to the other delivery stages. You learned how the Project Manager managed these other delivery stages in Chapter 10, "Managing the Middle of a Project Successfully with PRINCE2," but here's a brief summary. The Project Manager will plan the delivery stage in the previous Managing a Stage Boundary process and the Project Board will authorize the work in the Directing a Project process. When the stage starts, the Project Manager will use the Controlling a Stage process to manage the work and the teams will deliver the specialist products by using the Managing Product Delivery process.

The difference between the final delivery stage and the other delivery stages is that at the end of the final stage, instead of using the Managing a Stage Boundary process to prepare for an end-stage assessment, the Project Manager uses the Closing a Project process to prepare for the end of the project.

The Project Manager uses the activities in the Closing a Project process to prepare to meet the Project Board and ask for permission to shut down the project. These activities include ensuring that the customer accepts the project's products as complete, evaluating the project against its objectives, and assigning responsibility for the post-project benefit reviews.

After the Closing a Project process, the Project Board uses the Directing a Project activity Authorize project closure to make the final decision whether the project can now close.

Common Pitfalls with the Closing a Project Process

There are three common mistakes students make with the end of a PRINCE2 project. First, candidates think that the project is closed in Closing a Project. Given the name of the process, this is a reasonable assumption! But unfortunately, PRINCE2 hasn't named the process very well. What the process should be called is something like "Preparing for the Closing of a Project" because the project is closed after Closing a Project, by the Project Board in the Directing a Project activity authorize project closure.

Second, candidates mistakenly think that the Project Board carries out the activities in Closing a Project. It is the Project Manager who is responsible for this process.

Third, some candidates mistakenly think that Closing a Project is a stage in itself. This isn't the case. The Closing a Project activities are only part of the final delivery stage. In that final delivery stage, there will also be work to deliver various specialist products.

The Closing a Project Process

The Closing a Project process provides a fixed point in time at which acceptance of the main outputs of the project can be confirmed. If the project were to build a hotel, it would be during the Closing a Project process that the hotel is officially "signed off." In PRINCE2 terms, this final signing off on the project's products is called *obtaining acceptances*. This is where ownership of these products is transferred from the project team to the clients or operational teams.

Acceptance will need to be obtained from anyone who has acceptance responsibilities. The Project Product Description describes who these people are. You learned about the Project Product Description in Chapter 6, "Quality Theme." It describes the overall products and outlines measurable acceptance criteria that these products must meet, how the product should be checked against these criteria, and who should do the checking.

There could be a number of types of people who have acceptance responsibilities. They could be the ultimate clients, who might be internal or external to the organization running the project. In the hotel project, the customers might be senior directors of the hotel chain. They could also be the teams who will operate or maintain the products. In the hotel example, they could be the team who will run the hotel.

In Chapter 10, "Managing the Middle of a Project Successfully with PRINCE2," you learned that Closing a Project isn't the only place where products might be handed over to the clients or the operational teams. In some projects, there might be interim deliverables that are accepted by the clients or the operational teams in the Managing a Stage Boundary process at the end of a particular stage.

The Closing a Project process is also a time when the project is reviewed against its original objectives to see how successful it has been. For example, how long did the project take compared to the original estimates, and how much did it cost compared to the original budget? During the project, these original objectives might have been subject to some approved changes. If this is the case, obviously, these changes need to be taken into account when reviewing the project.

Figure 11.2 shows the main activities of the Closing a Project process. You can see that there are five activities that are mainly the responsibility of the Project Manager:

- Prepare planned closure
- Prepare premature closure
- Hand over products
- Evaluate the project
- Recommend project closure

FIGURE 11.2 Overview of Closing a Project

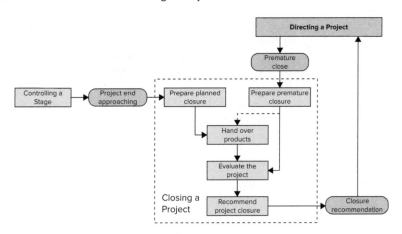

Based on Cabinet Office PRINCE2® material. Reproduced under licence from the Cabinet Office.

The first activity that the Project Manager will do in the Closing a Project process will depend on whether this is a planned or a premature closure. If the project is closing when it was originally planned to close, the Project Manager will do the Prepare planned closure activity. If the project is closing earlier than originally planned, a *premature closure*, the Project Manager will carry out the Prepare premature closure activity. After either one of these activities, the Project Manager will then do the final three Closing a Project activities: Hand over products, Evaluate the project, and Recommend project closure.

You will learn about each of these activities in this section. Read through this section and make sure you understand the general idea of Closing a Project, but you don't necessarily have to remember all the details. At the end of this section is a key facts table to show you what would be useful to memorize for the exams.

Prepare Planned Closure

Before arriving at this activity, the Project Manager would have been using the Controlling a Stage process to manage the final delivery stage. When he realizes that the final delivery stage is nearing completion, he will want to start preparing for the end of the project by using the Closing a Project process. In this situation, the first Closing a Project activity the Project Manager will do is Prepare planned closure.

The Project Manager updates the Project Plan with the progress updates from the final stage. He requests a Product Status Account to ensure that all the products from the final stage have been approved by the relevant people outlined in their Product Descriptions.

Finally, the Project Manager notifies the Project Board that the resources used in the final stage are about to be released from the project.

Prepare Premature Closure

This will be the first Closing a Project activity if the Project Board has instructed the Project Manager to close the project prematurely. The Project Manager will request a Product Status Account and review the current state of the products. In particular, he will look for products that could be useful to other projects or parts of the organization (even if the project hasn't finished them yet) and/or products that need to be made safe or put into storage.

For example, say the project is to create some new apartments for a construction firm. The construction firm may decide that because of poor economic conditions, they will prematurely close the project and restart it when conditions improve. In this case, some additional work will be needed to put security around the unfinished site and weatherproof the buildings.

The Project Manager will then create additional estimates for the work needed to finish potentially useful products or to put products into storage. The Project Manager will need to present these additional work estimates (maybe in the form of an Exception Plan) to the Project Board for authorization.

The Project Manager will also update the Issue Register to record the premature closure request and also update the Project Plan with the progress updates from the final stage.

Finally, he will notify the Project Board that the resources used in the final stage are about to be released from the project.

Hand Over Products

In this activity, the Project Manager hands over the project's products to the operational and maintenance teams. The Project Manager reviews the Configuration Management Strategy to understand any special procedure for this handover. The Project Manager should collect acceptance records from the operations and maintenance teams as proof that they have taken on responsibility for the products. After the products have been handed over, the Project Manager ensures that relevant Configuration Item Records are updated with the change of status.

Some products, such as IT systems, need a lot of support and maintenance in their operational life after the project. In this case, the Project Manager ensures that there is a suitable service agreement or contract between the operational team and the end users. This service agreement should have been a specialist product that was delivered as part of the project.

The Project Manager passes on any Follow-on Action Recommendations for the products to the operations team. These can be things such as known product errors, requests for change that were considered but never implemented, and/or known issues or risks for the products.

The Project Manager reviews the Benefits Review Plan to ensure that post-project benefit reviews have been planned. In addition to reviewing the benefits derived from the products, these reviews focus on how the products performed in their operational life.

In Chapter 10, "Managing the Middle of a Project Successfully with PRINCE2," you learned that some projects might hand over interim releases at the end of some of the stages. If this was the case, then at this point, the remainder of the products will be handed over.

Evaluate the Project

In this activity, the Project Manager will create the *End Project Report*. This report compares the project's actual achievements against the objectives set in the original version of the Project Initiation Documentation created in the initiation stage. One caveat to this is if these original objectives have been subject to an approved change—in that case, the amended objectives will be used.

The End Project Report focuses on how the project performed against its planned targets for time, cost, quality, scope, benefits, and risk. Of course, at this point in time, not all the benefits might have been achieved, since many benefits don't occur until after the project. So all that can be done at this point is review any benefits that occurred during the project and ensure post-project benefit reviews are described in the Benefits Review Plan.

You can see the composition of the End Project Report in Figure 11.3.

FIGURE 11.3 Composition of the End Project Report

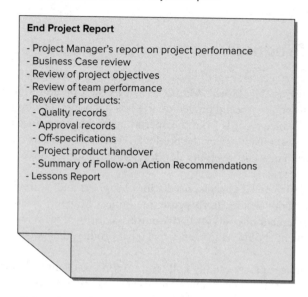

One of the aims of this activity is to provide useful feedback to corporate or programme management that will help in managing future projects. For example, by comparing estimates versus actual results, the organization might see ways to improve its estimating techniques.

The End Project Report contains a Lessons Report for the project, which can show corporate or programme management what worked well or worked badly in managing this project. For example, it could look at how PRINCE2 was implemented and suggest improvements in its use for future projects. (You learned about the Lessons Report in Chapter 10, "Managing the Middle of a Project Successfully with PRINCE2.")

Recommend Project Closure

In this activity, the Project Manager confirms to the Project Board that the project is ready to be closed. The Project Manager creates a draft project closure notification for the Project Board to review.

The Project Manager then reviews the Communication Management Strategy to see who needs to be informed that the project is about to close.

Finally, the Project Manager ensures that all the project's issues and logs are closed and that all the project documentation is archived in accordance with the procedure described in the Configuration Management Strategy.

Key Facts for Closing a Project

For the exams, you do not need to memorize all the Closing a Project activity details contained in the previous sections. Read through those sections and make sure you understand the basic concepts and then just learn the key facts for this process described in Table 11.1.

TABLE 11.1   Closing a Project—key process facts

Activity	Key facts
Prepare planned closure	The Project Manager requests a Product Status Account to check that the project's products meet all their quality criteria and have been approved by the appropriate authorities.
	Project Manager updates the Project Plan with actual progress from the last delivery stage.
Prepare premature closure	Project Manager updates the Project Plan with actual progress from the last delivery stage.
	The Project Manager requests a Product Status Account to understand which products have been completed.
	Project Manager prepares additional work estimates for unfinished products that could be useful for other projects or for products that need to be stored or made safe.
Hand over products	Project Manager ensures that all products are handed over to the operations and maintenance teams and acceptance records are obtained as proof.
	The Project Manager checks the Benefits Review Plan to ensure it includes all post-project activities to confirm benefits that cannot be measured until some time after the project.
Evaluate the project	Project Manager creates the End Project Report that evaluates how the project performed against the planned objectives outlined in the initial Project Initiation Documentation.
	Project Manager creates a Lessons Report to show useful experience learned during the project.
Recommend project closure	Project Manager sends a draft project closure notification to the Project Board.
	Project Manager ensures that the project documentation is archived according to the approach outlined in the Configuration Management Strategy.

Authorize Project Closure

The final activity in the PRINCE2 process model is the Directing a Project activity, Authorize project closure. This is where the Project Board reviews the outputs from the Closing a Project process and decides whether the project can finally close.

This is the Project Board's last activity before the body is disbanded. The decision may need further authorization from corporate or programme management. The Project Board may also use Project Assurance to review the End Project Report and validate its accuracy.

During this activity, the Project Board reviews the project against its original objectives (or, as stated previously, any approved amendments to these original objectives). They ensure that any post-project benefit reviews are planned and pass on the responsibility for these reviews to corporate or programme management. They also ensure that useful experience highlighted in the Lessons Report is passed on to the relevant authorities.

Finally, the Project Board issues the project closure notification in accordance with the procedure described in the Communication Management Strategy.

Using the Themes to Close the Project

This section looks at how the themes are used at the end of the project. It is important for you to understand this, as this will be a potential topic for exam questions.

Business Case Theme

During the Closing a Project process, the Project Manager updates the Benefits Review Plan with any further planned post-project benefit reviews and also reviews any benefits that have occurred during the project.

During the Directing a Project process, the Project Board ensures that corporate or programme management assumes responsibility for the post-project benefits reviews and reviews the achievement of any benefits during the project.

Organization Theme

The Project Manager uses the Communication Management Strategy to determine who needs to be notified that the project is ending. After the Directing a Project activity, Authorize project closure, the project management team is disbanded. The responsibility for post-project benefit reviews is given to the corporate or programme management team. The responsibility for the project's products is handed over to the operations and maintenance team.

Quality Theme

During the Closing a Project process, the Project Manager ensures that all the products from the final stage have been approved by the appropriate authorities highlighted in their

Product Descriptions. The Project Manager ensures that the authorities defined in the Project Product Description review the final outputs from the project against the acceptance criteria and give acceptances for those products. The Project Manager should obtain acceptance records as proof that this has happened.

Plans Theme

The Project Manager updates the Project Plan with details of what happened in the final stage during the Closing a Project process. If the project has closed prematurely, the Project Manager may need to create an Exception Plan to ask for authorization for any additional work, such as finishing products that might be useful for the organization or for storing products.

Risk Theme

The Project Manager passes on details of any relevant operational risks to the group who will maintain the products in their operational life. These risks are passed on as Follow-on Action Recommendations during the Closing a Project process.

The Project Manager closes and archives the Risk Register in the Closing a Project process.

Change Theme

During the Closing a Project process, the Project Manager will report any off-specifications, concessions, and approved requests for change in the End Project Report and archive the Issue Register and Issue Reports.

The Project Manager will pass on any relevant issues to the operational team as follow-on action recommendations.

Progress Theme

The End Project Report acts as a major project control, helping the Project Board to monitor the results of the project. The Lessons Report is another project control, helping the project management team capture and disseminate useful experiences from the project.

Using the Principles to Close the Project

All of the seven principles are used to some extent at the end of the project, but the three main ones are as follows:

Focus on Products   The Project Manager ensures that acceptance is obtained for the final outputs of the project and ensures that these products are reviewed against their acceptance criteria described in the Project Product Description.

Learn from Experience   The Project Manager creates a final Lessons Report and passes it on to the Project Board, who will, in turn, pass it on to the group that is focused on organizational improvement.

Continued Business Justification   The Project Manager ensures that the benefit objectives are reviewed and that post-project benefit reviews are planned.

Summary

In this chapter, you have seen how PRINCE2 can be used to manage the end of a project. You saw that there are two main processes involved: the Closing a Project process and the Directing a Project process.

The Closing a Project process ensures that there is a fixed point in time to review the outputs from the project and review the achievement (or lack of it) of the project's objectives. The Project Manager is responsible for Closing a Project, and its main output is the End Project Report.

You learned that after the Closing a Project process, the Project Board uses the Directing a Project activity Authorize project closure to review the End Project Report and decide whether the project is able to close. The Project Board ensures that corporate or programme management accepts responsibility for any post-project benefit reviews.

Finally, you saw that all the themes and principles are used at the end of the project.

Exam Essentials

Know the purpose, objectives, and context of the Closing a Project process.   The purpose of the Closing a Project process is to provide a fixed point at which acceptance of the project's products is confirmed and to review whether the project's objectives have been achieved. The objectives of the process are to gain user and operational acceptance for the products, review the project against its baseline, and ensure post-project benefit reviews are planned. The Closing a Project process occurs at the end of the final stage.

Understand the activities of the Closing a Project process and know which role has responsibilities within each activity.   There are five activities in the Closing a Project process: Prepare planned closure, Prepare premature closure, Hand over products, Evaluate the project, and Recommend project closure. The Project Manager is responsible for each of these activities.

Understand how the seven themes may be applied within the Closing a Project processes.   All seven themes are applied throughout the end of the project.

Know the purpose and composition of the End Project Report and understand in which processes it is developed, used, and reviewed, and which roles are responsible for each.   The End Project Report is used to review how the project performed against the planned objectives in the original Project Initiation Documentation. It is created by the Project Manager in the Closing a Project process and reviewed by the Project Board in the Directing a Project process in order for them to decide whether the project can close.

Review Questions

The rest of this chapter contains mock exam questions, first for the Foundation exam and then for the Practitioner exam.

Foundation Questions

1. What is a purpose of the Closing a Project process?
   A. Enable the Project Manager to review whether the project has anything further to contribute.
   B. Enable the Project Board to make the decision about whether or not to close the project.
   C. Enable the Project Manager to manage the final delivery stage.
   D. Enable the delivery team to create the specialist products of the final stage.

2. Which statement does **NOT** correctly describe when the Closing a Project activity might be used in a project?
   A. Directly following a request from the Project Board to close the project earlier than expected.
   B. Directly following a review of the status of the final delivery stage by the Project Manager.
   C. Directly preceding the decision by the Project Board about whether or not to close the project.
   D. Directly following the planning for the final stage of the project.

3. Which of the following are a purpose of the End Project Report?
   1. Compare the achievement of the project with the forecast objectives described in the version of the Project Initiation Documentation used to authorize it.
   2. Document lessons that could be applied to other projects.
   3. Show how and when the achievement of the post-project benefits can be made.
   4. Pass on details of ongoing risks.
   A. 1, 2, 3
   B. 1, 2, 4
   C. 1, 3, 4
   D. 2, 3, 4

4. Which of the following is a purpose of the Lessons Report?
   A. Recommend post-project actions specific to the project's products.
   B. Plan how and when the project's benefits will be reviewed.
   C. Collate lessons that could be usefully applied to the current project.
   D. Provoke action to embed positive experience into the organization's way of working.

5. Which is an objective of the Closing a Project process?

   A. Prepare a Stage Plan for the early phases of operational support for the project's products.

   B. Request authorization to start the final stage of the project.

   C. Provide authority to close the project.

   D. Ensure that any continuing threats to the project's products are highlighted in the Follow-on Action Recommendations.

6. How might the Project Manager use the Project Plan during the Closing a Project process?

   A. To update with actuals from the final stage

   B. To update with forecasts for the final stage

   C. To plan the work to review the post-project benefits

   D. To control and monitor the work of the final stage

7. When preparing the End Project Report, the Project Manager would **NOT** review the _____?

   A. Project Initiation Documentation

   B. Lessons Log

   C. Follow-on Action Recommendations

   D. Project Brief

8. Which of the following activities is carried out in the Closing a Project process?

   A. Design and appoint the project management team.

   B. Review the Configuration Management Strategy to understand how to hand over the project's products to the operational teams.

   C. Plan the final stage of the project.

   D. Review the Project Initiation Documentation to understand how to control the delivery of the specialist products.

9. Which of the following statements represents how the Closing a Project process helps to implement the Risk theme?

   A. Describes the activity where the procedure for managing threats for the project is defined

   B. Describes the activity where ongoing opportunities for the project's products are passed on to the operational and maintenance teams

   C. Describes the activity where the delivery teams report risks to the Project Manager

   D. Describes the activity where risks are captured in the Risk Register

10. How is the Quality theme used in the Closing a Project process?

    A. The Project Manager uses the Configuration Management Strategy to understand how to hand over the products to the operational team.

    B. The Project Manager requests a Product Status Account to check that all the project's products have their requisite approval.

    C. The Project Manager updates the Benefits Review Plan with any new benefit reviews planned for after the project.

    D. The Project Manager creates the End Project Report, which allows the Project Board to review the project's achievements of its objectives.

Practitioner Questions

The following Practitioner questions are divided into three sections by question type and are based on the Practitioner exam scenario that you will find in this book's Introduction.

Section 1: Practitioner Matching Questions about the Themes

Column 1 is a list of actions that occurred at the end of the Quality Furniture website project. For each action in Column 1, select from Column 2 the appropriate PRINCE2 theme that is being used. Each selection from Column 2 can be used once, more than once, or not at all.

Column 1	Column 2
1. The Project Manager refers to the Communication Management Strategy to identify who needs to know the project is closing.	A. Business Case
2. The Project Manager reviews the Benefits Review Plan to check that there is a planned review of online sales in six months' time.	B. Organization
3. First Tech highlights an ongoing security threat to the website. The Project Manager passes this on as a Follow-on Action Recommendation to the IT personnel who will operate and maintain the site.	C. Quality
4. The Project Manager discusses with the marketing director whether she agrees that the website has met all its acceptance criteria.	D. Plans E. Risk F. Change G. Progress

Section 2: Practitioner Matching Questions about the End Project Report

Column 1 is a list of **true statements** to be included in the End Project Report for the Quality Furniture website project. Column 2 is a selection of End Project Report headings. For each statement in Column 1, select from Column 2 the End Project Report heading under which it should be recorded. Each selection from Column 2 can be used once, more than once, or not at all.

Column 1	Column 2
1. The PRINCE2 method worked well but the project team felt that training in their PRINCE2 roles would have been useful early in the project. This should be considered for future PRINCE2 projects.	A. Review of Business Case
2. The acceptance criteria stated that all the information on the website could be reached in four clicks of the user's mouse from the home page. This was not quite achieved; the Project Board agreed five clicks were adequate in some cases.	B. Review of project objectives
3. Online sales are forecast to be $200,000 in year 1, $300,000 in year 2, and $400,000 in year 3.	C. Review of team performance
4. The project was delivered two weeks late.	D. Review of products
	E. Lessons Report

Section 3: Practitioner Assertion/Reason Questions

The Quality Furniture project is about to close and the Project Manager is preparing for the final end project assessment meeting with the Project Board.

Rows 1 to 6 in the following table consist of an assertion statement and a reason statement. For each line, identify the appropriate option, from options A to E, that applies. Each option can be used once, more than once, or not at all.

A. The assertion is true and the reason is true, *and* the reason explains the assertion.

B. The assertion is true and the reason is true, *but* the reason does not explain the assertion.

C. The assertion is true and the reason is false.

D. The assertion is false and the reason is true.

E. Both the assertion and the reason are false.

Assertion		Reason
1. During stage 5, the Project Board asked for a review of the monthly number of website visitors in six months' time. The Project Manager should add this to the Benefits Review Plan.	BECAUSE	The Project Manager creates the Benefits Review Plan in the Closing a Project process.
2. The internal IT team will maintain the website. It would be a good idea for the Project Manager to agree to service-level objectives with the IT team as part of the handover of the website.	BECAUSE	When a product requires a lot of support and maintenance, the Project Manager should ensure that a suitable service agreement is in place with the operations and maintenance team.
3. If the Project Board is satisfied that the project has nothing further to contribute, they should authorize the closure of the project in the Closing a Project process.	BECAUSE	The Project Board is responsible for the decision regarding whether the project can finish.
4. The Project Manager will create an End Stage Report during Closing a Project to review stage 5.	BECAUSE	At the end of every delivery stage, the Managing a Stage Boundary process is used to review the stage.

Chapter

12

Tailoring PRINCE2 to the Project Environment

PRINCE2 EXAM OBJECTIVES COVERED IN THIS CHAPTER:

- ✓ Understand the difference between tailoring and embedding PRINCE2.

- ✓ Understand the relationship between a programme's Business Case and a project's Business Case.

- ✓ Understand the general approach to tailoring PRINCE2.

- ✓ Understand that the PRINCE2 principles are not tailored.

- ✓ Understand how the themes, processes, management products, terminology, and roles and responsibilities can be tailored to suit various project situations.

- ✓ Be able to describe situations where PRINCE2 can be tailored.

In this chapter, you'll look at how PRINCE2 can be tailored to suit different environments and different types of projects. Before any project begins, the project management team needs to consider how to customize the method so that it improves the likelihood of project success without introducing unnecessary bureaucracy.

In this chapter, you will learn about the general concepts of tailoring PRINCE2, see how to modify different parts of the method, and learn how PRINCE2 can be tailored for large and small projects and those that involve different commercial organizations.

General Approach to Tailoring PRINCE2

Now that you have studied PRINCE2, you can see that there are many different parts to the method. For example, you have seen that there are 26 management products, 9 project roles, a process model with 7 processes, and numerous activities. Many people naturally ask, "Do we really need all this for every project?" By asking this question, they are starting to think about how to tailor the method.

For large, detailed, politically important projects, it may be necessary to use all the features of the method to the degree described in this study guide and in *Managing Successful Projects with PRINCE2* (Stationery Office, 2009). But for smaller projects, it would probably be better to apply many of the areas in a broader, more informal way. The key to tailoring PRINCE2 is not to completely omit any element, but to apply it to the necessary degree. For example, in a small project, it may not be necessary to create a formal Business Case with all the contents defined in PRINCE2; instead, it might be sufficient to provide some simple business justification, no matter how this is documented.

When it comes to tailoring, the general approach is to get a balance between an overly detailed implementation of the method and a lax application. An overly detailed implementation creates an unnecessary management overhead. For example, if the project management team dictated that every one of the 26 management products had to be documented in detail for a small project, the team would probably spend more time creating documents than managing the project. The opposite of this situation is where the method is hardly applied at all. This can lead to a chaotic project, where no one understands what they are supposed to be doing or why they are doing it. The idea behind tailoring PRINCE2 is to get the correct balance between these two extremes. PRINCE2 describes this balance as applying the method with a "lightness of touch." This happy medium doesn't introduce unnecessary overhead to the project but controls the project to just enough of a degree to bring about a major increase in the likelihood of project success.

In addition to the project's size, many other factors should be taken into account when deciding how to apply PRINCE2. Is the project part of a programme of projects? What industry-specific approaches might need to be used? Is the project being run in a public-or private-sector environment, and how might this affect the project? Does the project involve personnel from just one organization or many commercial organizations? All of these factors affect how the project is managed and thus how PRINCE2 is applied.

How to apply PRINCE2 to many different environments is a big topic. Many books, training courses, and consultancy services are focused on answering this question. It takes several years of experience in using PRINCE2 to fully understand how to tailor the model to work in multitudes of environments. Luckily, the PRINCE2 accreditation exams do not expect this degree of understanding. All you will need to understand is the overall tailoring concepts and how to tailor the method to some basic situations such as small projects and projects within programmes. This chapter will only cover the tailoring essentials needed for the Foundation and Practitioner exams. However, once you have passed the exams, I recommend that you investigate this topic further. It will greatly increase your success as a PRINCE2 Project Manager.

 **Real World Scenario**

The Reality of Tailoring PRINCE2

Over the years, I have seen many ways of applying PRINCE2, some more successful than others. I think the most important thing to consider when applying PRINCE2 is to remember that it is simply a means to an end rather than the end itself. Some Project Managers I have seen seem more concerned with implementing the method correctly than delivering the objectives of the project. Remember, a project that poorly implements PRINCE2 but creates a great set of products that bring the expected benefits is far better than one with a perfect set of 26 management products that didn't deliver what was required!

One example of focusing too much on the means rather than the end was a project I worked on for a local UK government organization. To apply PRINCE2, they had created a set of management product templates that had to be filled out at various times in the project. For example, there was a template for the Project Initiation Documentation that had to be filled out before the project budget was released.

Templates can be useful to remind the project team what information needs to be gathered, but they often turn into bureaucratic forms, which people fill out regardless of the need for the information. The purpose behind the management product gets lost. The local government organization had fallen into exactly that situation. Every project, regardless of size, needed a completely detailed Project Initiation Documentation. This led to unnecessary time being spent gathering information for quite small initiatives.

The other extreme of the previous situation is where there is no project method at all. I spent a number of years in the late 1990s working for Internet start-up companies in the dot-com boom. In the early days of these companies, there was very little project management discipline. This led to many problems: uncoordinated work, scope creep, poor risk management, and so on. One fundamental problem was that many projects were started without a good business rationale. This led ultimately to the bankruptcy of one of the businesses. Even a rudimentary application of the PRINCE2 Business Case theme might have avoided this. It could have ensured that each project was considered on its investment merits, rather than whether it used the latest Internet technology.

There are many projects I have worked on that have been far more successful in applying PRINCE2 to the right degree. For example, one project that I was involved with a few years ago created a UK-wide database containing syllabus and curriculum information for British schools. Teachers could access the database via the Internet, and those in charge of syllabus information at the Department of Education could upload new data via a content management system.

There were a number of things that worked very well on this initiative. The chief executive of the government department became the Executive for the project. He understood his primary role as project leader. However, he did not burden the project with too many meetings and was content to delegate the day-to-day management to the Project Manager and his team. He proved useful a number of times when we hit some large problems, getting involved and using his positional power to move issues forward.

The project used no templates and had very little documentation. There was a succinct Project Initiation Documentation that covered just enough detail for the stakeholders to understand and agree to the project definition. There was a broad Project Plan and more detailed Stage Plans for the delivery teams. One log contained all the risks and issues. As PRINCE2 puts it, "lightness of touch" was very much applied to the management products.

At the end of each stage, all the stakeholders that made up the Project Board attended the end-stage assessments. They were all interested in reviewing the previous stage and understanding and giving their opinion about what was involved in the next one. I always think one way of predicting project success is how many people on the Project Board turn up at the end-stage assessments!

The project was very successful, delivering on time and (more or less) within budget. I am convinced that the PRINCE2 ideas of strong governance from the Project Board, managing by stages, and creating just enough management products helped contribute considerably to this result.

Embedding vs. Tailoring

PRINCE2 uses two important terms in connection with tailoring the method. *Embedding* is the term used when an organization adopts PRINCE2 as the standard for project management. Table 12.1 shows how an organization might embed PRINCE2. For example, they could train Project Managers in PRINCE2, they could align current organizational processes (such as financial or procurement processes) to the PRINCE2 processes, or they could appoint a person or group to review each project's compliance to the method.

TABLE 12.1   Embedding and tailoring

Embedding	Tailoring
Done by the organization to adopt PRINCE2	Done by the project management team to adapt the method to the context of a specific project
Focus on: - Process responsibilities - Scaling rules/guidance (e.g., score card) - Standards (templates, definitions) - Training and development - Integration with business processes - Tools - Process assurance	Focus on: - Adapting the themes (through the strategies and controls) - Incorporating specific terms/language - Revising the Product Descriptions for the management products - Revising the role descriptions for the PRINCE2 project roles - Adjusting the processes to match the above
Guidance in *PRINCE2 Maturity Model* (Office of Government Commerce, 2010).	Guidance in *Managing Successful Projects with PRINCE2*

Based on Cabinet Office PRINCE2® material. Reproduced under licence from the Cabinet Office.

Once the method has been embedded into an organization, PRINCE2 needs to be tailored for each project. *Tailoring* ensures the method is applied in the right way given the environmental and project factors that face the project management team. Table 12.1 shows the different ways PRINCE2 can be tailored, such as adapting the management products, the themes, or the processes. You will learn more about these approaches in the following sections.

Tailoring the Elements of PRINCE2

In this section, you will learn which areas of PRINCE2 can be tailored and which areas cannot. You will see the general approaches to tailoring various parts of the method such as the themes, the processes, the PRINCE2 terms, the management products, and the roles and responsibilities.

Applying the Principles

The one area of PRINCE2 that cannot be modified is the principles. As you learned in Chapter 1, "Overview of PRINCE2," these are the core concepts that run through the entire method. For example, all PRINCE2 projects must be managed by stages, everyone in the project must consider past experience, and the Project Manager must ensure that everyone is clear about their role and what responsibilities they have within the project. No matter what type of project the team is facing and no matter what environment the initiative is operating within, all of the PRINCE2 principles will be applied.

Adapting the Themes

The themes are adapted to suit a particular project by creating strategies and project controls suitable for the situation. Here are a few examples of modifying the themes for certain situations:

- An organization uses a particular risk identification technique that is focused on identifying common threats within its industry. The technique could be highlighted in the project's Risk Management Strategy under the Tools and Techniques section.

- An organization uses a particular approach to constructing plans. These planning standards could be described in the project controls section of the Project Initiation Documentation that shows how the project will be monitored.

- A project is part of a programme, and benefit reviews are the responsibility of the programme management team and not the Executive as is usual in PRINCE2. The Executive job description in the Project Initiation Documentation would be a tailored version of the standard PRINCE2 Executive role description and would show that benefit reviews are not an Executive responsibility. Correspondingly, the project management team should ensure that the programme team understands that benefit reviews are *their* responsibility.

Adapting the Terminology

Many organizations have their own project terms and phrases that are either particular to their industry or maybe just to their own organization. For example, in the UK, architects talk about creating a "programme," which is their word for a plan. Of course, in PRINCE2, *programme* means an entirely different thing—a collection of projects being managed together. I have heard many variations for the management product that PRINCE2 calls a Project Initiation Documentation, such as "terms of reference," "project charter," and "project mandate." All of these different terms can cause a lot of confusion and miscommunication, so it is important at the outset of the project to agree on a project lexicon. One approach would be to create a project glossary, communicate this to the project management team, and make sure everyone uses the terms consistently.

Adapting the Management Products

Some projects will only use a subset of the management products, with many of them being much broader in detail than suggested by PRINCE2. For example, rather than having three registers and two logs, these products could be combined under one register. On a small project, it might not be necessary to produce detailed Product Descriptions for each product—one high-level Product Description might provide enough detail for planning and quality control purposes. In a programme situation, there may be no Business Case for each project, just one for the whole programme. The most important thing when adapting the management products is ensuring everyone is still clear on the purpose and composition of each new product.

Another area to consider is how the management products will be implemented. Do they need to be documented? Is there a requirement for an audit trail? On a small, more informal project, the information in the management products might be agreed to verbally.

Adapting the PRINCE2 Roles and Responsibilities

As you have seen, the PRINCE2 project management team structure ensures that there are people carrying out all the necessary directing, managing, and delivering roles within a project. The structure will probably need to be adapted to suit the project environment and the people carrying out the roles. However, when you are tailoring the roles, it is important not to lose the benefits that the Organization theme brings—such as having a single accountable individual for the project (the Executive), having a single responsibility for coordination and communication in the project (the Project Manager), and having a broad range of perspectives represented when making key project decisions (the Project Board).

One way of adapting this area of PRINCE2 is to combine roles. For example, on a smaller project, one individual could carry out the Project Manager, Team Manager, and Project Support roles. It's important when combining roles not to create conflict of interests. For example, Project Assurance checks on the effectiveness of the Project Manager, so one individual shouldn't carry out both of those roles.

Another way of adapting the roles is to amend the responsibilities suggested by PRINCE2. For example, if the project is part of a programme, the responsibility for ensuring that benefit reviews occur during the project might lie at the programme management level rather than with the Executive role.

Adapting the Processes

All the activities in the PRINCE2 processes need to be done on any project. What might vary from project to project is which roles are responsible for carrying out particular activities and which management products are used. For example, if a project is part of a programme, then the programme management team might perform the Starting up a Project process. If this is the case, the programme management team will decide what projects are viable and worthwhile for the programme, and then design and appoint the project management team. The first responsibility for the project management team in this situation would be the Initiating a Project process.

Adapting the processes might also involve doing each activity to a greater or lesser degree. For example, in a smaller project, it may not be necessary to have a formal Starting up a Project process. All that might be required is to ensure that relevant stakeholders have considered the sort of information that would go into the Project Brief; have thought about the project from the perspectives of the business, user, and supplier; and have decided to give authorization for the initiative. It might not even be necessary to create a Project Brief document; instead, the Project Board can just discuss and agree on the usual areas the Project Brief contains, such as the rationale for the project, the project definition, and what the project will deliver. However, PRINCE2 recommends providing some simple documentation at least regarding the justification for the project.

Examples of Adapting PRINCE2

For the accreditation exams, you need to understand how PRINCE2 could be adapted for a programme situation, for a small project, and for a project involving a number of commercial organizations. You will learn how this can be done in this section.

Adapting PRINCE2 to a Programme Environment

The PRINCE2 definition of a programme is as follows:

> A programme is a temporary, flexible, organization structure created to coordinate, direct and oversee the implementation of a set of related projects and activities in order to deliver outcomes and benefits relating to an organization's strategic objectives. A programme may have a life that spans several years.

What this means in practice is that a programme contains a number of related projects that are being coordinated together as a unit. An example of a programme is the work done for the London 2012 Olympics. Numerous projects were involved in that initiative: the creation of the main stadium, the cycling track, the Olympic London 2012 website, and so on. Each project was run as an individual unit under the overall governance of a programme board.

Table 12.2 shows the main differences between a PRINCE2 project and a programme.

TABLE 12.2   Comparison between projects and programmes

Projects	Programme
Driven by deliverables	Driven by vision of "end state"
Finite—defined start and finish	No predefined path

Projects	Programme
Bounded and scoped deliverables	Changes to the business capability
Delivery of product	Coordinated outputs delivery—includes projects not directly delivering benefits
Benefits usually realized after project closure	Benefits realized during the programme and afterwards
Shorter timescale	Longer timescales

PRINCE2 can be modified in many ways to work effectively in a programme situation. For example, there might be a programme strategy for managing areas such as risk, change, and quality. In this case, there is no need to create project strategies but simply to ensure that the project management team understands the programme approaches to these areas.

There may be an overarching Business Case for the entire programme, which the project's Business Case can refer to or use to highlight the programme's benefits that the project is delivering. The detailed project Business Case might therefore be created prior to the initiation stage. Some projects within a programme might deliver no benefits in themselves, just inputs into other projects. There also might be an overarching programme plan that the project's Project Plan needs to align to.

The project management team structure will have to fit into the programme management team structure. Figure 12.1 shows a simple example of this. In this programme, there are three distinct projects, all governed by their own Project Boards. Each of these Project Boards reports to a higher-level programme board. Some people on the Project Boards might also be represented on the programme board. For example, the Executives for each project might also sit on the programme board. Programme boards often have a role whose responsibility is to forecast and track the programme's benefits. This person (or people) might take on a Senior User role in one or more of the projects.

FIGURE 12.1 Programme management organization structure

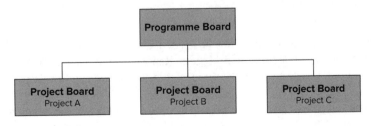

Some roles might be carried out at a programme level. For example, it might make sense to have a programme-wide Project Support person or group.

In a programme, the Starting up a Project process would probably be tailored. Remember that Starting up a Project focuses on answering the question, "Is the project viable and worthwhile?" For projects within a programme, this question might now be answered at a programme level. In this case, the Project Manager would start his work at the initiation stage (although the Project Manager will probably still be responsible for creating a Stage Plan for the initiation stage).

It may be that there are management products with the same name at a programme level and a project level; for example, a programme Quality Management Strategy and a project Quality Management Strategy. If this is the case, it is important to prefix each management product with "project" or "programme" to distinguish between the two.

Adapting PRINCE2 for Smaller Projects

There are a number of ways of simplifying PRINCE2 for a smaller project. First, the PRINCE2 roles could be combined. One person could take on the responsibility for the Project Manager, the Team Manager, and the Project Support role. If the Executive and the Senior User are both from the customer environment, one person could carry out both roles. The Project Board members could do their own Project Assurance.

The themes could also be implemented in a minimal way. For example, the Business Case could be a statement of the justification for the project, no matter how this is documented. One simple Project Plan could be produced to track and monitor work, eliminating the need for Stage Plans and Team Plans. The project could be run over a single delivery stage. Quality could be an understanding of the level of quality needed for each product and thus eliminate the need for documented Product Descriptions.

All the processes remain relevant, although on a small project, Starting up a Project could be of short duration and done in an informal way.

Many of the management products can be combined. It is actually possible to manage a PRINCE2 project with just the following four sets of documents:

- Project Initiation Documentation, which contains all the usual sections plus the Benefits Review Plan

- Highlight Report

- Daily Log, which combines the information for all the other logs, registers, and the Configuration Item Records

- End Project Report

Many management products might not be needed at all. For example, if there is just one delivery stage, a Stage Plan and an End Stage Report are not needed. If the Project Manager is managing the teams directly, there is no need for Checkpoint Reports and Work Packages.

For a very small, informal project, it may not be necessary to create any of the management products in document form—the information could be verbally agreed upon.

Very small projects might be dealt with as a task. In this case, there might be a one-person Project Board where the Executive is the Project Manager's line manager. The Project Manager might also do the work itself. In this case, all that is needed from PRINCE2 is the Work Package product with the associated Product Descriptions, logs/registers, and Checkpoint Reports.

Other Examples of Tailoring PRINCE2

PRINCE2 can also be tailored for commercial customer/supplier environments. For example, a company might ask a supplier to create a website for them. In this case, there may be a number of adaptations to the method. Work Packages between the customer and the commercial supplier would take the form of a legal contract. The Starting up a Project process might take place before any contract is signed between the customer and the supplier, in which case the Project Brief could be a proposal for the work from the supplier to the customer. The customer and the supplier will have different Business Cases for the project. In this case, the customer's rationale for a new website will be about improving efficiencies or selling products off the site, whereas the supplier's will be about making a profit on the building the website for the customer.

Some projects involve multiple organizations. For example, I have done a lot of work with NATO, where decision making is complicated by the fact that there are personnel from many different countries' military forces. In these cases, the challenge is to adapt the Project Board so that it is still a quick decision-making unit, either through identifying a single accountable owner for each project or by following consensus decision-making processes.

PRINCE2 is often used in many different industries that have their own life-cycle models for particular types of projects. For example, in IT, there is an approach called agile development, which has several characteristics. One example is that the project tries to create lots of interim releases of the final product, so that the customer can review it and give feedback quickly. This reduces the risk of the customer seeing the product only at the final delivery and only then realizing it has been specified incorrectly. PRINCE2 can fit cohesively with such industry-specific life-cycle approaches. Broadly, PRINCE2 can deal with the governance and project management aspects of the project, whereas the life-cycle approaches can be used to deal with the delivery of the products.

Finally, many organizations use project management bodies of knowledge such as the Project Management Institute's *A Guide to the Project Management Body of Knowledge (PMBOK® Guide)*. These bodies of knowledge provide a wealth of specialist project techniques in areas such as risk evaluation, planning, and people management. These techniques can work effectively with the PRINCE2 model. PRINCE2 can be thought of as a framework of *what* needs to be done, by *whom*, and *when*, whereas a body of knowledge provides a range of techniques that describes *how* those things can be done.

Summary

In this chapter, you learned how PRINCE2 can be tailored to many different situations. First, you saw that the general approach to tailoring PRINCE2 is to ensure that there is the right balance between not creating overly bureaucratic project management and not being too lax in controlling the project. PRINCE2 should be applied with a lightness of touch that provides real benefits in the control of a project and increases its likelihood of success without introducing unnecessary management overhead.

You saw that there is a difference in PRINCE2 between embedding and tailoring. Embedding is where an organization adopts PRINCE2 as the common standard for project management, whereas tailoring is adapting the method for the various projects that the organization must deliver.

You learned that there are many areas of PRINCE2 that can be tailored. However, you saw that a project management team should not tailor the seven PRINCE2 principles—these must be implemented on all projects.

You learned that each of the seven themes can be adapted to suit the project situation by creating specific strategies and project controls for each project. You saw that the PRINCE2 terminology might be tailored by substituting more commonly understood organizational terms for the PRINCE2 terms. This chapter described how the management products could be combined or implemented more broadly to suit the situation as well as how the PRINCE2 roles can be combined and responsibilities adapted. Finally, you saw that the process model could be customized for various situations. You learned that whereas all the activities in the process model are always necessary for each project, who is responsible for each activity might vary.

The last thing this chapter described were some situations that PRINCE2 can be tailored for. For example, PRINCE2 can be adapted for projects running in a programme environment, smaller projects, commercial customer/supplier projects, multiple organizational projects, and projects that use other approaches such as industry-specific life-cycle models or project management bodies of knowledge.

Exam Essentials

Understand the difference between tailoring and embedding PRINCE2.   The adoption of PRINCE2 across an organization is known as embedding, whereas the adaptation of PRINCE2 to suit a particular environment is known as tailoring.

Understand the relationship between a programme's Business Case and a project's Business Case.   The project's Business Case will be aggregated into the overall programme Business Case and is likely to be reduced in content. Know that the project's Business Case may only comprise a list of benefits with a statement as to how the project is contributing to the overall programme Business Case.

Understand the general approach to tailoring PRINCE2. The general approach to tailoring PRINCE2 is to consider external and project factors and then use the method with a lightness of touch that provides necessary control without introducing unnecessary bureaucracy. Tailoring does not consist of omitting PRINCE2 elements but involves applying the whole method to the degree required.

Understand that the PRINCE2 principles are not tailored. The PRINCE2 principles are universal, will always apply, and are not tailored.

Know how the themes can be tailored to suit various project situations. The themes are adapted by creating tailored strategies and project controls.

Understand how PRINCE2 terminology can be tailored to suit various project situations. The PRINCE2 terminology can be adapted to incorporate an organization's terms and languages if that improves communication and understanding among the stakeholders and the project management team.

Know how the management products can be tailored to suit various project situations. Management products can be adapted to suit particular project situations by modifying their Product Descriptions. If a management product is adapted, its purpose and composition should remain clear to the project management team.

Understand how the roles and responsibilities can be tailored to suit various project situations. PRINCE2 roles can be adapted to match an individual's actual capability and authority within the context of the project. Any adaptation of the PRINCE2 roles should ensure that all necessary directing, managing, and delivering roles are still carried out and that important PRINCE2 organizational constraints such as one Executive and one Project Manager are still adhered to.

Know how the processes can be tailored to suit various project situations. All the PRINCE2 process activities need to be done on any project, but the responsibilities for performing the activities and the use of management products might be changed to suit the context of the project.

Be able to describe sample situations where PRINCE2 can be tailored. PRINCE2 can be tailored to suit all projects. It can be tailored to suit smaller projects, projects in a programme environment, projects in a commercial customer/supplier environment, projects that use an industry-specific life-cycle model, and projects that use techniques outlined in project management bodies of knowledge.

Review Questions

The rest of this chapter contains mock exam questions for the Foundation exam.

Foundation Exam Questions

1. Which of the following terms describes the adoption of PRINCE2 across an organization?
   A. Embedding
   B. Tailoring
   C. Project management
   D. Adaptation

2. Which of the following is an example of adapting a PRINCE2 theme to suit a project environment?
   A. Substituting the term Project Charter for the Project Initiation Documentation
   B. Making the programme management team responsible for answering the question, "Is this project worthwhile and viable?"
   C. Combining issues and risks into one register
   D. Referring to the organization's quality management process in the Quality Management Strategy

3. Amending the project's progress reports so that they adhere to the organization's internal communication standards is an example of which of the following?
   A. Adapting the principles to suit the project environment
   B. Adapting the management products to suit the project environment
   C. Adapting the themes to suit the project environment
   D. Adapting the processes to suit the project environment

4. Which of the following is a characteristic of a programme?
   A. Driven by deliverables
   B. Driven by vision of "end state"
   C. Managed entirely by PRINCE2
   D. Initiatives with a shorter timescale

5. In a programme environment, the programme management team might carry out most of the activities of which of the following PRINCE2 processes?
   A. Starting up a Project
   B. Initiating a Project
   C. Controlling a Stage
   D. Managing Product Delivery

6. Which of the following describes how PRINCE2 might be tailored for a programme situation?

   1. Create the project Business Case in detail before the initiation of the project.

   2. Integrate the project management team structure into the programme management team structure.

   3. Derive the project strategies from the programme strategies.

   4. Run the programme using only four sets of documentation.

   A. 1, 2, 3

   B. 1, 2, 4

   C. 1, 3, 4

   D. 2, 3, 4

7. If a project is so small it can treated as a task, which of the following PRINCE2 managementv products might not be needed?

   A. Work Package

   B. Daily Log

   C. Product Descriptions

   D. Project Initiation Documentation

8. How can other project management bodies of knowledge work effectively with PRINCE2?

   A. By replacing some of the processes in the PRINCE2 method

   B. By providing a range of techniques showing how things can be done with the PRINCE2 framework

   C. PRINCE2 cannot work with other project management bodies of knowledge

   D. By creating an effective governance structure

9. Which of the following is **NOT** a characteristic of a programme?

   A. Introduce changes to the business capability

   B. Benefits realized both during and after the programme

   C. Focus on the delivery of products

   D. Longer timescales

10. Which of the following options does **NOT** show how the PRINCE2 roles can be tailored?

   A. Allow the Project Manager to carry out the role of Team Manager.

   B. In a programme, provide Project Support at a programme-wide level.

   C. On a large project, have several Executives.

   D. On a small project, combine the roles of the Senior User and the Executive.

Appendix A

Answers to Review Questions

Chapter 1: Overview of PRINCE2

Foundation Exam Answers

1. B. The Quality theme focuses on the work to first define the project's products with the appropriate people and then to ensure that the project delivers these definitions of the project's products.

2. A. There are four integrated elements of PRINCE2: principles, themes, processes, and tailoring to the project environment.

3. C. The expected returns from the project are the forecast benefits that occur as a result of the outcome of the project.

4. B. Projects often involve work that spans a number of functional divisions and possibly spans across a number of organizations.

5. A. The "defined roles and responsibilities" principle ensures that all necessary perspectives and people are involved with the management of the project.

6. D. Management by exception is the approach whereby one management level delegates work to the management level below by defining constraints around the lower level's authority. The standard way of defining this authority is by setting out what costs and timescales the lower level must work within. If the lower level realizes they cannot meet their constraints, they must escalate the situation to the management level above.

7. B. Manage by stages breaks up the project into time sections. The project is planned in summary form from beginning to end. Detailed planning is done only for each stage ahead, just before that stage starts.

8. A. The three types of management products are baseline, reports, and records.

9. C. The processes provide a set of activities to be done by defined project roles throughout the life of the project.

10. C. You can use the PRINCE2 best-practice framework to view a real project and identify ways to improve the project management approach.

Chapter 2: Starting a Project Successfully with PRINCE2

Foundation Exam Answers

1. B. The initial version of the Project Initiation Documentation is used at the end of the project to assess how the project performed. This assessment becomes part of the End Project Report.

2. D. Option D is correct—the Project Plan is created in the Initiating a Project process. This collates information about the work that needs to be done. Options A and B are purposes of the Starting up a Project process, and Option C is a purpose of the Directing a Project process.

3. C. The Project Product Description sets out the level of quality required from the major product(s).

4. C. Option 1 is correct—the Quality Management Strategy is created in the Initiating a Project process. This defines how to ensure that the quality required from the products is achieved. Option 2 is also correct—the Communication Management Strategy is created in the Initiating a Project process. This defines all the communication needs of the project management team and stakeholders who are external to the team. Finally, Option 4 is also correct—the Risk Management Strategy is created in the Initiating a Project process. This defines how risks will be managed during the project and, in particular, it will set out a risk management procedure showing how to identify, assess, and control risks. Option 3 is the incorrect option. The Starting up a Project process defines all the necessary authorities for initiating the project. Authorizing the initiation of the project occurs immediately prior to the Initiating a Project process.

5. A. The Project Initiation Documentation defines how PRINCE2 will be tailored for the needs of the project.

6. B. As the project progresses, the project management team will gain a better understanding of the challenges ahead. It might be useful to reevaluate previous experience to help with these new challenges.

7. D. The Project Product Description defines the specification for the major product or products that the project will create. It is the Senior User's role to ensure that the project creates products that meet their needs.

8. D. The Progress theme defines how the Project Board will control the project by authorizing the Project Manager to manage a stage at a time.

9. B. The Starting up a Project process creates the Project Brief. This provides base information about the project that the Project Board uses to decide whether to commission the first stage of the project.

10. A. Option A is correct—the project approach is created in the Starting up a Project process. This evaluates how the project's products can be delivered and recommends an approach. Option B is incorrect because this is an objective of the Initiating a Project process. The Project Board decides whether to appoint a Change Authority during the Prepare the Configuration Management Strategy activity. Option C is incorrect because this is an objective of the Initiating a Project process. The Project Manager creates the Quality Management Strategy that sets out how quality will be achieved. Finally, Option D is incorrect because this is an objective of the Initiating a Project process. The Project Manager creates the Benefits Review Plan that defines how to measure the achievement of the project's benefits.

Practitioner Exam Answers

Answers to Section 1: Classic Multiple Choice Questions on PRINCE2 Theory

1. A. Option A is correct—the Organization theme describes how a stakeholder analysis needs to take place while creating the Communication Management Strategy, which sets out the information needs of all those impacted by the project. Option B is incorrect because the team's lack of experience may affect the project objectives. It is an uncertain event, so it is a risk. Identifying risks is described in the Risk theme. Option C is incorrect because the establishment of a Change Authority is described in the Change theme. Option D is incorrect because the Progress theme defines how one level of management escalates major problems, or in PRINCE2 terms, escalates a forecast breach of tolerance.

2. B. Option B is correct—the Issue Register is created while the Project Manager is preparing the Configuration Management Strategy. It is used to record all off-specifications during the project. *Off-specifications* are products that are forecast not to comply with their Product Descriptions. (See Chapter 8, "Change Theme.") Option A is incorrect because the Product Descriptions of the major products will be created in the Project Plan, but they can change after this, as long as appropriate authorization for the change has been given. This is an incorrect explanation of the Change theme. Option C is incorrect because Configuration Item Records for *all* the project's products are not created during initiation. Each product's Configuration Item Record is created as soon as the need for that product has been identified, which might be during the creation of any of the project's plans. This is an incorrect explanation of the Change theme. Finally, option D is incorrect because the Marketing Director's lack of experience is a threat to the project's objectives, so recording this in the Risk Register is implementing the Risk theme.

Answers to Section 2: Classic Multiple Choice Questions Based on Applying PRINCE2 to the Scenario

1. A. Option A is correct—corporate or programme management appoints the Executive, and then the Executive appoints the Project Manager. Option B is incorrect because the Project Manager is appointed before the project starts, in the Starting up a Project process. Option C is incorrect because the Project Manager does not appoint the Executive; this is done by corporate or programme management. Option D is incorrect because during the activity "design and appoint the project management team," the Project Manager and the Executive work together to appoint the rest of the project management team.

2. C. Option C is correct—the Project Manager creates the Project Product Description during the "prepare the outline Business Case" activity, which occurs in the Starting up a Project process. Option A is incorrect because during the "prepare the outline Business Case" activity, two management products are created: the outline Business Case and the Project Product Description. Option B is incorrect because it is the Project Manager who creates the Project Product Description, although he should consult with the Senior Users in order to do so. Option D is incorrect because those who will be using the project's products and those who will be maintaining them give ultimate approval of the project's products. (See Chapter 6, "Quality Theme.")

3. C. Option C is correct—the outline Business Case sets out how the project will be funded in the Investment Appraisal section. (See Chapter 4, "Business Case Theme.") Option A is incorrect because although Starting up a Project is a lighter process, how the project can be funded must be determined in order to understand whether the project is viable and worthwhile (the main aims of this process). Option B is incorrect because corporate or programme may have secured the funds, but not always. Option D is incorrect because the project's funds are released to the Project Manager on a stage-by-stage basis.

4. B. Option B is correct—the Project Plan is created in the Initiating a Project process. Option A is incorrect because although the statement is correct in saying no, it gives the wrong reason why the statement is wrong, which is that the Project Plan does not get created during the Starting up a Project process. Option C is incorrect because although the Project Manager does consider key delivery milestones during the Starting up a Project process, these go into the Project Product Description, not the Project Plan. Option D is incorrect because the Project Plan is not part of the Project Brief; it is part of the Project Initiation Documentation.

Answers to Section 3: Practitioner Assertion/Reason Questions

1. D. **Assertion**: False. PRINCE2 separates out the directing level of management that contains the Executive from the management level that contains the Project Manager. The Executive should be a different person from the Project Manager.

Reason: True. The Executive is the single point of accountability for the project.

2. A. **Assertion**: True. The assertion describes a potential threat to the project. Threats are risks. During the Starting up a Project process, the Risk Register that is usually used to record risks has not been created. It is created later in the initiation stage. The Daily Log is used to record risks until the Risk Register is created.

Reason: True. See previous explanation for the assertion. As the reason explains the assertion, the answer is option A.

3. E. **Assertion**: False. The detailed specifications for the tender documents will be created when their Product Descriptions are created during the planning for stage 2.

Reason: False. The Project Product Description will define high-level specifications for the major outputs of the project.

4. A. **Assertion**: True. How the project will be delivered is defined in the Project Brief in the project approach section.

Reason: True. The Project Brief contains the project approach and this explains the delivery solution, or put another way, how the project will deliver the project's products. This is an explanation of the assertion, so the answer is A.

5. D. **Assertion**: False. The Communication Management Strategy should consider the information needs of all stakeholders within the project, some of whom may be external to Quality Furniture, such as the clients of Quality Furniture or the software development company.

Reason: True. A stakeholder is any individual or group that will be affected by, can affect, or perceives itself to be affected by a project.

6.   D. **Assertion:** False. The Project Manager should only prepare the Stage Plan for the first delivery stage following the Initiating a Project process. This is created in the Managing a Stage Boundary process.

   Reason: True. The Project Plan is created in the initiation stage, specifically in the Create the Project Plan activity in the Initiating a Project process.

Chapter 3: Organization Theme

Foundation Exam Answers

1.   B. The Executive represents the business interest on the project. It is his responsibility to secure the funding for the project.

2.   B. In the Organization theme, PRINCE2 states that Team Managers might be appointed because of a large team, a team sited in another geographic area, and/or a team using specialist skills (among other reasons).

3.   A. The only role that does not have any authority to authorize changes to the project's products is the Team Manager.

4.   B. Corporate or programme management is responsible for ensuring that post-project benefit reviews take place. The Senior User is responsible for demonstrating that forecast project benefits have occurred, many of which will probably happen post-project. Both of these responsibilities are covered in depth in Chapter 4, "Business Case Theme." Quality assurance is a group of people outside of the project management team who carry out a quality auditing role on the entire organization's activities. One of their focuses might be to review the way the project is being managed on behalf of corporate or programme management. For a full discussion of quality assurance, refer to Chapter 6, "Quality Theme."

5.   C. The Communication Management Strategy contains two sections relevant to stakeholders: the stakeholder analysis section—which identifies key interested parties in the project—and the information needs for each interested party section—which shows how the project will communicate with them.

6.   D. The Executive (or corporate or programme management) appoints the Project Manager.

7.   D. A Senior User could represent a number of different ways of using the products. First, they might represent people who will buy the products for their own use (Option 3). Second, they might represent those who will use the products to derive benefits, such as the marketing person in Option 4. Third, they might represent people who will maintain or operate the products after the project (Option 2). Option 1, someone who can assess and confirm the viability of the project approach, would be a Senior Supplier.

8. B. Project Assurance will check and monitor the project on behalf of the Project Board, including how Project Support is performing. Therefore, there would be a conflict of interest if Project Support were carrying out Project Assurance.

9. C. One purpose of the Organization theme is to make certain that the project management team is regularly reviewed to ensure that it is still relevant. Option A is a purpose of the Risk theme (see Chapter 7, "Risk Theme"), Option B is a purpose of the Plans theme (see Chapter 5, "Plans Theme"), and Option D is a purpose of the Quality theme (see Chapter 6, "Quality Theme").

10. C. On a small project, the Project Support and the Project Manager roles can be combined.

Practitioner Exam Answers

Answers to Section 1: Practitioner Sequence Questions

1. D. The stakeholder engagement procedure is documented in the "Prepare the Communication Management Strategy" activity in the Initiating a Project process. The other three actions occur in the Starting up a Project process that takes place before Initiating a Project. It is therefore the last action.

2. A. The Executive is appointed in the first activity of the first process of PRINCE2, in the "Appoint the Executive and Project Manager" activity in the Starting up a Project process. During this activity, corporate or programme management appoints the Executive, who then appoints the Project Manager.

3. C. Creating the Senior User role description occurs in the "design and appoint the project management team" activity in the Starting up a Project process.

4. B. The Project Manager is appointed in the first activity of the first process of PRINCE2, in the "Appoint the Executive and Project Manager" activity in the Starting up a Project process. During this activity, corporate or programme management appoints the Executive, who then appoints the Project Manager.

Answers to Section 2: Practitioner Multiple Response Questions

1. A, C. Option A is correct, because the Executive role is responsible for securing the funding for the project. Option C is also correct because the Executive represents the business interests in the project. As a major shareholder, the Chief Executive will be interested in the project's return on investment. Option B is incorrect, because the Executive role must represent the business interests of the project, not knowledge of PRINCE2. Option D is incorrect, because if the IT Manager is supplying resources to build the website, he might take on a Senior Supplier role; or if he is going to maintain the website in its operational life, he could take on the Senior User role. Being responsible for an initiative is not the same thing as focusing on the business return of an initiative. Finally, option E is incorrect, because those who are impacted by the project might take on a Senior User role.

2. B, C. Option B is correct, because the Senior User should represent those who will use the products to deliver benefits. Option C is also correct, because the Senior User should represent those who maintain the products post-project. Option A is incorrect, because this

reason would justify why the CEO should be the Executive, not the Senior User. Option D is also incorrect, because this reason does not show that the HR Director will be using the website either directly or indirectly. And finally, option E is incorrect because this is a justification for the Operations Director of Digital Design to be a Senior Supplier, not a Senior User.

3. D, E. Option D is correct, because when projects involve third-party suppliers, those procuring suppliers can represent the Senior Supplier. Option E is also correct, because Digital Design will be supplying products and services to create the products of the project. Option A is incorrect, because those who represent operations and maintenance of the project's products post-project should be Senior Users. Option B is also incorrect, because this project's scope is focused on supplying a website, not on the ongoing work of supplying furniture to Quality Furniture's clients. And finally, option C is incorrect because the project was preceded by the recommendations from FirstTech, but it is not supplying those recommendations during the project.

4. A, B. Option A is correct, because it is the role of the supplier assurance to advise on the project's products. Option B is also correct, because it is the role of supplier assurance to check that any third-party suppliers involved with the project are being realistic in their delivery proposals. Option C is incorrect, because this project scope does not include creating furniture. Option D is also incorrect, because checking that the project is delivering value-for-money is the role of the business assurance. And finally, option E is incorrect, because checking that the project can achieve the forecast benefits is the role of the user assurance.

Answers to Section 3: Practitioner Matching Questions

1. C. It is the responsibility of the Executive to secure the funding for the project.

2. D. It is the responsibility of the Senior User to demonstrate that the expected benefits from the project are realized.

3. A. It is the responsibility of the Senior Supplier to ensure that the project approach is viable.

4. B. It is the responsibility of the Project Manager to delegate work to the teams by authorizing all the Work Packages.

Chapter 4: Business Case Theme

Foundation Exam Answers

1. D. Corporate or programme management is responsible for ensuring that post-project reviews occur. (The Senior User will be involved in the post-project reviews to demonstrate that the benefits have occurred, but they are not responsible for the review.)

2. A. The Benefits Review Plan describes both how and when the benefits will be reviewed and also how the performance of the project's products will be reviewed.

3. C. Option C is correct; the Business Case is updated and reviewed at the end of each management stage. The Project Manager updates the Business Case in the Managing a Stage Boundary process and then the Project Board reviews the Business Case in the Directing a Project process when deciding whether to authorize the next stage. Options A and B are incorrect; the Business Case will be reviewed but not updated when carrying out an impact analysis of an issue or an assessment of a risk. Option D is incorrect; the Business Case is not updated after the project, although it may be reviewed at a benefit review.

4. A. The Executive will create the outline Business Case during the Starting up a Project based on any project justification information created by corporate or programme management in the project mandate.

5. B. An output from a project is the specialist products that the project produces. Option B, new computer software, might be an output from a project. Option A, Benefits Review Plan, is an example of a management product, not a specialist product. Option C is the result of the change of using some products, so it's an outcome. Option D is the measurable positive consequence of a project, so it's a benefit.

6. B. The Project Manager creates the Benefits Review Plan during Initiating a Project.

7. B. The detailed Business Case is created in the Initiating a Project process.

8. A. The Executive drafts the outline Business Case in the Starting up a Project process.

9. A. Option A is correct. The Executive creates the outline Business Case in the Starting up a Project process. This is part of developing the Business Case. Option B is incorrect. This is an example of a verify activity. Option C is incorrect. This is an example of a confirm activity. Option D is incorrect. This is an example of a maintain step.

10. A. The Senior User is responsible for both forecasting the benefits from the project and then demonstrating that the benefits have (or have not) been realized.

Practitioner Exam Answers

Answers to Section 1: Practitioner Multiple Response Questions

1. C, E. The Reasons section explains the background to the project. It is focused on what has happened. Options C and E fit this description. Option A is a forecast benefit, option B is a reason to select the website business option, and option D is the current sales figure.

2. A, D. The Business Options section shows the alternatives considered to meet the business challenge set out in the Reasons section. PRINCE2 states that the "do nothing" option should always be considered, which is option A. Option D is the chosen option. Options B and C describe how the chosen solution will be delivered, so they belong in the project approach. Option E describes how the project will be controlled, so it belongs in the project controls section of the Project Initiation Documentation.

3. A, B. Benefits are the forecast measurable result of the outcome of the project. Options A and B fit this description. Options C, D, and E are positive effects of the project, but they need to be stated in an objective way in order to be project benefits.

4. D, E. A dis-benefit is an actual consequence of the project perceived as negative by one or more project stakeholders. Options D and E fit this description. Options A and B contain an element of uncertainty, so they are risks. Option C is the project cost.

5. A, D. The timescale section states the duration of the project and over what period the project benefits will be measured. Options A and D fit that description. Option B is an estimate of an individual task, option C is a timescale for another potential follow-on project, and option E is a risk that might impact time.

6. B, C. The Costs section states the project costs and the cost of maintaining and operating the project's products. It also describes how funding will be arranged for the project. Option B describes the funding arrangement, and option C specifies the ongoing maintenance costs. Option A refers to the costs of the potential follow-on project; option D describes a risk, which may have a cost impact; and option E describes a financial benefit of this project.

7. A, B. The Risks section should include a summary of the aggregated risk situation and highlight any major risks. Options A and B fit that description. Options C and E are consequences of this project where there is no uncertainty, so they are dis-benefits. Option D is a risk, but to the potential follow-on project.

Answers to Section 2: Practitioner Assertion/Reason Questions

1. A. **Assertion:** True. The current level of sales should be measured so as to see the improvement the project brings.

    Reason: True. This is one of the key composition points of the Benefits Review Plan. In this case, the reason explains the assertion.

2. E. **Assertion:** False. The Chief Executive holds the Executive role for the project, so he or she is responsible for the Benefits Review Plan *during* the project.

    Reason: False. It is the role of the Senior User to demonstrate that forecast benefits have been realized.

3. D. **Assertion:** False. Authorized change to the project might involve updates to the Business Case, but these will be done during the Managing a Stage Boundary process.

    Reason: True. The costs of the project are set out in the Costs section of the Business Case.

4. D. **Assertion:** False. The Project Board authorizes Quality Furniture's Business Case.

    Reason: True. In a PRINCE2 project, there may be multiple customers and suppliers, each with their own Business Case that justifies their project involvement.

5. E. **Assertion:** False. It will not be until after the project has finished and the Project Board has been disbanded that all the project benefits can be assessed.

    Reason: False. Before authorizing project closure, the Project Board will not be able to review post-project benefits.

Chapter 5: Plans Theme

Foundation Exam Answers

1. D. The Project Plan ends at the end of the project, so it would not include activities to carry out post-project reviews. These would be detailed in the Benefits Review Plan.

2. C. The manage by exception is implemented by specifying that each PRINCE2 plan includes time, cost, and scope tolerances. Option A describes how the Plans theme implements the learn by experience principle. Option B describes how the Plans theme implements the manage by stages principle. Finally, Option D describes how the Plans theme implements the focus on products principle.

3. C. The Team Plan may be created by a different organization that is not using the PRINCE2 methodology, so PRINCE2 does not prescribe a particular format or composition for this level of plan.

4. A. Exception Plans are not produced following breaches in Work Package tolerance levels. Instead, the Project Manager takes corrective actions by updating the Work Package or issuing a new Work Package.

5. B. Each PRINCE2 plan contains information on plan prerequisites that show any fundamental aspects that must be in place and remain in place for the plan to succeed.

6. D. The Business Case theme establishes mechanisms to judge whether the project is desirable, viable, and achievable.

7. C. Identifying uncertainties in the plan takes place in the Analyze the risks step in the PRINCE2 approach to planning, not in the Design the plan step.

8. B. The product-based planning technique is recommended to help define and analyze products.

9. D. An external product is a product that already exists or is being created outside the scope of the plan. The Project Manager is not accountable for the creation of the external products; however, the external products will be needed in order to deliver a particular plan's work.

10. A. Product-based planning produces Product Descriptions for the project's products that identify who is responsible for approving a product.

Practitioner Exam Answers

1. C. The standard terms of conditions are being revised outside the scope of this stage's plan as they are being changed in another project. Products that are needed for a plan but for which the Project Manager is not accountable for delivering are external dependencies.

2. E. The Personal Assistant's experience is a lesson that can be usefully applied when scheduling this stage's activities.

3. G. The $5,000 to fund an advertisement is an amount of money used to fund a fallback response to the risk that no suitable tender responses will be received. Any money set aside to fund specific management responses to threats to the success of the plan should be itemized under the "budgets" heading as the risk budget.

4. B. The approval of the Project Initiation Documentation must occur before the activities of stage 2 can commence. Plan prerequisites are any fundamental aspects that must be in place for the plan to begin.

5. F. The Highlight Reports are one method that the Project Board can use to monitor the progress of the stage.

Answers to Section 2: Classic Multiple Choice Type

1. A. Option A is correct, because products that are required in order to create or modify the product being described in the Product Description should be listed under the "derivation" heading. Option B is incorrect, because the "procurement standards" are not going to be a component of the "request to tender documents." Option C is incorrect, because only products that will form a part of the product being described in the Product Description should be itemized under the "composition" heading. Option D is also incorrect, because although it is true that the dependency can be shown on the product flow diagram, that doesn't mean it can't also be shown under the "derivation" section of the Product Description.

2. B. Option B is correct, because the "Quality Furniture corporate brochure" will be part of the "request to tender documents" and, as such, it should go into the "composition" heading for the Product Description for the "request to tender documents." The "composition" section of the Product Descriptions shows the parts of the product. Option A is incorrect, because although the "Quality Furniture corporate brochure" is needed before creating the "request to tender documents," it will form part of the "request to tender documents" and therefore should be included in the "composition" section of the Product Description of the "request to tender documents." Option C is incorrect, because external products can be a part of product. Option D is incorrect, because the "quality method" heading shows how a product will be checked to see if it is fit for its purpose and will show the activities that need to be done in order to verify that the product matches its quality criteria.

3. C. Option C is correct, because products are only external if they are created outside the scope of the plan. In this case, the Project Manager will need to delegate the work to create the "list of suppliers" to FirstTech, so it is a product that the Project Manager is accountable for the delivery of and is within the scope of the Stage 2 Plan. Therefore, the "list of suppliers" is not external. Option A is incorrect, because products created by external organizations are not necessarily external. Option B is incorrect—products are not external because they contain information about external organizations. Option D is also incorrect—the reason that it is not external is not because it will be needed by the Personal Assistant.

4. B. Option B is correct. External products are ones that the Project Manager is not accountable for. In this case, the Project Manager won't be involved with managing the work of the suppliers responding to the tender—that is for the suppliers to do themselves. Option A is incorrect, because external products are not necessarily ones that are created or modified by other organizations. Option C is incorrect—"tender responses" are needed for the delivery of stage 2, but internal or external products might be needed in order to deliver a plan's work. Option D is incorrect, because the Project Manager might still need to check whether external products have been delivered by whomever is accountable to do so.

5. A. Option A is correct. External products are created outside the project management team, so the Project Manager does not have as much control over their creation; therefore, the risk is greater that they could be delivered late or incorrectly. They are a threat to the success of the plan and should be listed as a risk in the Risk Register. Option B is incorrect, because PRINCE2 specifically says that external products should always be listed as risks and, although some internal products could be seen as risks as well, not all products are necessarily risks. Option C is incorrect, because part of the PRINCE2 planning procedure is the activity Analyze the risks. Option D is incorrect, because it is the responsibility of the Project Manager to identify all risks to the project, even if another person is best placed to manage that risk.

6. D. Option D is correct—only products are shown in the product flow diagram (and also the product breakdown structure), not activities. Options A and B are incorrect, because "review tender responses" is an activity and so should not be shown in the product flow diagram. Option C is incorrect, because the "derivation" heading should only show products that are needed in order to create the "short list of potential suppliers."

7. A. Option A is correct, because the additional information states that "The Chief Executive needs to approve the selected supplier before the final contracts and purchase orders are sent." The activity of approving the supplier will create an output that would be an "approved selected supplier," which is needed before the "final contracts" are sent. Option B is incorrect, because even though the "final contracts" are needed at the end of the stage, it does not necessarily mean that the "approved selected supplier" is needed before them. Option C is incorrect—approving the selected supplier is an activity, but the question refers to the output of that activity: "approved selected supplier." Option D is incorrect—"approved selected supplier" is the output to the activity of approving suppliers, so it's a product.

Chapter 6: Quality Theme

Foundation Exam Answers

1. D. The Project Manager creates Product Descriptions when they are creating the Project Plan or Stage Plans. The Project Manager may liaise with other roles in order to create the Product Descriptions, but it is their responsibility to create them.

2. A. The four recommended quality review team roles are chair, presenter, reviewer, and administrator. Scribe is not a recommended team role (although in earlier editions of PRINCE2, it was).

3. B. Option 1 is true—both types of assurance will check that the project is being run to corporate standards. Option 2 is true—Project Assurance, although it is part of the project management team, is independent of the managing level because they will be checking the performance of the Project Manager. Quality assurance is not just independent of the Project Manager, but also independent of the whole project management team. Option 3 is incorrect—only Project Assurance is done on behalf of the Project Board. Quality assurance is carried out on behalf of the wider corporate or programme organization and is independent of the Project Board, because one of their functions is to check how the Project Board is directing the project. Option 4 is true—both Project Assurance and quality assurance check that quality management is being carried out properly.

4. C. Option C is correct—the quality review technique defines a series of activities that confirms that a product is complete and is ready for its final approval. Option A is incorrect—the product is reviewed by the quality review technique *after* it has been created. Option B is incorrect—a customer's quality expectations describe the overall outputs from the project, not an individual product. Quality criteria describe the characteristics of an individual product, but these are not defined as part of the quality review technique; instead, the product is checked to see if it conforms to these quality criteria during this process. Option D is incorrect—standard quality methods to be used by the project are defined in the Quality Management Strategy created by the Project Manager during the Initiating a Project process.

5. B. Quality control is about checking that the project's products have been created correctly. This is done by using quality methods, which are different ways of comparing a product to its quality criteria. Quality control implements the quality methods, monitors their implementation to check they are being done correctly, and records the results in quality records and the Quality Register.

6. A. Option A is correct—the Project Product Description defines what the project will need to deliver in order for it to be acceptable to the users. Option B is incorrect—it is the Quality Management Strategy that defines how the project will be managed in a way that ensures products that are fit for their purpose are delivered. Option C is incorrect—the Risk Management Strategy defines how the project will control uncertainty. Option D is incorrect—it is the Configuration Management Strategy that defines how the project will track, protect, and control the project's products. (See Chapter 8, "Change Theme.")

7. B. Quality planning involves defining the specifications of the products required. In PRINCE2, this is done by creating a Project Product Description with measurable acceptance criteria for the overall outputs of the project, and at a lower level, Product Descriptions containing quality criteria. Quality planning is also about defining how the products will be checked for conformity to their Product Descriptions. Quality methods are used to check a product. Quality planning is not about planning the activities to build the product—this is done when the Project Manager creates either the Project Plan or the Stage Plans and sometimes when the Team Managers create their Team Plans.

8. C. Quality records provide evidence that the quality checks in the Quality Register have been carried out.

9. B. Acceptance criteria should be measurable.

10. C. The Work Package given to the Team Manager from the Project Manager contains all the details that the Team Manager needs to know in order to create the products. This includes details of how to carry out quality activities, such as updating the Quality Register.

Practitioner Exam Answers

Answers to Section 1: Multiple Response Questions

1. B, D. Option B is correct—when creating the Stage Plan, the Project Manager will update the Quality Register with the details of planned quality activities such as quality checks. Option D is also correct—when accepting a Work Package, the Team Manager will consult with Project Assurance to check that no new reviewers are required for the planned quality activities, and if necessary, update the Quality Register with their names. Option A is incorrect—the Quality Register has not been created at the Starting up a Project point. It is created in the Initiating a Project process. Option C is incorrect—the Project Manager will review the Quality Register while reviewing Work Package status to assess the progress of quality activities, but will not update it. Option E is incorrect—the Quality Register is not used when handing over products. The Project Manager will need to get acceptance records, but they are not tracked in the Quality Register.

2. C, D. Option C is correct—the Project Manager updates the Quality Register when planning quality activities for a stage. Option D is also correct—the Team Manager updates the Quality Register when adding other suitable reviewers to planned quality checks as well as when updating the Quality Register with the results of quality checks. Option A is incorrect—the Executive is not involved with creating management products apart from during the Starting up a Project process when he prepares the outline Business Case. Option B is incorrect—the Senior User does not create management products, although they may be consulted in the creation of the Project Product Description and Product Descriptions. Option E is incorrect—Project Assurance reviews the Quality Register but does not update it.

Answers to Section 2: Sequence Type

1. A
2. D
3. C
4. B
5. G
6. E

The order of events is as follows:

1. The Project Product Description is created during the Starting up a Project process (the first action listed in the table). This management product defines the scope of the project by setting out all the major products that will be created in the composition section.

2. The Quality Management Strategy is created in the Initiating a Project process (the fourth action listed in the table). This management product shows how the project will be managed to ensure quality products. One aspect of this strategy is considering the various types of quality methods that will be employed to check a product's conformity with its Product Description.

3. The next activity in the sequence is to create a Product Description for the request for tender document (the third action listed in the table). This management product might be created when the Project Manager is creating the Project Plan or when the Project Manager is creating the Stage Plan for stage 2.

4. The request for tender document is checked using the quality review technique during the Managing Product Delivery process to see whether it conforms to its Product Description (the second action listed in the table).

5. The final activity is that the Team Manager for the product needs to obtain an approval record to provide evidence that the product has been signed off (the sixth action in the table).

The fifth action listed in the table would not be appropriate for Quality Furniture's web project. Acceptance records are obtained for the ultimate approval of the project's products. In this case, an acceptance record is obtained for the whole website when it goes into operation, not for an individual product like the tender document. Acceptance records are not obtained from the Project Board but from the users, customers, or operations and maintenance teams.

Answers to Section 3: Multiple Response Type

1. B, E. Option B is correct—the Daily Log says that the IT manager will be the reviewer of the designs. The presenter role should represent those who have produced the product. Option E is also correct—the quality records section can include references to any quality inspection documentation used during the quality check. Option A is incorrect—the quality review technique can be used for any product that takes on the form of a document or similar item. Option C is incorrect—someone on the project management team can take on the chair role. The only constraint is that the person does not represent the chair, who has an interest in the creation of the product. Option D is incorrect—the sign-off on the product can be carried out before the forecast date.

2. A, E. Option A is correct—the quality method should only refer to how the product will be checked to ensure that it conforms with its Product Description, not how it will be created. Option E is also correct—acceptance records are obtained when products from the project are handed over to the ultimate clients. For an individual quality check, the products are not handed over to the client, so only quality records are obtained for each quality check. After all the quality checks of a product have been done, an approval record for the product will be obtained. Option B is incorrect—the quality review technique could only have two people: one person taking on the chair and the reviewer roles, and one person taking on the presenter and the administrator roles. Option C is incorrect—the approval of all the web page designs takes place after the quality checks on all the individual web page designs have happened. This entry is only about a quality check of one particular web page design. Option D is incorrect—the sign-off can happen after the review of the product.

3. C, E. Option C is correct—if a product fails a quality review, another separate entry should be created in the Quality Register to show the details of the reassessment. Option E is also correct—details of the reassessment quality review should be contained in a separate Quality Register entry. Option A is incorrect—the Executive can take on the reviewer role. Option B is incorrect—the presenter role can be represented by anyone as long as that person has does not also take on a reviewer role. Option D is incorrect—the quality records can include details of any actions required to correct errors in the product.

4. A, D. Option A is correct—the Daily Log states that this product will be checked using the Quality Furniture's standard technical review process, not the PRINCE2 quality review technique. Option D is also correct—this entry should only refer to the first quality check, not the reassessment. Option B is incorrect—external suppliers can review the project's products, as long as they haven't built them themselves. Option C is incorrect—quality activities following the PRINCE2 quality review technique need a chair, but this quality check is not following that approach. Option E is incorrect—the quality records can also include information referring to any quality inspection documentation used during the quality check.

Chapter 7: Risk Theme

Foundation Exam Answers

1. B. Impact Analysis is a part of the change management procedure, not the risk management procedure. The other three options, along with assess and plan, are the five steps to the risk management procedure.

2. D. When you invest in anything, there is a certain amount of uncertainty about whether you will get the returns you are forecasting. A key way of controlling that uncertainty and increasing the likelihood of those returns is through effective risk management. Therefore, only by adhering to the ideas in the Risk theme can you be certain that a project is viable in business terms.

3. A. The risk tolerance defines the amount of risk that one management level is allowed to take on before escalating to the level of management above. The amount of risk the teams are allowed to take on is set by the Project Manager in the Work Package. Remember, there is also the amount of risk the Project Manager is allowed to take on. This is the stage level of risk tolerance and is set out in the Risk Management Strategy. Similarly, a project level of risk tolerance is set out in the Risk Management Strategy. Stage or team level risk tolerances may also be specified in the Stage Plans and the Team Plans respectively.

4. D. When the project management team identify context (during the identify step in the risk management procedure), they consider general characteristics about the project and the environment that might make it riskier than others. For example, a project with a large number of stakeholders will probably be riskier. This is a major determinant of how the project management team will manage risk, which is specified in the Risk Management Strategy.

5. C. Even though the question concerns risks, not issues, the Team Manager will raise an issue. By raising an issue, the Team Manager can escalate a number of types of concerns to the Project Manager such as risks, issues, problems, or concerns or request for changes. Option B, Risk Report, might sound more intuitive, but unfortunately doesn't exist in PRINCE2. Remember that the Exception Report is only used by the Project Manager to escalate concerns to the Project Board.

6. A. Buying the futures will help you reduce the financial impact on the project if the yen appreciates. It is a form of insurance, giving a payout if the worst happens. It is therefore a transfer response.

7. A. The risk budget is used to fund responses to risks but not any of the work to analyze the risk situation such as running risk management workshops. PRINCE2 suggests that the weighted cost of the major risks could be used to calculate a risk budget. The other three options are all inputs into the calculation of such a weighted cost.

8. A. For this question, the PRINCE2 semantics of the words are very important. In everyday speech, you could get away with using the word "estimating." In PRINCE2, the word "evaluating" is reserved for the task of weighing the overall risk situation.

9. C. The Project Manager wants to ensure that the risk management work is not too narrowly focused on any particular perspective of the project. A quick scan through the categories of all the risks currently identified in the Risk Register might reveal that he hasn't been taking a wide enough outlook on where risks could occur.

10. B. The Executive has a prime responsibility for ensuring that the project adheres to the strategic direction of the organization that the project is sitting within.

Practitioner Exam Answers

Answers to Section 1: Practitioner Multiple Response Questions

1. A, D. The risk management procedure sets out general risk management activities that need to be done during the project. Options A and D fit this description. Option B belongs in the Configuration Management Strategy, which I cover in Chapter 8, "Change Theme." Option C belongs in the Risk Management Strategy's timing of risk management activities section, and Option E belongs in the Risk Management Strategy's Reporting section.

2. B, C. The Records section sets out how to record information on all the risks that are identified. Both Option B and Option C do this. Option B states where the risk information should be recorded, and Option C states what types of information should be stored. Option A belongs under the Reporting heading, Option D belongs in the Configuration Management Strategy's Records heading, and Option E is an example of an early warning indicator.

3. A, B. The Reporting section sets out information on how the project reports on risks. Both Options A and B do this. Option A shows how the third-party supplier will report on risks; Option B defines who Highlight Reports, which include risks to the Business Case, should go to. Option C describes a repeatable risk management activity, so it belongs under the Risk Management Procedure heading; Option D refers to quality reporting, so it belongs in the Quality Management Strategy's Reporting heading. I cover off-specifications and the Quality Management Strategy in Chapter 6, "Quality Theme." Option E belongs under the Roles and Responsibilities heading.

4. D, E. Option D and Option E are risk management responsibilities for the Project Manager and the Executive. Option C is a change control responsibility for the Project Manager, so it belongs in the Configuration Management Strategy. I cover the issue and change control process in Chapter 8, "Change Theme." Option A belongs under the Timing of Risk Management Activities section, and Option B belongs under the Risk Categories section.

5. C, E. The Scales heading in the Risk Management Strategy shows how the project will scale each risk's probability and impact. Option C and option E fit this description. Option A shows how the project will scale each risk's proximity, so it belongs in the proximity heading. Option B identifies the probability for an individual risk and option D identifies the impact of an individual risk; both of these belong in the Risk Register.

6. D, E. The Risk Tolerance section sets out risk thresholds for corporate and programme management and the Project Board. If the levels are exceeded, the risk needs to be escalated. The tolerance could set an overall threshold level, or it could describe a type of risk that, if identified, needs escalating. Option D and option E fit this description. Option A is an example of a stage cost tolerance and belongs in the relevant stage plan, option B refers to a cost tolerance around the project's risk budget and belongs in the Project Plan, and option C is a team-level risk tolerance and belongs in a Work Package.

Answers to Section 2: Practitioner Matching Questions

1. D. By adding the clause in the contract with the software supplier, the Project Manager is transferring some of the financial risk to that supplier.

2. B. By bringing in an expert in the area of IT procurement, the Project Manager is reducing the likelihood of choosing an inappropriate supplier.

3. A. This seems rather strange, but the fact is that if the project is canceled, the risk is eradicated. The impact of a poor supplier is avoided by not having a project that necessitates selecting one.

4. C. Fallback responses are always reactive. The Project Manager waits until the risk occurs and then, if it does, does something.

5. E. When the Project Manager makes a conscious decision to do nothing about the risk, this is accept.

6. B. By splitting up the tender into several parts, the Project Manager is spreading the risk of a poor supplier. He may still pick a poor supplier, but it is less likely that he will do so for all the work. He reduces the likelihood of the risk.

Chapter 8: Change Theme

Foundation Exam Answers

1. B. Options 1, 2, and 4 are correct. An off-specification is a product that should be delivered by the project but has not been (or is forecast not to be) provided. This could be a missing product or one that doesn't meet its specification. Option 3 refers to a product that, even though it will be late, will be delivered, so it is not an off-specification.

2. B. During the identification activity, a coding system is developed that can be used to uniquely identify each of the configuration items in the project. This coding system consists of a project identifier, an item identifier, and the current version—the first three sections of the Configuration Item Record.

3. B. Option B is correct. The change budget can be used to fund the analysis of the potential impact of a request for change. Option A is incorrect—threats to the project are risks, and assessing risks is funded from the project budget. Option C is incorrect—reducing the probability of a threat would be done by carrying out a risk countermeasure that would be funded using the risk budget. Option D is incorrect—actions following a quality review would be funded from the project budget.

4. A. The Configuration Management Strategy describes how configuration management and issue and change control will be carried out on the project. Options 1 and 3, which refer to how products will be stored and how products will be identified, are configuration management activities, and option 2 is a change control activity. Option 4 would be described in the Quality Management Strategy.

5. A. Project Support maintains the Configuration Item Records, which hold information on the status of all the project's configuration items.

6. D. A Product Status Account provides the Project Manager with information on the status of all (or a specified subset of) the products. It is a useful source of information when the Project Manager creates a Highlight Report (option 2), prepares to close the project (option 3), or prepares an End Stage Report (option 4). It would not be created when preparing the Configuration Management Strategy; however, the Configuration Management Strategy would describe how to create Product Status Accounts during the project and who should be responsible for doing so.

7. C. A product that does not meet its specification is called an off-specification. Information on all the off-specifications in the project can be found in the Issue Register. Option B is incorrect, because an Issue Report would potentially hold information on just one particular off-specification, not all of them.

8. A. A concession occurs when the Project Board authorizes a product that does not comply with the specification described in that product's Product Description.

9. D. Project Support is not responsible for authorizing changes in a project. Instead, they are responsible for providing support for the issue and change control procedure, such as maintaining the Issue Register, and for providing support for the configuration management procedure, such as maintaining Configuration Item Records and creating Product Status Accounts.

10. C. A configuration item can be a product (either management or specialist), or a component of a product, or a group of products released together to the users (a release). Option C refers to a suggestion to change a product.

Practitioner Exam Answers

Answers to Section 1: Classic Multiple Choice Type

1. A. Option A is correct—product security is part of configuration management, so any security standards to be followed should be described in the configuration management procedure section. Option B is incorrect—how to capture requests for change is described in the issue and change control procedure section of the Configuration Management

Strategy. Option C is incorrect—uncertainties are risks, and how to assess risks is described in the risk management procedure in the Risk Management Strategy. Option D is incorrect—the timing of configuration audits is described in the timings section of the Configuration Management Strategy.

2. B. Option B is correct—one step in the issue and change control procedure is to examine the issue, which is done by performing an impact analysis. Option A is incorrect—the procedure to hand over the project's products is described in the configuration management procedure. Option C is incorrect—the format of the Issue Register should be in the records section. Option D is incorrect—any metrics to be employed in order to carry out the quality control activities should be in the quality management procedure in the Quality Management Strategy.

Answers to Section 2: Sequence Type

1. C
2. B
3. D
4. G
5. A
6. G

The order of events is as follows:

1. The first step in the issue and change control procedure is to "capture" the issue. In this case, it is a request for change, so it is a formal issue. The Project Manager creates an entry in the Issue Register as well as a corresponding Issue Report. The Project Manager may ask the person who raised the issue to create the initial Issue Report, which he does in this case (the fifth action listed in the table).

2. The second step in the issue and change control procedure is to "examine" the issue. At this time, an impact analysis will be carried out, looking at how the issue will affect the project objectives such as time, cost, benefits, risks, scope, and quality. The Project Manager might do this by chairing a meeting with the project management team (the second action listed in the table).

3. The third step in the issue and change control procedure is to consider alternative options to deal with the issue in the Propose activity. There is no corresponding action for this step in the question. After "Propose," the next step is Decide. Here, the Project Manager either takes corrective action to deal with the issue or, if he does not have the authority, escalates the issue to the relevant Change Authority or the Project Board. In this case, the request for change will cost more than the Change Budget the Project Manager has been allocated, so he will have to escalate the situation to the Project Board (the first action listed in the table).

4. The final step of the issue and change control procedure is to implement the actions to resolve the issue. Either the Project Manager can do this himself or, if he does not have the authority, he will need to create an Exception Plan, which needs to be authorized by the Project Board (the third action listed in the table).

The following options are *not* appropriate actions to handle this issue:

- The fourth action listed in the table. The Project Manager details the issue and change control procedure for the whole project during the initiation stage when he creates the Configuration Management Strategy. There is no individual issue and change control procedure for each issue.

- The sixth action listed in the table. This issue is a request for change so it should not be implemented using the cost tolerance, but it should be funded by the Change Budget.

Answers to Section 3: Practitioner Assertion/Reason Questions

1. D. **Assertion:** False. The document management system is a configuration management system, so this statement should be recorded under the Tools and Techniques section of the Configuration Management Strategy.

    Reason: True. The configuration management procedure includes five activities: planning, identification, control, status accounting, and verification and audit. The control activity should cover a number of areas such as storage and retrieval, security, and handover procedures.

2. B. **Assertion:** True. The DOCINFO is recording information on configuration items within the project. In effect, it is a set of Configuration Item Records. The format and composition of Configuration Item Records is recorded in the "records" section.

    Reason: True. Information on off-specifications is stored in the Issue Register. The "records" section records the format and composition of the Issue Register. The reason is about the Issue Register, whereas the assertion is about the Configuration Item Records, so the reason does not explain the assertion.

3. B. **Assertion:** True. The review of the accuracy of the information on the documents is effectively carrying out a configuration audit. The timings of configuration audits are recorded in the "timings" section.

    Reason: True. Configuration audits are part of the verification and audit step of the configuration management procedure. The reason does not explain the assertion.

4. E. **Assertion:** False. The administration assistant's responsibility to maintain the DOCINFO spreadsheet is a configuration management responsibility, so it should be recorded under the Roles and Responsibilities section in the Configuration Management Strategy.

    Reason: False. Maintaining information on the project's configuration items is a configuration management activity.

Chapter 9: Progress Theme

Foundation Exam Answers

1. C. The Project Manager allocates the Work Package tolerances for the team when they authorize a Work Package.

2. C. The Daily Log is used to capture actions and significant events not caught by the other PRINCE2 registers or logs. Option 1 is correct, because risks and issues identified in the Starting up a Project process are put temporarily into the Daily Log and then later transferred over into the relevant register in Initiating a Project. Option 3 is correct, because all informal issues are placed in the Daily Log. Finally, Option 4 is correct, because personal actions for the Project Manager are placed in the Daily Log. Option 3 is incorrect, because requests for changes are added to the Issue Register.

3. A. Option A is correct—the Lessons Log is used to collate experience and lessons that could be useful for the current project. Option B is incorrect—the Project Manager uses an Exception Report to escalate forecast breaches in stage or project tolerances to the Project Board. Option C is incorrect—the Issue Register captures requests for change, off-specifications, or problems or concerns. Option D is incorrect—the Project Initiation Documentation is used as the main terms of reference for the project.

4. C. Option A is a benefit of management stages—at the end of each stage, the Project Board reviews how external influences could affect the project. Option B is also a benefit—at the end of each stage, the Project Board reviews the project and decides whether to authorize the next stage. Option D is a benefit as well—the Project Board delegates stage tolerances to the Project Manager at the beginning of each stage. Option C is not a benefit of management stages—although specialist work may be a factor to consider when defining management stages, it should not drive the control of the project.

5. D. Scope tolerances define any flexibility in what will be delivered. Scope tolerance can be defined at three different levels—project level, stage level, and Work Package level—and is documented in the Project Plan, Stage Plan, and Work Package, respectively.

6. B. Option B is not true—management stages are a project control, because they relate to commitment of resources and authority to spend. Technical stages are not used to control a project—they are simply major pieces of work that could be contained in one management stage or span several management stages.

7. B. The configuration management requirements section in the Work Package describes standards relating to version control and storage of the specialist products to be delivered by the teams. The Configuration Management Strategy contains information on how to carry out configuration management throughout the whole project, but the teams do not refer to this management product. The Configuration Item Record stores status information on each product but does not show how to configuration-manage each product. The Quality Register contains details of quality checks on the products.

8.   D. The Lessons Report is used to pass on lessons from the project that could be usefully applied to other projects or parts of the organization. An organization's quality assurance department would probably be focused on improving an organization's operations by using experiences from many sources, including lessons learned on projects.

9.   A. There is no need for the Project Board to carry out regular progress meetings in a PRINCE2 project; Highlight Reports and End Stage Reports keep them updated on the progress of the project.

10.   B. Opportunities are a type of risk. A threshold over which risks need to be escalated to the next level of management is an example of a risk tolerance.

Practitioner Exam Answers

Answers to Section 1: Multiple Response Questions

1.   B, D. Option B is correct, because this section should only include processes that the team will use to create the designs, not ones that the Project Manager will use to manage the teams. Option D is also correct, because this section should include any standards to be followed when creating the specialist products. Option A is incorrect, because the designs are not a product that will go into an operational environment. Option C is incorrect, because accessibility standards should be followed when creating the designs. Option E is incorrect, because this information should be placed in the "Development interfaces" section.

2.   A, D. Options A and D are correct, because the Marketing Director and the photographer are people with whom Digital Design will need to liaise during the completion of the designs. Option B is incorrect, because Checkpoint Reports are sent to the Project Manager, not to other stakeholders. Option C is incorrect, because the "Operations and maintenance interfaces" section should only include products that the specialist products being developed in the Work Package will work with when in operations. Option E is incorrect, because the design software is a tool used to develop the designs and therefore should be placed under the heading "Techniques, processes, and procedures."

3.   A, C. Option A is correct, because the person who approves the products should be described in "Approval method." Option C is correct, because this section should describe security and access requirements for the Work Package's products. Option B is incorrect, because this section should include how the products will be stored. Options D and E are incorrect because this section should describe how the person responsible for configuration management will be updated about status changes to the products.

4.   C, D. Option C is correct, because there is a separate section in the Work Package where tolerances are described. Option D is also correct, because this section should include details of key milestones for the Work Package's work. Option A is incorrect, because there is a separate section for tolerances. Option B is incorrect, because this section should not include tolerance information. Option E is incorrect, because this section shows agreements on the work's effort, cost, and schedule, not on the management method to be used.

5. B, D. Option B is correct, because Checkpoint Reports are sent to the Project Manager. Option D is also correct, because this section should cover regular reporting, not ad hoc issue reporting. Option A is incorrect, because the teams are not responsible for creating Highlight Reports. Option C is incorrect, because this section should not cover problem handling, which is covered in the "Problem handing and escalation" section. Option E is incorrect, because the teams will not access the Communication Management Strategy to see how they should report on their work—all the details they need on reporting should be in the Work Package.

6. B, C. Option B is correct, because how a product will be checked to see if it is fit for its purpose is described in the "quality method" section of the Product Description. Option C is also correct, because this section should include details of who should approve the completed products. Option A is incorrect, because how the product will be checked should be described in the "quality method" section of the Product Description. Option D is incorrect, because this section should show who should approve the products. Option E is incorrect, because this section should include a description of how the Project Manager will be notified of the completion of the products.

Answers to Section 2: Assertion/Reason Questions

1. E. **Assertion:** False. A Work Package does not need to contain the work to deliver all the products of one stage.

   Reason: False. In any one stage, the Project Manager might issue a number of Work Packages to a number of teams.

2. B. **Assertion:** True. Where the Project Manager needs to delegate work to an external third party, it is likely that the Work Package may take the form of a legal contract.

   Reason: True. The Project Initiation Documentation should show how a project would be tailored to its particular environment. However, this reason does not explain why the Digital Design Work Package might be a legal contract, because Digital Design is a commercial organization that is separate from Quality Furniture.

3. D. **Assertion:** False. Forecast breaches in tolerance should be escalated immediately to the next level of management, not in the next regular progress report.

   Reason: True. Checkpoint Reports are time-driven controls, because they are used at a regular frequency in time.

4. E. **Assertion:** False. Multiple Work Packages can be delivered concurrently.

   Reason: False. Technical stages can overlap; it is management stages that cannot overlap.

5. A. **Assertion:** True. A Work Package will contain the Product Descriptions for the specialist products to be created. The descriptions will help a team understand quality expectations for those products.

   Reason: True. Quality criteria are a set of measurable attributes that show the specification required for a particular product. They are contained in a product's Product Description. In this case, the reason explains the assertion, so the answer is A.

6. **B. Assertion:** True. The Work Package contains the development interfaces that show who the teams need to liaise with during the creation of the specialist products.

   Reason: True. The Work Package shows the techniques, processes, and procedures to be followed in order to create the specialist products. However, this is not the section that shows the teams who they need to liaise with; that information goes into the "Development interfaces" section, so the answer is B.

Chapter 10: Managing the Middle of a Project Successfully with PRINCE2

Foundation Exam Answers

1. B. Option 2 is incorrect—the Starting up a Project process provides the Project Board with information so that it can assess whether the project is worthwhile and viable and should be commissioned.

2. A. Option A is not an objective of the Controlling a Stage process. The Project Manager produces the End Stage Report in the Managing a Stage Boundary process.

3. C. The Project Manager primarily carries out the activities of the Managing a Stage Boundary process. However, the Senior User may be involved when creating the Stage Plans to confirm or direct the production of Product Descriptions, and the Executive may be involved with any updates of the Business Case.

4. C. The Project Manager uses Checkpoint Reports, the Quality Register, and Configuration Item Records for the products being delivered to review the progress of the Work Package. The Lessons Log is used to collate experience that may be useful for future work.

5. C. Taking corrective action to ensure the stage remains within tolerance is a purpose of the Controlling a Stage process.

6. D. Option D is not a purpose of the Controlling a Stage process. The Project Manager uses Managing a Stage Boundary to provide the information to the Project Board that they use to decide whether to authorize the next stage.

7. A. Option A is correct. The Managing Product Delivery activity Accept a Work Package ensures that the teams understand the expected effort, time, and cost needed to deliver the Work Package's products. Option B is an objective of the Starting up a Project process (the project approach evaluates how the project will be delivered). Option C is an objective of the Initiating a Project process (the Quality Management Strategy describes how quality management will be carried out). Option D is an objective of the Managing a Stage Boundary process.

8. B. The Quality Register contains the details of those who will review the products during their quality checks.

9. C. Option C is correct—the Project Manager should review the quality activities and ensure that all products in the current stage have been approved. Option A is incorrect—the Starting up a Project process is used to ensure that there is business justification for initiating the project. Option B is incorrect—the products for any stage are approved in the Managing Product Delivery process. Option D is incorrect—the Directing a Project process is used to communicate to corporate or programme management.

10. D. The Project Manager sends an Exception Report to the Project Board in order to escalate an issue.

Practitioner Exam Answers

Answers to Section 1: Matching Events with Themes

1. G. The Progress theme describes how the Project Manager uses the Work Package as a way of controlling the work of the teams. The Work Package gives official authorization for the teams to start creation of the specialist products and ensures that they start work at the correct time.

2. F. The Change theme covers configuration management. Configuration management is used to administer the storage, security, and issuing of project documents.

3. E. Digital Design has spotted what PRINCE2 calls an "opportunity." Opportunities are types of risks that may affect the project in a favorable way. Risks are assessed using the Risk theme.

4. C. Reviewing products after they have been created is a quality control activity that is covered by the Quality theme.

Answers to Section 2: Matching Actions with Controlling a Stage Activities

1. A. The Project Manager authorizes teams to carry out their work in the "Authorize a Work Package" activity.

2. E. The Project Manager regularly reports progress of the stage by creating a Highlight Report in the Report highlights activity. This Highlight Report will be sent to the Project Board and any other recipients highlighted in the Communication Management Strategy.

3. F. The Marketing Director is raising a request for change. Requests for changes are treated as issues and are immediately logged in the Issue Register during the Capture and examine issues and risks activity.

4. G. If more resources are needed than were originally authorized, this means that there is a forecast breach in stage tolerances. The Project Manager must escalate this to the Project Board by using an Exception Report.

Answers to Section 3: Classic Multiple Choice Questions

1. C. The order of events should be as follows: the Project Manager creates the Stage Plan for a stage during the Managing a Stage Boundary process; then the Project Board authorizes the Stage Plan during the Directing a Project process; and finally, the Project Manager manages the stage using the Controlling a Stage process, part of which will be authorizing Work Packages for the teams.

2. A. The Project Manager will initially plan quality reviews and checks on the stage's products while creating the Stage Plan during the Managing a Stage Boundary process. However, the Team Manager and the teams should review these quality checks with Project Assurance when they are accepting a Work Package during the Managing Product Delivery process. At this point, Project Assurance may recommend adding some extra reviewers to certain quality checks.

3. D. All requests for change of baselined products, no matter how small, must follow the PRINCE2 issue and change control procedure: capture the issue in the Issue Register, create an Issue Report, carry out an impact analysis, and then authorize the change at the right level of Change Authority.

4. B. The Project Manager might create a Lessons Report at various times in the project, such as when creating an End Stage Report, a Highlight Report, or the End Project Report. So it is appropriate for the Project Manager to create a Lessons Report and append it to the End Stage Report.

Chapter 11: Managing the End of a Project Successfully with PRINCE2

Foundation Exam Answers

1. A. Option A is correct—the Closing a Project process is used to review a project's achievements against its objectives and see if it has anything further to contribute. Option B is incorrect—the Project Board's decision to close the project is made in Directing a Project. Option C is incorrect—the Project Manager uses the Controlling a Stage process to manage the final delivery stage (as well as all the other delivery stages). Option D is incorrect—the delivery teams use the Managing Product Delivery process to create the specialist products of the final stage (as well as the specialist products for all the other stages).

2. D. Option D is incorrect—the planning for the final stage of the project will take place in the Managing a Stage Boundary process, which will be followed by the Directing a Project process, during which the Project Board will decide whether to authorize the final delivery stage of the project.

3. B. Option 3 is incorrect. The Benefits Review Plan shows how and when the achievement of the post-project benefits can be made. The Benefits Review Plan is passed along with the End Project Report to the Project Board for them to consider when authorizing the closure of the project.

4. D. Option D is correct. The Lessons Report passes on useful experience to those who have responsibility for quality improvement within an organization. Option A is incorrect—post-project actions specific to the project's products are described in the Follow-on Action Recommendations. Option B is incorrect—the Benefits Review Plan plans how and when the project's benefits will be reviewed. Option C is incorrect—the Lessons Log is used to collate lessons that could be applied to the current project.

5. D. Option D is correct. In the Closing a Project process, the Project Manager creates the Follow-on Action Recommendations, which will include continuing threats to the project's products in their operational life. Option A is incorrect—PRINCE2 does not manage the operational phase for the project's products. Option B is incorrect—the Managing a Stage Boundary process is used to request authorization to start the final stage. Option C is incorrect—the Directing a Project process enables the Project Board to provide authority to close the project.

6. A. Option A is correct—during Closing a Project, the Project Manager updates the Project Plan with the actuals from the final stage. Option B is incorrect—the Project Manager would update the Project Plan with forecasts for the final stage when using the Managing a Stage Boundary process just before the final stage. Option C is incorrect—the Benefits Review Plan is used to plan the work to review the post-project benefits. Option D is incorrect—the Project Manager uses the Stage Plan for the final stage to control and monitor the work of the final stage.

7. D. Option D is correct. The Project Initiation Documentation supersedes the Project Brief, so the Project Manager would only review the Project Initiation Documentation.

8. B. Option B is correct—the Closing a Project process includes the activity Hand over products, where the Project Manager reviews the Configuration Management Strategy to understand how to hand over the project's products to the operational teams. Option A is incorrect—the Starting up a Project process covers the activity of designing and appointing the project management team. Option C is incorrect—the Managing a Stage Boundary process covers the activity of planning the delivery stages. Option D is incorrect—the the Project Manager would review the "project controls" section of the Project Initiation Documentation when authorizing Work Packages in the Controlling a Stage process in order to understand how to control the teams.

9. B. Option B is correct. The Closing a Project process passes on Follow-on Action Recommendations that could include ongoing risks to the product in their operational phase. Option A is incorrect—the procedure for managing threats is defined in the Risk Management Strategy that is created in the Initiating a Project process. Option C is incorrect—the Managing Product Delivery process describes how the teams use Checkpoint Reports to report risks to the Project Manager. Option D is incorrect—the Controlling a Stage process describes where risks are captured in the Risk Register.

10. B. Option B is correct—the Project Manager checking the approval of the project's products is an example of the Project Manager checking the implementation of quality control.

Practitioner Exam Answers

Answers to Section 1: Practitioner Matching Questions about the Themes

1. B. The Organization theme describes how to use the Communication Management Strategy to detail all the project's stakeholders and their information needs from the project. This will include identifying who will need to be informed when the project is finishing.

2. A. The Business Case theme describes how the Benefits Review Plan is used to plan how and when reviews of the project's benefits will take place.

3. E. The Risk theme describes how to manage threats to the project's products.

4. C. The Quality theme describes how to use the acceptance criteria detailed in the Project Product Description to confirm that the project has produced products that are fit for their purpose.

Answers to Section 2: Practitioner Matching Questions about the End Project Report

1. E. The Lessons Report should show what went well, what went badly, and any recommendations that the project management team would make for future projects.

2. D. The review of the products should contain a review of any concessions. These are products that did not meet their original requirements (off-specifications) but that the Project Board or Change Authority has authorized.

3. A. The review of the Business Case should contain a review of the residual benefits expected after the project has finished.

4. B. The review of project objectives will review how the project performed against its planned targets for time, cost, quality, scope, benefits, and risks.

Answers to Section 3: Practitioner Assertion/Reason Questions

1. C. **Assertion:** True. During the Closing a Project process, the Project Manager will update the Benefits Review Plan with details of any new post-project reviews of the performance of the project's products.

   Reason: False. The Benefits Review Plan is created in the Initiating a Project process.

2. A. **Assertion:** True. As part of the Closing a Project activity Hand over products, the Project Manager should ensure that there is a support contract in place.

   Reason: True. This statement is true for the same reason that the assertion is true. The reason explains the assertion, so the answer is A.

3. D. **Assertion:** False. The Project Board authorizes the closure of the project during the Directing a Project process.

    Reason: True. The Project Board is responsible for authorizing the end of the project.

4. E. **Assertion:** False. The Project Manager reviews the final stage using the End Project Report.

    Reason: False. The Managing a Stage Boundary process is used at the end of every delivery stage apart from the final one, where the Closing a Project process is used instead.

Chapter 12: Tailoring PRINCE2 to the Project Environment

Foundation Exam Answers

1. A. Embedding is done by an organization when they adopt PRINCE2 across their organization. There are many ways to embed PRINCE2, such as training and development, creating scaling rules, and using process assurance.

2. D. Option D is correct. One way the PRINCE2 themes are adapted is by incorporating relevant organizational and programme standards into the project strategies. Option A is an example of adapting the PRINCE2 terminology. Option B is an example of adapting the PRINCE2 processes because the responsibility for the Starting up a Project process has been transferred to the programme management team. Option C is an example of adapting the management products.

3. B. The Highlight Reports, Checkpoint Reports, and End Stage Reports are all examples of progress reports. These are all management products.

4. B. Option B is correct—programmes tend to focus on a vision of an end state. Option A is incorrect—projects focus on deliverables or products. Option C is incorrect—the projects within a programme may be managed by PRINCE2, but at a programme management level, other approaches such as Managing a Successful Programme might be used. Option D is incorrect—projects tend to have shorter timescales.

5. A. In a programme environment, the programme management team might carry out most of the activities of the Starting up a Project process.

6. A. Option 4 is incorrect. This is a way of tailoring PRINCE2 for a small project.

7. D. A very small project could be treated as a task, in which case, the Project Board might consist of just one person, the Executive, who authorizes the Project Manager to deliver a Work Package. The Project Manager then does the specialist work himself. The Project Manager needs only Work Packages, log/registers, Product Descriptions, and Checkpoint Reports to manage the project.

8. B. PRINCE2 provides a framework showing what needs to be done, by whom, and when, whereas bodies of knowledge can provide a range of techniques showing how things can be done.

9. C. Projects focus on the delivery of products, whereas programmes focus on the delivery of a vision or end state.

10. C. There can only ever be one Executive.

Appendix B

Management Products in PRINCE2

In this appendix, you will find information on all 26 of the PRINCE2 management products. You were introduced to management products in Chapter 1, "Overview of PRINCE2." You saw that each management product contains information that helps the project management team deliver the project. You learned that in many projects, the management products will be documents, but in some circumstances, such as a small informal project, the information could be agreed to verbally.

Management products might be used for the following:

- Reporting information to various people both inside and outside the project management team

- Recording information on items such as risks, issues, lessons, and actions

- Planning the work that needs to be done

- Defining how the project should be managed

- Documenting the business justification for the project

- Outlining the specifications for products

- Tracking the status of the products

- Documenting and agreeing to the project definition and scope of work

Throughout this study guide, you have learned about each one of the 26 management products. In particular, you have learned about the purpose and composition of each management product. You also saw which roles create, update, and review each management product and in which of the processes this work is done.

In this appendix, you will find a brief outline of each management product and a reference to which chapter discusses it in detail.

Benefits Review Plan The Benefits Review Plan outlines how and when the benefits from the project will be reviewed. It also plans reviews of how the project's products have performed in their operational environment. It is created by the Project Manager in the initiation stage and updated at each stage boundary. The reviews that it plans may occur both during and after the project. You can learn more about this management product in Chapter 4, "Business Case Theme."

Business Case The Business Case documents the business justification for the project. The Executive creates an outline Business Case in the Starting up a Project process. The Project Manager adds more information in the initiation stage to create the first detailed Business Case. The Business Case is updated at each stage boundary and is a key input into the Project Board's decisions about whether to authorize initiation, the project, and each delivery stage. You can learn more about this management product in Chapter 4, "Business Case Theme."

Checkpoint Report The Team Manager (or the team members if there is no Team Manager) sends a regular Checkpoint Report to the Project Manager. Checkpoint Reports update the Project Manager on the progress of the Work Package that the team is delivering. The Work Package outlines how often the Project Manager wishes to receive Checkpoint Reports. The Team Manager creates Checkpoint Reports in the Managing Product Delivery process, and the Project Manager reads them in the Controlling a Stage process. You can learn more about this management product in Chapter 10, "Managing the Middle of a Project Successfully with PRINCE2."

Communication Management Strategy The Communication Management Strategy outlines how the project will approach communication between the members of the project management team. It also contains a stakeholder analysis showing all those outside the project management team who wish to be updated on the progress of the project and how they wish to receive those updates. The Project Manager creates the Communication Management Strategy in the initiation stage, and it forms part of the Project Initiation Documentation. It may be updated at each stage boundary with information on new stakeholders or project management team members. You can learn more about this management product in Chapter 3, "Organization Theme."

Configuration Item Record A Configuration Item Record contains information on the latest status of a particular product (which could be a management or specialist product). It also shows the owner of the product, who holds copies of the products, and which other products need to be considered if a change is made to this product.

The Project Manager uses Configuration Item Records to track the status of products. In some circumstances, the Project Manager might want to track the status of a component of a product or a group of products. If this is the case, there might be Configuration Item Records for these components or groups of products.

Every time the need for a product (or a component or group of products) is identified, a Configuration Item Record should be created to track its status. This record is created when the Project Manager is creating a Project Plan, Stage Plan, or Exception Plan, or when the Team Manager is creating a Team Plan.

You can learn more about this management product in Chapter 8, "Change Theme."

Configuration Management Strategy The Configuration Management Strategy outlines how a number of areas of the project will be managed: how to manage proposed changes to the project's products, how to manage products that do not meet their specifications, how to manage issues, and how to carry out configuration management. Configuration management involves managing versions of the products, storing and securing products, and reporting on the status of the products. The Project Manager creates the Configuration Management Strategy in the initiation stage, and it forms part of the Project Initiation Documentation. The Configuration Management Strategy might be updated at a stage boundary. You can learn more about this management product in Chapter 8, "Change Theme."

Daily Log   The Project Manager creates the Daily Log in the Starting up a Project process and uses it to record personal actions and informal issues. It also acts as a temporary repository of issues and risks in the Starting up a Project process, until the Risk Register and the Issue Register are created in the initiation stage. The Daily Log is sometimes known as the Project Manager's project diary. You can learn more about this management product in Chapter 9, "Progress Theme."

End Project Report   The Project Manager creates the End Project Report in the Closing a Project process. It reviews the project's performance against its objectives that were outlined in the original Project Initiation Documentation (or against any approved changes to the original objectives). The Project Board reviews the End Project Report when they are considering whether to authorize the closure of the project in the Directing a Project process. You can learn more about this management product in Chapter 11, "Managing the End of a Project Successfully with PRINCE2."

End Stage Report   The Project Manager creates an End Stage Report in the Managing a Stage Boundary process. The report reviews the performance of a stage. The Project Board reviews the End Stage Report during the Directing a Project process when they are considering whether to authorize the next stage. You can learn more about this management product in Chapter 10, "Managing the Middle of a Project Successfully with PRINCE2."

Exception Report   The Project Manager sends the Project Board an Exception Report if he is forecasting a breach in stage or project tolerances. The report details the problem that has caused the exception, gives a number of options to resolve the situation, and recommends one or more of the options. The Project Manager creates Exception Reports when necessary in the Controlling a Stage process. The Project Board reviews Exception Reports in the Directing a Project process and then must make a decision about what to do next. You can learn more about this management product in Chapter 9, "Progress Theme."

Highlight Report   The Project Manager sends regular Highlight Reports to the Project Board and any other stakeholders identified as recipients in the Communication Management Strategy. Highlight Reports update the Project Board and stakeholders of a stage's progress. The Communication Management Strategy defines the frequency of Highlight Reports. The Project Manager creates Highlight Reports in the Controlling a Stage process, and the Project Board reads the reports in the Directing a Project process. You can learn more about this management product in Chapter 10, "Managing the Middle of a Project Successfully with PRINCE2."

Issue Register   The Issue Register records issues throughout the project. The Project Manager is responsible for regularly monitoring and updating the Issue Register. There are three types of issues recorded in the Issue Register: requests for changes, off-specifications, and problems or concerns. The Project Manager creates the Issue Register in the initiation stage. You can learn more about this management product in Chapter 8, "Change Theme."

Issue Report   An Issue Report is created for any issue that will be handled formally. It contains a description of the issue, an impact assessment, and recommendations. The Project Manager creates Issue Reports during the Controlling a Stage process when capturing and examining issues. Issue Reports are updated throughout the life of the issue. You can learn more about this management product in Chapter 8, "Change Theme."

Lessons Log   The Lessons Log is used to record experience learned on previous projects that might be useful for the current project. It also acts as a repository for experience gained on the current project that might be useful for other projects. The Project Manager creates the Lessons Log in the Starting up a Project process and updates it throughout the project. You can learn more about this management product in Chapter 9, "Progress Theme."

Lessons Report   The Lessons Report is used to pass on useful experience from the current project to those in the organization who are focused on quality improvement. The Project Manager might create a Lessons Report at the end of each stage as well as at the end of the project. You can learn more about this management product in Chapter 9, "Progress Theme."

Plan   A plan defines what products will be delivered within the plan's scope and what activities and resources are needed to deliver those products. There are three levels of plans in PRINCE2: Project Plan, Stage Plan, and Team Plan. Each plan level follows the same composition.

The Project Plan shows the major products to be delivered for the entire project and what major activities and resources are needed to deliver those products. It will probably be at a fairly high level. The Project Manager creates the Project Plan in the initiation stage and updates it with progress information at the end of each stage. The Project Board uses the Project Plan to monitor the progress of the project during the Directing a Project process.

Stage Plans shows the products to be delivered for a particular management stage and what activities and resources are needed to deliver those products. It will probably be more detailed than the Project Plan. The Project Manager creates Stage Plans during the Managing a Stage Boundary process. The Project Board reviews the Stage Plan when considering whether to authorize the next stage. The Project Manager uses the Stage Plan to monitor the progress of a stage during the Controlling a Stage process.

Team Plans show the products to be delivered for one or more Work Packages and what activities and resources are needed to deliver those products. The Team Manager (or team member if there is no Team Manager) creates Team Plans and uses them to monitor the team's work in the Managing Product Delivery process.

After an exception situation, the Project Board might request that the Project Manager create an Exception Plan. This will show how the Project Manager proposes that the project recover from a project- or stage-level forecast breach of tolerance, and if approved by the Project Board, the Exception Plan will replace the Project Plan or Stage Plan, respectively.

You can learn more about this management product in Chapter 5, "Plans Theme."

Product Description   A Product Description defines the specification for a particular product. The product could be a specialist or a management product. A Product Description shows the measurable quality criteria that the product needs to conform to, what quality methods to use to check the product, and who is responsible for reviewing and approving the product. The Project Manager creates Product Descriptions when creating a Project Plan, Exception Plan, or Stage Plan. The Team Manager might also create Product Descriptions when creating a Team Plan. When creating Product Descriptions, the Project Manager (or Team Manager) will probably need to liaise with the users of the products and those with specialist knowledge of the products. You can learn more about this management product in Chapter 6, "Quality Theme."

Product Status Account   A Product Status Account shows the current status information on all, or a subset of, the project's products. This status information is sourced from the Configuration Item Records. The Project Manager creates (or asks Project Support to create) a Product Status Account at various times in the project, such as when creating a Highlight Report or an End Stage Report or when preparing to close the project. You can learn more about this management product in Chapter 8, "Change Theme."

Project Brief   The Project Manager creates the Project Brief in the Starting up a Project process. The Project Brief defines and scopes the project at a high level. It answers the basic questions such as why the project is being done, what the project is to deliver, who will be involved with the project, when the project will start and finish, and what approach will be used to deliver the products. The outline Business Case and the Project Product Description are both within the Project Brief.

The Project Board reviews the Project Brief during the Directing a Project process when they are considering whether to authorize the initiation stage of the project. You can learn more about this management product in Chapter 2, "Starting a Project Successfully with PRINCE2."

Project Initiation Documentation   The Project Manager creates the Project Initiation Documentation during the initiation stage. The Project Initiation Documentation builds on the information in the Project Brief to further define and scope the project. The Project Initiation Documentation also contains a set of strategies showing how the project will be managed as well as the Project Plan and the project controls.

The Project Manager updates the Project Initiation Documentation at the end of each stage. The Project Board reviews the latest version of the Project Initiation Documentation when considering whether to authorize the project or the next stage. You can learn more about this management product in Chapter 2, "Starting a Project Successfully with PRINCE2."

Project Product Description   The Project Manager, with the help of the Senior Users and the Executive, creates the Project Product Description in the Starting up a Project process. It describes the main outputs of the project. It contains the customer quality expectations and measurable acceptance criteria for the products. It also shows how the products will be checked to see whether they conform to the acceptance criteria and who is responsible for officially accepting the products.

The Project Product Description is used when deliverables are handed over to the client or the operations team to confirm that the products have been created correctly. This handing over of deliverables might happen at the end of a stage or the end of the project.

You can learn more about this management product in Chapter 6, "Quality Theme."

Quality Management Strategy   The Quality Management Strategy outlines how the project management team will approach quality planning, quality control, and quality assurance throughout the project. It shows how the project will be managed in such a way as to ensure that the products are fit for their purpose. The Project Manager will create the Quality Management Strategy in the initiation stage and it will form part of the Project Initiation Documentation. The Quality Management Strategy might be updated at a stage boundary. You can learn more about this management product in Chapter 6, "Quality Theme."

Quality Register   The Quality Register records information on the quality activities that take place during the project. Each quality check should have a corresponding entry in the Quality Register that provides information such as when the check took place, who was involved, and whether the check passed or failed. The Project Manager creates the Quality Register in the initiation stage and updates it with planned quality activities when planning a stage. The Quality Register will be updated with the results of the quality activities in the Managing Product Delivery process. The Work Package will define who should update the Quality Register with the results of the quality activities. You can learn more about this management product in Chapter 6, "Quality Theme."

Risk Management Strategy   The Risk Management Strategy outlines how the project management team will approach managing threats and opportunities throughout the project. It shows how the project will be managed in a way that decreases the likelihood and/or impact of threats and increases the likelihood and/or impact of opportunities. The Project Manager creates the Risk Management Strategy in the initiation stage, and it forms part of the Project Initiation Documentation. The Risk Management Strategy might be updated at a stage boundary. You can learn more about this management product in Chapter 7, "Risk Theme."

Risk Register   The Risk Register records information on the threats and opportunities that the project faces. Each entry will record information such as a description of the risk, the risk's likelihood and impact, and countermeasures to address the risk. The Project Manager creates the Risk Register in the initiation stage and updates it regularly throughout the project. You can learn more about this management product in Chapter 7, "Risk Theme."

Work Package   The Work Package is an agreement between the Project Manager and the Team Manager (or the team members if there is no Team Manager) that the team will deliver a set of specialist products. The Work Package describes the time and cost that the products must be delivered within and whether there are any tolerances around these objectives. The Work Package is created between two activities in the process model: when the Project Manager authorizes a Work Package in the Controlling a Stage process, and when the Team Manager accepts a Work Package in the Managing Product Delivery process. You can learn more about this management product in Chapter 9, "Progress Theme."

Appendix C

Passing the Accreditation Exams

There are two things that will greatly increase your chances of becoming PRINCE2-accredited: first, you need to learn the method, and second, you must understand the style and format of the two exams.

Studying a method with as much detail as PRINCE2 provides can be quite a challenge. But the good news is that you don't need to remember everything. The basic Foundation exam will not test you in the detailed aspects of the method. The more difficult Practitioner level allows you to use the PRINCE2 manual *Managing Successful Projects with PRINCE2* (Stationery Office, 2009) during the exam. In this appendix, you will see what you need to remember for the Foundation examination and how to use the PRINCE2 manual for the Practitioner exam.

You should also know how to tackle the exam formats. The Practitioner exam in particular has a unique style. If the first time you see this style is on the exam day, a good knowledge of PRINCE2 might not be enough to ensure that you pass. In this appendix, I will give you a whole range of tips and tactics to improve your chances of successfully negotiating the Foundation and Practitioner exam formats.

Preparing for the Exams

As with any exam, the better you prepare, the more likely you are to pass. In this section, you will see where you need to focus your study time, for both the Foundation and the Practitioner exams.

Preparing for the Foundation Level

The Foundation exam is the easier of the two qualification levels. It tests to see if you can remember the PRINCE2 methodology rather than the more difficult skill of whether you can apply the methodology. However, you do need to be fully prepared in order to pass. As I mentioned in the introduction, you don't have to remember everything for this exam. In this section, I will show you what you should memorize in order to pass the Foundation exam.

It is also very important to practice taking as many Foundation mock questions as you can before taking the real exam. There are plenty of practice questions for you to try, both in this book and on the companion website for this study guide (www.sybex.com/go/prince2studyguide). In this section, I will also discuss the best way to use these practice questions.

Syllabus Topics Tested During the Foundation Exam

There are 15 separate syllabus areas in the Foundation exam. On average, there will be about five questions on each of these topics. The syllabus area topics are as follows:

Overview, Principles, and Tailoring of PRINCE2   I covered this topic in Chapter 1, "Overview of PRINCE2." This topic includes the characteristics of a project, the six aspects of project performance that need to be managed, the four integrated elements of PRINCE2, the benefits of PRINCE2, and the seven principles of PRINCE2.

The Seven Themes   I have covered each one of these in a separate chapter throughout the book.

The Seven Processes   This study guide has covered the processes as follows: Directing a Project is covered in Chapter 1, "Overview of PRINCE2"; Starting up a Project and Initiating a Project are covered in Chapter 2, "Starting a Project Successfully with PRINCE2"; Controlling a Stage, Managing Product Delivery, and Managing a Stage Boundary are covered in Chapter 10, "Managing the Middle of a Project Successfully with PRINCE2"; and Closing a Project is covered in Chapter 11, "Managing the End of a Project Successfully with PRINCE2."

Each of these 15 syllabus topics needs to be learned to a medium level of detail for the Foundation exam. Over the next six sections, I will describe what "medium level of detail" means in practice.

Learning the Overview of PRINCE2 for the Foundation Exam

This syllabus topic was covered in Chapter 1, "Overview of PRINCE2." You need to be able to identify the following:

- The characteristics that distinguish a project from business as usual: change, temporary, cross-functional, unique, and uncertainty.

- The four elements of PRINCE2: principles, themes, processes, and the project environment.

- The benefits of PRINCE2. There are quite a few; see the list in Chapter 1, "Overview of PRINCE2."

- The seven principles of PRINCE2: continued business justification, learn from experience, defined roles and responsibilities, manage by stages, manage by exception, focus on products, and tailor to suit the project environment.

You could be lucky, and the "overview" Foundation questions that you will have to answer might simply ask you to identify some of the information in the preceding list. This information is usually the first thing people learn about PRINCE2, and by the time they take the exam, they've forgotten it. Make sure you don't fall into that trap!

Some "overview" Foundation questions are a little more complicated. You might need to explain how the PRINCE2 principles are supported and implemented by the rest of the methodology. For example, which theme primarily supports the "manage by exception" principle? The answer is the Progress theme (covered in Chapter 9, "Progress Theme") because it explains the use of tolerances that implement management by exception. Another example would be, which theme primarily supports the "focus on products" principle? The answer is the Quality theme (covered in Chapter 6, "Quality Theme") because it explains how to use Product Descriptions to specify a product. These sorts of questions require a little bit more thought.

Learning the Process Model for the Foundation Exam

The PRINCE2 model contains seven processes, and within those processes are 40 separate activities. Within each activity, various roles do various actions that are carried out using the management approaches set out in the themes and using the various PRINCE2 management products. This is obviously a lot of detail to remember.

My advice for learning the process model for the Foundation exam is that the vast majority of questions can be answered by knowing the model down to the process level, not to the activity level. For example, rather than trying to remember that the Project Manager creates the Daily Log during the Appoint the Executive and the Project Manager activity, it is enough to remember that this occurs in the Starting up a Project process. So for each of the seven processes, memorize what management products are created, reviewed, or updated; what themes are used; and what roles are involved.

You should also understand the sequence in which the processes are used throughout the life of a project. The "An End-to-End Walk-through of PRINCE2" section in Chapter 1, "Overview of PRINCE2," is an excellent source of information for this.

The process key facts tables provided in this book are also useful for preparing for the Foundation exam. You will find these tables in the following chapters:

- In Chapter 2, "Starting a Project Successfully with PRINCE2," you'll find key facts tables for the Starting up a Project and Initiating a Project processes.

- In Chapter 10, "Managing the Middle of a Project Successfully with PRINCE2," are key facts tables for the Controlling a Stage, Managing Product Delivery, and Managing a Stage Boundary processes.

- In Chapter 11, "Managing the End of a Project Successfully with PRINCE2," there is a key facts table for the Closing a Project process.

Learning the Roles for the Foundation Exam

It is very important to understand the PRINCE2 roles and responsibilities. These are covered in detail in Chapter 3, "Organization Theme," but here's a quick rundown of what you need to know about them for the exam:

- Understand that there are three main stakeholder interests represented in the PRINCE2 project management team: the user, the supplier, and the business.

- Know the four levels of the PRINCE2 project management structure: the corporate or programme management level, the directing level represented by the Project Board, the managing level represented by the Project Manager, and the delivering level represented by the Team Manager and the teams. Understand how these levels interact with each other throughout the project.

- Understand the project management team organization chart. Figure 3.3 in Chapter 3, "Organization Theme," shows how the various PRINCE2 roles report to and work with each other.
- Understand the responsibilities of each PRINCE2 role.

The Organization theme topic spans the entire PRINCE2 method. In every single process, theme, or activity, various roles do various things. With every management product, various roles are involved with the product's creation, review, and update. This makes the Organization theme one of the most important topics to learn.

Learning the Themes for the Foundation Level

Ironically, I have the least amount to say about how to learn the themes for the Foundation exam. It's ironic because most of your preparation time should be focused on understanding the seven themes, but there are no shortcuts with this topic. Make sure you read through the relevant chapters in this study guide to fully understand how each of the themes describes how to manage the project using its particular area of project management and how this theme relates to the rest of the PRINCE2 model.

Learning the Management Products for the Foundation Exam

There are 26 PRINCE2 management products, each one with about 10 different sections of information. That is a lot of information to remember. For the Foundation exam, for most of these management products, I wouldn't recommend memorizing all the sections of all the products. What you do need to know is each product's purpose, an overview of the information they contain, and what processes they are created and updated within. In Appendix B, "Management Products in PRINCE2," you'll find a reference list for all 26 management products that tells you where they are described in this study guide. However, with some management products, it is more important to remember exactly what they contain. I recommend memorizing the composition of the following:

- Business Case
- Product Description
- Project Product Description
- Project Brief
- Project Initiation Documentation
- Work Package

Learning the PRINCE2 Terminology

It is very important to understand the PRINCE2 terminology. One of the benefits of PRINCE2 is that it provides a common project management language, but for this to be useful, you need to be able to speak that language! This can be challenging to learn for a number of reasons:

▪ Before studying PRINCE2, candidates may have managed projects using a different approach, either one created specifically for their workplace or one of the other available project management best practice approaches such as the Project Management Institute's *A Guide to the Project Management Body of Knowledge, 4th Edition (PMBOK® Guide)*. Candidates then confuse the terminology between PRINCE2 and the other approach.

▪ A number of PRINCE2 terms are used in a different way in everyday speech. For example, "risks" in PRINCE2 are not just potential bad things that might happen, but also potential opportunities (see Chapter 7, "Risk Theme"). The "reason" for doing the project is always what has happened before the project started to trigger the initiative, not the predicted value that the project might bring (see Chapter 4, "Business Case Theme"). And "quality" doesn't mean luxurious; it means a product that is fit for the purpose it will be used for (see Chapter 6, "Quality Theme.")

The meaning of a Foundation question can change if the candidate misunderstands the meaning of just one word. It is important to learn all the PRINCE2 terminology by using the Glossary, which can be found on this book's companion website (`www.sybex.com/go/prince2studyguide`).

Test Your Knowledge

In addition to doing all the exam preparation discussed previously, you should take as many practice Foundation questions as you can. You will find practice Foundation questions at the beginning of this book in the Assessment Test and at the end of each chapter in the Review Question sections. There are also two complete Foundation examinations with 75 questions each in Appendix D, "Sample Foundation Examinations." plus another bonus Foundation exam on this book's companion website (`www.sybex.com/go/prince2studyguide`).

I would recommend that you answer all of these questions.

Use the practice Foundation questions to focus your exam preparation. Look at the ones you are getting wrong and make sure you understand your mistakes. Look to see if there is any pattern to your mistakes—maybe there is a particular topic you are having trouble with. If this is the case, you obviously need to do further work in this area.

When you answer the practice Foundation questions, try to take them in the same amount of time that you will have for the real exam. You will only get one hour to do 75 questions, so that works out to less than a minute per question. Also try to answer the questions without referring to this study guide, any of your revision material, or *Managing Successful Projects with PRINCE2*.

Preparing for the Practitioner Exam

The Practitioner exam is the harder of the two PRINCE2 accreditation levels. It tests not only whether you understand the methodology, but also whether you know how to apply it. Obviously, the best way to understand how to apply PRINCE2 is to actually use it in practice. However, quite a number of candidates who take the Practitioner exam have never used the method and, for those who have, very few workplaces implement every aspect of PRINCE2. So how do you show how to apply the method if you have never or only partially used it? I suggest a number of approaches:

- Take plenty of Practitioner questions. The Practitioner style of exam gives you a project case study and then asks questions how to apply PRINCE2 to it. The more of these sorts of questions you take, the better your understanding will be on how to apply the method. I have given you example Practitioner questions at the end of most of the chapters of this book, and there is one further complete Practitioner exam on this book's companion website (www.sybex.com/go/prince2studyguide). I suggest you answer all of these questions.

- Read the case studies set out throughout this book. They show how PRINCE2 has been used in real projects.

- Read widely on the application of project approaches such as PRINCE2. If you search on the Web for PRINCE2 blogs, articles, and discussion forums (there are some particularly good ones on LinkedIn®), you will find plenty of resources to expand your knowledge.

- Implement some of the aspects of PRINCE2 in your workplace.

The Practitioner exam doesn't require you to memorize any more of the theory than you did for the Foundation level. Remember that the more detailed questions in the Practitioner exam can be answered by referring to *Managing Successful Projects with PRINCE2*, which you are allowed to take into the exam.

Using *Managing Successful Projects with PRINCE2*

You should know how to use the official PRINCE2 manual, *Managing Successful Projects with PRINCE2*, during the exam to help you answer the more detailed questions. The manual is useful for detailed questions such as what happens in a particular activity or what type of information goes into which particular section of one of the management products. I discuss how to use the manual during the exam in the "Taking the Practitioner Exam" section later in this appendix. But there are a number of things you can do before the exam that will make the manual easier to use *during* the exam:

- There isn't much time in the Practitioner exam, so you have to find the information in the manual quickly. Buy some sticky tabs and place them at the beginning of the chapters. You could tab the beginning of the processes and themes chapters and the beginning of the appendices. This will make it far easier to quickly find what you are looking for.

- The Practitioner exam rules state that you are not allowed to take any reference material other than the PRINCE2 manual into the exam. This includes not being allowed to insert sheets or anything larger than a section tab into the manual. However, one loophole in this rule is that you are allowed to write notes in the manual and highlight words. I recommend that you do this for any summary material that you have found useful in this study guide or from any other source that you feel will help you during the exam.

- When you answer the mock Practitioner exam questions in this study guide and its companion website (www.sybex.com/go/prince2studyguide), practice using the PRINCE2 manual.

Taking the Exams

Sooner or later, the dreaded exam day will arrive! If you have followed all the advice in this study guide, you will have an excellent chance of passing both levels of accreditation. Remember that before you sit for the Practitioner exam, you must first take and pass the Foundation exam.

Obviously, having a good knowledge of PRINCE2 is a prerequisite to passing the accreditation; however, approaching the exam in the right way will increase your chances of success. In this section, I have provided tips and tactics for dealing with the two exams that I have learned over the many years I have taught PRINCE2.

General Tips for Taking the Exams

There are a number of general tips that will be useful for both the Foundation and the Practitioner exams. They are all included in this section.

Read the Question!

When I teach PRINCE2 courses, "read the question" are three words that I repeat again and again throughout the week. It sounds so obvious and also rather patronizing. However, it is very easy, especially when you are under pressure, to skim the questions, misreading or missing essential words in a question, or changing the question into something you would rather have answered!

The PRINCE2 examinations are specifically worded. They use the PRINCE2 terminology in an exacting way. This makes it even more important than normal to carefully read the questions. It might help you during the exam to use a pen to underline or highlight key words in a question.

To illustrate how easy it is to misread the exam, take a look at the following question. It is from the mock Foundation exams in Appendix D, "Sample Foundation Examinations," and is about the Change theme.

> Which product would confirm the version numbers of all products being developed within a given stage?
>
> **A.** Configuration Item Record
>
> **B.** Product Status Account
>
> **C.** Stage Plan
>
> **D.** Work Package

Answer: B. Option B is correct. The Product Status Account provides a summary of the status information about a group of products. This status information is sourced from all those products' Configuration Item Records. Option A is incorrect. Each product has a corresponding Configuration Item Record that holds status information on that product, such as its latest version number. However, the question asks for the product that holds the version numbers of *all* the products in a stage, not just for one product. Option C is incorrect. The Stage Plan shows how the products will be created, not their version numbers. Option D is incorrect. The Work Package is the official instruction to the teams to build the products.

Did you get it right? Well done if you went for Product Status Account. If you went for Configuration Item Record, you just proved my point about reading the question! If you went for Stage Plan or Work Package, you probably need to reread Chapter 8, "Change Theme"!

The key word in this question is *all*. It is easy to miss such a small word and read the question as "Which product would confirm the version numbers of *a* product being developed within a given stage?" If the question had asked this, then the answer would be the Configuration Item Record.

Other common misread terms are confusing an Exception Plan with an Exception Report, Product Descriptions with the Project Product Description, and Issue Reports with Issue Registers.

Time Management

One of the major reasons that people fail the PRINCE2 exams is that they run out of time.

There are 75 questions on the Foundation exam that you need to answer in one hour. That is 48 seconds per question! Practice answering the mock questions until you can do them at this sort of pace.

There are nine main questions in the Practitioner exam that you have to answer in two and a half hours. Each of the nine questions is subdivided into 12 smaller ones. I recommend that you allocate 15 minutes per main question, which will leave you with a contingency of 15 minutes. Once again, when you answer the mock questions, practice doing them at this speed. Candidates generally find it harder to complete the Practitioner exam than the Foundation exam in the time available.

In either exam, if you get stuck on a particular question, you must move on. Leave it for any time you have left at the end. Keep moving through the exam at the right sort of pace so you have the best chance of answering as many questions as you can.

Marking the Answer Sheet

For both exams, you are given an answer sheet with a grid that you fill out to indicate which option you think is correct. All your hard revision work comes down to filling out this sheet correctly. Here are a few tips:

- Mark the answer sheet in pencil. The APMG (the organization that marks the papers) has stated that they might not mark answer sheets filled out in pen. The exam invigilator or proctor should remind you of this, and should provide spare pencils, but I wouldn't rely on him. Take plenty of spare pencils, an eraser, and pencil sharpeners to the exam.

- If you change your mind about an answer, erase the first option you chose carefully, and then fill out the new one. A computer scanner marks the papers, so if you haven't fully erased your first choice, the scanner might pick up your original answer. Be careful when you change an option, though—it has been proven that the majority of exam candidates who change their mind about an answer are changing it to the wrong one!

- Some candidates I see taking the exam mark the question paper with their choice and then transfer all their answers to the answer grid at the end of the exam. This is a ridiculously risky strategy! The APMG invigilators or proctors are under strict rules to give candidates only the allocated amount of time—they will have to take the answer sheet from you at the end of the exam time, whether or not you have completed it. Mark the answer sheet as you go through the questions. You can always erase wrong answers later.

- If you leave a question to come back to later, be careful that the next answer that you mark on the answer sheet takes account of the fact that you've skipped a question. I have seen candidates who have skipped a question near the beginning and then proceeded to mark the wrong answer numbers for the rest of the exam. Make sure that the answer you are marking on the answer sheet corresponds to the question you read on the question paper.

- For most questions in the PRINCE2 exams, there is one right option. However, there is one exception to this rule in the Practitioner exam: the multiple response question format. For this type of format, the question will clearly state the number of options you need to choose; however, under the pressure of the exam, it is all too easy to miss these instructions. Read the question carefully to make sure you are giving the right number of options per question.

- Always answer every single question. There is no negative marking, so you won't lose points for the wrong answers. If you run out of time, quickly guess the answers you have missed. If you can't understand one of the questions, guess and move on. You might get lucky and get a few more points!

Special Allowances for International and Disabled Candidates

I discussed earlier how challenging it can be to understand the PRINCE2 terminology. This is difficult enough for native English speakers; it is obviously even harder for someone who isn't. I regularly teach PRINCE2 courses across Europe for international bodies such as NATO and the United Nations. Although the exam is available in 16 different languages, my courses are always in English and the exams are worded in English. During these courses, I spend extra time making sure that the candidates understand the language of PRINCE2.

As of this writing, the APMG allows extra time for candidates taking the exam in English who are nonnative speakers of English, providing that they fulfill the following two criteria:

- They are nonnative speakers of English.
- They work in an environment where English is not the business language.

If the candidates meet both of these criteria, they can get an extra 15 minutes for the Foundation exam and an extra 30 minutes for the Practitioner exam. If you meet these criteria, *take* this extra time—every advantage helps! The APMG regularly updates these rules, so do check them with the organization that is providing your exam center. They will have an up-to-date copy of the APMG proctor or invigilator rules.

The exams have also been translated into 16 languages. You could also therefore check to see if the exam is available in your language. Once again, the organization that is providing your exam center will have all the latest details on this.

If you believe you have a disability that will affect your performance in the exam, contact your exam center and discuss this. The APMG makes all reasonable allowances for disabilities so that everyone can have a fair chance at taking the exams.

Raising Issues During or After the Exam

If there are any issues either before or during the exam that you feel would reasonably affect your performance, you should raise them with your exam invigilator or proctor. He will write them down and submit them, along with the exam papers, to the APMG.

Taking the Foundation Exam

Although the Foundation exam is considered the easier of the two levels, it can still represent a challenge for candidates. However, if you follow all of the preceding preparation tips, you will arrive at the exam well prepared.

There will be 75 multiple-choice questions. Each question gives four possible options, one of which is correct. The invigilator or proctor rules do not allow you to refer to any books or study notes during the exam. The exam tests to see if you know the methodology but not necessarily that you know how to apply it. (That comes later, in the Practitioner exam.) Fifty percent is the pass mark.

One slight complication is that in every Foundation exam, the APMG inserts five trial questions. Your answers to these questions do not count toward your final mark. The APMG is just trying out these trial questions to see if they might use them for future exams. You will not know which of the 75 questions are the trial ones, so don't try to figure this out—just answer as many of the 75 questions as possible. And keep in mind that you need to get 35 out of the 70 nontrial questions to get the 50 percent pass mark.

Foundation Question Formats

There are four types of Foundation questions: standard, negative, missing word, and list. Let's look at each in turn and talk about how you should tackle them.

Standard Foundation Question Type

The standard type is the easiest. Here is an example taken from the mock Foundation exams in Appendix D, "Sample Foundation Examinations":

> Which is one of the six aspects of project performance that needs to be managed?
>
> **A.** Customers
>
> **B.** People
>
> **C.** Benefits
>
> **D.** Processes
>
> **Answer:** C. Six aspects of project performance need to be managed: time, cost, benefits, risk, quality, and scope. (See Chapter 1, "Overview of PRINCE2.")

Unless the question itself is difficult, you should be able to quickly answer questions in this format.

Negative Foundation Question Type

Under exam conditions, you may easily miss the word "not" in these types of questions, which, of course, will lead you to the wrong answer. However, the exam should highlight "**NOT**" by capitalizing and putting it in bold. Here is an example taken from the mock Foundation exams in Appendix D, "Sample Foundation Examinations":

> Which is **NOT** a recommended response type to respond to a threat?
>
> **A.** Avoid
>
> **B.** Reject
>
> **C.** Share
>
> **D.** Transfer
>
> **Answer:** B. This is a question about risk responses, which were covered in Chapter 7, "Risk Theme." To answer this question, you need to learn the risk threat responses (avoid, reduce, fallback, transfer, share, or accept) and the risk opportunity responses (exploit, enhance, share, or reject).

Missing Word(s) Question Type

Here is an example of this type of question taken from the mock Foundation exams in Appendix D, "Sample Foundation Examinations":

> Identify the missing word(s) in the following sentence:
>
> Quality planning provides the definition of the required products with their _____ as a foundation for Project Board agreement.
>
> **A.** Customer's quality expectations
>
> **B.** Quality test results
>
> **C.** Quality criteria
>
> **D.** Owners
>
> **Answer:** C. The quality criteria of each product define the measurable specification for that product, which can then be agreed to by the Project Board. (See Chapter 6, "Quality Theme.")

I think this type of question is fairly straightforward. Just be careful to remember that sometimes there is a missing word and sometimes there is a missing partial sentence.

List Question Type

The list type of Foundation question takes more time than the other types, because there is more to read. Here is an example of this type of question taken from the mock Foundation exams in Appendix D, "Sample Foundation Examinations":

Which of the following roles can the Project Manager also perform?

1. Change Authority

2. Project Assurance

3. Project Support

4. Team Manager

A. 1, 2, 3

B. 1, 2, 4

C. 1, 3, 4

D. 2, 3, 4

Answer: C. The Project Manager cannot carry out the Project Assurance role, because one of the responsibilities of Project Assurance is to check and audit the work of the Project Manager.

To answer these questions quickly, read through the four options and find which one is wrong. In this case, it is the second one, Project Assurance. Now all you need to do is find the combination that doesn't contain the wrong option, in this case Option C.

Taking the Practitioner Exam

The Practitioner exam is the harder of the two PRINCE2 accreditation levels. It is not just testing whether you know the theory, but whether you understand how to apply it. A prerequisite for taking the Practitioner exam is that you must have passed the Foundation exam.

There are nine main questions, each focusing on a different one of the following syllabus topics:

- Starting up a Project/Initiating a Project. (If both of these processes are examined, they are always grouped together in one main question.)

- Managing a Stage Boundary/Closing a Project/Directing a Project. (If all of these processes are examined, they are always grouped together in one main question.)

- Controlling a Stage/Managing Product Delivery. (If both of these processes are examined, they are always grouped together in one main question.)

- Business Case.

- Organization.

- Plans.

- Progress.
- Change.
- Quality.
- Risk.

Usually, seven of the questions ask about the themes (one question for each theme), and then the other two questions focus on the process combinations—so one of the process combinations is generally left out.

Each of the nine main questions is subdivided into 12 mini-questions. You get a point for correctly answering each of the mini-questions, so there is a total of 108 marks available. You need to get 55 percent to pass.

The Practitioner exam consists of three booklets:

- A scenario booklet with additional information for some of the questions. (I will describe how to deal with this in the next subsection.)
- A question paper.
- An answer sheet.

Dealing with the Scenario and Additional Information

When you take the Practitioner exam, you will get a separate booklet containing a scenario of about a page in length and some additional information. The additional information is usually divided up into four or five sections. Some of the nine main questions will refer to one or more of these additional information sections.

It will always say clearly at the top of any question whether you need to refer to a section of the additional information in order to answer that question. One common mistake Practitioner candidates make is trying to answer a question without referring to any necessary additional information.

As you can imagine, with only two and a half hours to finish the whole exam, you don't have a great deal of time to read this additional information. I recommend that as soon as you start the exam, you should quickly read through the scenario. The exam will refer to the scenario throughout all the nine questions, whereas the additional information sections are generally needed for only one particular question, so you need a fairly good grasp of the scenario right away. Highlight any significant points and aim to understand broadly what is happening, but on this first read-through, don't concern yourself with all the scenario details. As you move through the exam, you can fill in the gaps in your knowledge. Also, at this point, you don't know what is important about the scenario until you see the questions.

Once you have read quickly through the scenario, move on to the questions. Don't read any of the additional information until you come to a question that refers to it. Even then, you should first read the question and then read the relevant section of the additional information. Using this approach, you can frame how you read the information, focusing only on what you need to answer the question.

Dealing with the Various Practitioner Question Formats

There are five possible Practitioner exam question formats:

Classic Multiple Choice   Similar to the Foundation questions; you are given a question with three or four possible answers. You need to pick the correct option.

Matching   You are given two lists, and you have to match one set of list items with the other set of list items.

Sequence   You are given a list of project activities that you need to put into the correct order.

Multiple Response   You are given a question with four or five possible answers. You need to pick the two or three correct options.

Assertion/Reason   You are given two statements: one is an assertion about how you should manage a project, and the other is a reason that might justify the assertion. You have to work out whether the assertion and reason are true.

Over the next few sections, you will see how to tackle each of these question types. I will use some example Practitioner questions taken from the review question sections at the end of the chapters. If you haven't reviewed all of these questions yet, don't worry—you don't need to in order to understand this section. The Practitioner exam scenario for these questions concerns a furniture manufacturing company called Quality Furniture that has started a project to create a new website. The website will sell their furniture products.

Classic Multiple Choice Question Type

The classic multiple choice format is the easiest type of Practitioner question. Here is a sample question taken from Chapter 8, "Change Theme":

> What information should be recorded under the issue and change control procedure heading in the Configuration Management Strategy?
>
> **A.**   Information on how to hand over the website to the operational team
>
> **B.**   A reference to Quality Furniture's standard impact analysis procedure
>
> **C.**   The format of the Issue Register
>
> **D.**   Any metrics to be employed in order to verify the product's fitness for purpose
>
> **Answer:** B. Option B is correct—one step in the issue and change control procedure is to examine the issue, which is done by performing an impact analysis. Option A is incorrect—the procedure to hand over the project's products is described in the configuration management procedure. Option C is incorrect—the format of the Issue Register should be in the records section. Option D is incorrect—any metrics to be employed in order to carry out the quality control activities should be in the quality management procedure in the Quality Management Strategy.

These types of questions should be the quickest to answer. Save time on these questions—time that you can then use for the harder formats, such as the multiple response or the assertion/reason.

Matching Question Type

In the matching type of question, you are given two lists. For each option in the first list, you have to choose an option from the second list. The following is an example taken from Chapter 7, "Risk Theme."

The request for tender has been sent out to a number of software suppliers who could build the website. The Executive is concerned that because of Quality Furniture's lack of experience in IT and the Internet, there is a risk that they will choose an inappropriate or poor supplier for the work. If this happens, a number of the project's objectives, such as the timeline, costs, and the anticipated benefits, could be impacted.

Column 1 contains a list of risk responses identified by the Project Manager following an assessment of this risk. Column 2 contains a list of threat response types. For each risk response in Column 1, select from Column 2 the type of response it represents. Each option from Column 2 can be used once, more than once, or not at all.

Column 1	Column 2
1. Add a clause in the supplier contract that makes the supplier financially liable if certain cost, quality, and time criteria are not met.	A. Avoid
2. Recruit a specialist in IT procurement and give him the role of supplier assurance on the project.	B. Reduce
3. Decide that the risk of choosing the wrong supplier is too high, cancel the project, and continue to use the old website.	C. Fallback
4. Wait for the software development stage and if the supplier starts to deliver poor quality, terminate the supplier's contract and use a recommended IT contractor to finish the work.	D. Transfer
5. Decide that the cost of mitigating this risk does not outweigh the benefit of doing so.	E. Accept
6. Decide to split the tender into several parts and allocate the work to several different suppliers.	F. Share

How did you do? Here are the answers and explanations:

1. D. By adding the clause in the contract with the software supplier, the Project Manager is transferring some of the financial risk to that supplier.

2. B. By bringing in an expert in the area of IT procurement, the Project Manager is reducing the likelihood of choosing an inappropriate supplier.

3. A. This seems rather strange, but the fact is that if the project is canceled, the risk is eradicated. The impact of a poor supplier is avoided by not having a project that necessitates selecting one.

4. C. Fallback responses are always reactive. The Project Manager waits until the risk occurs and then, if it does, does something.

5.   E. When the Project Manager makes a conscious decision to do nothing about the risk, he is using the accept response type.

6.   B. By splitting up the tender into several parts, the Project Manager is spreading the risk of a poor supplier. He may still pick a poor supplier, but it is less likely that he will do so for all the work. He reduces the likelihood of the risk.

One potential pitfall that exam candidates sometimes fall into is believing that all the options in Column 2 have to be used. As you can see from the previous example, this is not always the case. In this example, the share (Option F) was not used and the answers to two of the questions was reduce (Option B). At the top of these sorts of questions, a statement such as "Each selection in Column 2 can be used once, more than once, or not at all" will appear that explains this.

Sequence Question Type

The sequence type of question is a special case of the matching format. The first list will be a set of activities carried out in a project; the second will be a list of sequence numbers. You have to match the activities with the sequence number to show the order in which the activities are done. The following example is taken from Chapter 3, "Organization Theme." The question focuses on what needs to be done during the Starting up a Project and Initiating a Project processes.

Column 1 is a list of actions that, according to PRINCE2, need to be carried out in the project. For each action in Column 1, indicate in which order these actions should occur by selecting the appropriate option from Column 2.

Column 1	Column 2
1. Document the stakeholder engagement procedure.	A. First
2. Appoint the Executive.	B. Second
3. Create the role descriptions for the Senior User.	C. Third
4. Appoint the Project Manager.	D. Fourth

How did you do? Here are the answers and explanations:

1.   D. The stakeholder engagement procedure is documented in the "Prepare the Communication Management Strategy" activity in the Initiating a Project process. The other three actions occur in the Starting up a Project process that takes place before Initiating a Project. It is therefore the last action.

2.   A. The Executive is appointed in the first activity of the first process of PRINCE2, in the "Appoint the Executive and Project Manager" activity in the Starting up a Project process. During this activity, corporate or programme management appoints the Executive, who then appoints the Project Manager.

3. C. Creating the Senior User role description occurs in the "Design and Appoint the Project Management Team" activity in the Starting up a Project process.

4. B. The Project Manager is appointed in the first activity of the first process of PRINCE2, in the "Appoint the Executive and Project Manager" activity in the Starting up a Project process. During this activity, corporate or programme management appoints the Executive, who then appoints the Project Manager.

When answering these questions, write directly on the question paper, next to each item in column 1, the ordering of the items. Once you have worked out the ordering of the Column 1 items, it is then much easier to match those items with the sequence numbers in Column 2.

Multiple Response Question Type

In the multiple response questions, you are given a question with a number of possible answers (usually there are four or five options). Out of the available options, you need to choose two or sometimes three correct responses.

I think this is the hardest type of question. Many candidates initially disagree with me, arguing that the assertion/reason type is more difficult. (You'll see the assertion/reason type in the next section.) Initially, they do appear very difficult, because the question style is quite unusual; however, they become easier with practice.

Each multiple response question is worth one mark. To get the one mark, you must choose all the right options. So if the question asks for two correct options, you must select both to get the mark. If only one of your options is correct, you don't get any marks.

The following example question is taken from Chapter 3, "Organization Theme."

The following question gives a possible candidate supported by *true* statements for the Executive role. In the context of PRINCE2, only two of the candidates along with the supporting statements are appropriate for that role.

1. Which of the following 2 statements give possible alternative candidates for the role of the Executive?

   A. The Marketing Director, because she will fund the project from the marketing budget

   B. The Personal Assistant to the CEO, because she has recently attended a PRINCE2 seminar

   C. The Chief Executive of Quality Furniture, because he is a major shareholder in the company

   D. The IT Manager, because he is responsible for all major IT initiatives within Quality Furniture

   E. The Operations Manager, because he will be impacted by the project if sales increase

   Answer: A, C. Option A is correct, because the Executive role is responsible for securing the funding for the project. Option C is also correct because the Executive represents the business interests in the project. As a major shareholder, the Chief Executive will be interested in the project's return on investment. Option B is incorrect, because the Executive role must represent the business interests of the project, not knowledge of PRINCE2. Option D is incorrect, because if the IT Manager is supplying resources to build the website, he might take on a Senior Supplier role; or if he is going to maintain the website in its operational life, he could take on the Senior User role. Being responsible for an initiative is not the same thing as focusing on the business return of an initiative. Finally, Option E is incorrect, because those who are impacted by the project might take on a Senior User role. These questions require a lot of reading—there is the question itself and then all the five options (or sometimes four). When you are managing your time in the exam, be aware that the multiple responses will need more time than, for example, the classic multiple choice type. For added security, always also check that the options you are not choosing are the wrong ones.

As you saw from the previous example, sometimes for the multiple response questions, a statement such as the following will appear at the top of the question:

"The following question gives a possible candidate supported by *true statements* for the Executive role."

The words "*true statements*" are very important. They mean that the examiner can introduce new information about the project scenario within the body of the question. This new information may not have appeared in either the project scenario or the additional information. For example, the fact that the Marketing Director will fund the project from the marketing budget may be completely new to you prior to reading this question. As a result, some candidates might disregard this information because they don't believe it is true. But of course it is, because the question states that each option is a *true statement*.

Assertion/Reason Question Type

Out of all the question formats, the assertion/reason type causes the most amount of anguish in my PRINCE2 classes. It is quite an unusual style of question that takes a little time to understand. The good news is that once you have answered a few, they become a lot easier.

Each question gives you two statements: an assertion about the project, and a reason that might explain that assertion. There are two possible steps to answering these questions:

1. First, you need to treat the assertion statement and reason statement as two entirely unconnected sentences. In this step, you have to determine whether the assertion on its own is true or false and similarly if the reason on its own is true or false.

2. If and only if both the assertion and reason statements are true, you need to determine whether the reason statement explains the assertion statement.

After you've completed the previous two steps, you then need to choose one of five options:

A. The assertion is true and the reason is true, *and* the reason explains the assertion.

B. The assertion is true and the reason is true, *but* the reason does not explain the assertion.

C. The assertion is true and the reason is false.

D. The assertion is false and the reason is true.

E. Both the assertion and the reason are false.

One piece of good news is that these five options are always the same. So, for example, Option E always means that you think the assertion and the reason are false.

Try using the following methodology when answering these questions:

- For each question, first consider the assertion and reason as different statements. Forget about the possible link between them. Work out whether either statement on its own is true or false. On the question paper next to the assertion, mark a "T" if you think it's true or an "F" if you think it's false—and then do the same for the reason statement.

- Choosing the correct option is easier if either the assertion or reason is false. The answer must be Option C if the assertion is true and the reason is false, Option D if the assertion is false and the reason is true, or Option E if both statements are false. In these cases, you do not have to consider the linkages between the assertion and the reason.

- If both the assertion and the reason are true, you have a bit more thinking to do. Reread the assertion and ask yourself, "Why is this true?" If your answer resembles what's in the reason box, then the reason explains the assertion, and you should choose Option A. If your answer is different from what's in the reason box, the reason doesn't explain the assertion, and you should choose Option B.

The following example question is taken from Chapter 2, "Starting a Project Successfully with PRINCE2."

Rows 1 to 3 in the following table consist of an assertion statement and a reason statement. For each line, identify the appropriate option, from Options A to E, that applies. Each option can be used once, more than once, or not at all.

- **A.** The assertion is true and the reason is true, *and* the reason explains the assertion.
- **B.** The assertion is true and the reason is true, *but* the reason does not explain the assertion.
- **C.** The assertion is true and the reason is false.
- **D.** The assertion is false and the reason is true.
- **E.** Both the assertion and the reason are false.

Assertion		Reason
1. If the Chief Executive Officer feels this is a very important project, he should take on the Executive and the Project Manager role.	BECAUSE	The Executive is the single point of accountability for the project.
2. During the Starting up a Project process, the Project Manager should record in the Daily Log that Quality Furniture's procurement department has no experience in dealing with IT suppliers and this could lead to them selecting a poor supplier.	BECAUSE	The Daily Log acts as a repository for all project risks before the creation of the Risk Register.
3. The Project Manager will need to create detailed specifications for the tender documents during the Starting up a Project process.	BECAUSE	The Project Product Description that forms part of the Project Brief contains detailed descriptions of all the project's products.

How did you do? Here are the answers and some explanations:

1. D. **Assertion:** False. PRINCE2 separates out the directing level of management that contains the Executive from the management level that contains the Project Manager. The Executive should be a different person from the Project Manager.

   Reason: True. The Executive is the single point of accountability for the project.

2. A. **Assertion:** True. The assertion describes a potential threat to the project. Threats are risks. During the Starting up a Project process, the Risk Register that is usually used to record risks has not been created. It is created later in the initiation stage. The Daily Log is used to record risks until the Risk Register is created.

   Reason: True. See previous explanation for the assertion. As the reason explains the assertion, the answer is Option A.

3. E. **Assertion:** False. The detailed specifications for the tender documents will be created when their Product Descriptions are created.

   Reason: False. The Project Product Description will define high-level specifications for the major outputs of the project.

One thing that often confuses candidates about these types of questions is the use of the word *should*. Consider the following assertion statement:

> The development and building of the website should be planned and managed as two management stages.

When the exam uses the word *should,* it's saying that the PRINCE2 method states it has to be done this way. But since PRINCE2 does not, in fact, say that all website developments have to be run across two management stages, this statement is false.

Now consider the following statement, which is worded a bit differently:

> The development and building of the website *could* be planned and managed as two management stages.

This statement is true, because the development of the website could be run over two stages—it doesn't have to be, but it *could* be. Misreading just one word could lead to you losing a point.

Using *Managing Successful Projects with PRINCE2* during the Exam

Some questions are quite detailed, such as asking what type of information appears in a particular section of a particular management product. Unless you have a photographic memory and have memorized this entire study guide and/or memorized the entire official PRINCE2 manual (*Managing Successful Projects with PRINCE2*), you will not be able to answer these very detailed questions without referring to the PRINCE2 manual during the exam.

Here are a few tips about using the using the PRINCE2 manual during the exam:

- For questions about management products, refer to Appendix A in the PRINCE2 manual. The only caveat to this is that there is a better description of what is in the Business Case in the Business Case theme chapter. Appendix A shows you exactly what type of information goes into which section of each management product.

- For questions about roles and responsibilities, refer to Appendix C in the PRINCE2 manual. This appendix contains an easy-to-read list of responsibilities for each role. Also, the last page of each theme gives you a similar list, but just focusing on that theme's responsibilities.

- For questions about particular activities, use the relevant process chapter. The input/ output diagrams and the responsibilities tables for each activity in the process chapters are particularly easy to read and show you what management product is created, reviewed, or updated in which activity as well as which role is responsible.

- For questions about the Organization theme, you'll find useful the diagram in the Organization theme chapter that shows the project management team structure. It illustrates who reports to whom and how each role fits into the project management team.

- For questions on the Quality theme, you'll find useful the diagram in the Quality theme chapter that shows the quality audit trail. It pulls together all the aspects of quality management. You can annotate this diagram using what you learned in Chapter 6, "Quality Theme," in this study guide.

- For questions on the Plans theme, you'll find useful the diagram in the Plans theme chapter that shows the PRINCE2 levels of plans. It illustrates how the plans relate to each other. You can annotate this diagram using what you learned in Chapter 5, "Plans Theme," in this study guide.

- For questions on the Risk theme, you'll find useful the diagram in the Risk theme chapter that shows the threat and opportunity responses. It demonstrates how to respond to a risk. You can annotate this diagram using what you learned in Chapter 7, "Risk Theme," in this study guide.

- For questions on the Change theme, you'll find useful the diagram in the Change theme chapter that shows the issue and change control procedure. It shows how to respond to a change. You can annotate this diagram using what you learned in Chapter 8, "Change Theme," in this study guide.

Appendix
D

Sample Foundation Examinations

Sample Paper 1

June 2011 Release

Multiple Choice

1-hour paper

Instructions

1. All 75 questions should be attempted.
2. 5 of the 75 questions are under trial and will not contribute to your overall score. There is no indication of which questions are under trial.
3. All answers are to be marked on the answer sheet provided.
4. Please use a pencil and NOT ink to mark your answers on the answer sheet provided. There is only one correct answer per question.
5. You have 1 hour for this paper.
6. You must get 35 or more correct to pass.

Candidate Number: ....

1. Which is one of the six aspects of project performance that needs to be managed?
   A. Accuracy
   B. Reliability
   C. Scope
   D. Ease of use

2. What theme ensures the project is desirable, viable and achievable?
   A. Organization
   B. Progress
   C. Business Case
   D. Risk

3. What process is triggered by the Project Manager's request to initiate a project?
   A. Starting up a Project
   B. Initiating a Project
   C. Directing a Project
   D. Managing a Stage Boundary

4. The purpose of what theme is to establish mechanisms to monitor and compare actual achievements against those planned?

  A. Business Case

  B. Change

  C. Progress

  D. Quality

5. Which is an objective of the Closing a Project process?

  A. Check that all the project's products have been accepted by the users

  B. Prepare for the final stage of the project

  C. Capture the customer's quality expectations

  D. Ensure that all benefits have been achieved

6. Identify the missing words in the following sentence.

  A purpose of the Managing a Stage Boundary process is to provide the Project Board with sufficient information so that it can approve the [?] for the next stage.

  A. Work Packages

  B. Exception Report

  C. Stage Plan

  D. Project Brief

7. What theme provides information on what is required, how it will be achieved and by whom?

  A. Organization

  B. Plans

  C. Business Case

  D. Quality

8. Which is recommended as a possible risk response type for an opportunity?

  A. Reduce

  B. Transfer

  C. Reject

  D. Fallback

9. Basing projects on a 'management by exception' principle provides which benefit?

  A. Promotes consistency of project work and staff mobility

  B. Provides a common language

  C. Clarity of what a project will deliver, why, when and by whom

  D. Efficient and cost-effective use of management time

10. Identify the missing words in the following sentence.

    The purpose of the [?] process is to establish solid foundations for the project, enabling the organization to understand the work that needs to be done to deliver the project's products.

    A. Initiating a Project

    B. Starting up a Project

    C. Directing a Project

    D. Managing a Stage Boundary

11. Which is a purpose of the Managing Product Delivery process?

    A. Controls the link between the Project Manager and the Team Manager(s)

    B. Tracks the progress of a stage with the help of Checkpoint Reports

    C. Provides a link between the work of the Project Manager and the Project Board

    D. Maintains a focus on the delivery of benefits throughout the stage

12. Which role is responsible for authorizing and monitoring work to be completed and for taking corrective action within a stage?

    A. Project Manager

    B. Project Support

    C. Project Assurance

    D. Team Manager

13. Which fact is true of Project Assurance but not quality assurance?

    A. Responsible for monitoring the conduct of the project

    B. Independent of the Project Manager

    C. Appointed as part of the project management team

    D. Responsible for reviewing the project for compliance with corporate standards

14. Which is NOT a characteristic of a project?

    A. Has a higher degree of risk than business as usual

    B. Involves people with different skills introducing a change that will impact others outside of the team

    C. Has a lifespan that usually covers the delivery of the desired outcomes and the realization of all the expected benefits

    D. A temporary management structure created for the implementation of business products

15. What product forms the 'contract' between the Project Manager and the Project Board for the project?

    A. Project Plan

    B. Project Product Description

    C. Project Initiation Documentation

    D. Project Brief

16. Which is an objective of the Managing a Stage Boundary process?
    A. Enable the Project Board to commit resources and expenditure required for the initiation stage
    B. Review and, if necessary, update the Project Initiation Documentation
    C. Provides a break between those managing the project from those creating products
    D. Ensure a periodic review is held to approve the products created within the completed stage

17. How should a Team Manager escalate a suggestion for an improvement to a product?
    A. Include details in a Checkpoint Report
    B. Include details in a Highlight Report
    C. Raise an issue
    D. Raise an Exception Report

18. Which is a purpose of the Closing a Project process?
    A. Define the procedure for handing over products
    B. Provide a fixed point at which acceptance for the project product is confirmed
    C. Define formal requirements for the acceptance, execution and delivery of project work
    D. Confirm all project benefits have been achieved

19. Which is an objective of the Starting up a Project process?
    A. Confirm there are no known restrictions that would prevent the project from being delivered
    B. Ensure all Team Managers understand their responsibilities
    C. Get approval for the Project Plan from corporate or programme management
    D. Prepare the Project Initiation Documentation for authority to initiate the project

20. What process is used to provide an interface with corporate or programme management?
    A. Managing Product Delivery
    B. Directing a Project
    C. Controlling a Stage
    D. Managing a Stage Boundary

21. Which is NOT a purpose of an End Project Report?
    A. Compare project achievements against what was originally agreed
    B. Record information that will help future projects
    C. Prompt the Project Board to authorize the next stage
    D. Pass on details of any ongoing risks for those who will maintain and operate the finished product

22. Identify the missing word(s) in the following sentence.

If a baselined product requires modification, the [?] procedure should be applied in order to manage the modification.

A. risk management

B. exception

C. issue and change control

D. quality control

23. Which is a purpose of a Project Brief?

A. Describe an agreed position from which the project can be started

B. Describe the information needs of the project's stakeholders

C. Describe the configuration management procedure that will be used by the project

D. Describe the reporting requirements of the Project Board

24. Which is one of the four integrated elements within PRINCE2?

A. Quality

B. Role descriptions

C. Processes

D. Product Descriptions

25. Which of the following statements apply to a Stage Plan?

1. Is produced with the knowledge of earlier stages

2. Provides the basis for control by the Project Board

3. Is produced close to the time when the planned events will take place

4. Provides the basis for day-to-day control by the Project Manager

A. 1, 2, 3

B. 1, 2, 4

C. 1, 3, 4

D. 2, 3, 4

26. Identify the missing words in the following sentence.

Because the Project Board receives regular [?], there is no need for regular progress meetings.

A. End Stage Reports

B. Checkpoint Reports

C. Exception Reports

D. Highlight Reports

27. Which is a benefit of using the product-based planning technique?

    A. All the required products of the project will be delivered to time and to cost

    B. Clearly shows how long a project will take

    C. It removes the need for activity-based planning

    D. Reduces the risk of incorrectly scoping the project

28. Which of the following describe a purpose of the Risk theme?

    1. Identify risks that may have an impact on the project delivering its objectives

    2. Assess and evaluate the impact of the risks on the project delivering its objectives

    3. Manage risks at the corporate or programme level of the organization

    4. Implement risk management activities to improve the chances of the project delivering its objectives

    A. 1, 2, 3

    B. 1, 2, 4

    C. 1, 3, 4

    D. 2, 3, 4

29. What project management team role can trigger the premature closure of a project?

    A. Project Manager

    B. Project Board

    C. Project Support

    D. Project Assurance

30. Which is a purpose of the Organization theme?

    A. Set the tolerance on the cost of resources

    B. Provide project management training to those working within the project

    C. Define the structure of accountability and responsibilities on the project

    D. Implement the controls required to permit management by exception

31. Which process enables the Project Board to exercise overall control of a project?

    A. Directing a Project

    B. Controlling a Stage

    C. Starting up a Project

    D. Initiating a Project

32. Which is the first plan to be created?

    A. Project Plan

    B. Initiation Stage Plan

    C. Team Plan

    D. Exception Plan

33. What is the PRINCE2 definition of a project?
    A. A number of activities managed as a unit
    B. A unique undertaking that requires organization and resources
    C. An element of work that a Project Manager agrees to deliver
    D. A temporary organization created for the purpose of delivering business products

34. Which is NOT an objective of the Managing Product Delivery process?
    A. Ensure suppliers understand what is expected of them
    B. Ensure products of appropriate quality are delivered
    C. Ensure the Project Board is kept informed of progress on the products
    D. Ensure work for the team is agreed with the Project Manager

35. Which is an objective of the quality review technique?
    A. Involve key interested parties to promote wider acceptance of the product
    B. Develop and improve the specification of a product through continuous assessment
    C. Correct any errors found in a product during the quality review meeting
    D. Update the status information in the Configuration Item Record when a product is signed-off

36. Which is a purpose of the Communication Management Strategy?
    A. Identify how and by whom the project's products will be controlled and protected
    B. Define the method of communication between the project and its stakeholders
    C. Define the structure of responsibilities and accountabilities in support of effective decision making in a project
    D. Identify the communications required from the Team Manager(s) to the Project Board

37. Identify the missing words in the following sentence.
    Any requests for change, which require Project Board approval, should be recorded in the [?] and monitored by the Project Manager
    A. Product Description
    B. Issue Register
    C. Configuration Item Record
    D. Quality Register

38. Which is a recommended quality review team role?
    A. Senior User
    B. Presenter
    C. Project Support
    D. Project Assurance

39. If a product fails its quality check, what product should always be updated?

   A. Risk Register

   B. Issue Register

   C. Quality Register

   D. Lessons Log

40. In what product should the Project Manager enter the details of issues that are resolved without using the formal issue and change control procedure?

   A. Stage Plan

   B. Daily Log

   C. Configuration Item Record

   D. Checkpoint Report

41. Which of the PRINCE2 principles uses tolerances to establish the limits of delegated authority?

   A. Manage by stages

   B. Tailor to suit the project environment

   C. Focus on products

   D. Manage by exception

42. Which is a purpose of the Starting up a Project process?

   A. Ensuring that the prerequisites for initiating the project are in place

   B. Establishing that the Project Plan can meet the required target dates

   C. Creating the Project Initiation Documentation so the project can be initiated

   D. Confirming to corporate or programme management that quality expectations will be met

43. When should the project management team be reviewed?

   A. As and when new stakeholders are identified

   B. When planning a quality review

   C. When planning the next stage

   D. During product creation

44. Which is NOT a responsibility of the Project Board?

   A. Allocate tolerances to specialist teams

   B. Transfer ownership of the Benefits Review Plan to corporate or programme management

   C. Approve the Project Product Description

   D. Confirm the required frequency of Highlight Reports

45. Who sets the project tolerances?

   A. Project Board

   B. Corporate/programme management

   C. Executive

   D. Project Manager

46. PRINCE2 plans are carefully designed to meet the needs of the different levels in the project organization. Why is this a benefit?

   A. Ensures stakeholders are properly represented

   B. Improves communication and control

   C. Ensures that one plan will meet everyone's needs

   D. Reduces the levels of management required in the project organization

47. What levels of plan are recommended by PRINCE2?

   A. Project Plan

   B. Project Plan and Stage Plan

   C. Project Plan, Stage Plan and Team Plan

   D. Project Plan, Stage Plan, Team Plan and Exception Plan

48. Which of the following are described in a Product Description?

   1. The component parts of the product

   2. The products that are derived from this product

   3. The skills needed to create the product

   4. The method required to check the product

   A. 1, 2, 3

   B. 1, 2, 4

   C. 1, 3, 4

   D. 2, 3, 4

49. Which of the following is funded from a change budget?

   A. All changes to the baseline cost of the project

   B. Increased tolerance required by the Project Manager to complete a stage

   C. Changes to approved baselined products

   D. The correction of an off-specification

50. What is risk appetite?

   A. Part of the project budget, used to pay for any additional activities required to manage risks

   B. The funds the Project Board is willing to spend on the management of risk

   C. Permissible deviation from planned expenditure without the need to escalate to the next higher authority

   D. An organization's attitude towards risk-taking

51. Which role represents the 'delivering' level on the project management team?

    A. Project Board

    B. Project Manager

    C. Team Manager

    D. Project Support

52. Which is a purpose of the Benefits Review Plan?

    A. Document the justification for the undertaking of a project

    B. Describe only residual benefits and those that could not be achieved during the lifecycle of the project

    C. Provide a schedule for measuring the achievement of benefits

    D. Provide the reasons for the project, for entry into the Business Case

53. Which is a purpose of a Configuration Item Record?

    A. Provide a summary of the status of all products at any one time

    B. Provide any details of important links between configuration items

    C. Support the creation of the project product breakdown structure

    D. Include an analysis of an issue or risk which caused the product to change

54. Which is NOT a purpose of the Controlling a Stage process?

    A. Take corrective actions to control deviations from the Stage Plan

    B. Recommend the tolerances for the next stage

    C. Report progress to the Project Board

    D. Assign work to be done

55. Which is a true statement regarding stages?

    A. A project can be scheduled without management stages

    B. There can be several management stages within a technical stage

    C. Several management stages can be scheduled to run concurrently

    D. Technical stages and management stages should always end together

56. Which is a purpose of the Risk Management Strategy?

    A. Defines the techniques to be used when assessing project risks

    B. Summarizes exposure to strategic, programme, project and operational risks

    C. Recommends responses for each of the project risks

    D. Identifies suitable risk owners for each of the project risks

57. Which role can the Project Manager also perform?
    A. Executive
    B. Project Assurance
    C. Change Authority
    D. Senior User

58. What are the three recommended types of issue?
    A. Off-specification, request for change and concession
    B. Off-specification, request for change and problem/concern
    C. Request for change, problem/concern, and Issue Report
    D. Request for change, Issue Report and risk

59. Which of the following is established within the Initiating a Project process?
    A. The various ways in which the project can be delivered
    B. Those who require project information have been identified
    C. All of the information to develop the Project Brief is available
    D. Any constraints which could affect the project have been removed

60. What term is used to describe when a risk might occur?
    A. Impact
    B. Proximity
    C. Probability
    D. Evaluate

61. Within what process are Team Plans produced?
    A. Initiating a Project
    B. Controlling a Stage
    C. Managing a Stage Boundary
    D. Managing Product Delivery

62. Identify the missing words in the following sentence.

    If a Project Manager has the appropriate specialist skills and knowledge, they may also perform the role of [?] on the project.
    A. Senior Supplier(s)
    B. Team Manager(s)
    C. Project Assurance
    D. Senior User(s)

63. Which statement is true for project stakeholders?

    A. Some have decision-making authority within the project environment

    B. All are external to the corporate organization

    C. All are internal to the project management team structure

    D. None have decision-making authority within the project environment

64. Which of the following is funded from a risk budget?

    A. Potential changes that may be required as the project progresses

    B. Shortfall in estimating the development costs of the project's products

    C. Additional activities to reduce, avoid, fallback, transfer, share or enhance project risks

    D. Production of a Risk Management Strategy

65. Which is NOT an objective of the Controlling a Stage process?

    A. Produce the Stage Plan for the next stage

    B. Focus attention on delivery of the stage's products

    C. Escalate threats to tolerances

    D. Keep issues and risks under control

66. Which of the following describes an output?

    A. Any of the project's specialist products

    B. The result of the change derived from using the project's products

    C. The measurable improvement resulting from an outcome

    D. A negative outcome

67. Which is a purpose of the Quality theme?

    A. Define the way in which the project will ensure that all products of the project are fit for purpose

    B. Define the procedures and responsibilities for the creation, maintenance and control of project products

    C. Establish mechanisms to judge whether the project remains desirable and achievable

    D. Enable the assessment of continuing project viability

68. Which factor should influence the length of a management stage?

    A. Frequency of Highlight Reports

    B. The level of project risk

    C. Availability of the Project Board

    D. Requirement of a specialist team for an element of the development work

69. After the first stage, when are the Stage Plans for further stages produced?

    A. Near the end of the current stage

    B. After completion of the current stage

    C. When creating the Project Plan

    D. At the start of the initiation stage

70. What is a risk cause?

    A. Negative consequence of a threat occurring

    B. Explanation of the uncertainty which, should it occur, would create a problem

    C. Positive consequence of an exploited opportunity

    D. A known situation which creates uncertainty

71. Which product is a time-driven control?

    A. End Stage Report

    B. Exception Report

    C. Checkpoint Report

    D. Lessons Report

72. Which is a purpose of the Project Product Description?

    A. Define the quality checks that will be used for the project's products

    B. Explain what the project must handover to achieve customer approval

    C. Confirm the delivery timescales for the project's products

    D. Document the Project Manager's responsibilities for delivering the project's products

73. Which is a purpose of the Change Authority?

    A. Determine the change budget for a project

    B. Assess the impact of all requests for change

    C. Reduce the number of requests for change that need to be escalated to the Project Board

    D. Allow the Project Board to delegate the approval of all risks and Issue Reports

74. To which role does a Team Manager report an exception situation?

    A. Project Manager

    B. Project Board

    C. Project Assurance

    D. Project Support

75. What is the first step within the recommended risk management procedure?

    A. Assess

    B. Identify

    C. Implement

    D. Plan

Sample Paper 2

June 2011 Release

Multiple Choice

1-hour paper

This paper remains the property of The APM Group (APMG). This document is not to be reproduced or re-sold without express permission from The APM Group Ltd. PRINCE2® is a Registered Trade Mark of the Office of Government Commerce.

Instructions

1. All 75 questions should be attempted.

2. 5 of the 75 questions are under trial and will not contribute to your overall score. There is no indication of which questions are under trial.

3. All answers are to be marked on the answer sheet provided.

4. Please use a pencil and NOT ink to mark your answers on the answer sheet provided. There is only one correct answer per question.

5. You have 1 hour for this paper.

6. You must get 35 or more correct to pass.

Candidate Number: ....

1. Which is one of the six aspects of project performance that needs to be managed?
   A. Customers
   B. People
   C. Benefits
   D. Processes

2. What is the trigger for the Starting up a Project process?
   A. Project Brief
   B. Project Plan
   C. Project mandate
   D. Outline Business Case

3. Which is a purpose of the Business Case theme?
   A. Establish mechanisms to monitor and compare actual achievements against those planned
   B. Establish methods to judge whether the ongoing project is justified
   C. Assess and control uncertain events or situations
   D. Describe how, when and at what cost products can be delivered

4. What role is responsible for creating a Team Plan in the Managing Product Delivery process?

    A. Project Manager

    B. Team Manager

    C. Project Support

    D. Senior User

5. The incorporation of the primary stakeholders on the project management team supports what principle?

    A. Continued business justification

    B. Defined roles and responsibilities

    C. Manage by stages

    D. Learn from experience

6. Which describes risk appetite?

    A. An organization's attitude towards risk-taking

    B. Probable effect on the project delivering its objectives

    C. Probable timeframe within which a risk may occur

    D. Level of risk exposure that, when exceeded, triggers an exception

7. Identify the missing words in the following sentence.

    If the Project Manager needs to know the results of a quality review, the [?] will provide a summary together with the date of any follow-up meeting.

    A. Stage Plan

    B. Issue Register

    C. Daily Log

    D. Quality Register

8. How is the Project Initiation Documentation used during the Closing a Project process?

    A. As the basis for comparing the original aim of the project against what was actually achieved

    B. Provides the controls for the final stage of the project

    C. Updated to include relevant lessons from previous projects

    D. Provides the Project Product Description for approval by the Project Board

9. What role agrees the techniques, products and constraints for a Work Package with the Project Manager?

    A. Executive

    B. Project Assurance

    C. Senior Supplier

    D. Team Manager

10. Identify the missing word in the following sentence.

PRINCE2 recommends three levels of [?] to reflect the needs of the different levels of management involved in a project.

A. product

B. activity

C. plan

D. benefit

11. Which is a purpose of a Configuration Item Record?

A. Record quality issues found in a quality test of the product

B. Explain which procedure should be used for updating the Configuration Item Records of products completed in the stage

C. Explain which procedure should be used for transferring completed products into the operational and maintenance environment

D. Record the development status of products in a completed Work Package

12. When authorizing a stage, in which product would the Project Board look for an explanation of any deviations from the approved plans that are within tolerance?

A. Lessons Report

B. End Stage Report

C. Benefits Review Plan

D. Project Initiation Documentation

13. Which of the following are a purpose of the Benefits Review Plan?

1. Define how a measurement of the achievement of the project's benefits can be made

2. Define what benefits assessments need to be undertaken

3. Define the project, in order to form the basis for its management and an assessment of its overall success

4. Define the activities required to measure the expected project's benefits

A. 1, 2, 3

B. 1, 2, 4

C. 1, 3, 4

D. 2, 3, 4

14. Which is a purpose of the Organization theme?

A. Define the total resource requirements of the project

B. Capture the project acceptance criteria

C. Define the responsibilities for managing teams

D. Establish mechanisms to judge whether the project is desirable and achievable

15. Which is a purpose of a Project Brief?

   A. Define how and when a measurement of the achievement of the project's benefits can be made

   B. Define any lessons from previous projects and how they may affect this project

   C. Communicate the quality techniques and standards to be applied to achieve the required quality levels

   D. Provide sufficient information for the decision on whether to initiate the project

16. Which is a purpose of a Risk Management Strategy?

   A. Communicate how risk management will be implemented throughout the wider corporate organization

   B. Capture and maintain information on all identified risks relating to the project

   C. Document specific actions for responding to risks

   D. Describe the procedures and techniques for managing project risks

17. Which is **NOT** a purpose of the Plans theme?

   A. Facilitate communication

   B. Establish the project's structure of accountability

   C. Define the means of delivering the products

   D. Ensure targets are achievable

18. Which is a purpose of the Directing a Project process?

   A. Enable the Project Board to exercise overall control of a project

   B. Prepare a solid foundation for the project

   C. Establish the prerequisites for the initiation of a project

   D. Assign Work Packages

19. Which takes place within the Managing a Stage Boundary process?

   A. Periodic review of progress against the Stage Plan

   B. Obtain approvals for all completed products

   C. Escalation of Issue Reports created during the current stage

   D. Review of the business justification for the project

20. Which is a type of issue?

   A. Problem/concern

   B. Follow-on action recommendation

   C. Exception Report

   D. Identified threat

21. Which is a characteristic of a project?

    A. Low risk

    B. Avoids stresses and strains between organizations

    C. Business as usual

    D. Cross-functional

22. Which is **NOT** a recommended response type to respond to a threat?

    A. Avoid

    B. Reject

    C. Share

    D. Transfer

23. Which is an objective of the Managing a Stage Boundary process?

    A. Request authorization to start the next stage

    B. Ensure that all threats and opportunities for the current stage have been closed

    C. Make certain that work on products allocated to the team for the next stage is authorized and agreed

    D. Implement actions to resolve tolerance deviations from the Stage Plan

24. In what process are the project's risk management techniques and standards defined?

    A. Starting up a Project

    B. Directing a Project

    C. Initiating a Project

    D. Managing Product Delivery

25. Which is a purpose of a Daily Log?

    A. Record the products and activities planned for the stage

    B. Record informal issues

    C. Record and track the status of all products produced during a stage

    D. Update the Project Board on the progress of a stage

26. Which is an objective of the quality review technique?

    A. Determine whether a product has been created

    B. Agree the quality method that will be applied to a product

    C. Formulate ideas on how the product will be developed

    D. Provide consultation with a range of interested parties on a product's fitness for purpose

27. When does the Directing a Project process start?

    A. On completion of the Starting up a Project process

    B. On completion of the Initiating a Project process

    C. When the Starting up a Project process commences

    D. After the project has been authorized

28. What plan is mandatory?

    A. Team Plan

    B. Exception Plan

    C. Project Plan

    D. Programme Plan

29. On which environment is PRINCE2 based?

    A. Information technology

    B. Customer/supplier

    C. Procurement

    D. Programme

30. Which theme assesses and controls uncertainty within a project?

    A. Progress

    B. Risk

    C. Change

    D. Plans

31. Which of the following is funded from a change budget?

    A. Fallback plan

    B. Request for change

    C. Action to reduce a threat

    D. Change Authority

32. Which is an aim of the Starting up a Project process?

    A. Understand how and when the project's products will be delivered and at what cost

    B. Ensure that there is authority to deliver the project's products

    C. Do the minimum necessary in order to decide whether it is worthwhile to even initiate the project

    D. Create the set of management products required to control the project

33. Which is a responsibility of the Project Manager?

    A. Delegating responsibility for changes to the Change Authority

    B. Documenting the Communication Management Strategy

    C. Approving stage tolerances

    D. Approving the customer's quality expectations

34. Which is **NOT** a factor to consider when defining management stages?

    A. How long the project is

    B. When Team Managers are available

    C. When key decisions are required on the project

    D. The amount of risk within the project

35. What process ensures that plans for achieving the expected benefits are managed and reviewed?

    A. Managing Product Delivery

    B. Initiating a Project

    C. Directing a Project

    D. Starting up a Project

36. Which of the following are a purpose of an Issue Report?

    1. Document an off-specification

    2. Record an issue's resolution

    3. Capture all problems or concerns within the project

    4. Capture recommendations for handling a request for change

    A. 1, 2, 3

    B. 1, 2, 4

    C. 1, 3, 4

    D. 2, 3, 4

37. Which product establishes the baseline against which the project's actual performance is compared?

    A. Project Brief

    B. Product Status Account

    C. Project Initiation Documentation

    D. Configuration Item Record

38. Which is **NOT** identified when creating a product breakdown structure?

    A. Products to be created by internal resources

    B. Products to be modified

    C. Resources required to produce the products

    D. Products to be created by an external third party

39. Which statement regarding a project's outputs, outcomes and benefits is correct?

   A. All outputs have tangible benefits

   B. Outcomes are the long term results of benefits

   C. Outputs are changes in the way the project's products are used

   D. Benefits are improvements resulting from project outcomes

40. What process covers the acceptance and execution of project work by external suppliers?

   A. Controlling a Stage

   B. Managing a Stage Boundary

   C. Managing Product Delivery

   D. Directing a Project

41. Which is **NOT** a PRINCE2 integrated element?

   A. The principles

   B. The techniques

   C. The themes

   D. Tailoring to the project environment

42. What is the goal of the 'Identify context' step within the recommended risk management procedure?

   A. Identify responses to risks identified in the Business Case

   B. Understand the specific objectives that are at risk

   C. Gather information about risks for inclusion in Highlight Reports to the Project Board

   D. Identify the threats and opportunities that may affect the project's objectives

43. Which is a purpose of the Project Product Description?

   A. Defines the reporting structure to be used by the project

   B. Provides information on what the project is about and how it is being managed

   C. Describes what the project has to produce to obtain customer acceptance

   D. Provides input to the creation of the project mandate

44. Which is a purpose of the Controlling a Stage process?

   A. Agree, perform and deliver project work

   B. Draft a plan for the next stage

   C. Agree stage tolerances

   D. Take action to make sure that the stage remains within tolerance

45. Which of the following roles can the Project Manager also perform?

  1. Change Authority

  2. Project Assurance

  3. Project Support

  4. Team Manager

  A. 1, 2, 3

  B. 1, 2, 4

  C. 1, 3, 4

  D. 2, 3, 4

46. Which defines the sequence in which the products of a plan should be developed?

  A. Product Description

  B. Product breakdown structure

  C. Project Product Description

  D. Product flow diagram

47. If a Work Package is forecast to exceed its tolerances, how should a Team Manager inform the Project Manager?

  A. Raise an Exception Report

  B. Issue an Exception Plan

  C. Raise an issue

  D. Raise a risk

48. What process enables an organization to understand the work that needs to be done to deliver a project's products before it is approved?

  A. Directing a Project

  B. Initiating a Project

  C. Starting up a Project

  D. Controlling a Stage

49. Which is a responsibility of the Project Assurance role?

  A. Inform the Project Manager about the status of the project's products

  B. Document the Project Board's reporting needs

  C. Ensure the Project Manager is aware of the need to use any existing corporate standards

  D. Inform corporate or programme management about the project's status

50. When is it confirmed if a project's objectives have been achieved?

    A.   During the Closing a Project process

    B.   During the final end stage assessment

    C.   During the post-project review

    D.   During the Managing Product Delivery process

51. Which is a definition of a risk cause?

    A.   The impact of a risk on the stage and project tolerance

    B.   The source of a risk

    C.   The overall effect of a risk on the Business Case

    D.   How likely a risk is to occur in a given project situation

52. When would the Team Manager be required to produce a Checkpoint Report?

    A.   When a Work Package is being negotiated

    B.   At the frequency agreed in the Work Package

    C.   On completion of the quality-checking activities for each product

    D.   When reviewing how a stage is progressing

53. Which is a recommended quality review team role?

    A.   Project Manager

    B.   Presenter

    C.   Project Support

    D.   Producer

54. What PRINCE2 principle supports planning only to a level of detail that is manageable and foreseeable?

    A.   Continued business justification

    B.   Manage by exception

    C.   Focus on products

    D.   Manage by stages

55. In which situation might the Controlling a Stage process be used?

    A.   Managing a long initiation stage of a complex project

    B.   Managing the activities of a complex programme

    C.   Managing support activities following the handover of the products to the operational environment

    D.   Creating an Exception Plan to replace the current Stage Plan

56. Which is a responsibility of the business representative on the Project Board?

   A. Setting tolerance levels for the project

   B. Ensuring the project represents value for money

   C. Confirming the project delivers the required functionality

   D. Checking the required quality levels are achieved by the project's products

57. Which statement correctly describes the relationship between Project Assurance and quality assurance?

   A. Project Assurance provides assurance to the project's stakeholders whereas quality assurance provides assurance to the wider corporate or programme organization

   B. They are both the responsibility of the Project Board, but Project Assurance may be delegated.

   C. They are both independent of the project

   D. Project Assurance and quality assurance are both the responsibility of corporate or programme management

58. Which of the following assists the Project Board in assessing project viability at certain points as defined in the Project Plan?

   A. Receiving regular Checkpoint Reports

   B. Authorizing one stage at a time

   C. Creating Exception Reports when tolerances are threatened

   D. Authorizing project closure

59. Which is a purpose of the Change theme?

   A. Prevent change to anything agreed in the Project Initiation Documentation

   B. Ensure any potential changes to baselined products are controlled

   C. Assess and control uncertainty

   D. Assess changes to only the specialist products

60. What product would confirm the version numbers of all products being developed within a given stage?

   A. Configuration Item Record

   B. Product Status Account

   C. Stage Plan

   D. Work Package

61. Which is a benefit of using PRINCE2?

   A. Stakeholders are kept out of planning and decision-making

   B. Participants understand each other's roles and needs

   C. Stakeholders are not involved in assuring the project work

   D. All problems are escalated to all stakeholders

62. In what product would a product's quality tolerance be defined?

   A. Project Product Description

   B. Product Description

   C. Stage Plan

   D. Quality Management Strategy

63. When should the Managing a Stage Boundary process be undertaken?

   A. Close to the end of a management stage

   B. After the completion of each management stage

   C. At the end of the final stage

   D. At the end of project start-up

64. Which is a purpose of a risk budget?

   A. To fund risk management activities defined in the risk management procedure

   B. To fund the cost of analyzing requests for change while executing a Work Package

   C. Funds set aside from the project budget to cover the costs of implementing risk responses

   D. Funds set aside from the project budget to cover the costs of identifying risks to the project

65. Which role is part of the project management team?

   A. Corporate or programme management

   B. Quality assurance

   C. Stakeholder

   D. Business assurance

66. Identify the missing words in the following sentence.

   PRINCE2 management stages relate to the [?], which is a factor that differentiates them from technical stages

   A. use of a particular set of technical skills

   B. use of a specific set of Team Managers

   C. authorization from corporate or programme management

   D. commitment of resources

67. What principle is supported by the Project Product Description?

   A. Continued business justification

   B. Focus on products

   C. Learn from experience

   D. Manage by stages

68. Identify the missing word(s) in the following sentence.

Quality planning provides the definition of the required products with their [?] as a foundation for Project Board agreement.

    A. customer's quality expectations

    B. quality test results

    C. quality criteria

    D. owners

69. Which is a definition of risk probability?

    A. Scale of the risk should it occur

    B. Probable effect on the project delivering its objectives

    C. Probable timeframe within which the risk may occur

    D. A measure of the likelihood of the risk occurring

70. Which is **NOT** an event-driven control?

    A. Highlight Report

    B. Exception Report

    C. Project Initiation Documentation

    D. End of a stage

71. Identify the missing words in the following sentence.

The Project Board will allocate tolerances [?] to the Project Manager.

    A. for each Work Package

    B. for the project

    C. for each management stage

    D. for each technical stage

72. Which is **NOT** a purpose of a Product Description?

    A. Define the time and cost needed to produce the product

    B. Define the quality skills required to check the product

    C. Define the function and appearance of the product

    D. Define the development skills required to produce the product

73. Which is a purpose of a Communication Management Strategy?

    A. Ensuring the project team can use the required reporting tools

    B. Producing reports for the Project Board

    C. Defining the communication method between the Project Board and corporate or programme management

    D. Ensuring stakeholders are aware of their responsibilities

74. Identify the missing words in the following sentence.

During the Controlling a Stage process, the [?] is checked for any new or revised threats and their possible impact on the Business Case.

A. Benefits Review Plan

B. End Stage Report

C. Risk Register

D. Risk Management Strategy

75. In what plan should project closure activities be planned?

A. Closure Stage Plan

B. Stage Plan for the final management stage

C. Initiation Stage Plan

D. Team Plan

Sample Paper 1: Answer Key

1.	C	26.	D	51.	C
2.	C	27.	D	52.	C
3.	C	28.	B	53.	B
4.	C	29.	B	54.	B
5.	A	30.	C	55.	B
6.	C	31.	A	56.	A
7.	B	32.	B	57.	C
8.	C	33.	D	58.	B
9.	D	34.	C	59.	B
10.	A	35.	A	60.	B
11.	A	36.	B	61.	D
12.	A	37.	B	62.	B
13.	C	38.	B	63.	A
14.	C	39.	C	64.	C
15.	C	40.	B	65.	A
16.	B	41.	D	66.	A
17.	C	42.	A	67.	A
18.	B	43.	C	68.	B
19.	A	44.	A	69.	A
20.	B	45.	B	70.	D
21.	C	46.	B	71.	C
22.	C	47.	C	72.	B
23.	A	48.	C	73.	C
24.	C	49.	C	74.	A
25.	C	50.	D	75.	B

Sample Paper 2: Answer Key

1. C	26. D	51. B
2. C	27. A	52. B
3. B	28. C	53. B
4. B	29. B	54. D
5. B	30. B	55. A
6. A	31. B	56. B
7. D	32. C	57. A
8. A	33. B	58. B
9. D	34. B	59. B
10. C	35. C	60. B
11. D	36. B	61. B
12. B	37. C	62. B
13. B	38. C	63. A
14. C	39. D	64. C
15. D	40. C	65. D
16. D	41. B	66. D
17. B	42. B	67. B
18. A	43. C	68. C
19. D	44. D	69. D
20. A	45. C	70. A
21. D	46. D	71. C
22. B	47. C	72. A
23. A	48. B	73. C
24. C	49. C	74. C
25. B	50. A	75. B

Appendix E

About the Additional Study Tools

IN THIS APPENDIX:

- ✓ Additional study tools
- ✓ System requirements
- ✓ Using the study tools
- ✓ Troubleshooting

Additional Study Tools

The following sections are arranged by category and summarize the software and other goodies you'll find from the companion website. If you need help with installing the items, refer to the installation instructions in the "Using the Study Tools" section later in this appendix.

The additional study tools can be found at www.sybex.com/go/ prince2studyguide. Here, you will find instructions on how to download the files to your hard drive.

Sybex Test Engine

The files contain the Sybex test engine, which includes one bonus practice exam.

PDF of PRINCE2 Practitioner Exam

We have included a sample PRINCE2 Practitioner Exam in PDF format. You can view the electronic version of the exam with Adobe Reader.

Electronic Flashcards

These handy electronic flashcards are just what they sound like. One side contains a question or fill-in-the-blank question, and the other side shows the answer.

PDF of Glossary of Terms

We have included an electronic version of the Glossary in PDF format. You can view the electronic version of the Glossary with Adobe Reader.

Adobe Reader

We've also included a copy of Adobe Reader so you can view PDF files that accompany the book's content. For more information on Adobe Reader or to check for a newer version, visit Adobe's website at www.adobe.com/products/reader/.

System Requirements

Make sure your computer meets the minimum system requirements shown in the following list. If your computer doesn't match up to most of these requirements, you may have problems using the software and files. For the latest and greatest information, please refer to the ReadMe file located in the downloads.

- A PC running Microsoft Windows 98, Windows 2000, Windows NT4 (with SP4 or later), Windows Me, Windows XP, Windows Vista, or Windows 7
- An Internet connection

Using the Study Tools

To install the items, follow these steps:

1. Download the zip file to your hard drive, and unzip to the appropriate location. Instructions on where to download this file can be found here: `www.sybex.com/go/prince2studyguide`.

2. Click the `Start.exe` file to open the study tools file.

3. Read the license agreement, and then click the Accept button if you want to use the study tools.

The main interface appears. The interface allows you to access the content with just one or two clicks.

Troubleshooting

Wiley has attempted to provide programs that work on most computers with the minimum system requirements. Alas, your computer may differ, and some programs may not work properly for some reason.

The two likeliest problems are that you don't have enough memory (RAM) for the programs you want to use or you have other programs running that are affecting installation or running of a program. If you get an error message such as "Not enough memory" or "Setup cannot continue," try one or more of the following suggestions and then try using the software again:

Turn off any antivirus software running on your computer.   Installation programs sometimes mimic virus activity and may make your computer incorrectly believe that it's being infected by a virus.

Close all running programs.   The more programs you have running, the less memory is available to other programs. Installation programs typically update files and programs, so if you keep other programs running, installation may not work properly.

Have your local computer store add more RAM to your computer.   This is, admittedly, a drastic and somewhat expensive step. However, adding more memory can really help the speed of your computer and allow more programs to run at the same time.

Customer Care

If you have trouble with the book's companion study tools, please call the Wiley Product Technical Support phone number at (800) 762-2974, or visit them at `http://sybex` `.custhelp.com/`.

Index

G

H

F